HAWKMAN

WINGS OF FURY

HAWKMAN: WINGS OF FURY

Published by DC Comics. Cover and compilation copyright © 2005 DC Comics. All Rights Reserved.

Originally published in single magazine form in HAWKMAN 15-22, JLA A TO Z 1, 2. Copyright © 2003, 2004 DC Comics. All Rights Reserved. All characters, their distinctive likenesses and related elements featured in this publication are trademarks of DC Comics. The stories, characters and incidents featured in this publication are entirely fictional. DC Comics does not read or accept unsolicited submissions of ideas, stories or artwork.

DC Comics, 1700 Broadway, New York, NY 10019
A Warner Bros. Entertainment Company
Printed in Canada. First Printing.
ISBN: 1-4012-0467-8
Cover illustration by John Watson.

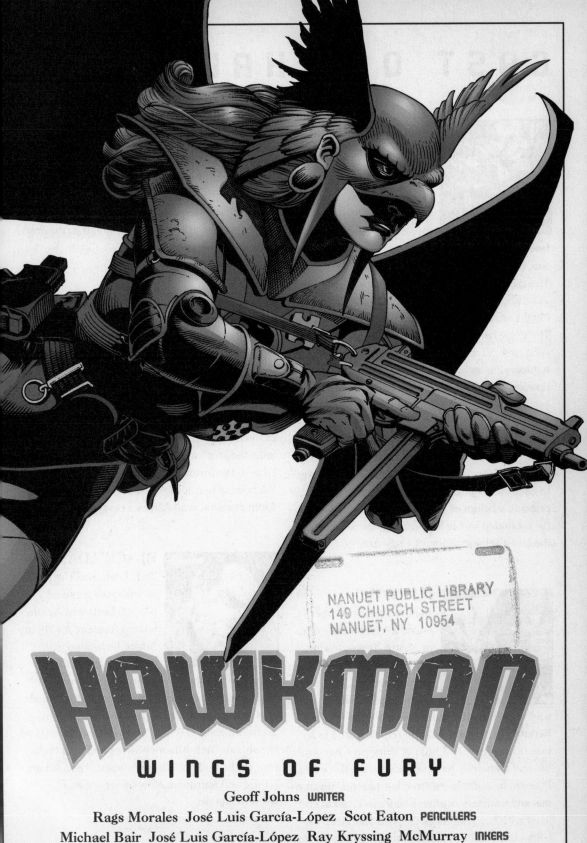

HAWKMAN

WINGS OF FURY

Geoff Johns WRITER

Rags Morales José Luis García-López Scot Eaton PENCILLERS

Michael Bair José Luis García-López Ray Kryssing McMurray INKERS

John Kalisz COLORIST Bill Oakley Ken Lopez LETTERERS

CAST OF CHARACTERS

HAWKMAN

Prince Khufu has lived a thousand lives, and in each one has waged a battle against evil. His journey began during the 15th Dynasty of Ancient Egypt. Hath-Set murdered Khufu, and his lover, Chay-Ara, but since both had been exposed to the alien Thanagarian *Nth metal* their souls were altered. Time and again, the lovers were reborn and fought against evil until death reclaimed them. The cycle has repeated over the centuries and each time, Khufu has emerged as a champion. A generation ago, Khufu fought as the first Hawkman, legendary warrior and member of the Justice Society of America. A temporal anomaly swallowed Khufu until his soul answered a higher calling and returned to earth, this time with the memories of all his previous lives intact. Once more he is Carter Hall, a.k.a. Hawkman, striving to balance his innate warrior's anger with the princely wisdom of his ancient beginnings. He is blinded by his love for Kendra Saunders, the latest reincarnation of Chay-Ara.

HAWKGIRL

Kendra Saunders experienced a frightening event in Austin, Texas, leading her to attempt suicide. This resulted in her body's becoming the home for the soul of an Egyptian princess (who was one of Kendra's ancestors). Midlife reincarnation is a rare occurrence, and little of Princess Chay-Ara's life and memories have surfaced since the event. Plagued by nightmares from her parents' mysterious and untimely deaths, Kendra left Austin and lived with her grandfather, Speed Saunders. He began training her for her destiny, to become the new Hawkgirl. Once she took flight, she grew to love the freedom it provided and she has since joined the Justice Society of America. Chay-Ara's eternal lover, Prince Khufu, recently returned to mortal form as Hawkman. He has struggled to accept that Kendra is just beginning to process the memories of her past lives and that for now their eternal love must wait.

THE ATOM

Ray Palmer is a scientist who harnessed the properties of a white dwarf star. This led to the creation of unique size and weight controls that enable him to reduce his physical form to the size of an atom, or even smaller. One of the first heroes to join after the Justice League of America's founding, he is in the forefront of this generation's heroes. Eschewing heroics for research and teaching, the Atom remains available as a reserve member.

BLACK ADAM

Teth-Adam was the first to wield the mystical powers bestowed by the wizard Shazam. As Mighty Adam, he battled evil during Egypt's 15th Dynasty until the power ultimately corrupted him. Shazam imprisoned Adam in a scarab that was lost for centuries. A few years ago, two archaeologists, C.C. and Mary Batson, unearthed the scarab. Teth-Adam's powers and soul took root in the body of his descendant, Theo Adam, a thief and murderer. Now he struggles for redemption.

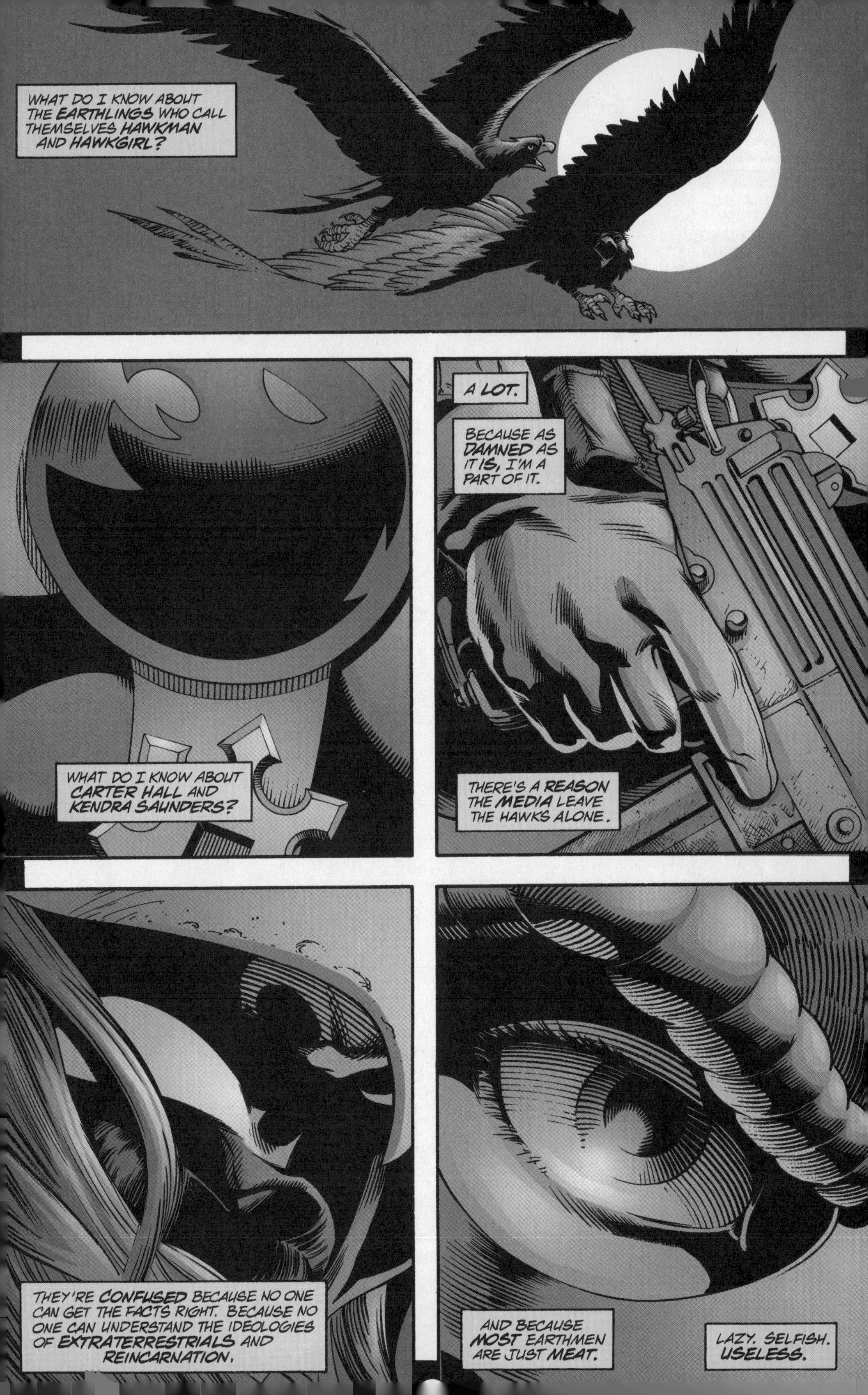
WHAT DO I KNOW ABOUT THE EARTHLINGS WHO CALL THEMSELVES HAWKMAN AND HAWKGIRL?
WHAT DO I KNOW ABOUT CARTER HALL AND KENDRA SAUNDERS?
A LOT.
BECAUSE AS DAMNED AS IT IS, I'M A PART OF IT.
THERE'S A REASON THE MEDIA LEAVE THE HAWKS ALONE.
THEY'RE CONFUSED BECAUSE NO ONE CAN GET THE FACTS RIGHT. BECAUSE NO ONE CAN UNDERSTAND THE IDEOLOGIES OF EXTRATERRESTRIALS AND REINCARNATION.
AND BECAUSE MOST EARTHMEN ARE JUST MEAT.
LAZY. SELFISH. USELESS.

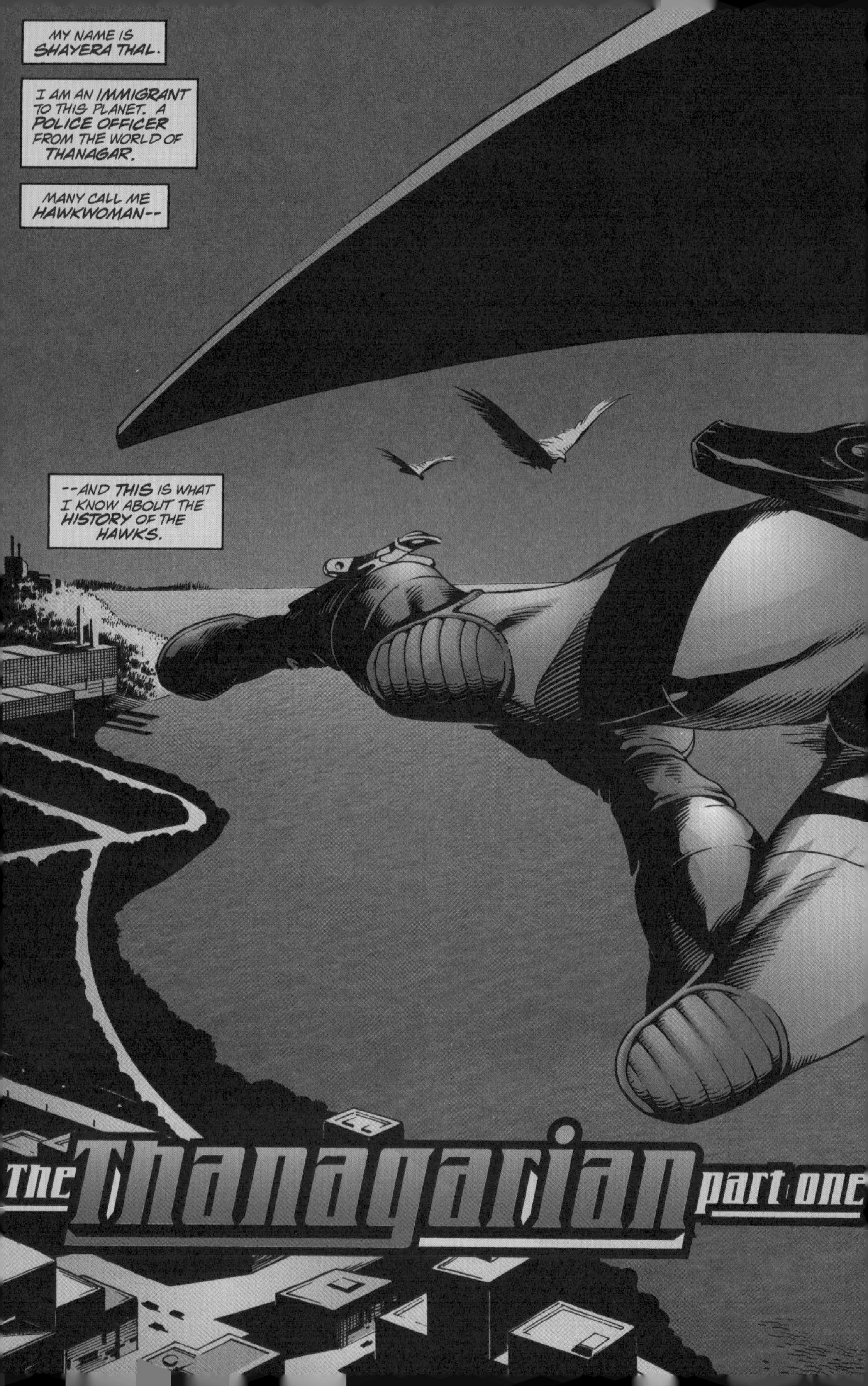
MY NAME IS SHAYERA THAL.
I AM AN IMMIGRANT TO THIS PLANET. A POLICE OFFICER FROM THE WORLD OF THANAGAR.
MANY CALL ME HAWKWOMAN--
--AND THIS IS WHAT I KNOW ABOUT THE HISTORY OF THE HAWKS.
The Thanagarian part one

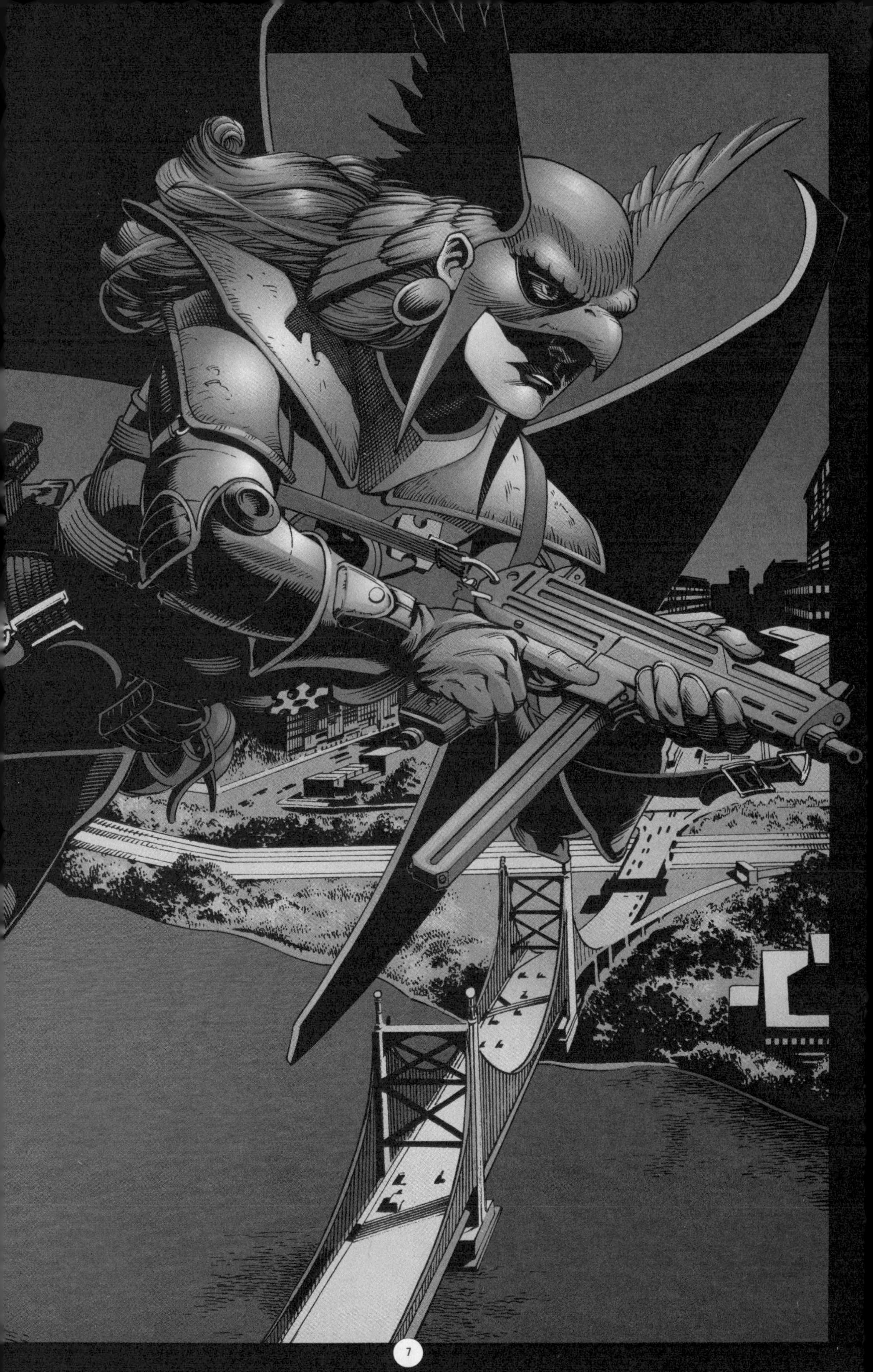

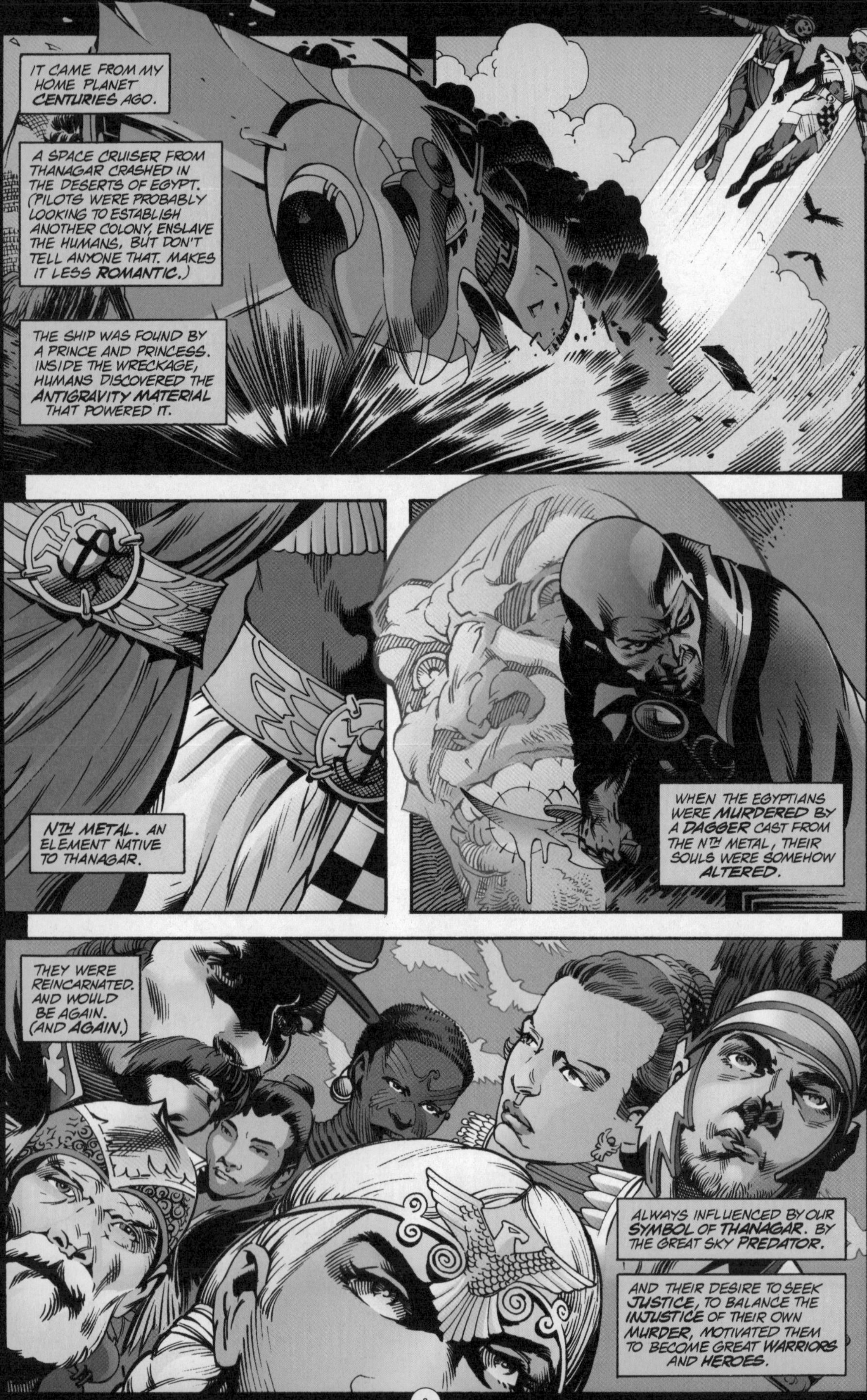
IT CAME FROM MY HOME PLANET CENTURIES AGO.
A SPACE CRUISER FROM THANAGAR CRASHED IN THE DESERTS OF EGYPT. (PILOTS WERE PROBABLY LOOKING TO ESTABLISH ANOTHER COLONY, ENSLAVE THE HUMANS, BUT DON'T TELL ANYONE THAT. MAKES IT LESS ROMANTIC.)
THE SHIP WAS FOUND BY A PRINCE AND PRINCESS. INSIDE THE WRECKAGE, HUMANS DISCOVERED THE ANTIGRAVITY MATERIAL THAT POWERED IT.
NTH METAL. AN ELEMENT NATIVE TO THANAGAR.
WHEN THE EGYPTIANS WERE MURDERED BY A DAGGER CAST FROM THE NTH METAL, THEIR SOULS WERE SOMEHOW ALTERED.
THEY WERE REINCARNATED. AND WOULD BE AGAIN. (AND AGAIN.)
ALWAYS INFLUENCED BY OUR SYMBOL OF THANAGAR. BY THE GREAT SKY PREDATOR.
AND THEIR DESIRE TO SEEK JUSTICE, TO BALANCE THE INJUSTICE OF THEIR OWN MURDER, MOTIVATED THEM TO BECOME GREAT WARRIORS AND HEROES.

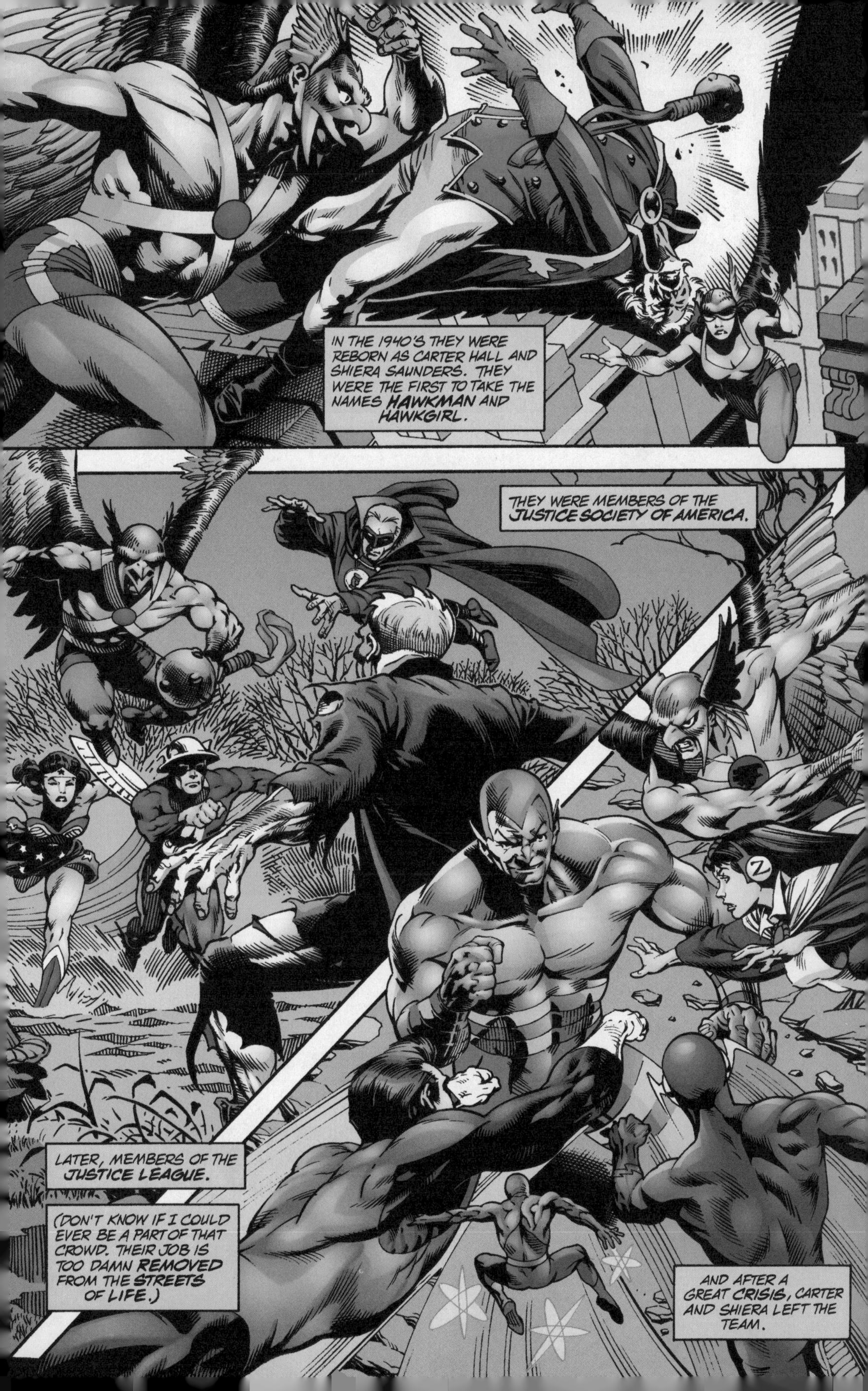
IN THE 1940'S THEY WERE REBORN AS CARTER HALL AND SHIERA SAUNDERS. THEY WERE THE FIRST TO TAKE THE NAMES HAWKMAN AND HAWKGIRL.
THEY WERE MEMBERS OF THE JUSTICE SOCIETY OF AMERICA.
LATER, MEMBERS OF THE JUSTICE LEAGUE.
(DON'T KNOW IF I COULD EVER BE A PART OF THAT CROWD. THEIR JOB IS TOO DAMN REMOVED FROM THE STREETS OF LIFE.)
AND AFTER A GREAT CRISIS, CARTER AND SHIERA LEFT THE TEAM.

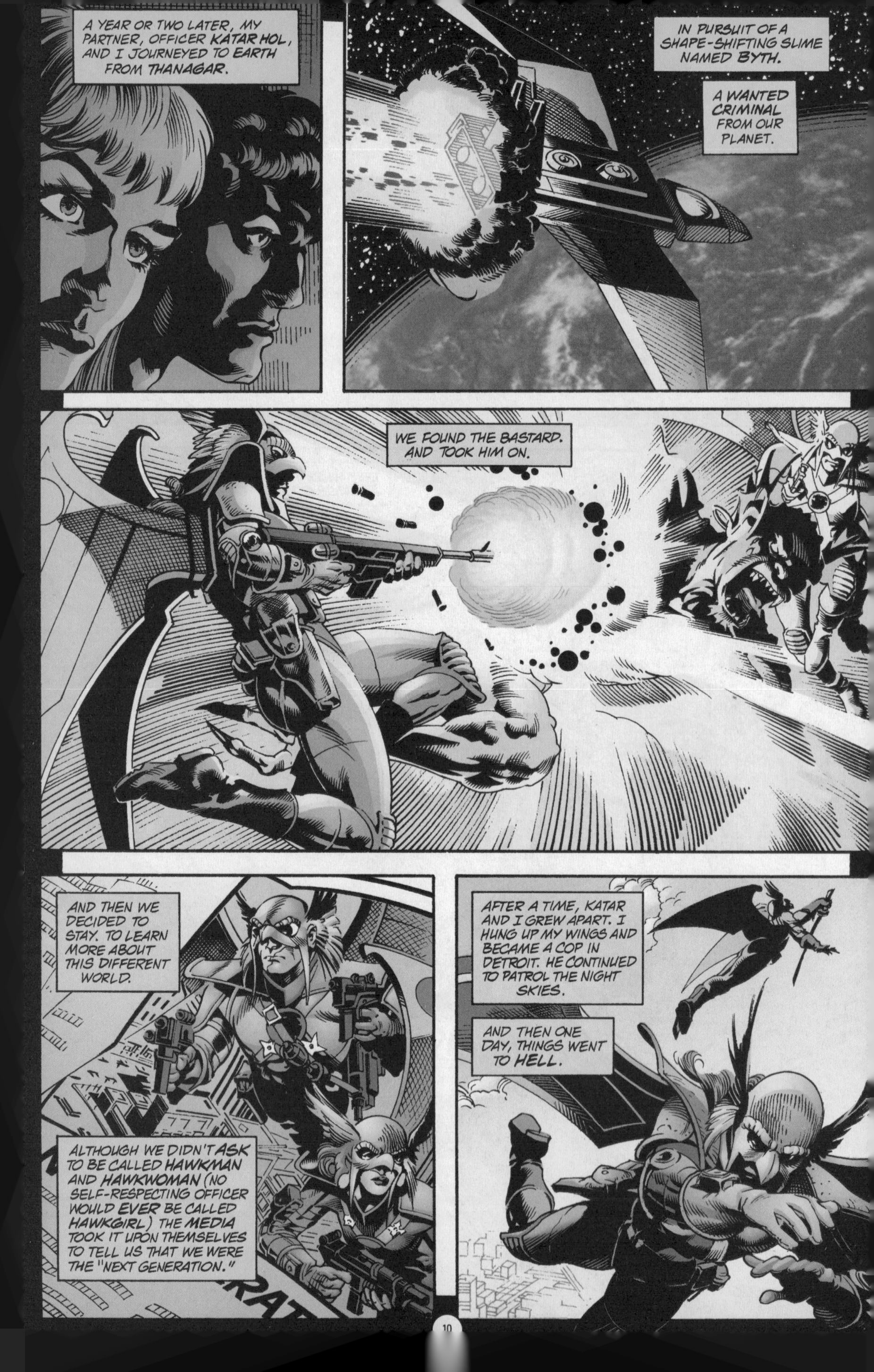
A YEAR OR TWO LATER, MY PARTNER, OFFICER KATAR HOL, AND I JOURNEYED TO EARTH FROM THANAGAR.
IN PURSUIT OF A SHAPE-SHIFTING SLIME NAMED BYTH.
A WANTED CRIMINAL FROM OUR PLANET.
WE FOUND THE BASTARD. AND TOOK HIM ON.
AND THEN WE DECIDED TO STAY. TO LEARN MORE ABOUT THIS DIFFERENT WORLD.
ALTHOUGH WE DIDN'T ASK TO BE CALLED HAWKMAN AND HAWKWOMAN (NO SELF-RESPECTING OFFICER WOULD EVER BE CALLED HAWKGIRL) THE MEDIA TOOK IT UPON THEMSELVES TO TELL US THAT WE WERE THE "NEXT GENERATION."
AFTER A TIME, KATAR AND I GREW APART. I HUNG UP MY WINGS AND BECAME A COP IN DETROIT. HE CONTINUED TO PATROL THE NIGHT SKIES.
AND THEN ONE DAY, THINGS WENT TO HELL.

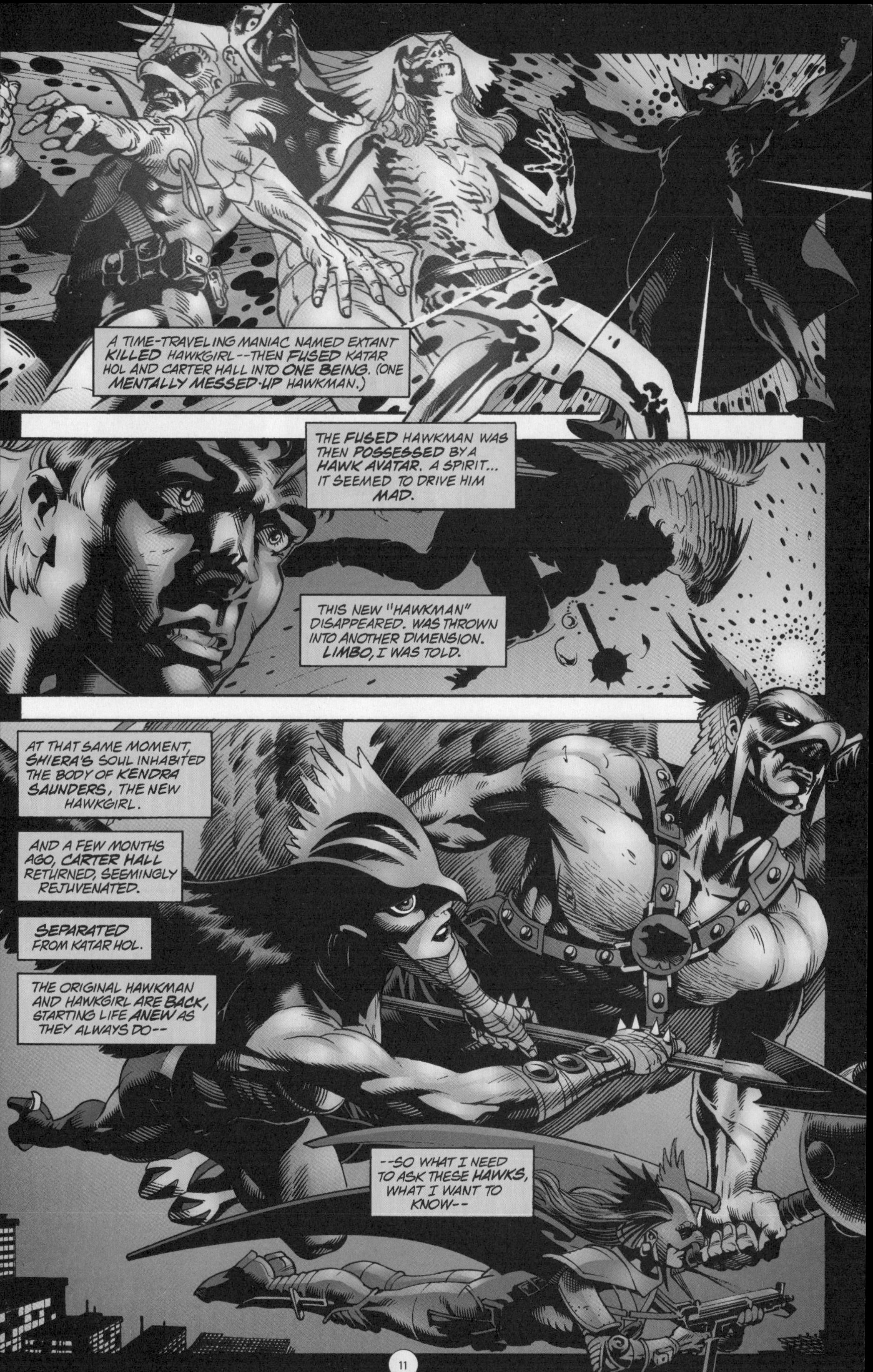
A TIME-TRAVELING MANIAC NAMED EXTANT KILLED HAWKGIRL--THEN FUSED KATAR HOL AND CARTER HALL INTO ONE BEING. (ONE MENTALLY MESSED-UP HAWKMAN.)
THE FUSED HAWKMAN WAS THEN POSSESSED BY A HAWK AVATAR. A SPIRIT... IT SEEMED TO DRIVE HIM MAD.
THIS NEW "HAWKMAN" DISAPPEARED. WAS THROWN INTO ANOTHER DIMENSION. LIMBO, I WAS TOLD.
AT THAT SAME MOMENT, SHIERA'S SOUL INHABITED THE BODY OF KENDRA SAUNDERS, THE NEW HAWKGIRL.
AND A FEW MONTHS AGO, CARTER HALL RETURNED, SEEMINGLY REJUVENATED.
SEPARATED FROM KATAR HOL.
THE ORIGINAL HAWKMAN AND HAWKGIRL ARE BACK, STARTING LIFE ANEW AS THEY ALWAYS DO--
--SO WHAT I NEED TO ASK THESE HAWKS, WHAT I WANT TO KNOW--

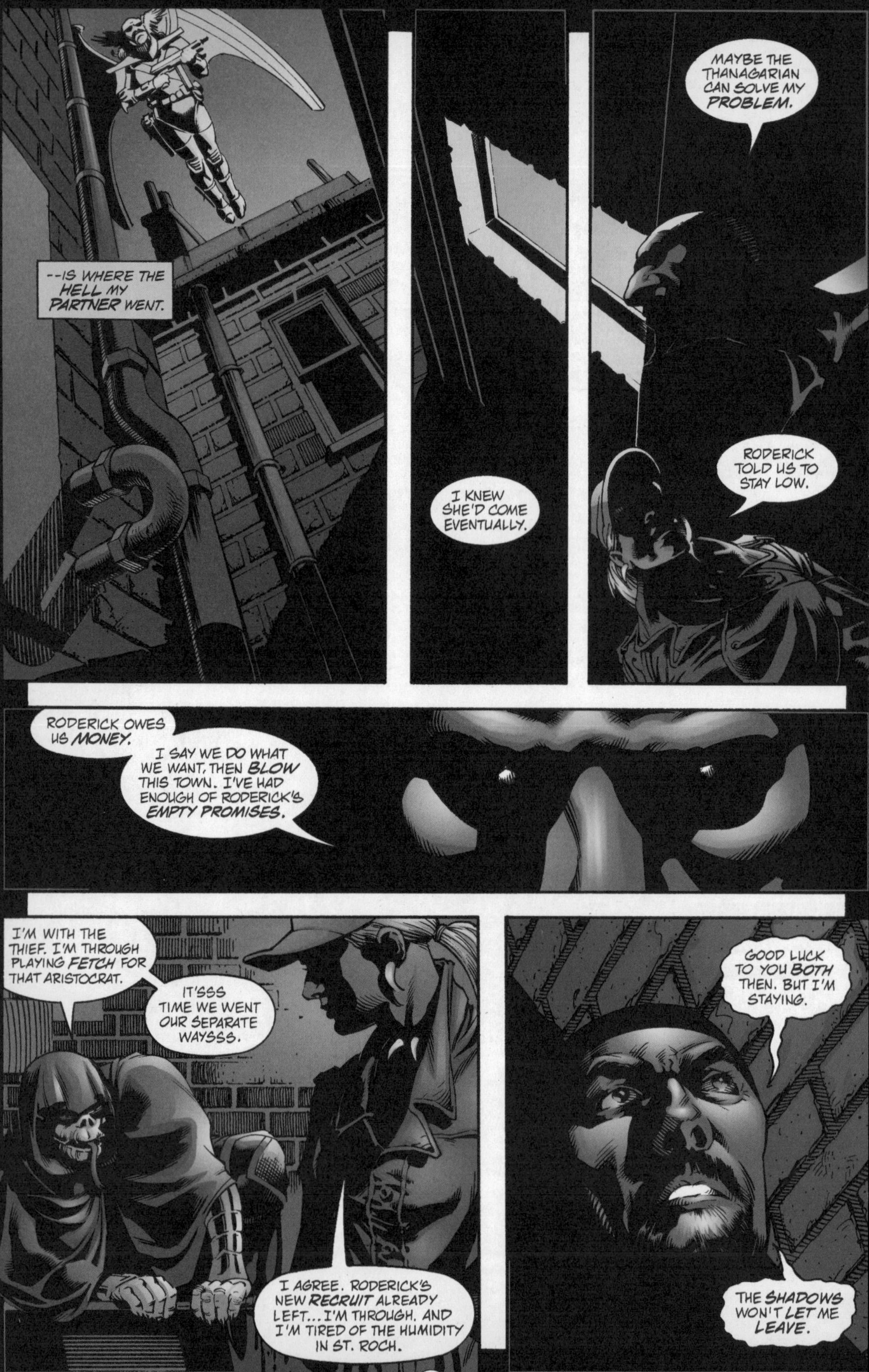
--IS WHERE THE HELL MY PARTNER WENT.
I KNEW SHE'D COME EVENTUALLY.
MAYBE THE THANAGARIAN CAN SOLVE MY PROBLEM.
RODERICK TOLD US TO STAY LOW.
RODERICK OWES US MONEY.
I SAY WE DO WHAT WE WANT, THEN BLOW THIS TOWN. I'VE HAD ENOUGH OF RODERICK'S EMPTY PROMISES.
I'M WITH THE THIEF. I'M THROUGH PLAYING FETCH FOR THAT ARISTOCRAT.
IT'SSS TIME WE WENT OUR SEPARATE WAYSSS.
I AGREE. RODERICK'S NEW RECRUIT ALREADY LEFT... I'M THROUGH. AND I'M TIRED OF THE HUMIDITY IN ST. ROCH.
GOOD LUCK TO YOU BOTH THEN. BUT I'M STAYING.
THE SHADOWS WON'T LET ME LEAVE.

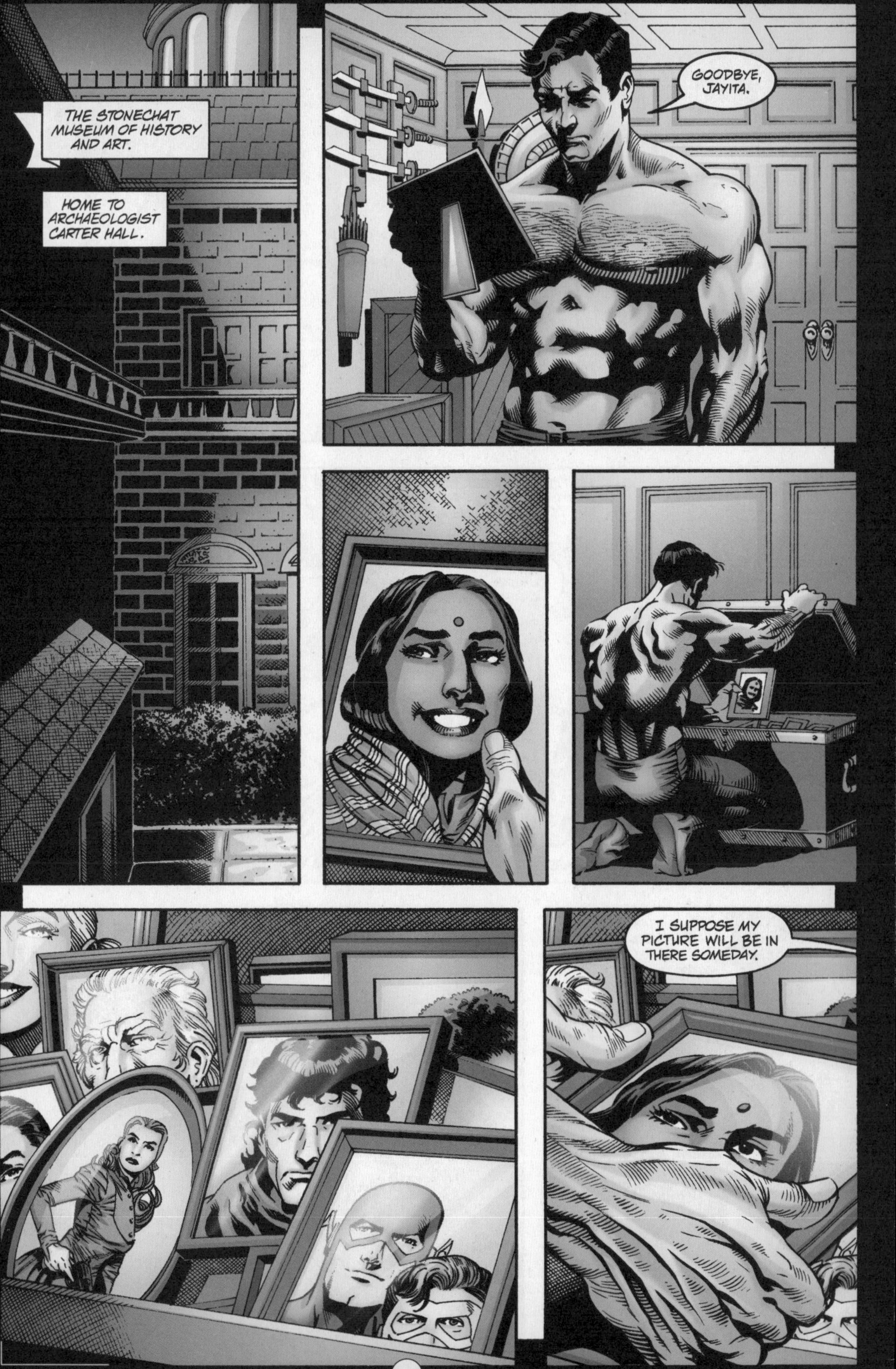
THE STONECHAT MUSEUM OF HISTORY AND ART.
HOME TO ARCHAEOLOGIST CARTER HALL.
GOODBYE, JAYITA.
I SUPPOSE MY PICTURE WILL BE IN THERE SOMEDAY.

**THOSE PICTURES. THEY'RE ALL PEOPLE YOU'VE KNOWN?**

**AND LOVED.**

MY FATHER AND OUR INTERNS SPENT FOUR DAYS LOCKED IN THE CELLAR. ALL BECAUSE OF THAT GHOST.

DAD'S STILL BLAMING HIMSELF FOR JAYITA'S DEATH. HE'S BACK ON THE JOB. BUT IT'S GOING SLOW.

I'M SORRY WE DIDN'T TELL YOU EARLIER ABOUT THE HAUNTINGS, BUT--

--WE DIDN'T WANT TO SCARE YOU AND HAWKGIRL AWAY FROM THE MUSEUM. WE WON'T HOLD ANYTHING BACK FROM YOU AGAIN.

GHOSTS DON'T SCARE ME.

**AND JAYITA'S DEATH WAS NO ONE'S FAULT, DANNY...**

IT WAS JUST--

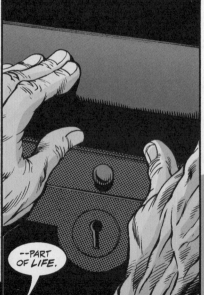**--PART OF LIFE.**

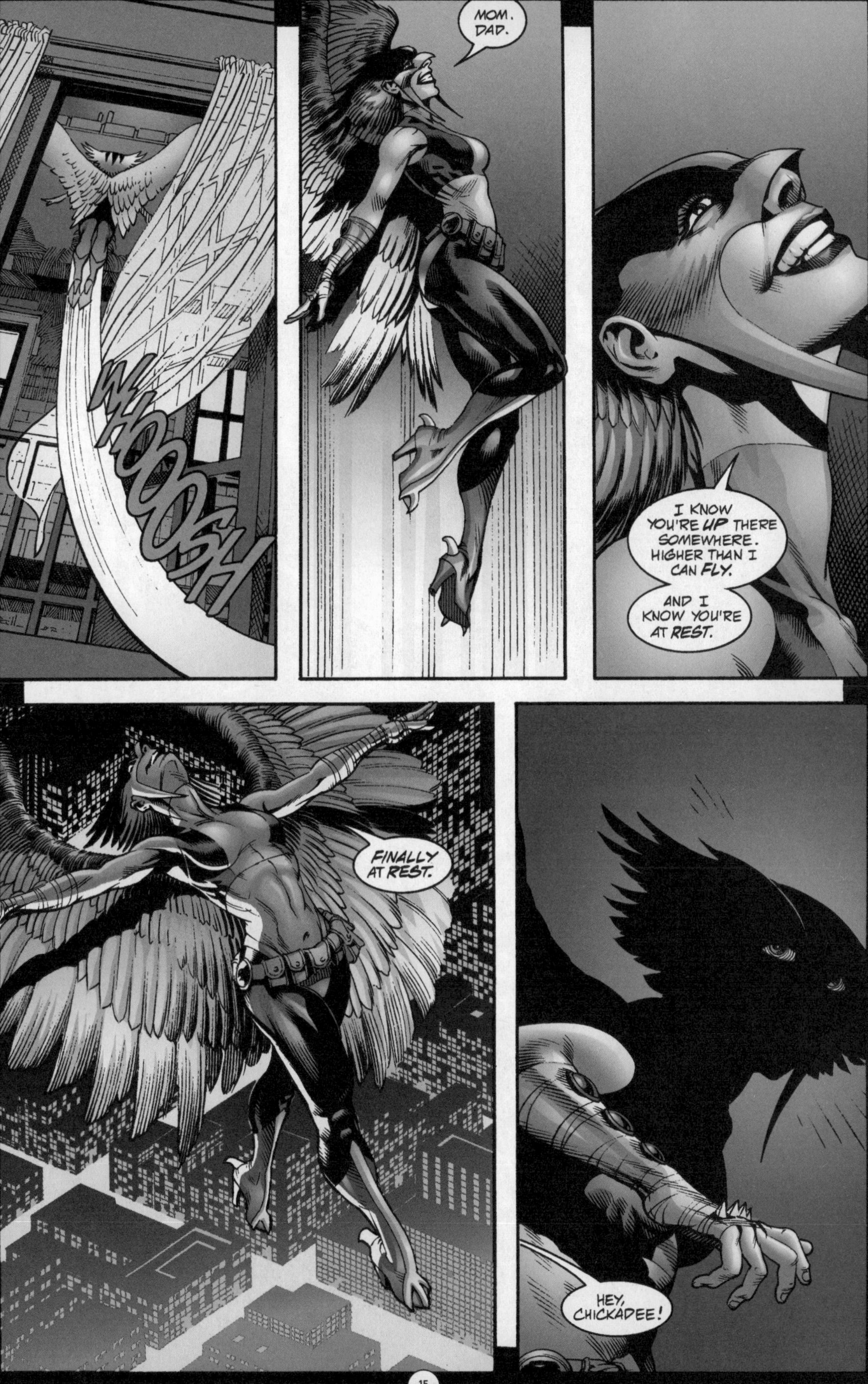
WHOOOSH
MOM. DAD.
I KNOW YOU'RE UP THERE SOMEWHERE. HIGHER THAN I CAN FLY.
AND I KNOW YOU'RE AT REST.
FINALLY AT REST.
HEY, CHICKADEE!

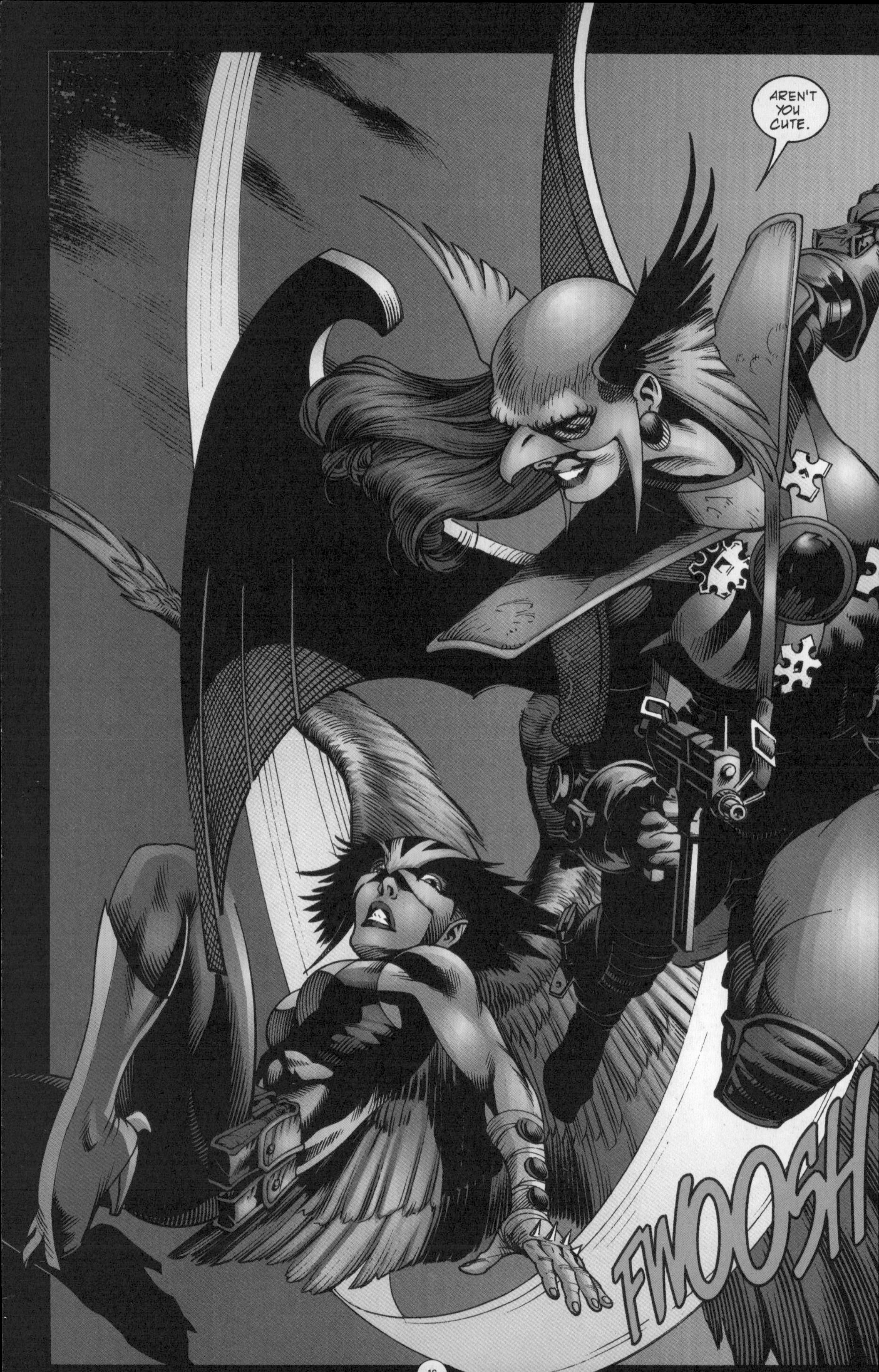
AREN'T YOU CUTE.
FWOOSH

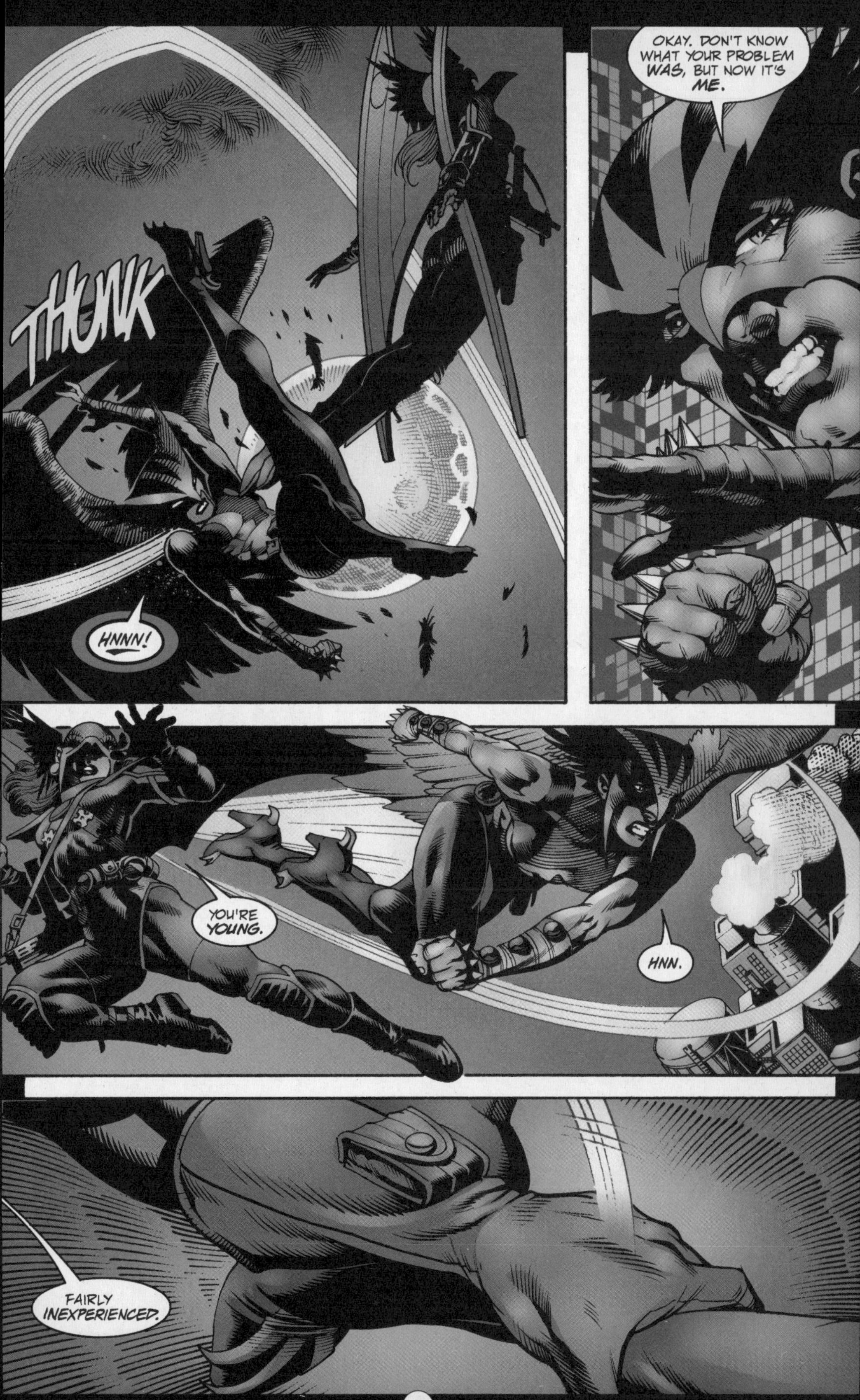
THUNK
HNNN!
OKAY. DON'T KNOW WHAT YOUR PROBLEM WAS, BUT NOW IT'S ME.
YOU'RE YOUNG.
HNN.
FAIRLY INEXPERIENCED.

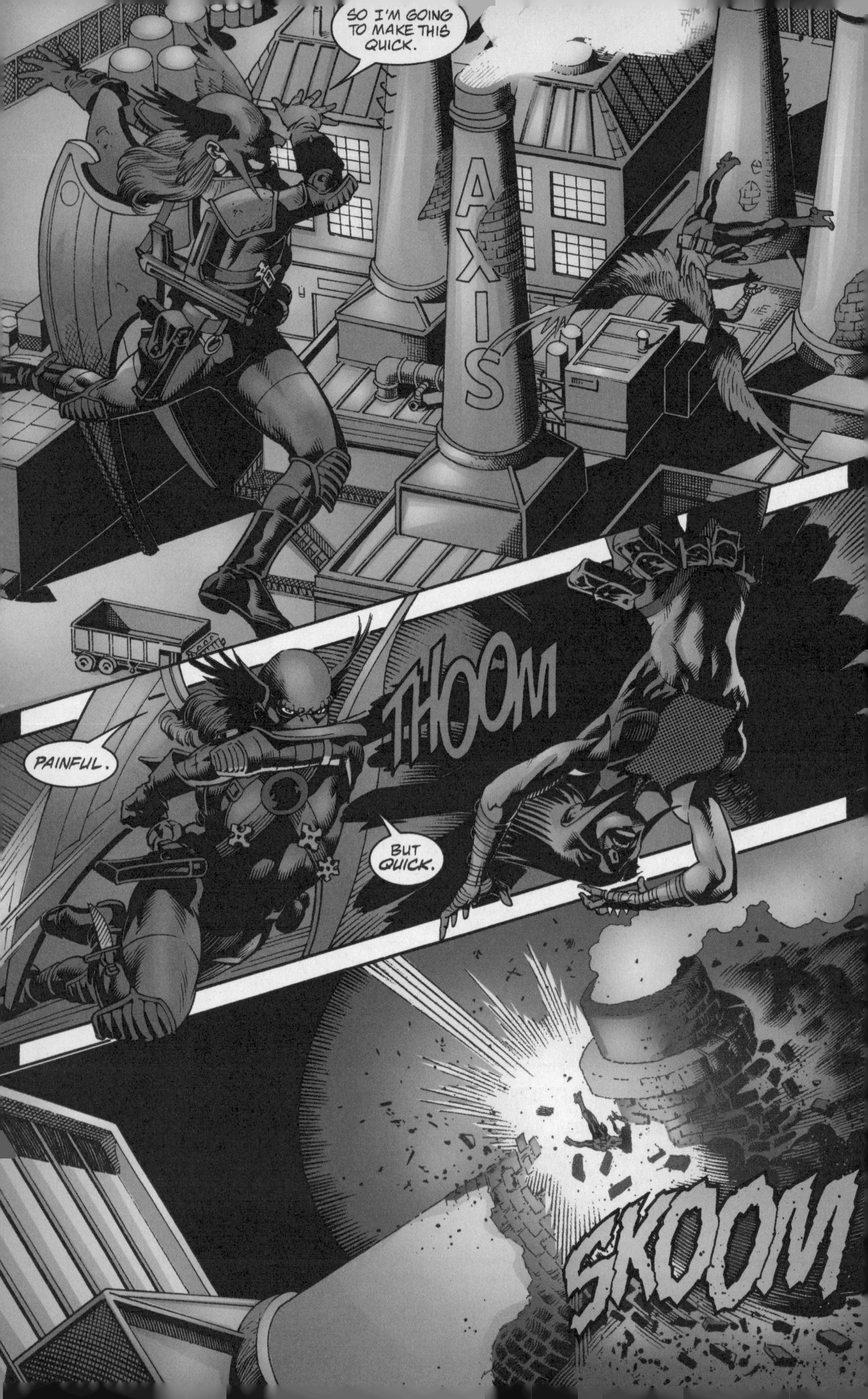
SO I'M GOING TO MAKE THIS QUICK.
THOOM
PAINFUL.
BUT QUICK.
SKOOM

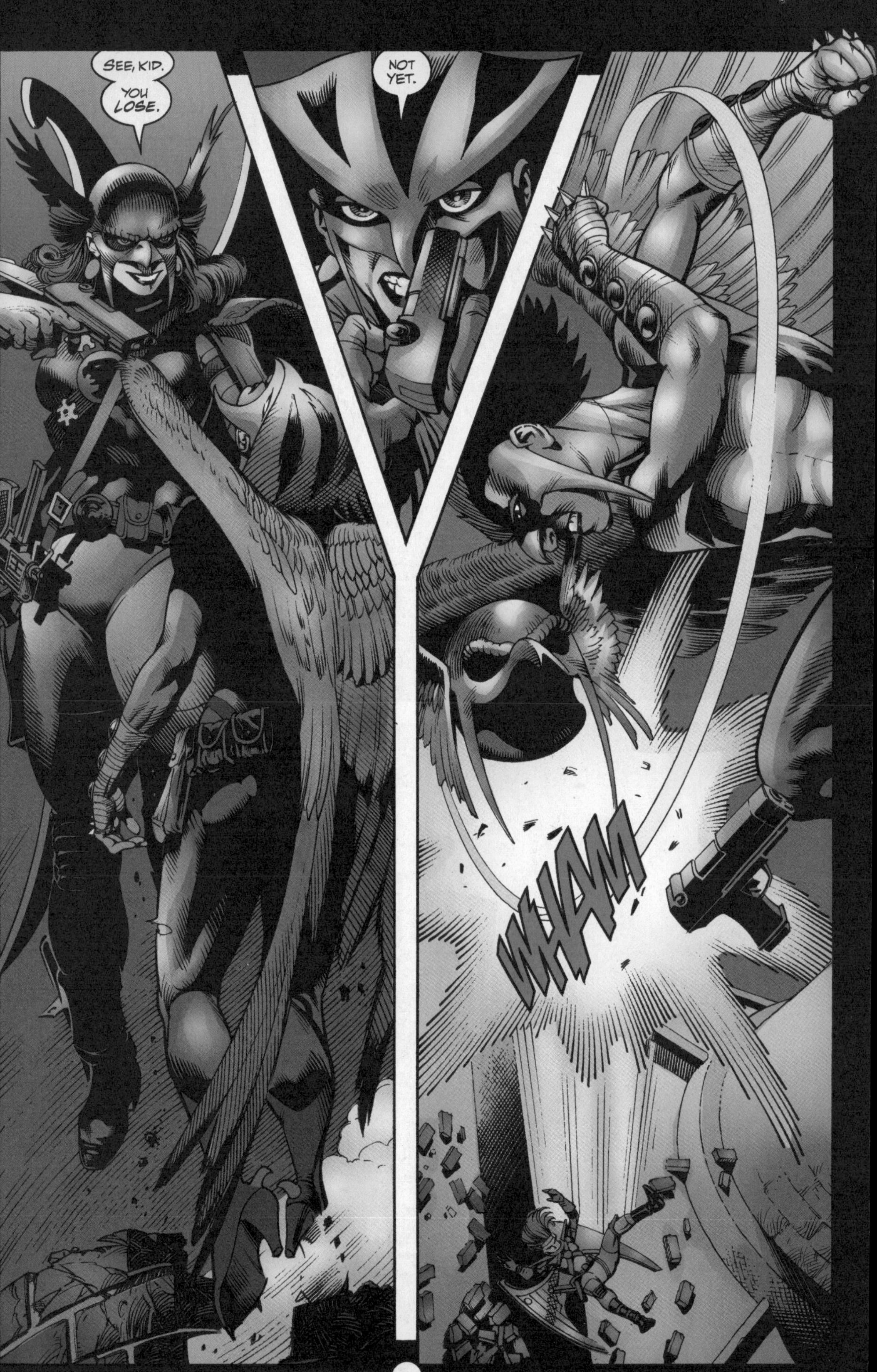
SEE, KID. YOU LOSE.
NOT YET.
WHAM

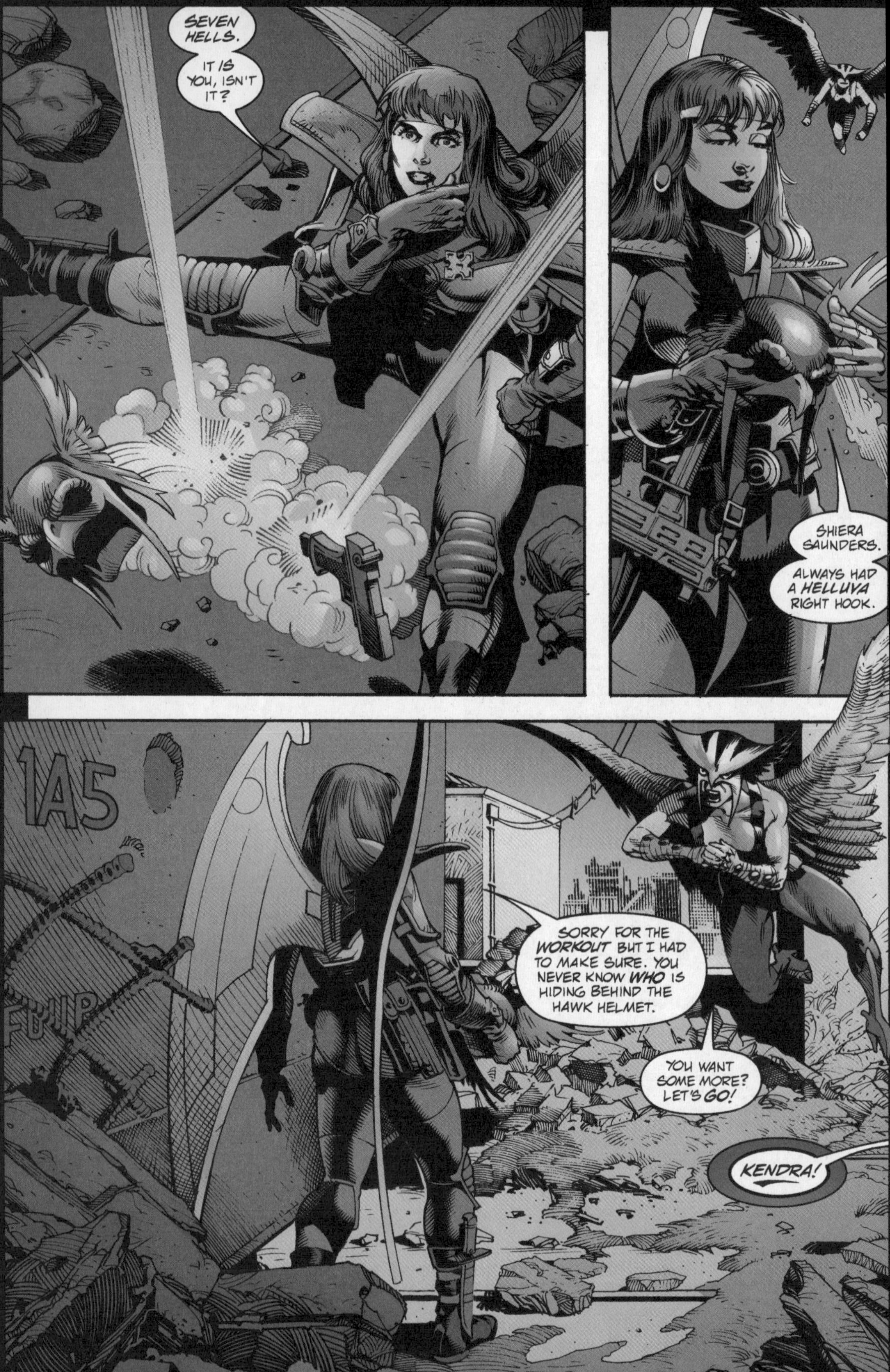
SEVEN HELLS.
IT IS YOU, ISN'T IT?
SHIERA SAUNDERS.
ALWAYS HAD A HELLUVA RIGHT HOOK.
1A5
SORRY FOR THE WORKOUT BUT I HAD TO MAKE SURE. YOU NEVER KNOW WHO IS HIDING BEHIND THE HAWK HELMET.
YOU WANT SOME MORE? LET'S GO!
KENDRA!

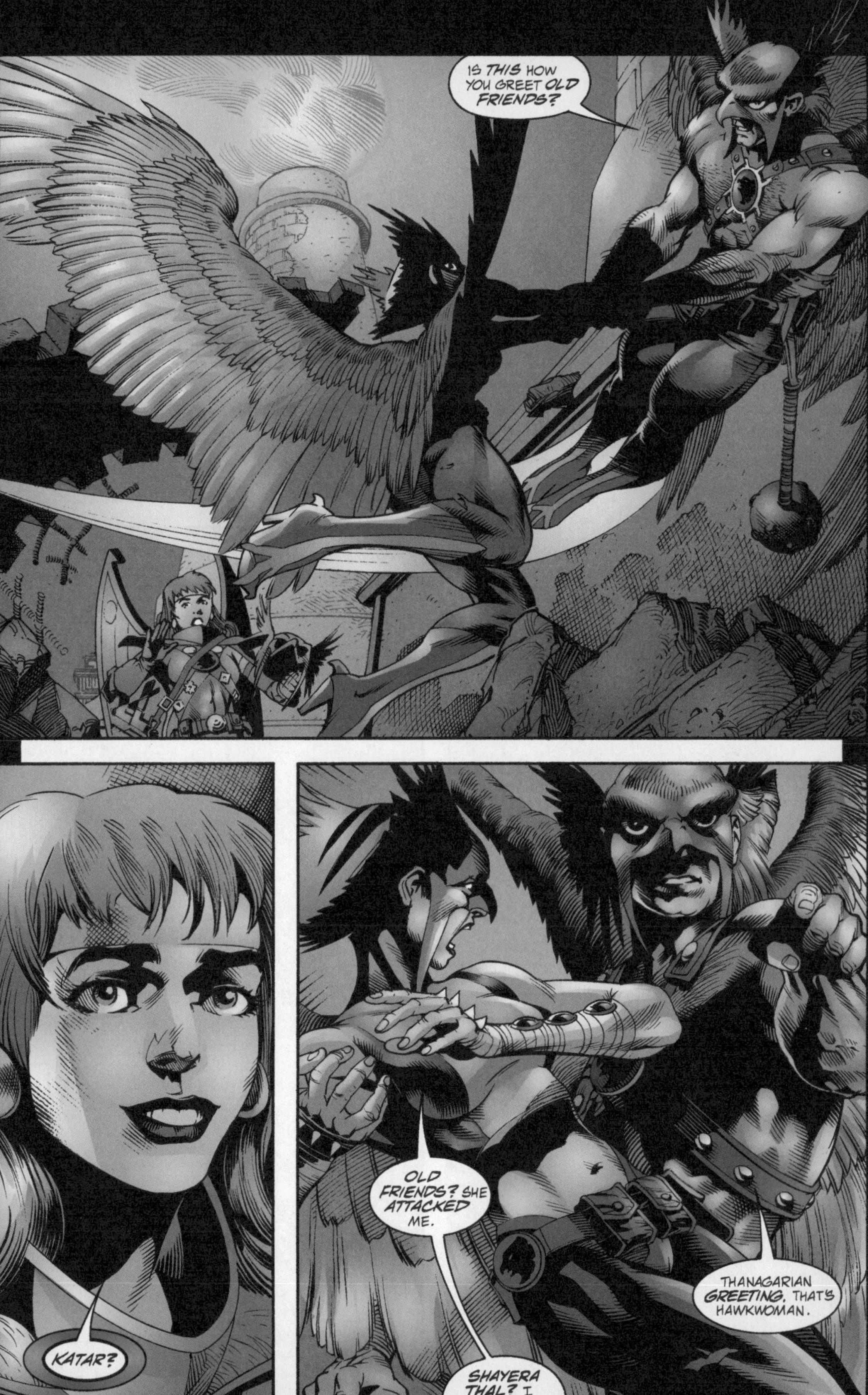
IS THIS HOW YOU GREET OLD FRIENDS?
KATAR?
OLD FRIENDS? SHE ATTACKED ME.
THANAGARIAN GREETING. THAT'S HAWKWOMAN.
SHAYERA THAL? I THOUGHT SHE RETIRED.

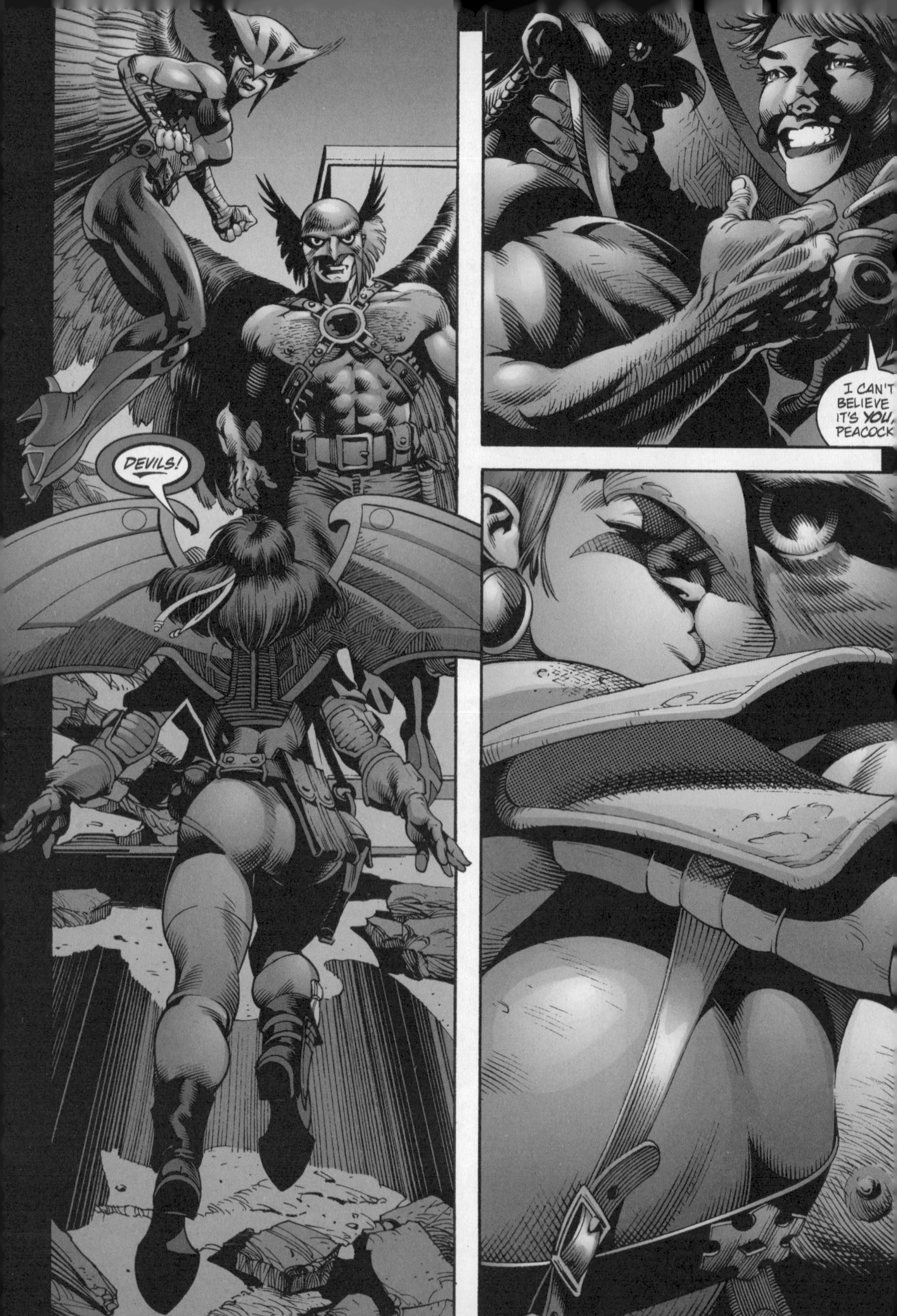
DEVILS!
I CAN'T BELIEVE IT'S YOU, PEACOCK

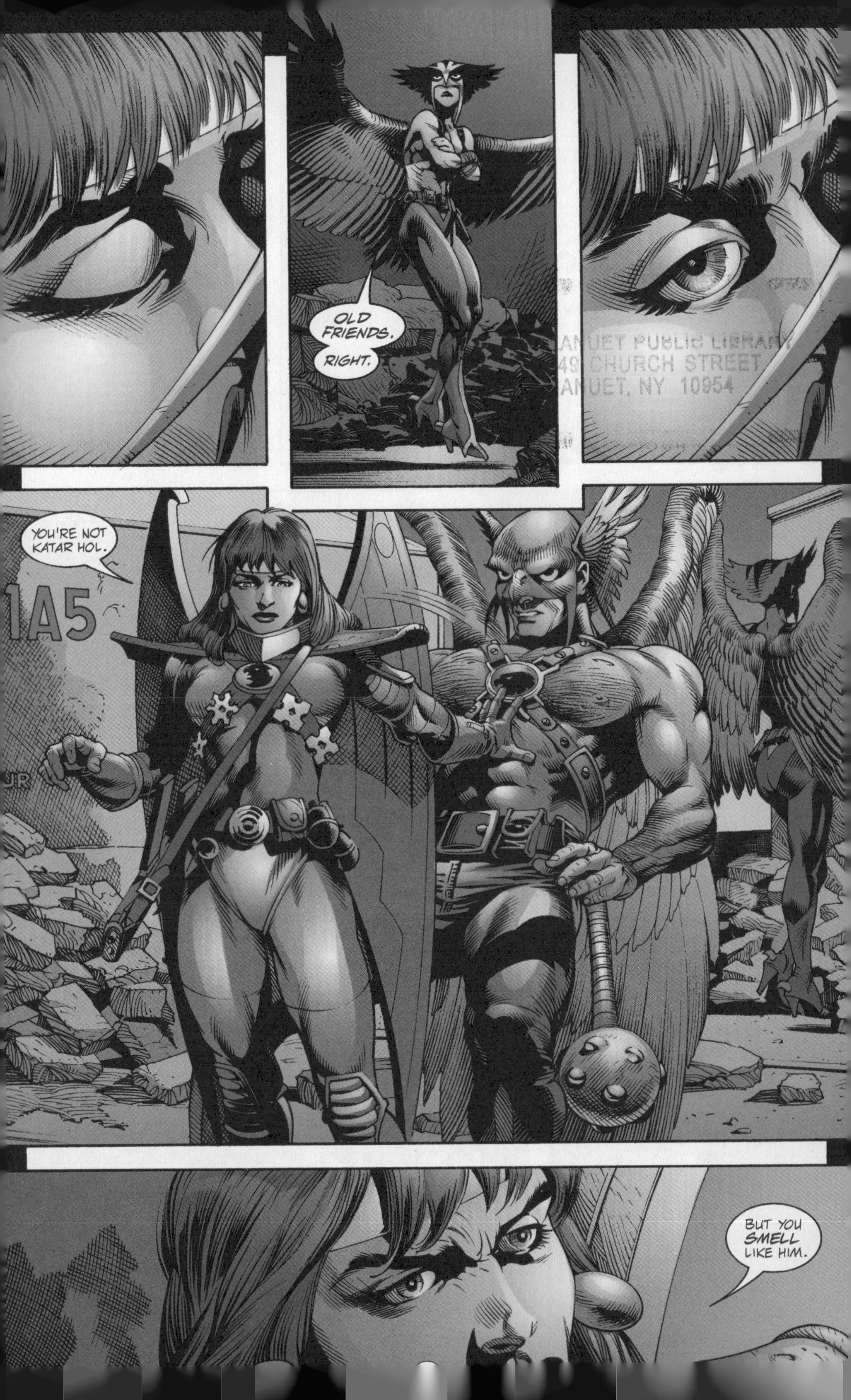

OLD FRIENDS.
RIGHT.
YOU'RE NOT KATAR HOL.
1A5
BUT YOU SMELL LIKE HIM.

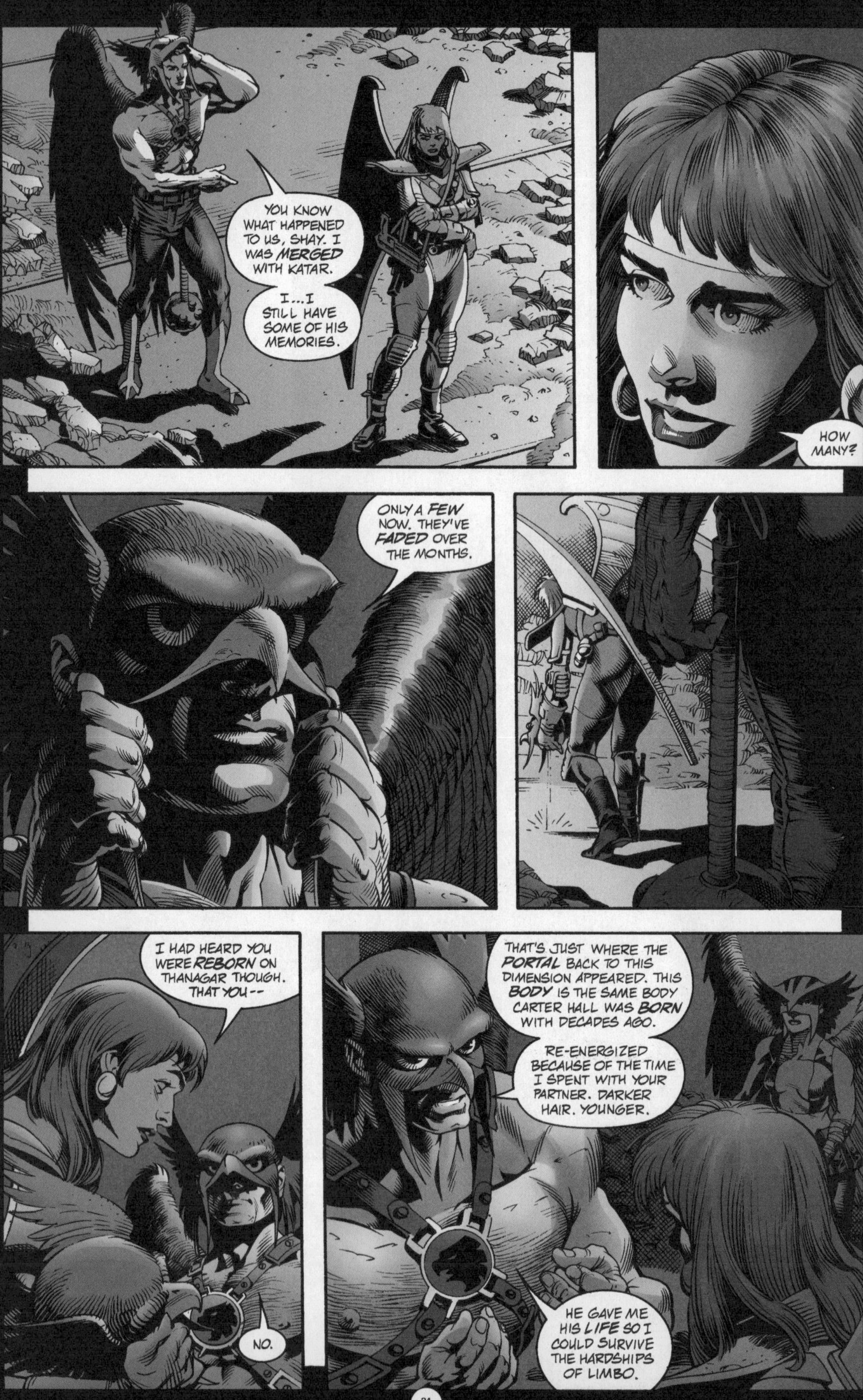

YOU KNOW WHAT HAPPENED TO US, SHAY. I WAS MERGED WITH KATAR.
I...I STILL HAVE SOME OF HIS MEMORIES.
HOW MANY?
ONLY A FEW NOW. THEY'VE FADED OVER THE MONTHS.
I HAD HEARD YOU WERE REBORN ON THANAGAR THOUGH. THAT YOU--
NO.
THAT'S JUST WHERE THE PORTAL BACK TO THIS DIMENSION APPEARED. THIS BODY IS THE SAME BODY CARTER HALL WAS BORN WITH DECADES AGO.
RE-ENERGIZED BECAUSE OF THE TIME I SPENT WITH YOUR PARTNER. DARKER HAIR. YOUNGER.
HE GAVE ME HIS LIFE SO I COULD SURVIVE THE HARDSHIPS OF LIMBO.

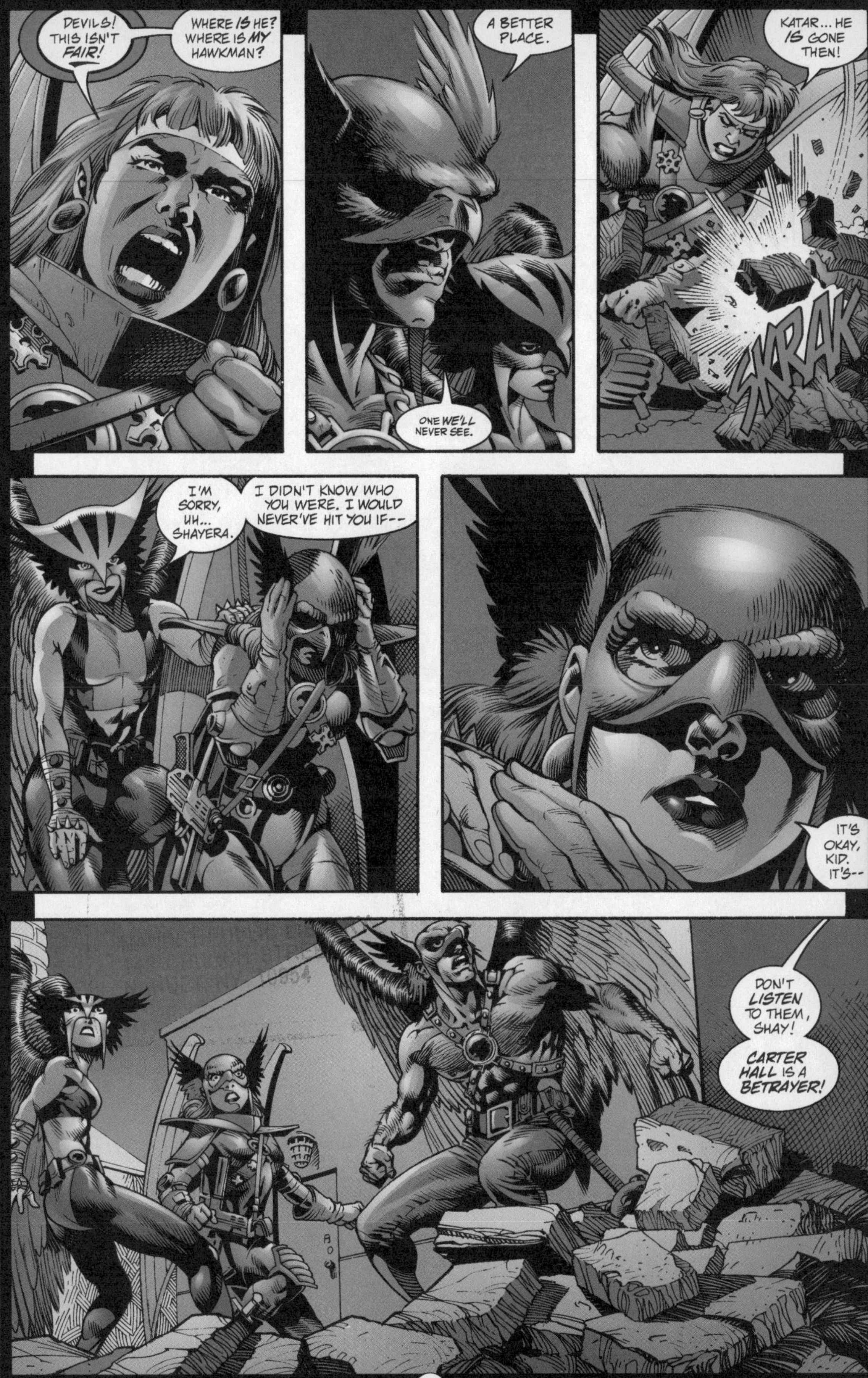
DEVILS! THIS ISN'T FAIR!
WHERE IS HE? WHERE IS MY HAWKMAN?
A BETTER PLACE.
ONE WE'LL NEVER SEE.
KATAR... HE IS GONE THEN!
SKRAK
I'M SORRY, UH... SHAYERA.
I DIDN'T KNOW WHO YOU WERE. I WOULD NEVER'VE HIT YOU IF--
IT'S OKAY, KID. IT'S--
DON'T LISTEN TO THEM, SHAY!
CARTER HALL IS A BETRAYER!

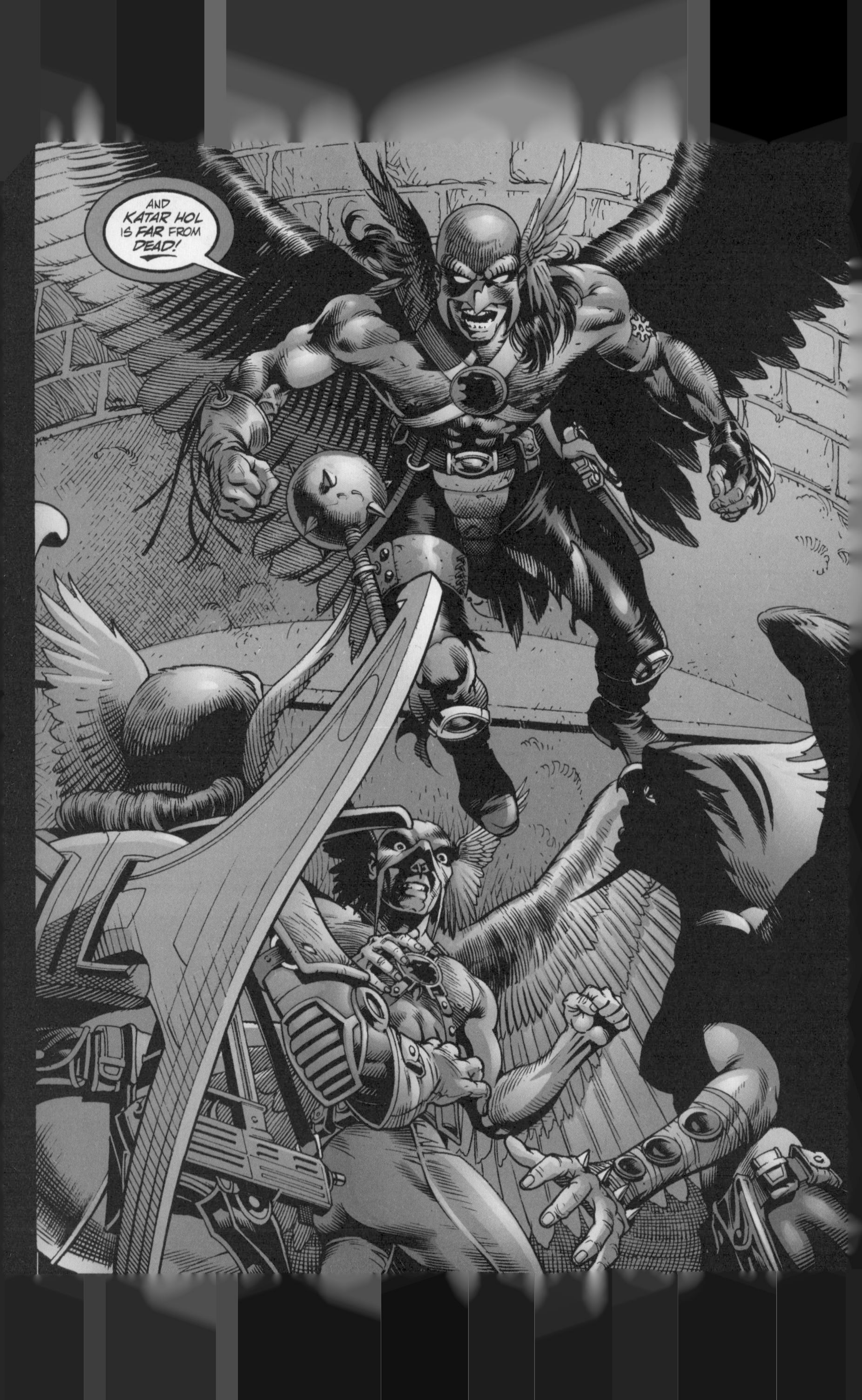
AND KATAR HOL IS FAR FROM DEAD!

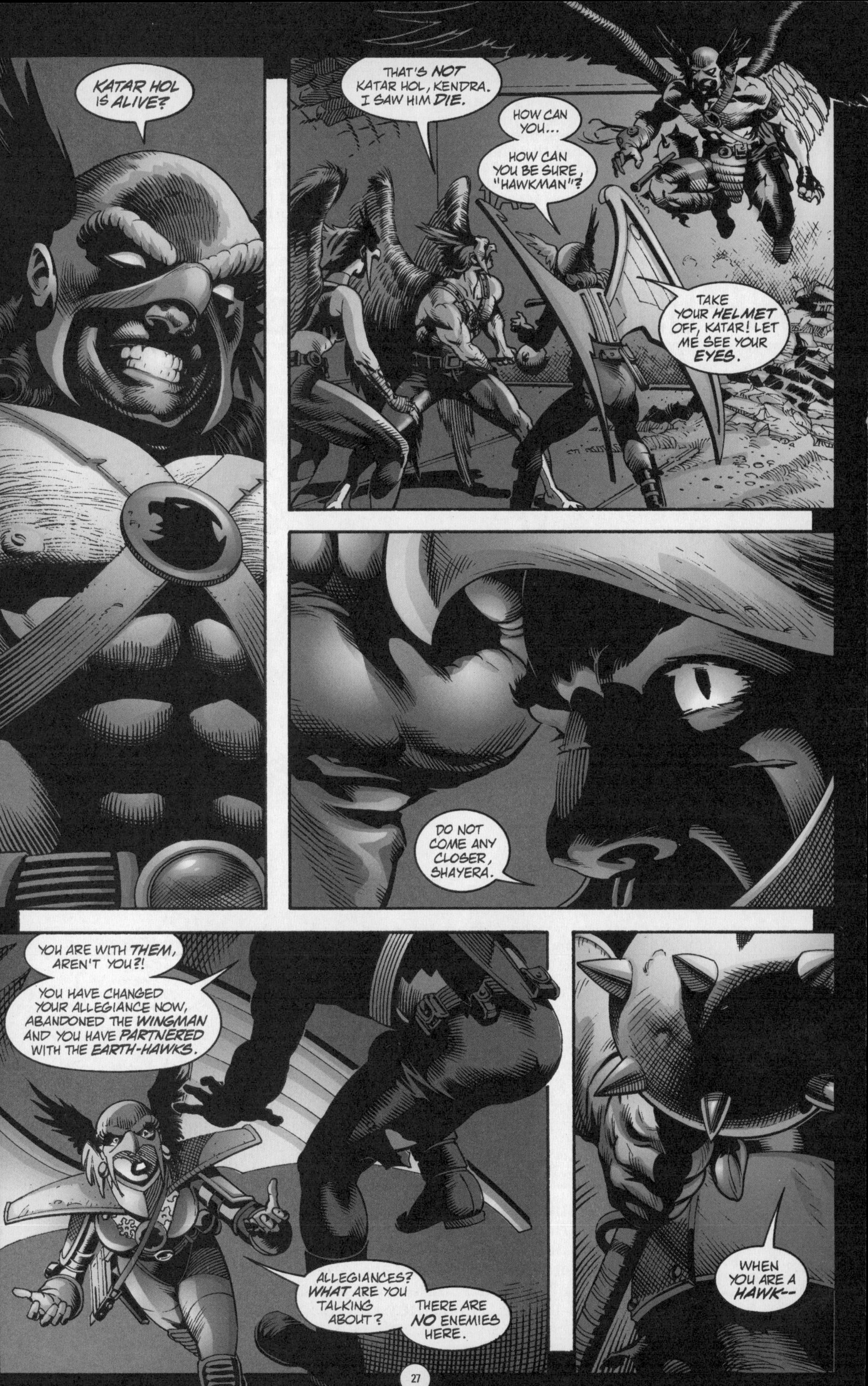
KATAR HOL IS ALIVE?
THAT'S NOT KATAR HOL, KENDRA. I SAW HIM DIE.
HOW CAN YOU...
HOW CAN YOU BE SURE, "HAWKMAN"?
TAKE YOUR HELMET OFF, KATAR! LET ME SEE YOUR EYES.
DO NOT COME ANY CLOSER, SHAYERA.
YOU ARE WITH THEM, AREN'T YOU?!
YOU HAVE CHANGED YOUR ALLEGIANCE NOW, ABANDONED THE WINGMAN AND YOU HAVE PARTNERED WITH THE EARTH-HAWKS.
ALLEGIANCES? WHAT ARE YOU TALKING ABOUT?
THERE ARE NO ENEMIES HERE.
WHEN YOU ARE A HAWK--

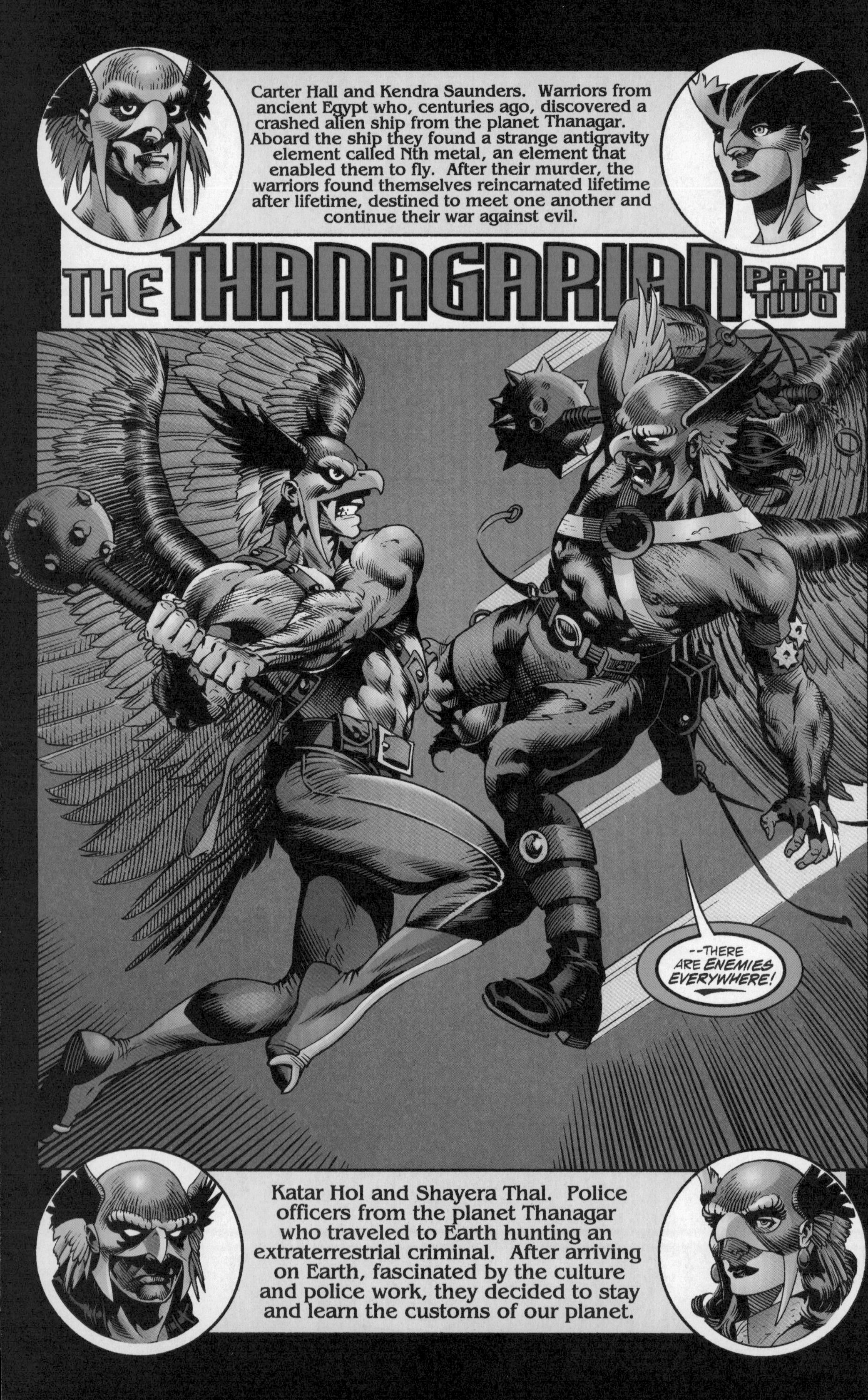
Carter Hall and Kendra Saunders. Warriors from ancient Egypt who, centuries ago, discovered a crashed alien ship from the planet Thanagar. Aboard the ship they found a strange antigravity element called Nth metal, an element that enabled them to fly. After their murder, the warriors found themselves reincarnated lifetime after lifetime, destined to meet one another and continue their war against evil.
THE THANAGARIAN PART TWO
--THERE ARE ENEMIES EVERYWHERE!
Katar Hol and Shayera Thal. Police officers from the planet Thanagar who traveled to Earth hunting an extraterrestrial criminal. After arriving on Earth, fascinated by the culture and police work, they decided to stay and learn the customs of our planet.

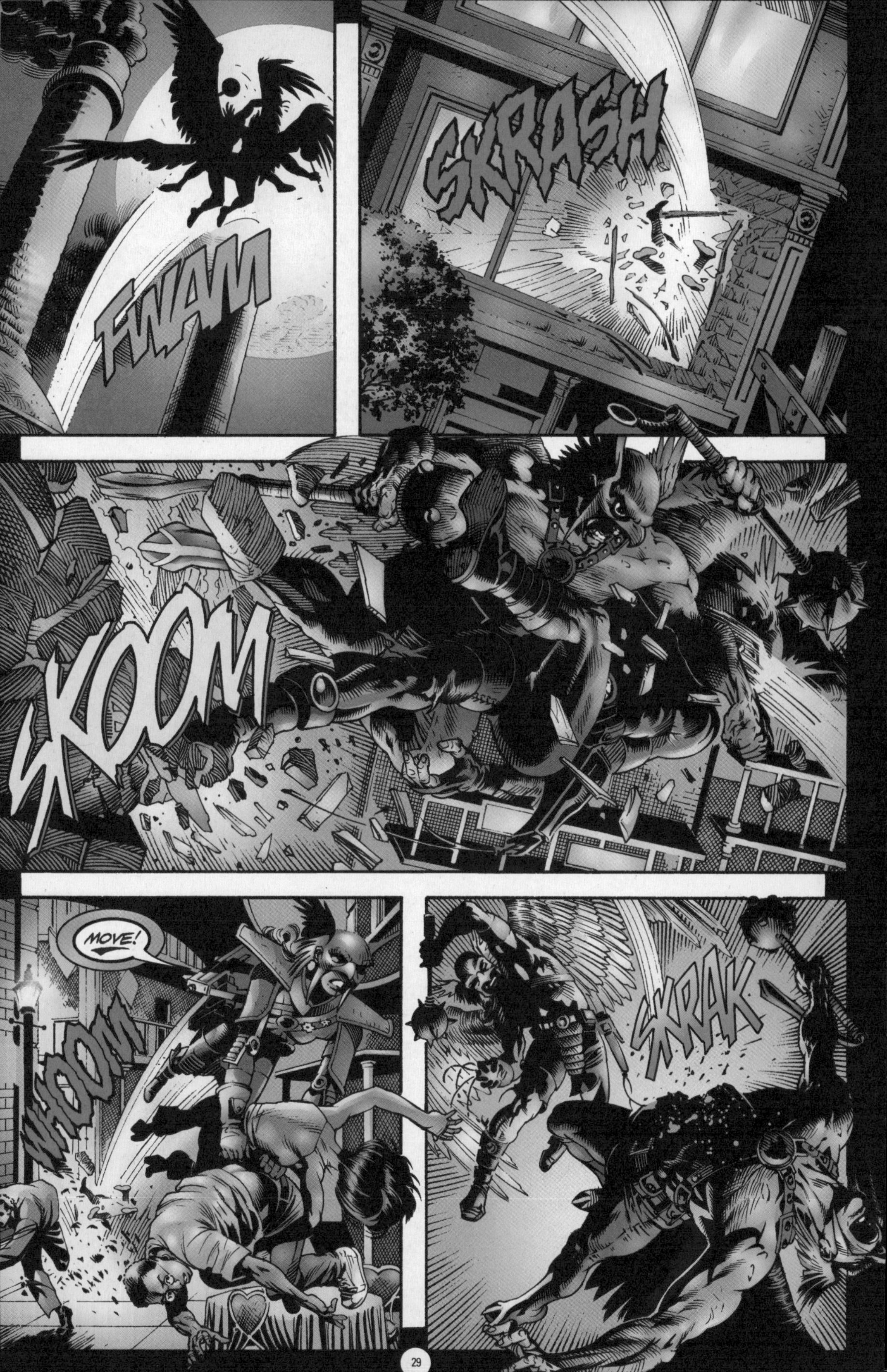
FWAM
SKRASH
SKOOM
MOVE!
WHOOM
SKRAK

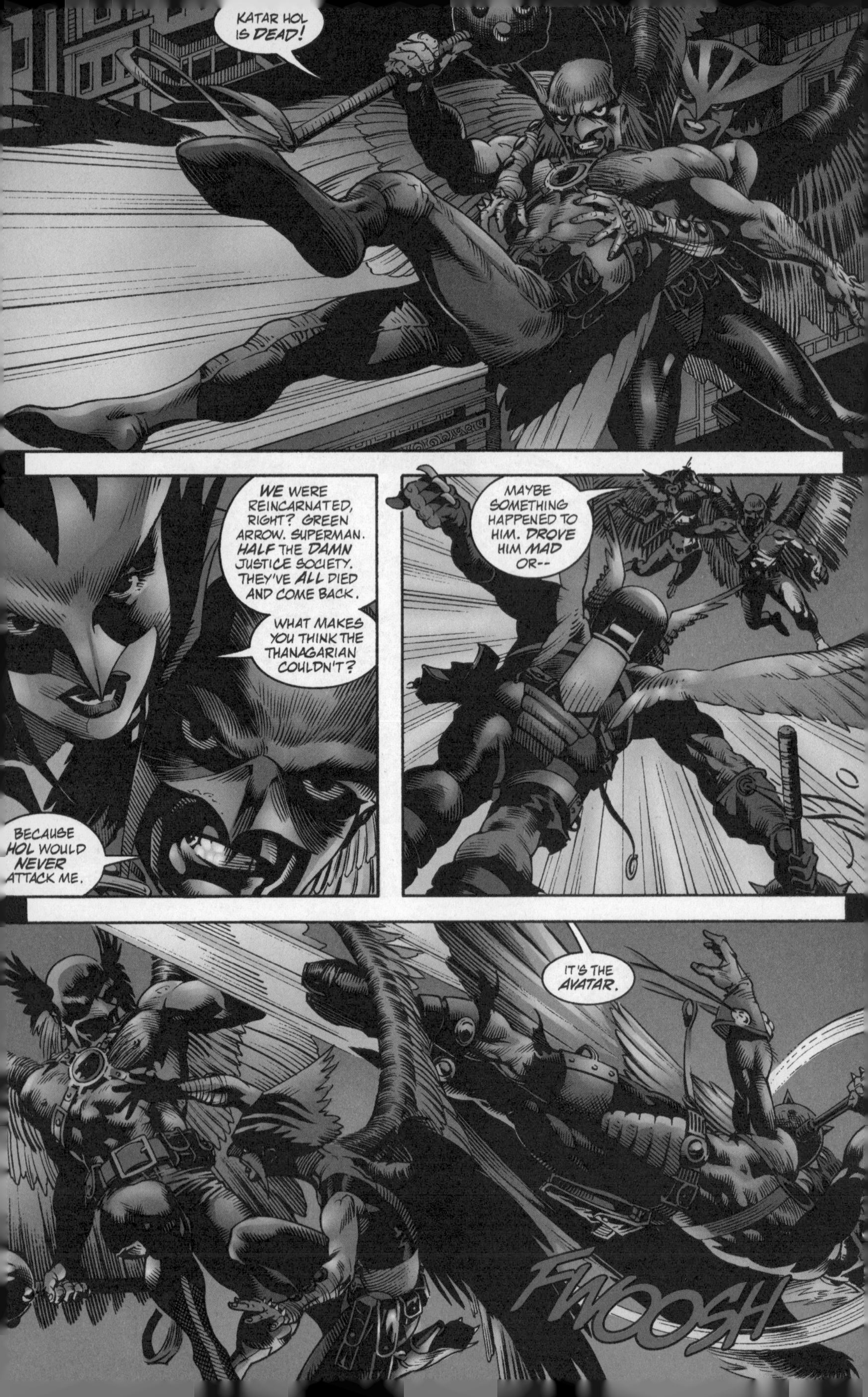

KATAR HOL IS DEAD!
WE WERE REINCARNATED, RIGHT? GREEN ARROW. SUPERMAN. HALF THE DAMN JUSTICE SOCIETY. THEY'VE ALL DIED AND COME BACK.
WHAT MAKES YOU THINK THE THANAGARIAN COULDN'T?
BECAUSE HOL WOULD NEVER ATTACK ME.
MAYBE SOMETHING HAPPENED TO HIM. DROVE HIM MAD OR--
IT'S THE AVATAR.
FWOOSH

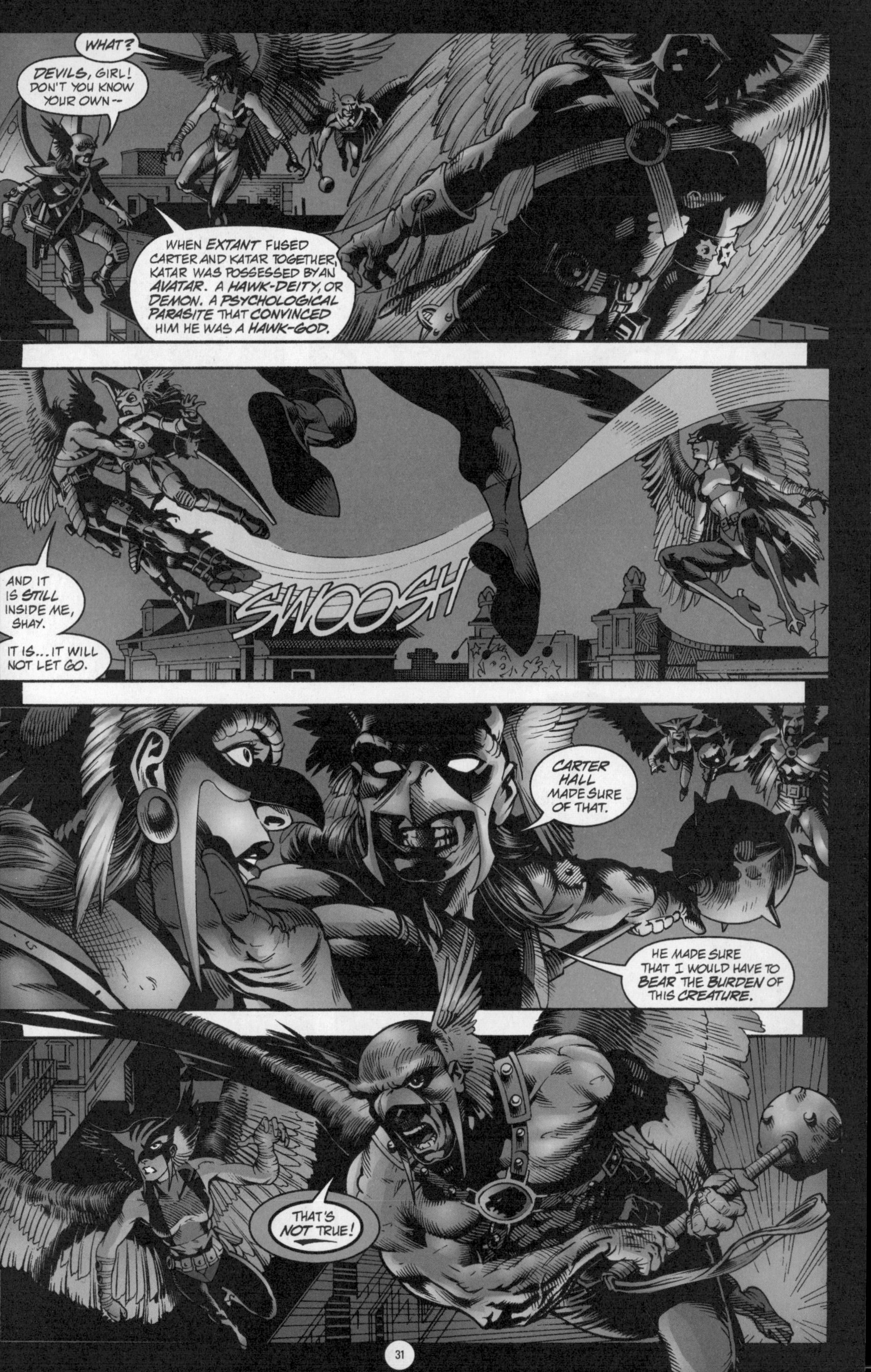
WHAT?
DEVILS, GIRL! DON'T YOU KNOW YOUR OWN--
WHEN EXTANT FUSED CARTER AND KATAR TOGETHER, KATAR WAS POSSESSED BY AN AVATAR. A HAWK-DEITY, OR DEMON. A PSYCHOLOGICAL PARASITE THAT CONVINCED HIM HE WAS A HAWK-GOD.
AND IT IS STILL INSIDE ME, SHAY.
IT IS... IT WILL NOT LET GO.
SWOOSH
CARTER HALL MADE SURE OF THAT.
HE MADE SURE THAT I WOULD HAVE TO BEAR THE BURDEN OF THIS CREATURE.
THAT'S NOT TRUE!

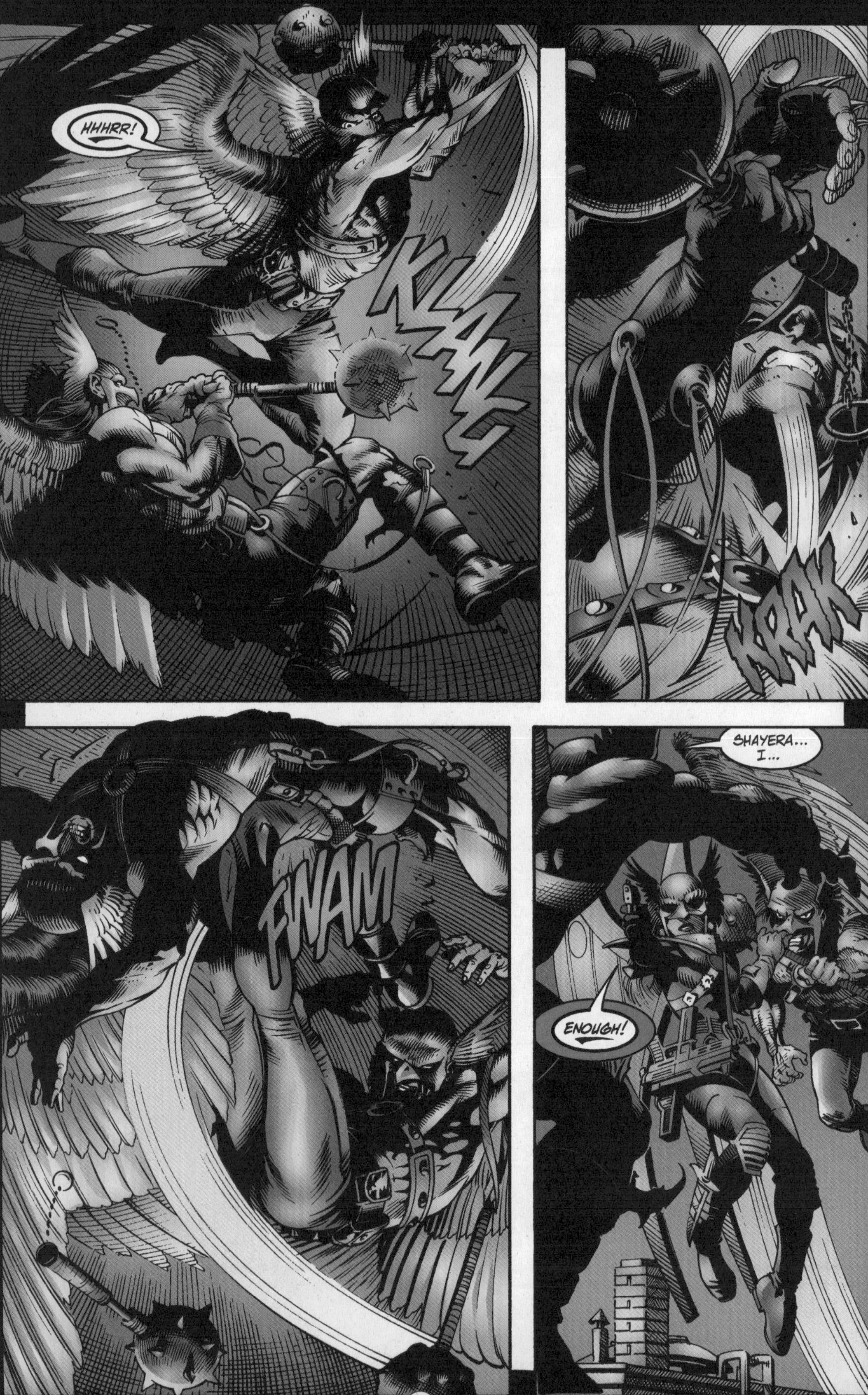
HHHRR!
KLANNG
KRAK
FWAM
SHAYERA... I...
ENOUGH!

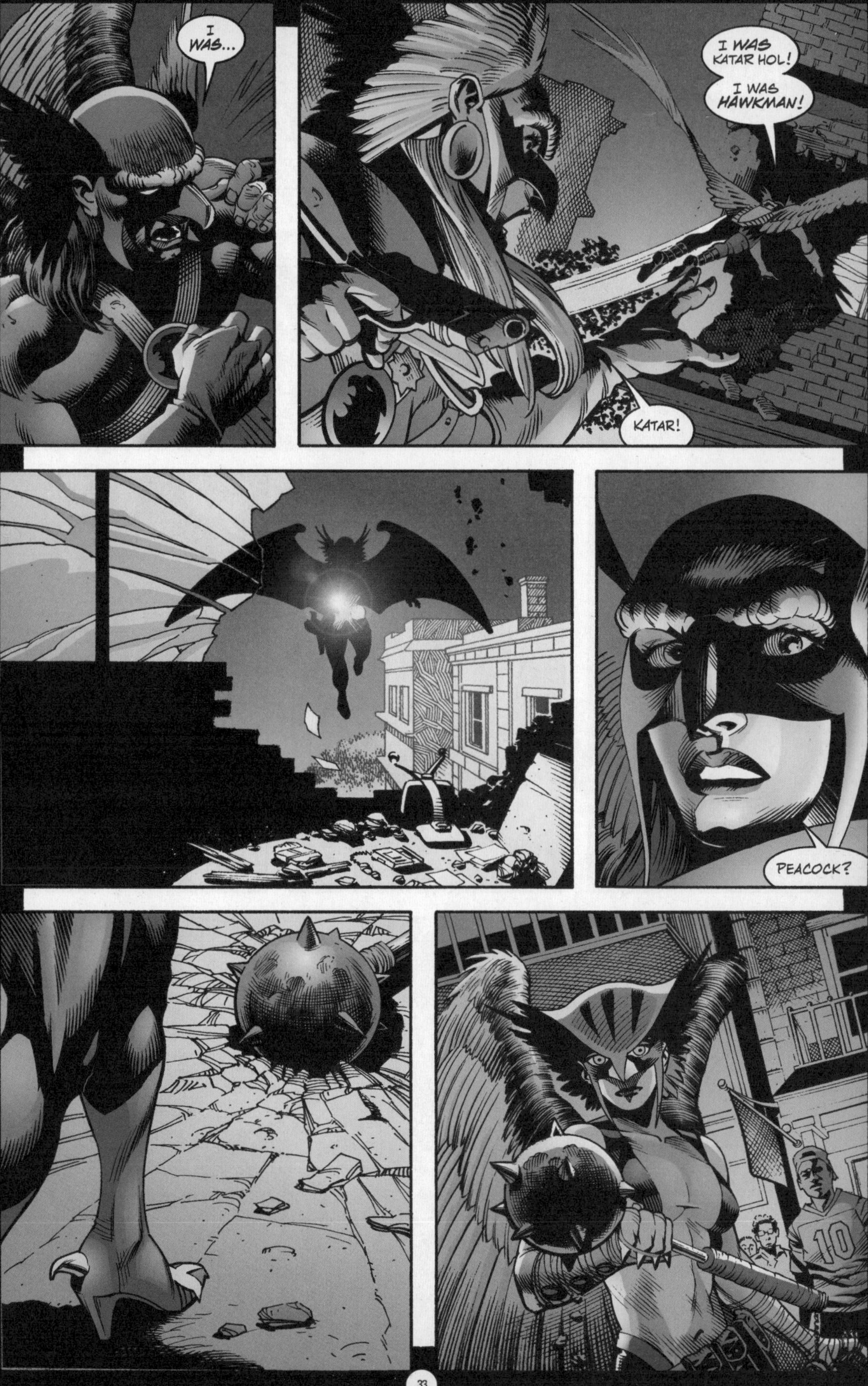
I WAS...
I WAS KATAR HOL!
I WAS HAWKMAN!
KATAR!
PEACOCK?
10

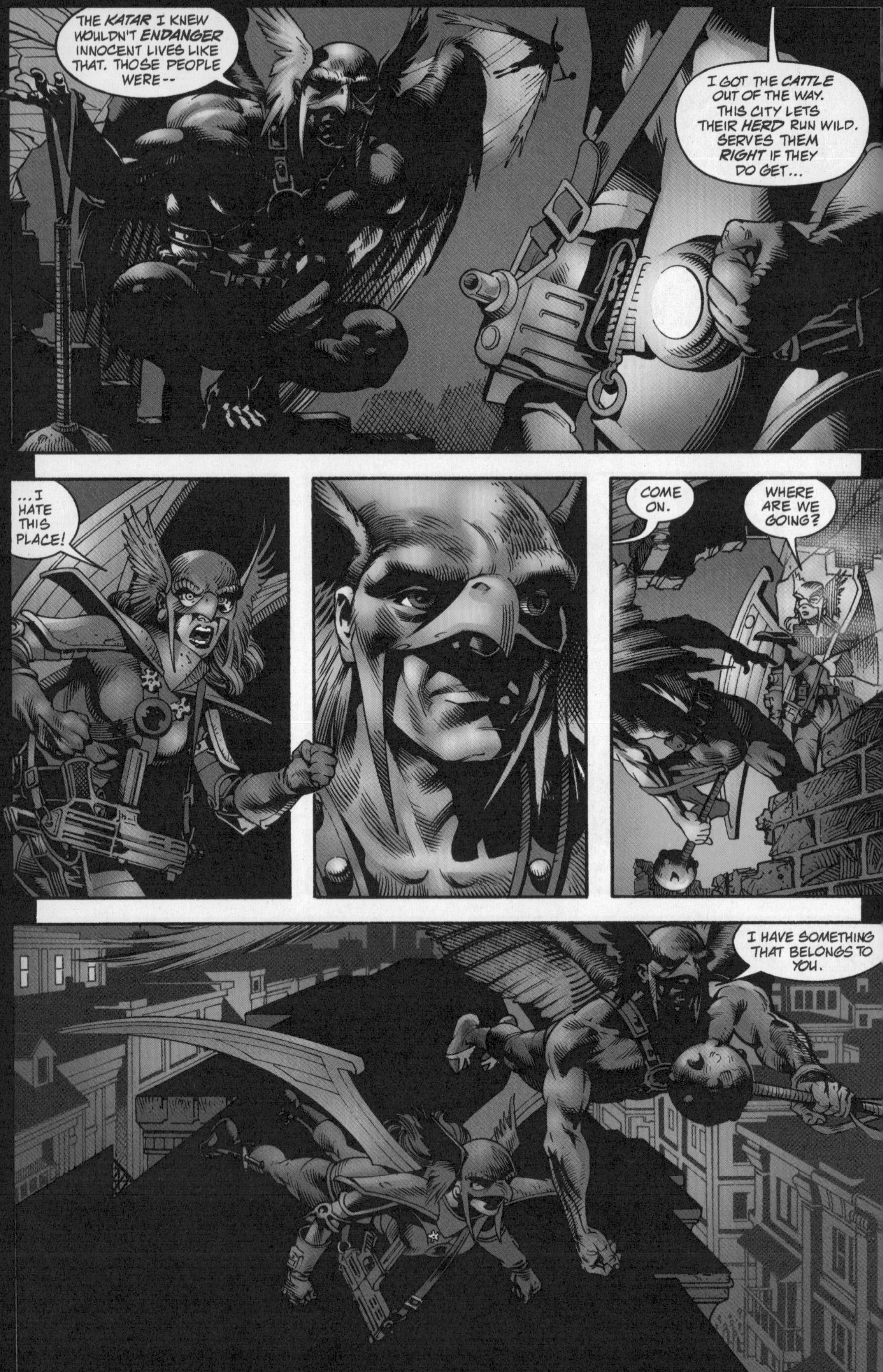
THE KATAR I KNEW WOULDN'T ENDANGER INNOCENT LIVES LIKE THAT. THOSE PEOPLE WERE--
I GOT THE CATTLE OUT OF THE WAY. THIS CITY LETS THEIR HERD RUN WILD. SERVES THEM RIGHT IF THEY DO GET...
...I HATE THIS PLACE!
COME ON.
WHERE ARE WE GOING?
I HAVE SOMETHING THAT BELONGS TO YOU.

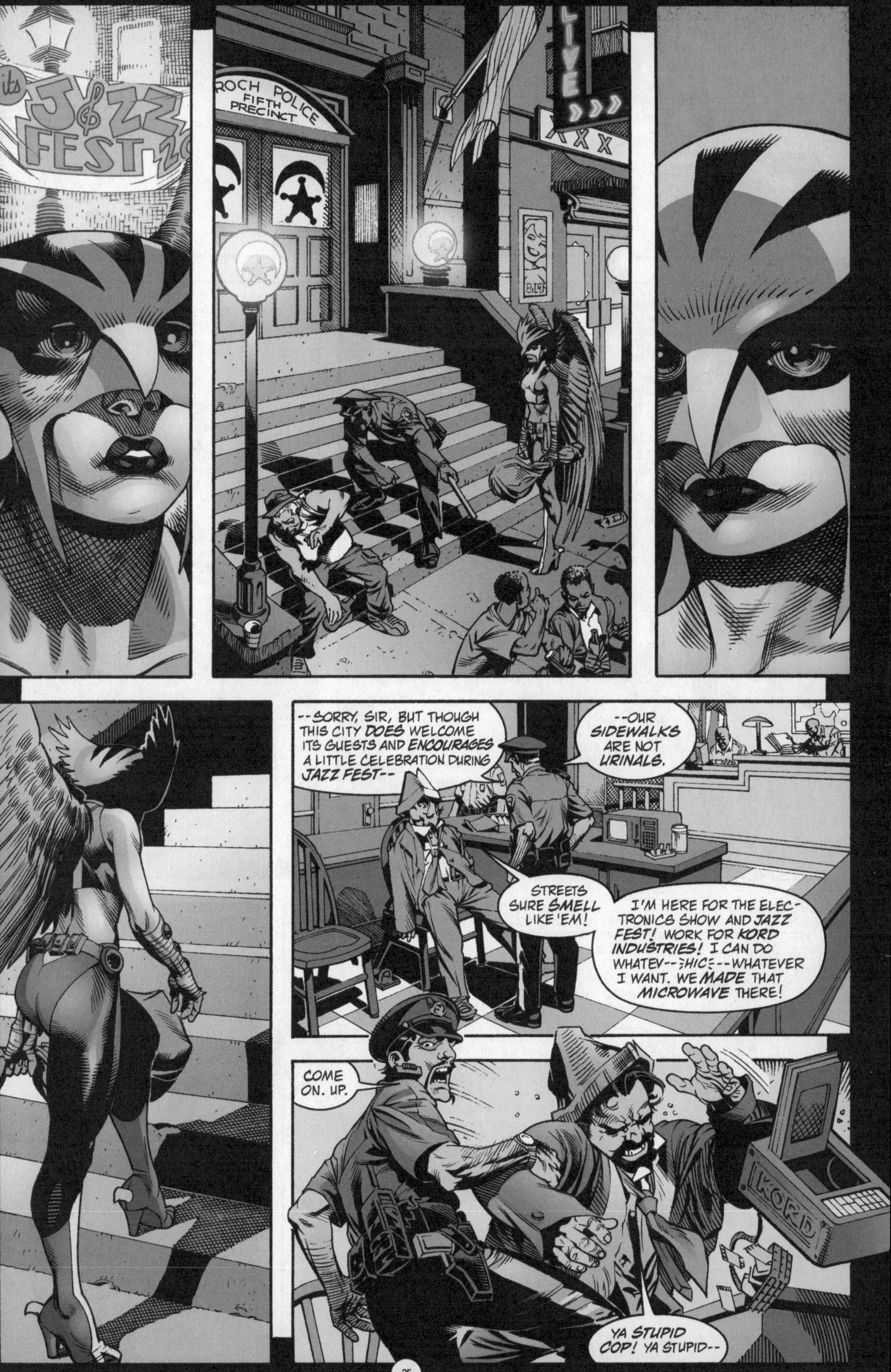
its
JAZZ
FEST 20
ROCH POLICE
FIFTH
PRECINCT
LIVE
XXX
--SORRY, SIR, BUT THOUGH THIS CITY DOES WELCOME ITS GUESTS AND ENCOURAGES A LITTLE CELEBRATION DURING JAZZ FEST--
--OUR SIDEWALKS ARE NOT URINALS.
STREETS SURE SMELL LIKE 'EM!
I'M HERE FOR THE ELECTRONICS SHOW AND JAZZ FEST! WORK FOR KORD INDUSTRIES! I CAN DO WHATEV--HIC--WHATEVER I WANT. WE MADE THAT MICROWAVE THERE!
COME ON. UP.
KORD
YA STUPID COP! YA STUPID--

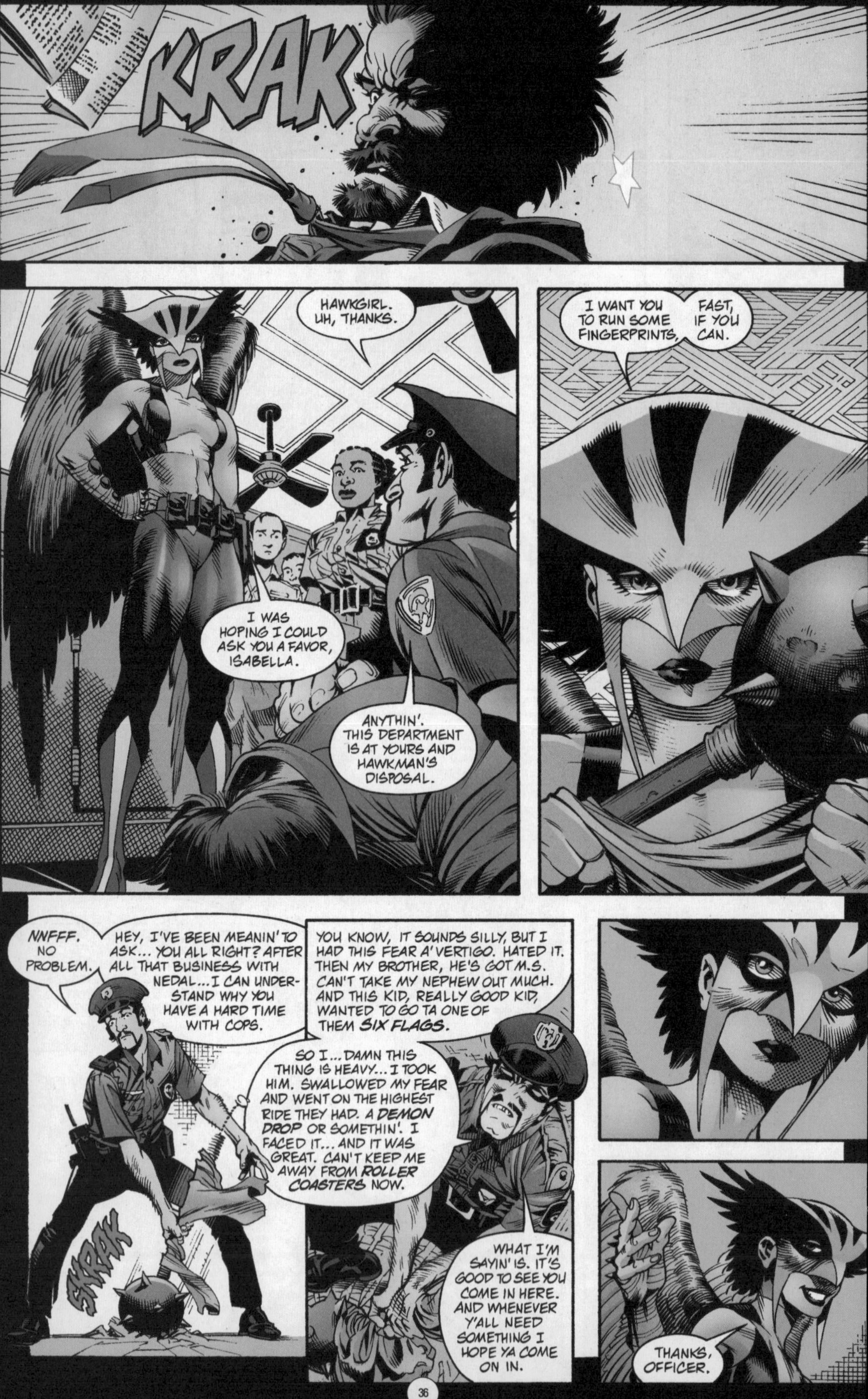
KRAK
HAWKGIRL. UH, THANKS.
I WANT YOU TO RUN SOME FINGERPRINTS,
FAST, IF YOU CAN.
I WAS HOPING I COULD ASK YOU A FAVOR, ISABELLA.
ANYTHIN'. THIS DEPARTMENT IS AT YOURS AND HAWKMAN'S DISPOSAL.
NNFFF. NO PROBLEM.
HEY, I'VE BEEN MEANIN' TO ASK... YOU ALL RIGHT? AFTER ALL THAT BUSINESS WITH NEDAL... I CAN UNDERSTAND WHY YOU HAVE A HARD TIME WITH COPS.
YOU KNOW, IT SOUNDS SILLY, BUT I HAD THIS FEAR A' VERTIGO. HATED IT. THEN MY BROTHER, HE'S GOT M.S. CAN'T TAKE MY NEPHEW OUT MUCH. AND THIS KID, REALLY GOOD KID, WANTED TO GO TA ONE OF THEM SIX FLAGS.
SO I... DAMN THIS THING IS HEAVY... I TOOK HIM. SWALLOWED MY FEAR AND WENT ON THE HIGHEST RIDE THEY HAD. A DEMON DROP OR SOMETHIN'. I FACED IT... AND IT WAS GREAT. CAN'T KEEP ME AWAY FROM ROLLER COASTERS NOW.
SKRAK
WHAT I'M SAYIN' IS. IT'S GOOD TO SEE YOU COME IN HERE. AND WHENEVER Y'ALL NEED SOMETHING I HOPE YA COME ON IN.
THANKS, OFFICER.

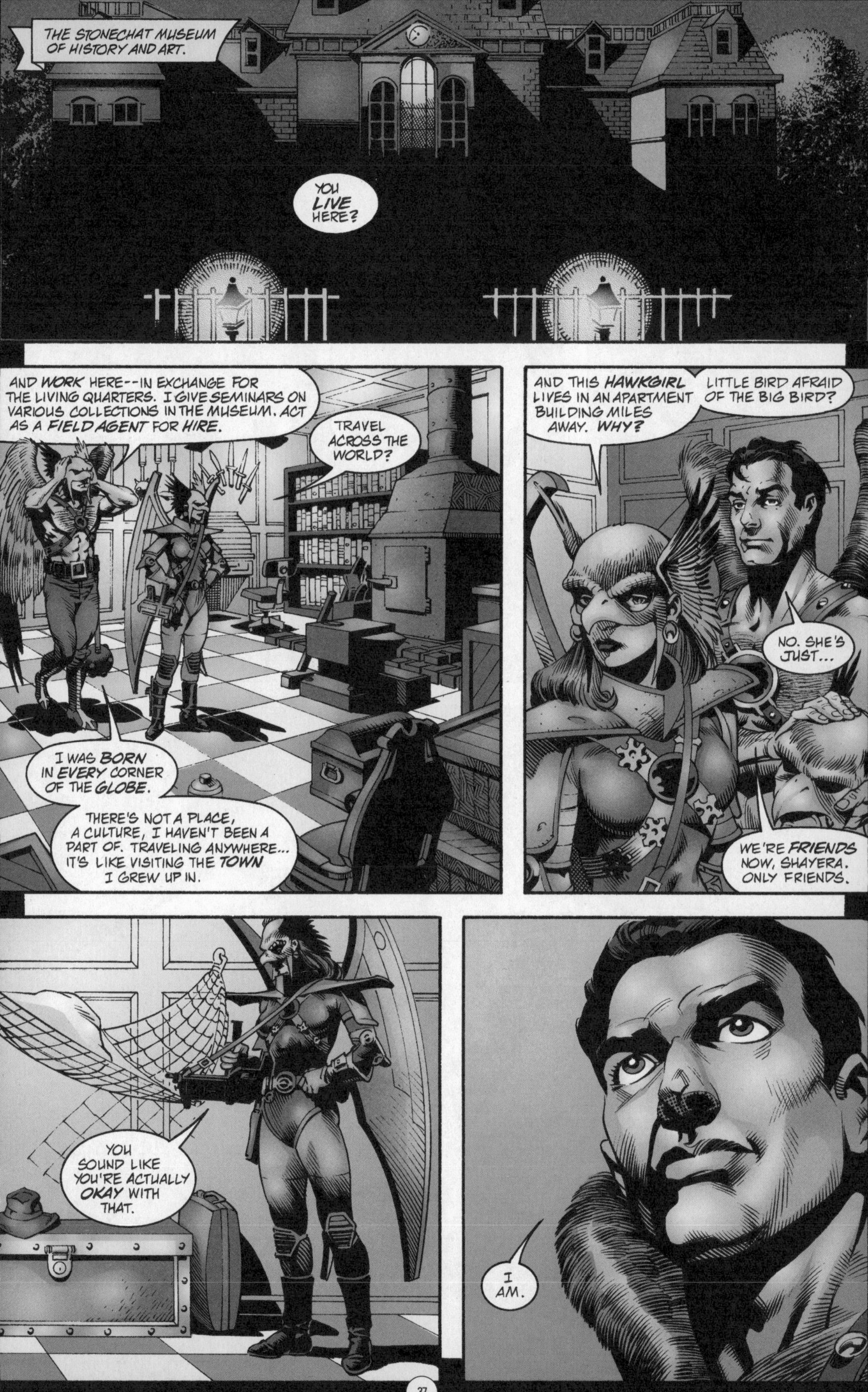
THE STONECHAT MUSEUM OF HISTORY AND ART.
YOU LIVE HERE?
AND WORK HERE--IN EXCHANGE FOR THE LIVING QUARTERS. I GIVE SEMINARS ON VARIOUS COLLECTIONS IN THE MUSEUM. ACT AS A FIELD AGENT FOR HIRE.
TRAVEL ACROSS THE WORLD?
I WAS BORN IN EVERY CORNER OF THE GLOBE.
THERE'S NOT A PLACE, A CULTURE, I HAVEN'T BEEN A PART OF. TRAVELING ANYWHERE... IT'S LIKE VISITING THE TOWN I GREW UP IN.
AND THIS HAWKGIRL LIVES IN AN APARTMENT BUILDING MILES AWAY. WHY?
LITTLE BIRD AFRAID OF THE BIG BIRD?
NO. SHE'S JUST...
WE'RE FRIENDS NOW, SHAYERA. ONLY FRIENDS.
YOU SOUND LIKE YOU'RE ACTUALLY OKAY WITH THAT.
I AM.

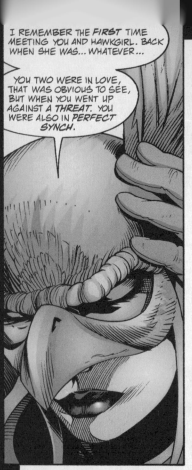

I REMEMBER THE *FIRST* TIME MEETING YOU AND HAWKGIRL. BACK WHEN SHE WAS... WHATEVER...

YOU TWO WERE IN LOVE, THAT WAS OBVIOUS TO SEE, BUT WHEN YOU WENT UP AGAINST A *THREAT*. YOU WERE ALSO IN *PERFECT SYNCH.*

I'M NOT ONE FOR *EMOTIONS*, NOT UNLESS THEY HELP ME IN A *FIGHT*--

--BUT DEVILS IF I DIDN'T, AT LEAST ONCE, FEEL A BIT *ENVIOUS.*

OVER HERE.

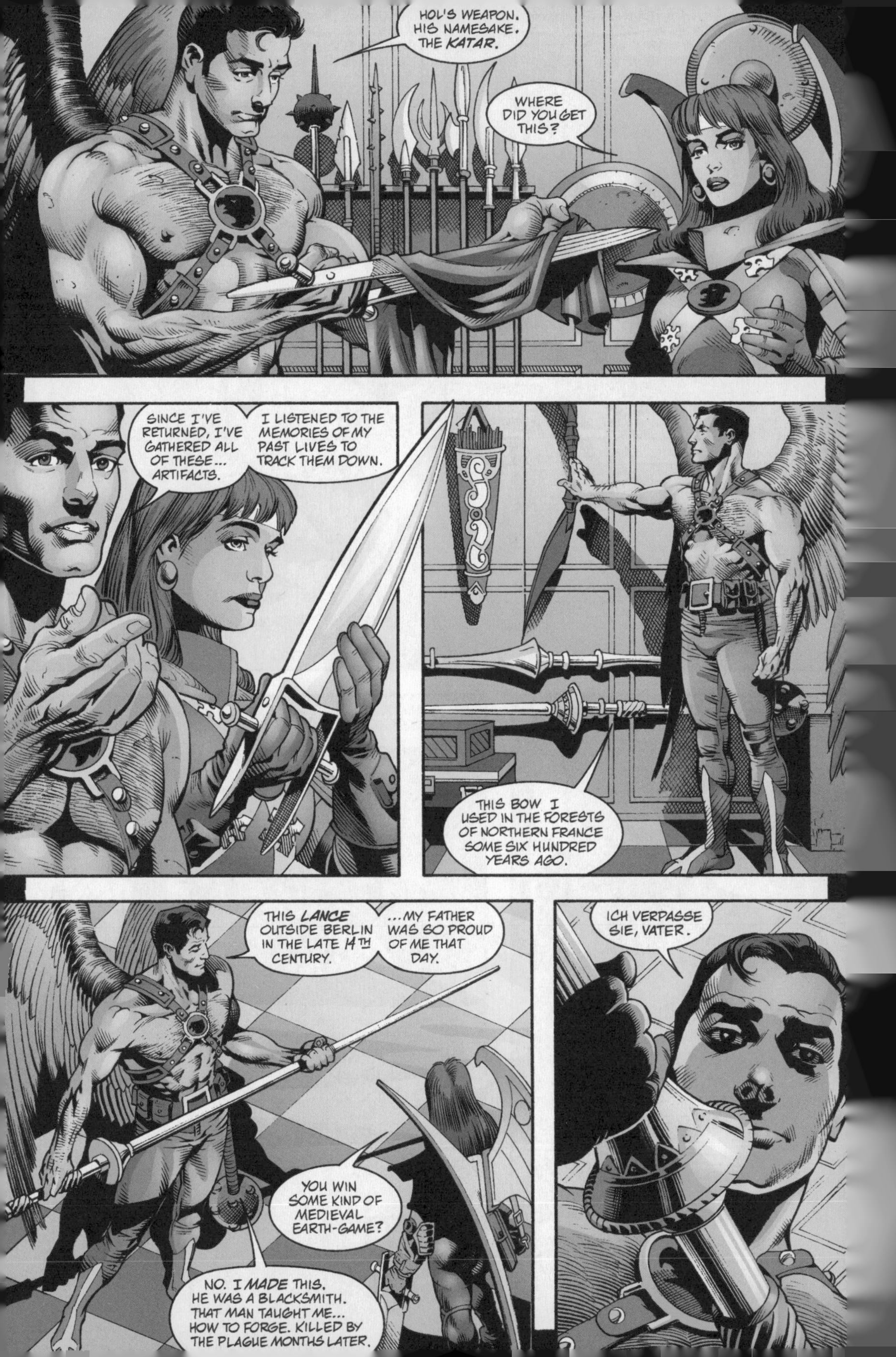
HOL'S WEAPON. HIS NAMESAKE. THE KATAR.
WHERE DID YOU GET THIS?
SINCE I'VE RETURNED, I'VE GATHERED ALL OF THESE... ARTIFACTS.
I LISTENED TO THE MEMORIES OF MY PAST LIVES TO TRACK THEM DOWN.
THIS BOW I USED IN THE FORESTS OF NORTHERN FRANCE SOME SIX HUNDRED YEARS AGO.
THIS LANCE OUTSIDE BERLIN IN THE LATE 14TH CENTURY.
...MY FATHER WAS SO PROUD OF ME THAT DAY.
YOU WIN SOME KIND OF MEDIEVAL EARTH-GAME?
NO. I MADE THIS. HE WAS A BLACKSMITH. THAT MAN TAUGHT ME... HOW TO FORGE. KILLED BY THE PLAGUE MONTHS LATER.
ICH VERPASSE SIE, VATER.

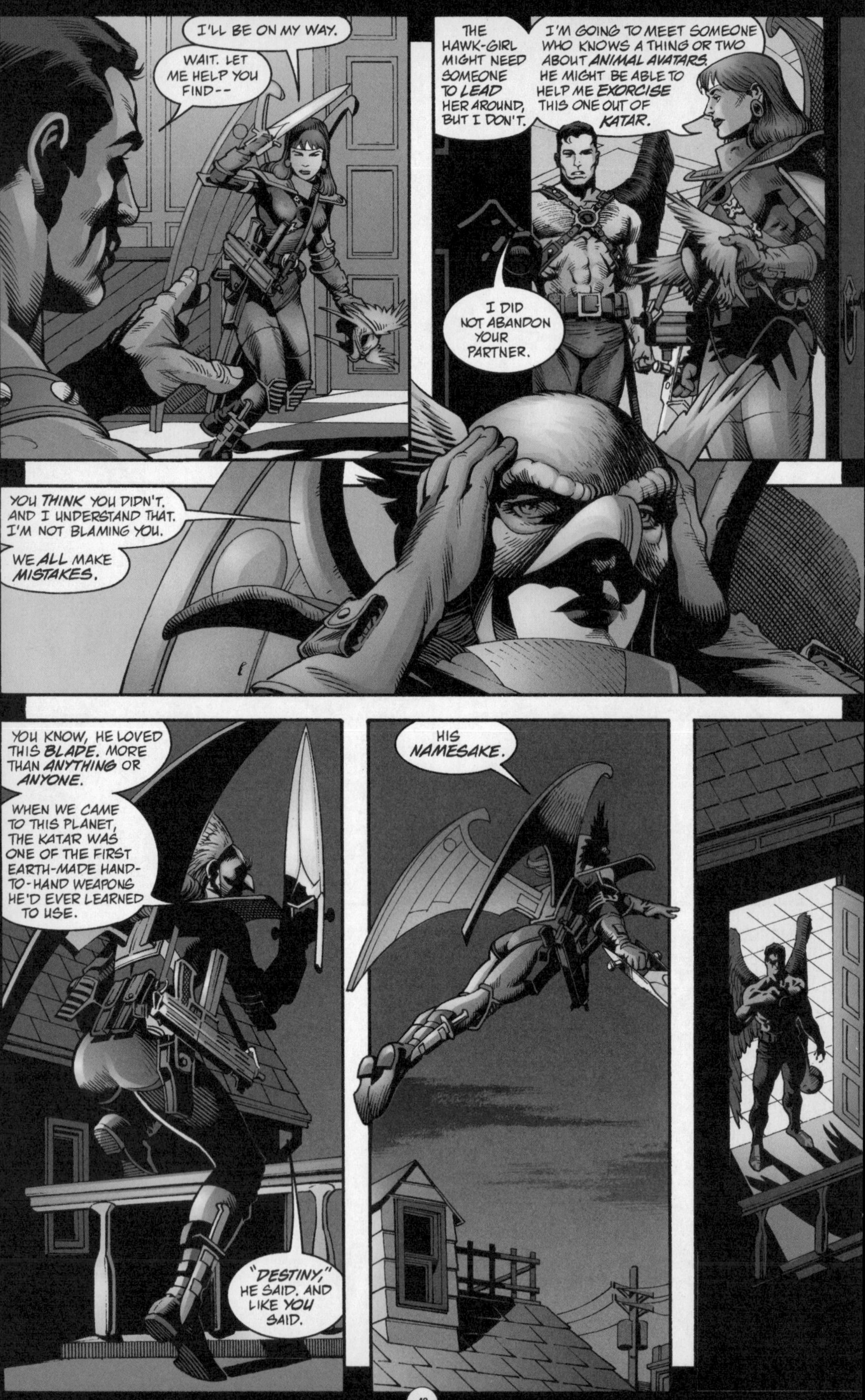

I'LL BE ON MY WAY.
WAIT. LET ME HELP YOU FIND--
THE HAWK-GIRL MIGHT NEED SOMEONE TO LEAD HER AROUND, BUT I DON'T.
I'M GOING TO MEET SOMEONE WHO KNOWS A THING OR TWO ABOUT ANIMAL AVATARS. HE MIGHT BE ABLE TO HELP ME EXORCISE THIS ONE OUT OF KATAR.
I DID NOT ABANDON YOUR PARTNER.
YOU THINK YOU DIDN'T. AND I UNDERSTAND THAT. I'M NOT BLAMING YOU.
WE ALL MAKE MISTAKES.
YOU KNOW, HE LOVED THIS BLADE. MORE THAN ANYTHING OR ANYONE.
WHEN WE CAME TO THIS PLANET, THE KATAR WAS ONE OF THE FIRST EARTH-MADE HAND-TO-HAND WEAPONS HE'D EVER LEARNED TO USE.
"DESTINY," HE SAID. AND LIKE YOU SAID.
HIS NAMESAKE.

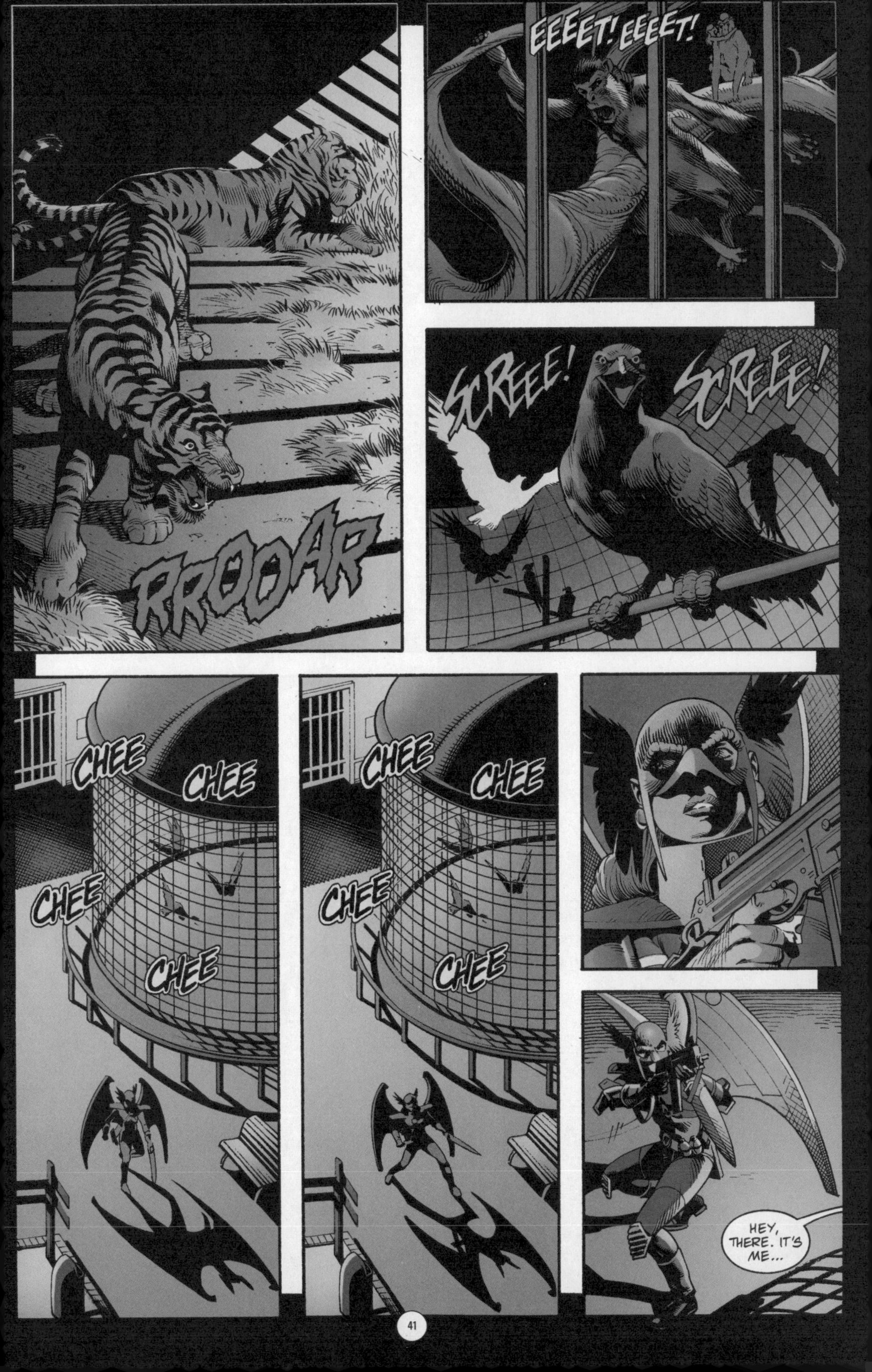
RROOAR
EEEET! EEEET!
SCREEE!
SCREEE!
CHEE
CHEE
CHEE
CHEE
CHEE
CHEE
CHEE
CHEE
HEY, THERE. IT'S ME...

Animal Man

I USUALLY DON'T DO *HOUSE CALLS*, BUT MARTIAN MANHUNTER SAID YOU NEEDED SOME INFORMATION.

I TOLD HIM I WASN'T TOO *ENTHUSIASTIC* ABOUT THANAGARIANS... I HELPED FIGHT OFF THAT *INVASION* SOME YEARS AGO... BUT THE *GREEN GUY* SPOKE VERY HIGHLY OF YOU--

--WHICH IS *WHY* I CAME.

NAME'S *BUDDY.* BUDDY BAKER.

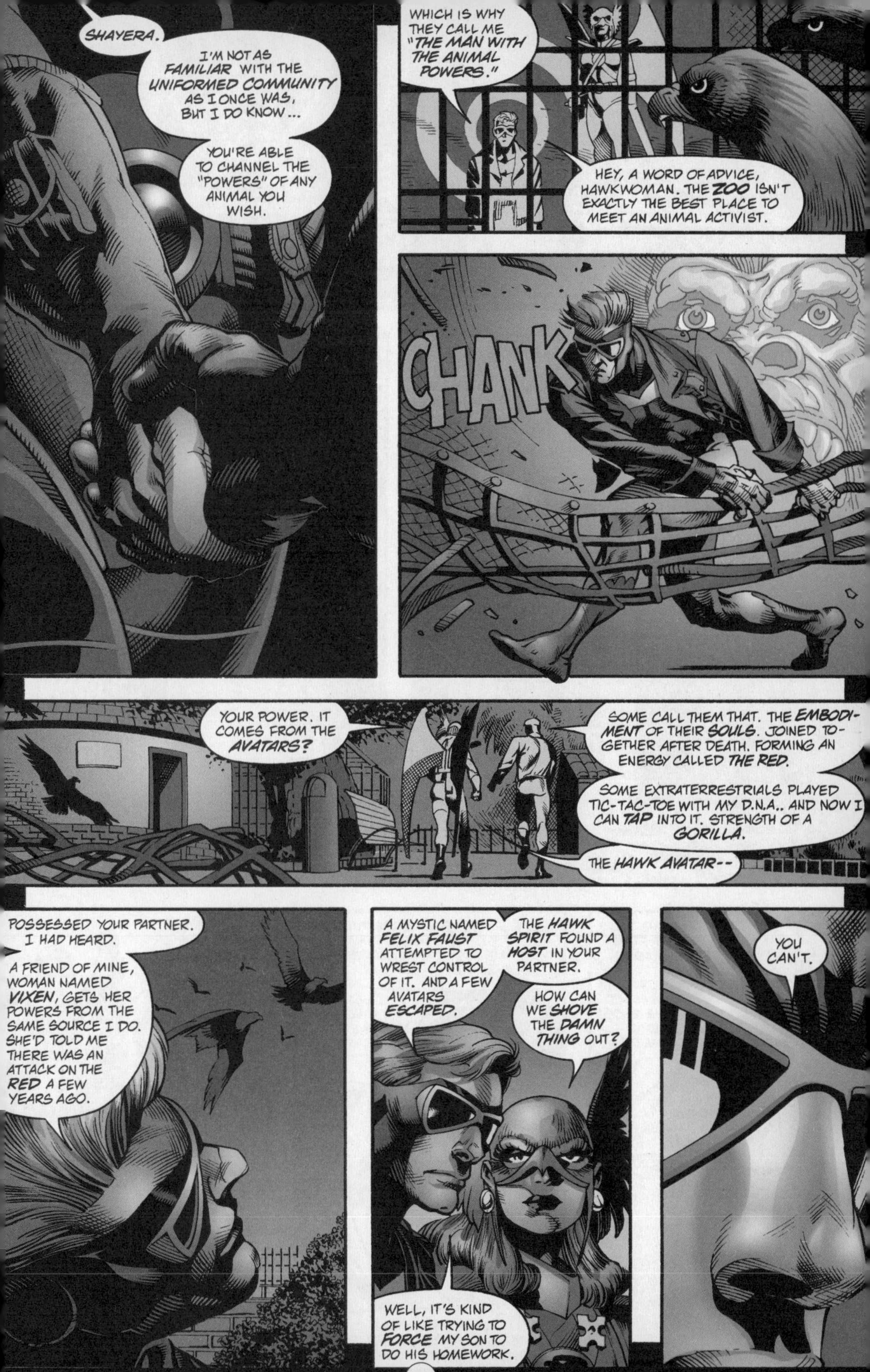
SHAYERA.
I'M NOT AS FAMILIAR WITH THE UNIFORMED COMMUNITY AS I ONCE WAS, BUT I DO KNOW...
YOU'RE ABLE TO CHANNEL THE "POWERS" OF ANY ANIMAL YOU WISH.
WHICH IS WHY THEY CALL ME "THE MAN WITH THE ANIMAL POWERS."
HEY, A WORD OF ADVICE, HAWKWOMAN. THE ZOO ISN'T EXACTLY THE BEST PLACE TO MEET AN ANIMAL ACTIVIST.
CHANK
YOUR POWER. IT COMES FROM THE AVATARS?
SOME CALL THEM THAT. THE EMBODIMENT OF THEIR SOULS. JOINED TOGETHER AFTER DEATH. FORMING AN ENERGY CALLED THE RED.
SOME EXTRATERRESTRIALS PLAYED TIC-TAC-TOE WITH MY D.N.A.. AND NOW I CAN TAP INTO IT. STRENGTH OF A GORILLA.
THE HAWK AVATAR--
POSSESSED YOUR PARTNER. I HAD HEARD.
A FRIEND OF MINE, WOMAN NAMED VIXEN, GETS HER POWERS FROM THE SAME SOURCE I DO. SHE'D TOLD ME THERE WAS AN ATTACK ON THE RED A FEW YEARS AGO.
A MYSTIC NAMED FELIX FAUST ATTEMPTED TO WREST CONTROL OF IT. AND A FEW AVATARS ESCAPED.
THE HAWK SPIRIT FOUND A HOST IN YOUR PARTNER.
HOW CAN WE SHOVE THE DAMN THING OUT?
WELL, IT'S KIND OF LIKE TRYING TO FORCE MY SON TO DO HIS HOMEWORK.
YOU CAN'T.

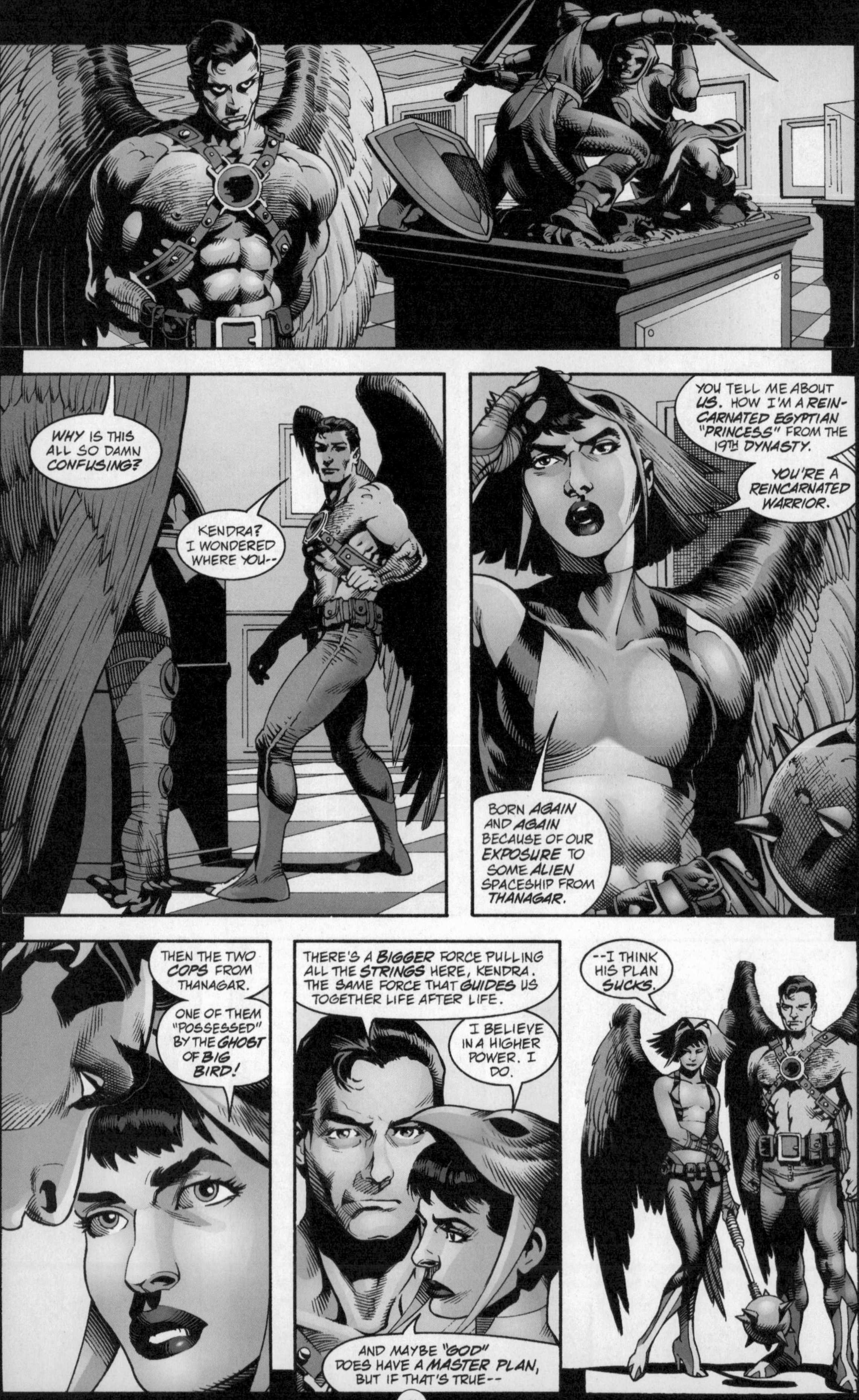
WHY IS THIS ALL SO DAMN CONFUSING?
KENDRA? I WONDERED WHERE YOU--
YOU TELL ME ABOUT US. HOW I'M A REINCARNATED EGYPTIAN "PRINCESS" FROM THE 19TH DYNASTY.
YOU'RE A REINCARNATED WARRIOR.
BORN AGAIN AND AGAIN BECAUSE OF OUR EXPOSURE TO SOME ALIEN SPACESHIP FROM THANAGAR.
THEN THE TWO COPS FROM THANAGAR.
ONE OF THEM "POSSESSED" BY THE GHOST OF BIG BIRD!
THERE'S A BIGGER FORCE PULLING ALL THE STRINGS HERE, KENDRA. THE SAME FORCE THAT GUIDES US TOGETHER LIFE AFTER LIFE.
I BELIEVE IN A HIGHER POWER. I DO.
AND MAYBE "GOD" DOES HAVE A MASTER PLAN, BUT IF THAT'S TRUE--
--I THINK HIS PLAN SUCKS.

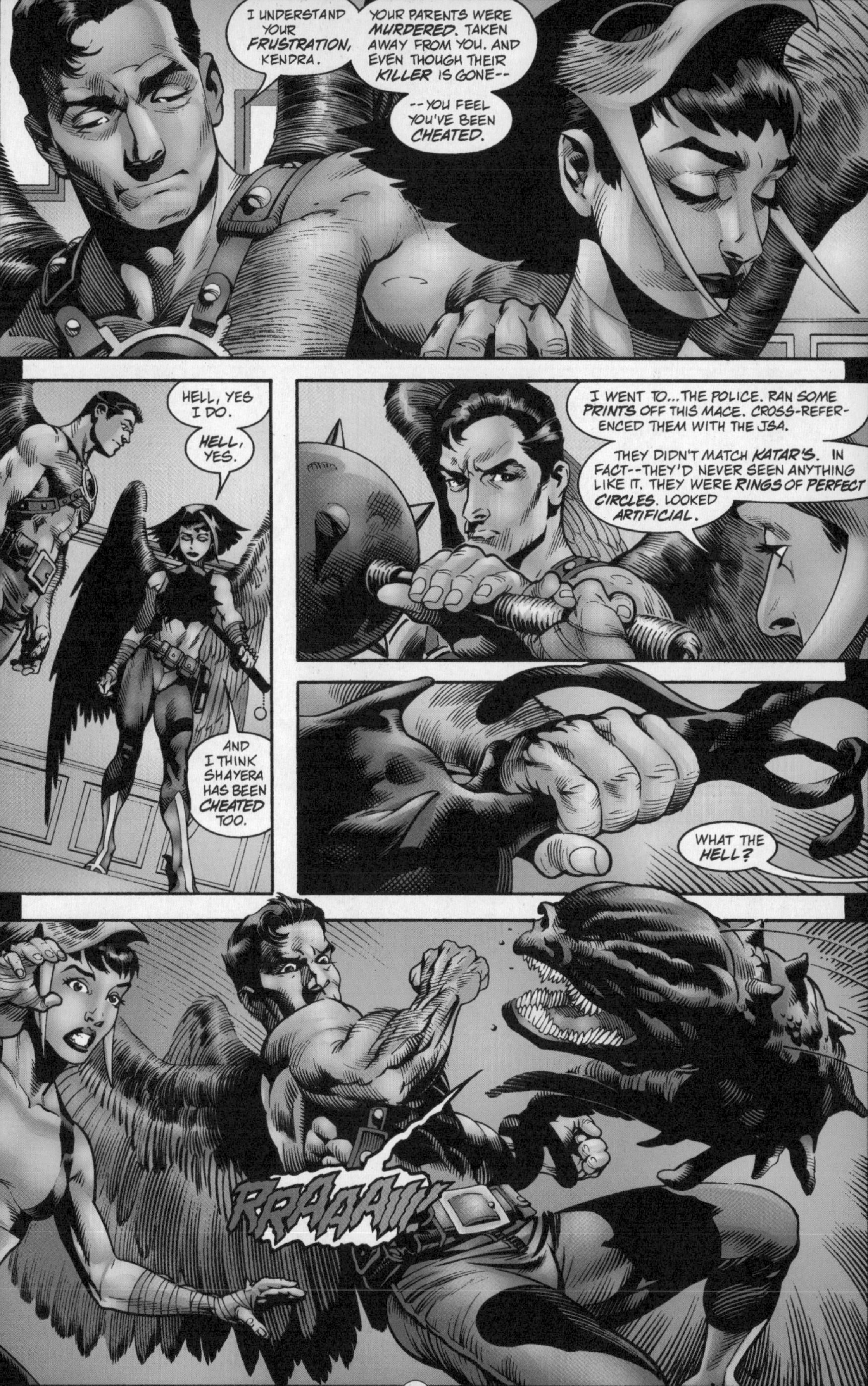
I UNDERSTAND YOUR FRUSTRATION, KENDRA.
YOUR PARENTS WERE MURDERED. TAKEN AWAY FROM YOU. AND EVEN THOUGH THEIR KILLER IS GONE--
--YOU FEEL YOU'VE BEEN CHEATED.
HELL, YES I DO.
HELL, YES.
AND I THINK SHAYERA HAS BEEN CHEATED TOO.
I WENT TO...THE POLICE. RAN SOME PRINTS OFF THIS MACE. CROSS-REFERENCED THEM WITH THE JSA.
THEY DIDN'T MATCH KATAR'S. IN FACT--THEY'D NEVER SEEN ANYTHING LIKE IT. THEY WERE RINGS OF PERFECT CIRCLES. LOOKED ARTIFICIAL.
WHAT THE HELL?
RRAAAII!

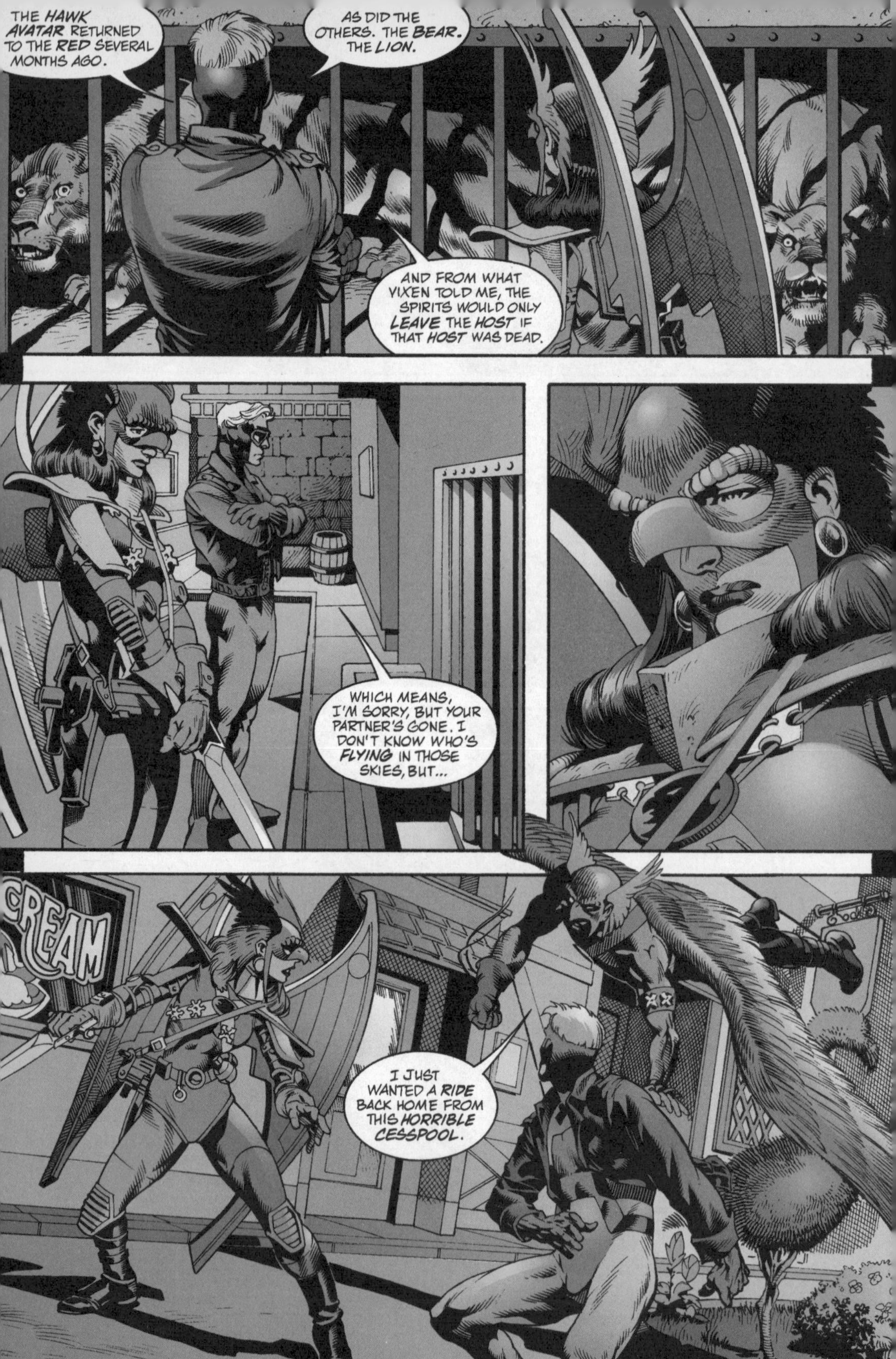
THE HAWK AVATAR RETURNED TO THE RED SEVERAL MONTHS AGO.
AS DID THE OTHERS. THE BEAR. THE LION.
AND FROM WHAT VIXEN TOLD ME, THE SPIRITS WOULD ONLY LEAVE THE HOST IF THAT HOST WAS DEAD.
WHICH MEANS, I'M SORRY, BUT YOUR PARTNER'S GONE. I DON'T KNOW WHO'S FLYING IN THOSE SKIES, BUT...
I JUST WANTED A RIDE BACK HOME FROM THIS HORRIBLE CESSPOOL.

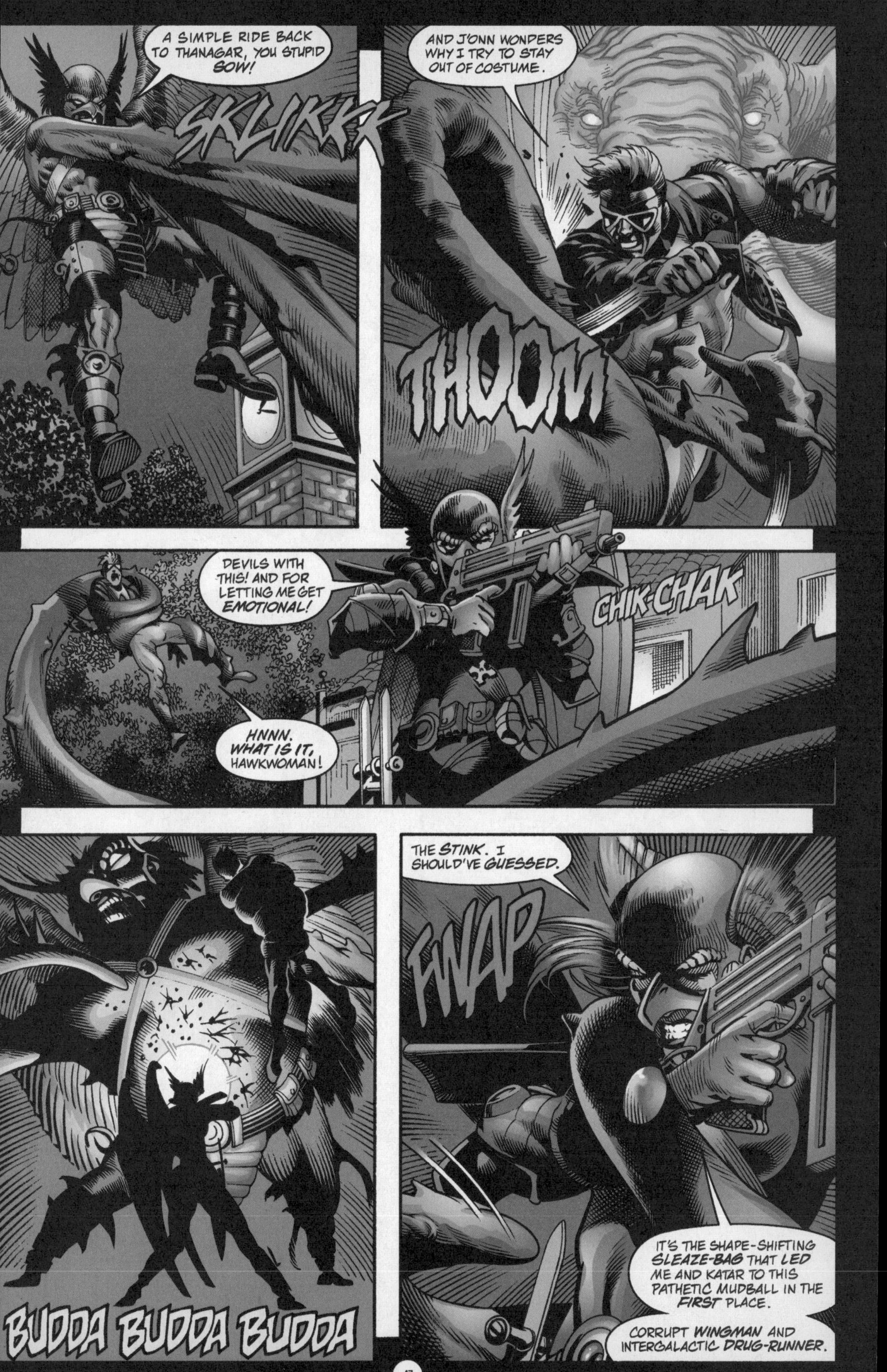
A SIMPLE RIDE BACK TO THANAGAR, YOU STUPID SOW!
SKLIKKK
AND J'ONN WONDERS WHY I TRY TO STAY OUT OF COSTUME.
THOOM
DEVILS WITH THIS! AND FOR LETTING ME GET EMOTIONAL!
CHIK-CHAK
HNNN. WHAT IS IT, HAWKWOMAN!
BUDDA BUDDA BUDDA
THE STINK. I SHOULD'VE GUESSED.
FWAP
IT'S THE SHAPE-SHIFTING SLEAZE-BAG THAT LED ME AND KATAR TO THIS PATHETIC MUDBALL IN THE FIRST PLACE.
CORRUPT WINGMAN AND INTERGALACTIC DRUG-RUNNER.

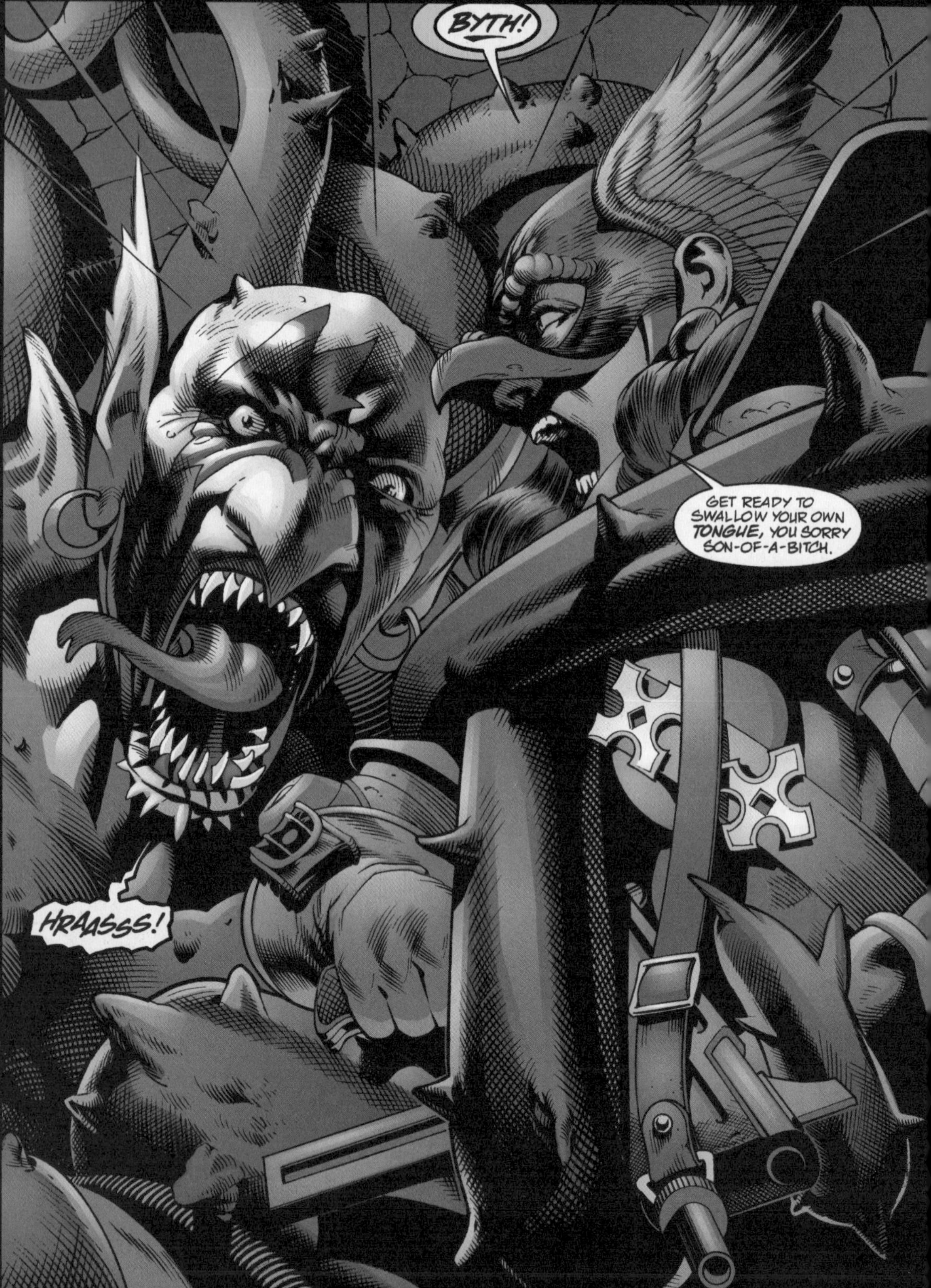
BYTH!
GET READY TO SWALLOW YOUR OWN TONGUE, YOU SORRY SON-OF-A-BITCH.
HRAASSS!

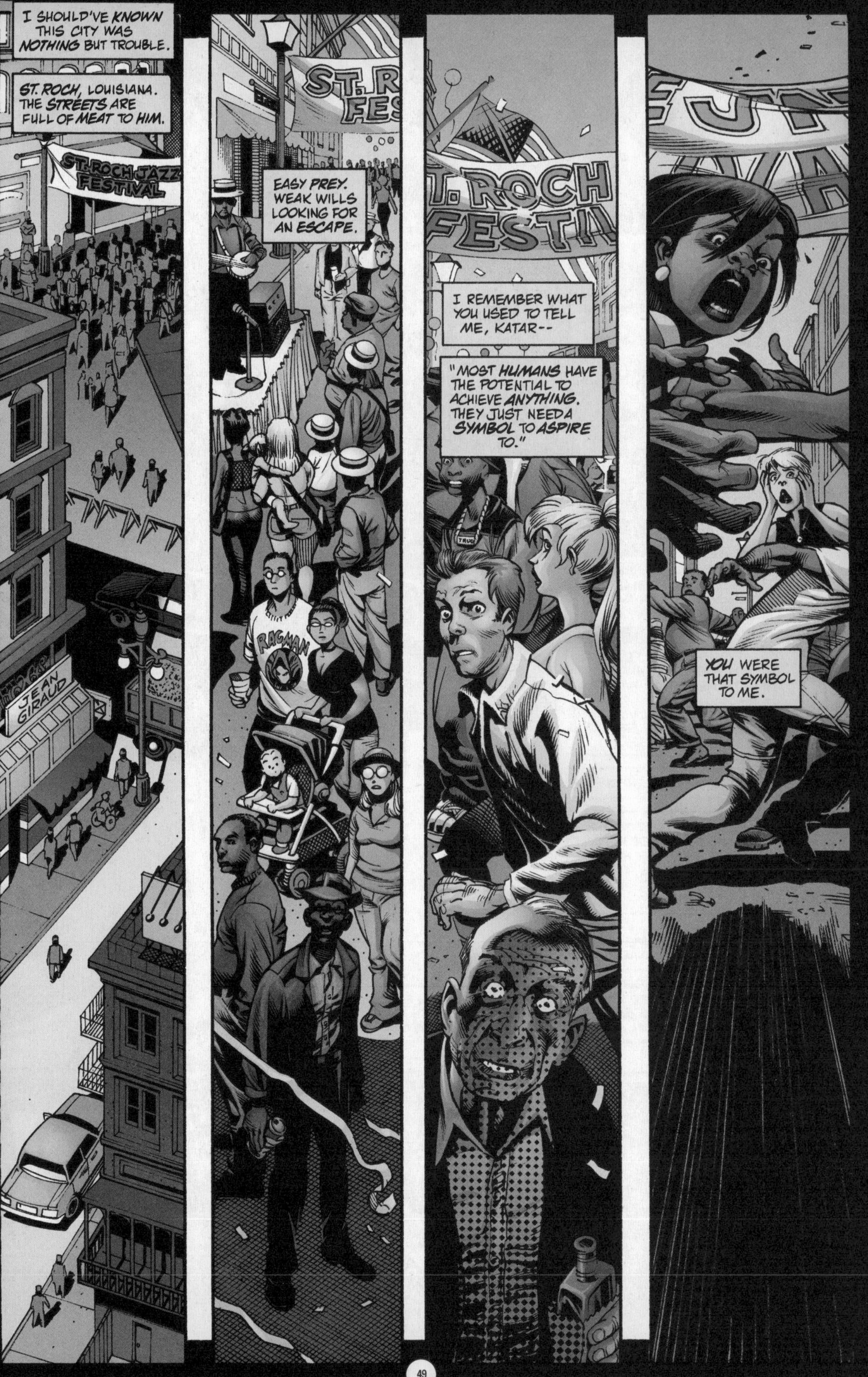

I SHOULD'VE KNOWN THIS CITY WAS NOTHING BUT TROUBLE.
ST. ROCH, LOUISIANA. THE STREETS ARE FULL OF MEAT TO HIM.
ST. ROCH JAZZ FESTIVAL
JEAN GIRAUD
ST. R FES
EASY PREY. WEAK WILLS LOOKING FOR AN ESCAPE.
RAGMAN
T. ROCH FESTI
I REMEMBER WHAT YOU USED TO TELL ME, KATAR--
"MOST HUMANS HAVE THE POTENTIAL TO ACHIEVE ANYTHING. THEY JUST NEED A SYMBOL TO ASPIRE TO."
YOU WERE THAT SYMBOL TO ME.

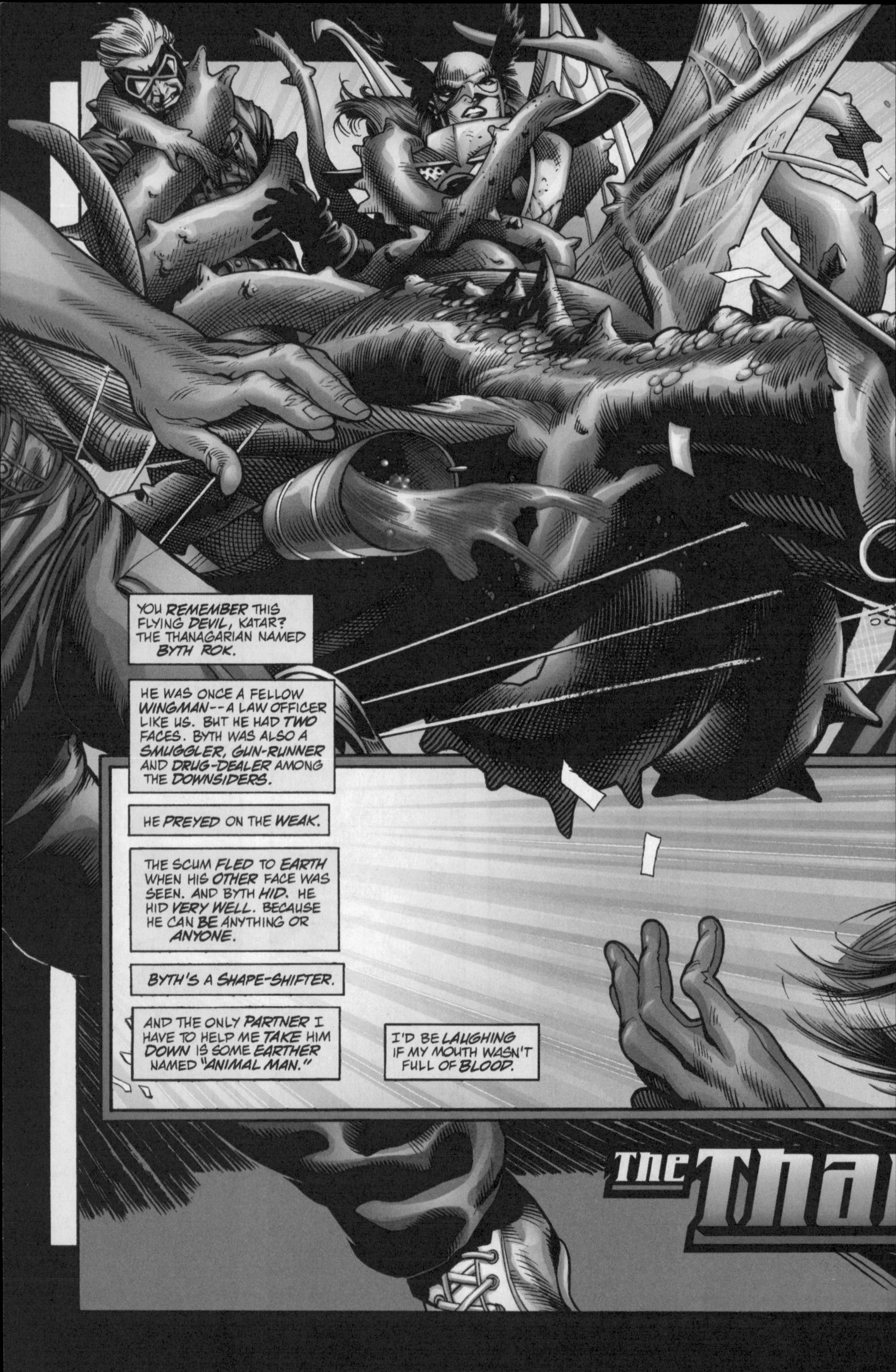
YOU REMEMBER THIS FLYING DEVIL, KATAR? THE THANAGARIAN NAMED BYTH ROK.
HE WAS ONCE A FELLOW WINGMAN--A LAW OFFICER LIKE US. BUT HE HAD TWO FACES. BYTH WAS ALSO A SMUGGLER, GUN-RUNNER AND DRUG-DEALER AMONG THE DOWNSIDERS.
HE PREYED ON THE WEAK.
THE SCUM FLED TO EARTH WHEN HIS OTHER FACE WAS SEEN. AND BYTH HID. HE HID VERY WELL. BECAUSE HE CAN BE ANYTHING OR ANYONE.
BYTH'S A SHAPE-SHIFTER.
AND THE ONLY PARTNER I HAVE TO HELP ME TAKE HIM DOWN IS SOME EARTHER NAMED "ANIMAL MAN."
I'D BE LAUGHING IF MY MOUTH WASN'T FULL OF BLOOD.
THE THA

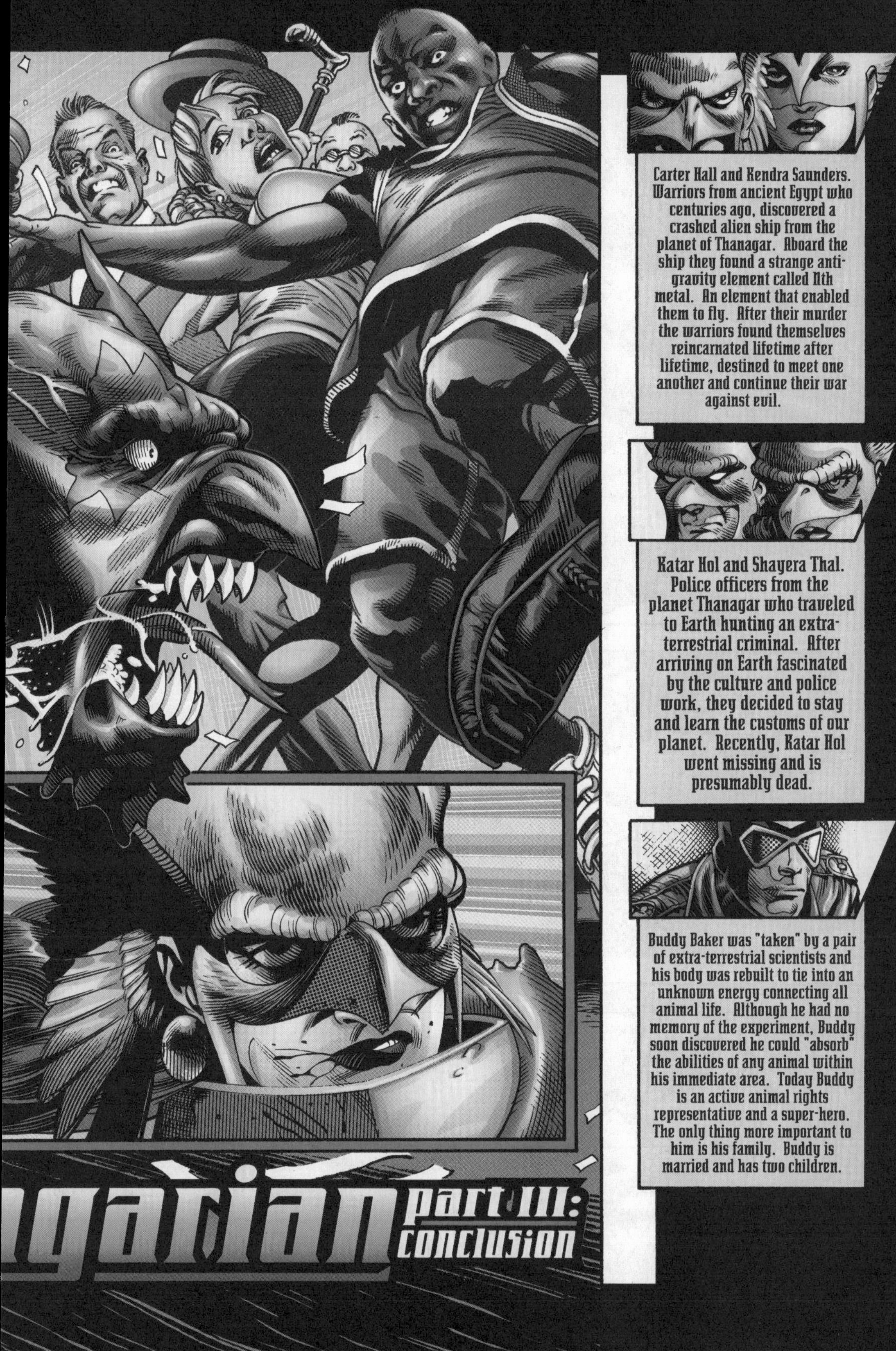
Carter Hall and Kendra Saunders. Warriors from ancient Egypt who centuries ago, discovered a crashed alien ship from the planet of Thanagar. Aboard the ship they found a strange anti-gravity element called Nth metal. An element that enabled them to fly. After their murder the warriors found themselves reincarnated lifetime after lifetime, destined to meet one another and continue their war against evil.
Katar Hol and Shayera Thal. Police officers from the planet Thanagar who traveled to Earth hunting an extra-terrestrial criminal. After arriving on Earth fascinated by the culture and police work, they decided to stay and learn the customs of our planet. Recently, Katar Hol went missing and is presumably dead.
Buddy Baker was "taken" by a pair of extra-terrestrial scientists and his body was rebuilt to tie into an unknown energy connecting all animal life. Although he had no memory of the experiment, Buddy soon discovered he could "absorb" the abilities of any animal within his immediate area. Today Buddy is an active animal rights representative and a super-hero. The only thing more important to him is his family. Buddy is married and has two children.
part III: conclusion

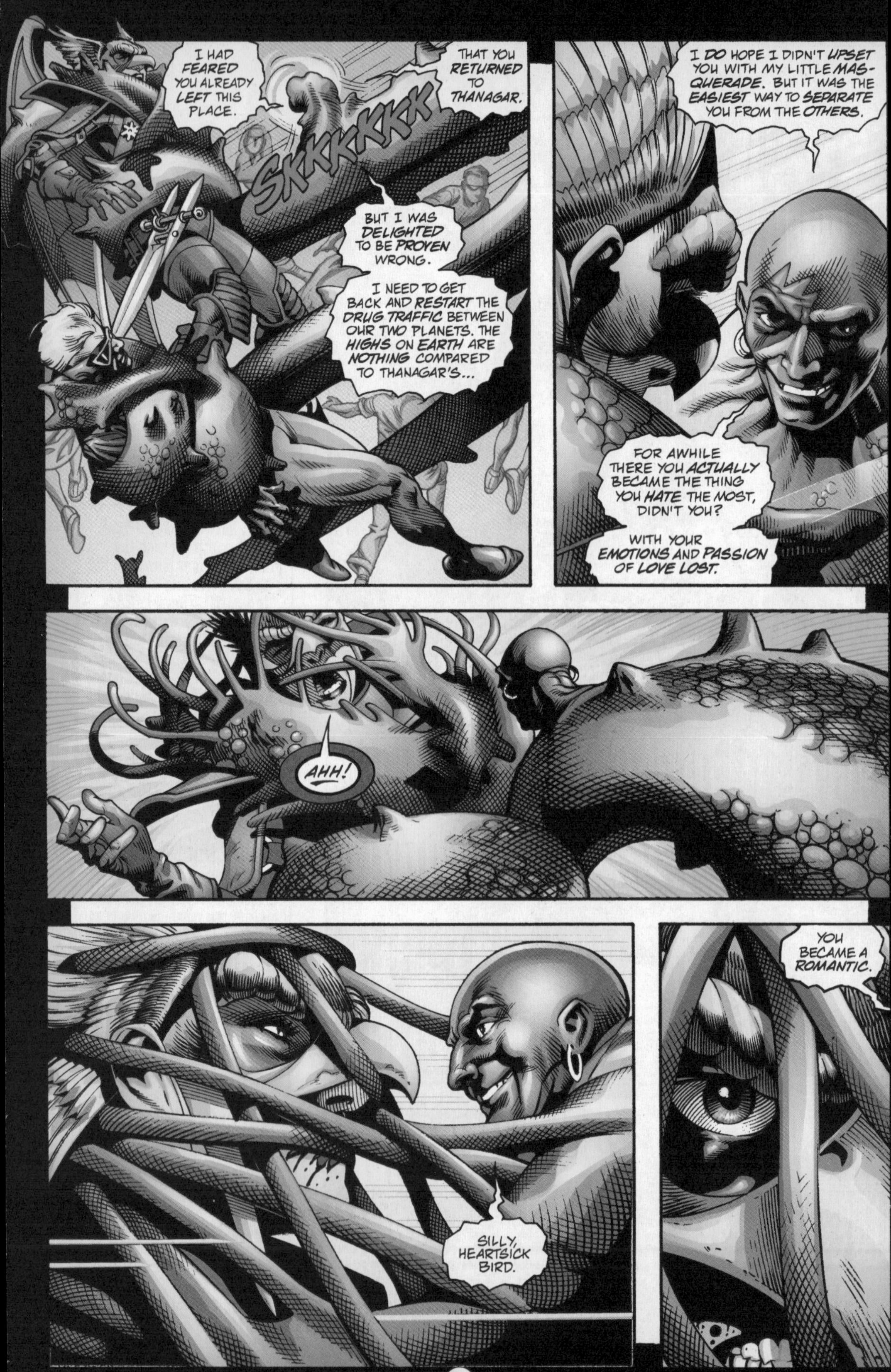
I HAD FEARED YOU ALREADY LEFT THIS PLACE.
THAT YOU RETURNED TO THANAGAR.
SKKKKKK
BUT I WAS DELIGHTED TO BE PROVEN WRONG.
I NEED TO GET BACK AND RESTART THE DRUG TRAFFIC BETWEEN OUR TWO PLANETS. THE HIGHS ON EARTH ARE NOTHING COMPARED TO THANAGAR'S...
I DO HOPE I DIDN'T UPSET YOU WITH MY LITTLE MAS-QUERADE. BUT IT WAS THE EASIEST WAY TO SEPARATE YOU FROM THE OTHERS.
FOR AWHILE THERE YOU ACTUALLY BECAME THE THING YOU HATE THE MOST, DIDN'T YOU?
WITH YOUR EMOTIONS AND PASSION OF LOVE LOST.
AHH!
SILLY, HEARTSICK BIRD.
YOU BECAME A ROMANTIC.

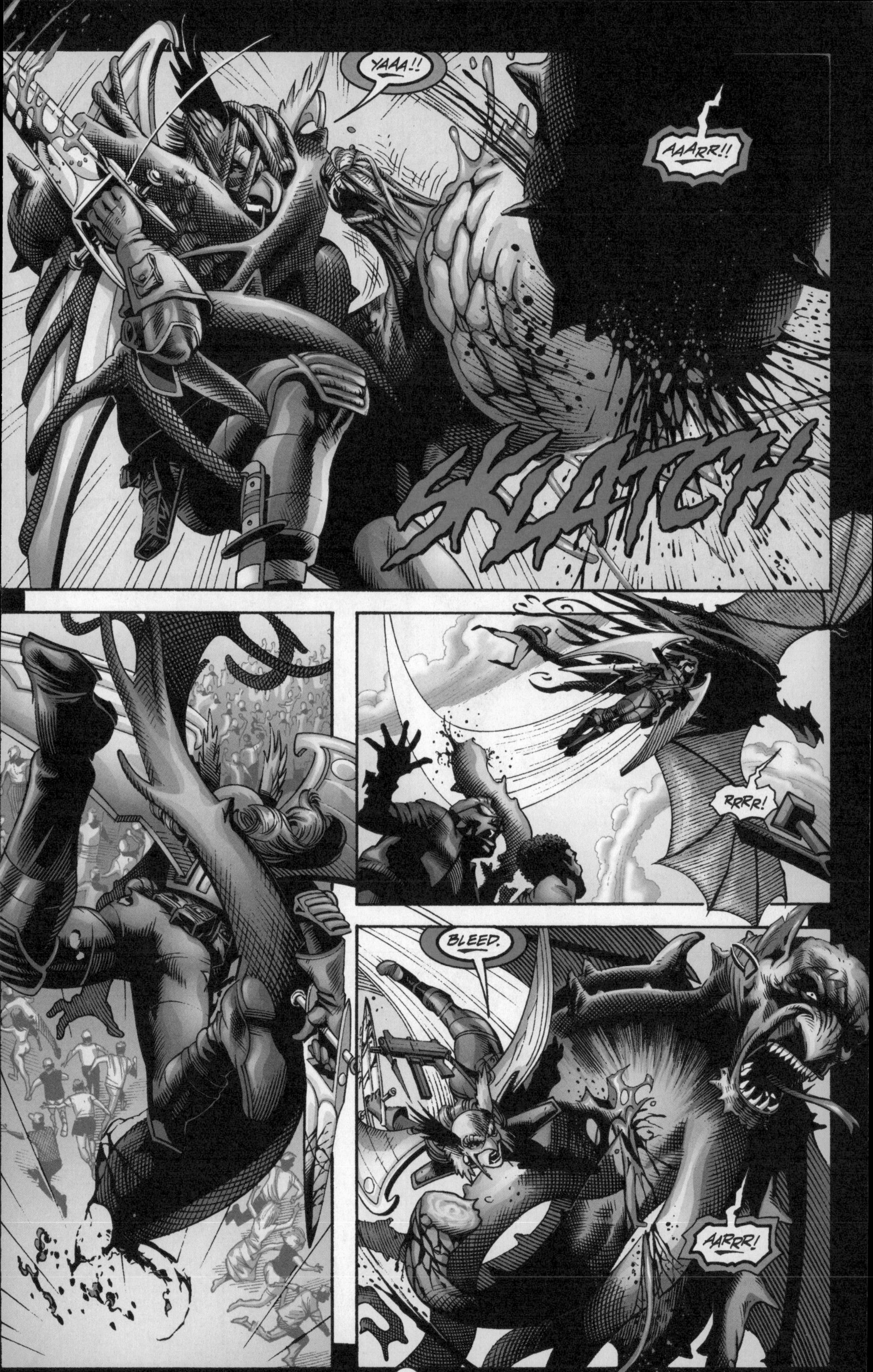
YAAA!!
AAARR!!
SKLATCH
RRRR!
BLEED.
AARRR!

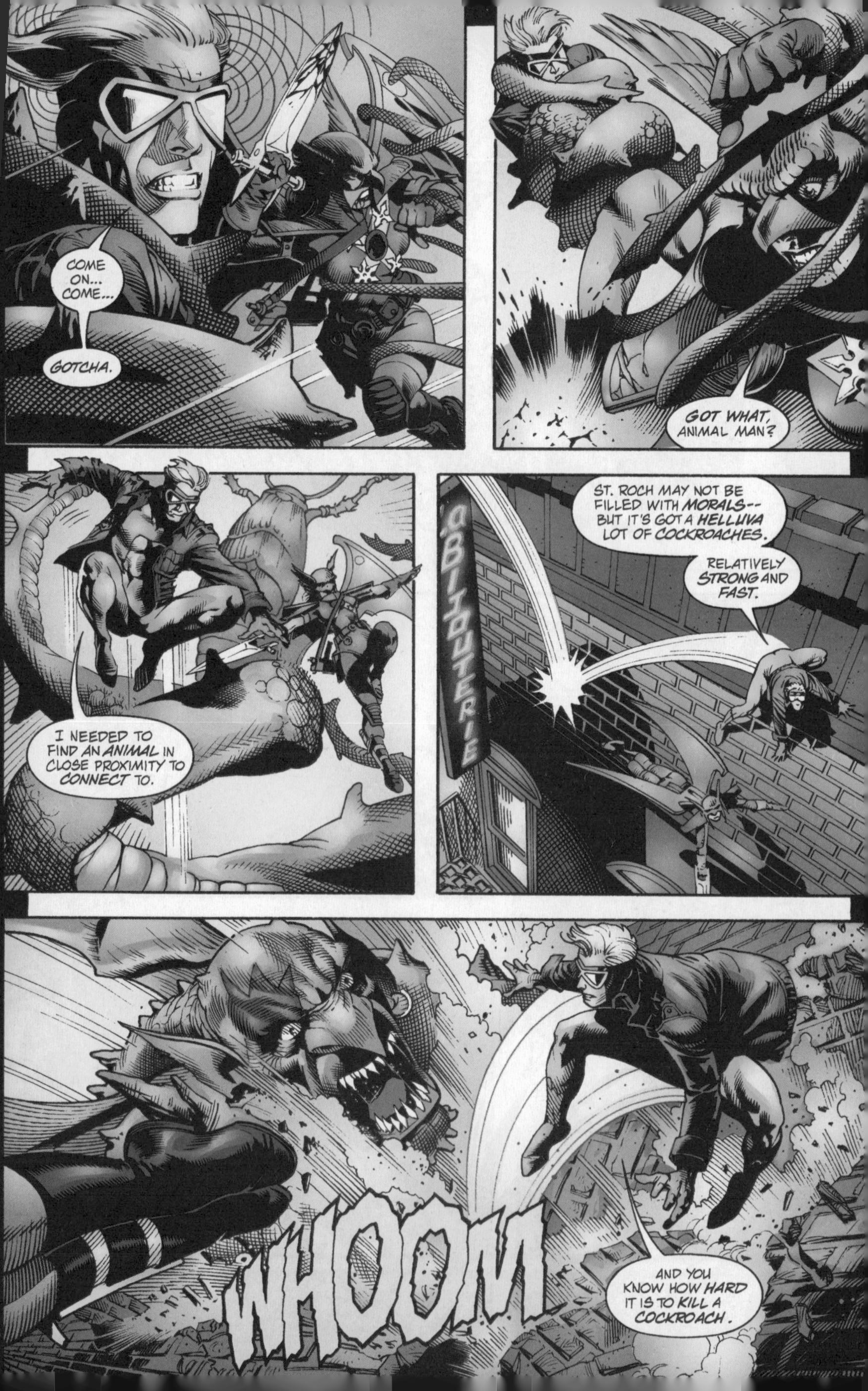
COME ON... COME...
GOTCHA.
GOT WHAT, ANIMAL MAN?
I NEEDED TO FIND AN *ANIMAL* IN CLOSE PROXIMITY TO *CONNECT* TO.
ST. ROCH MAY NOT BE FILLED WITH *MORALS*-- BUT IT'S GOT A *HELLUVA* LOT OF *COCKROACHES*.
BIJOUTERIE
RELATIVELY *STRONG* AND *FAST*.
WHOOM
AND YOU KNOW HOW *HARD* IT IS TO *KILL* A *COCKROACH*.

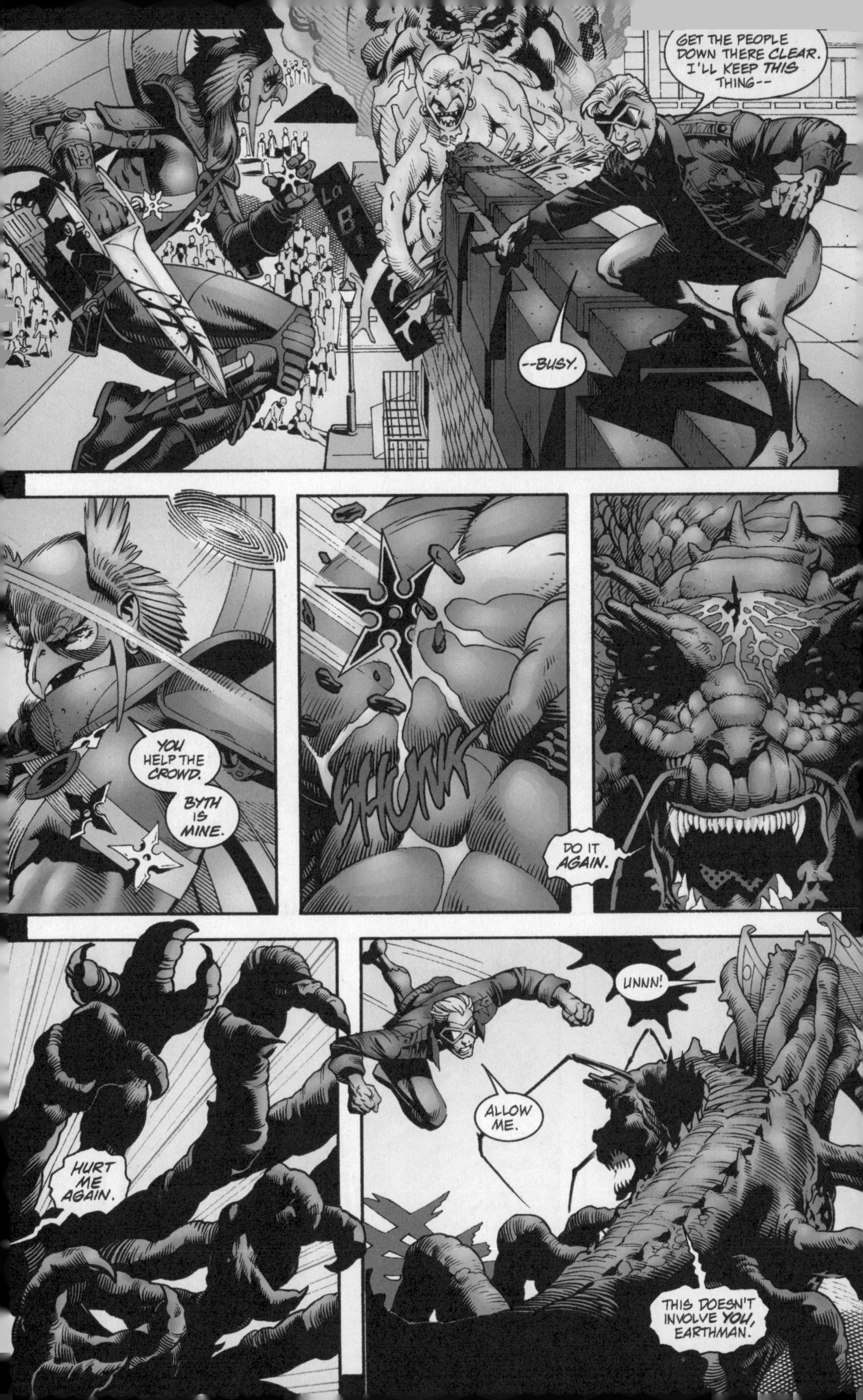
GET THE PEOPLE DOWN THERE CLEAR. I'LL KEEP THIS THING--
--BUSY.
YOU HELP THE CROWD.
BYTH IS MINE.
SHUNK
DO IT AGAIN.
HURT ME AGAIN.
UNNN!
ALLOW ME.
THIS DOESN'T INVOLVE YOU, EARTHMAN.

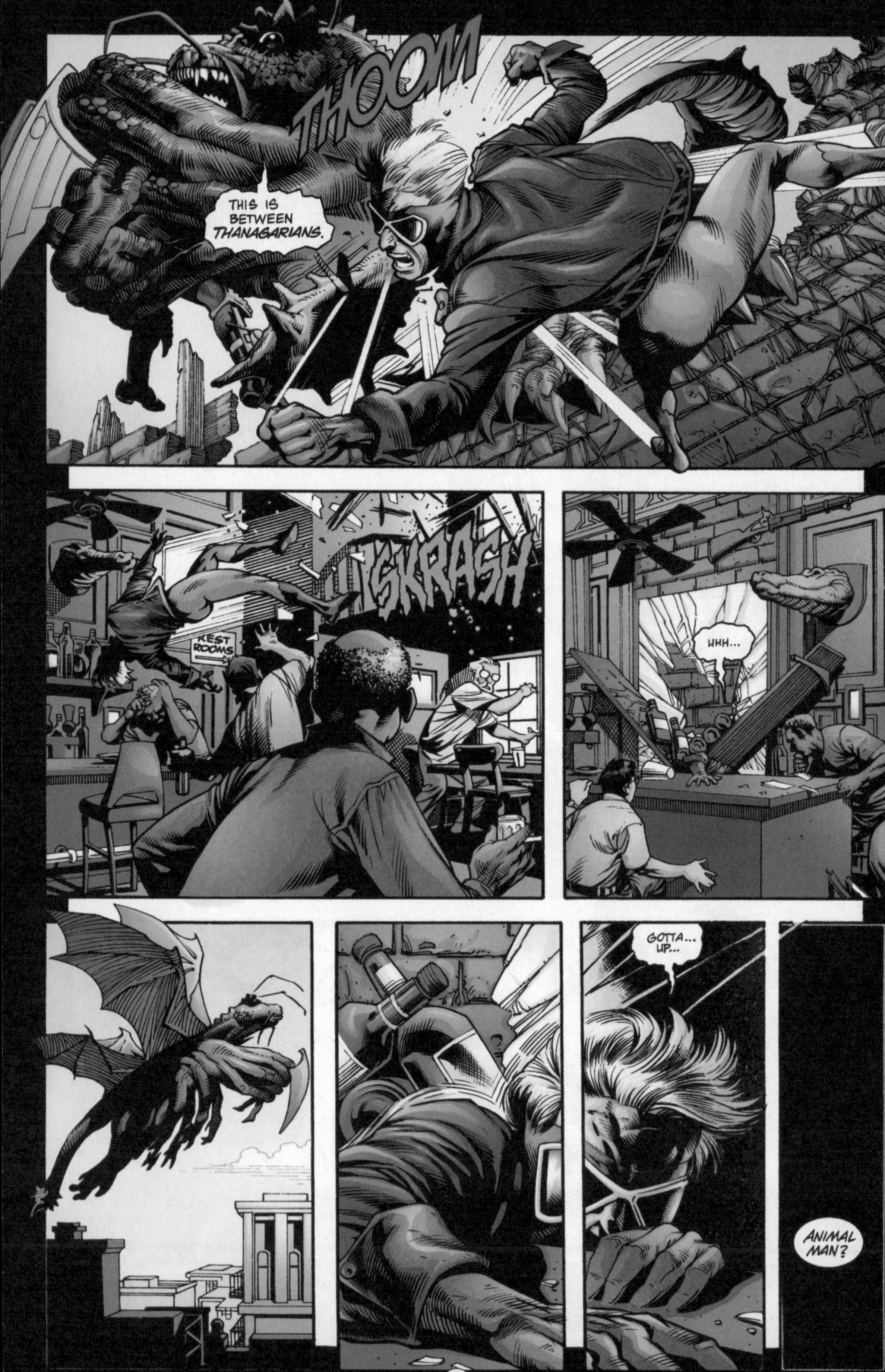
THOOM
THIS IS BETWEEN THANAGARIANS.
SKRASH
REST ROOMS
UHH...
GOTTA... UP...
ANIMAL MAN?

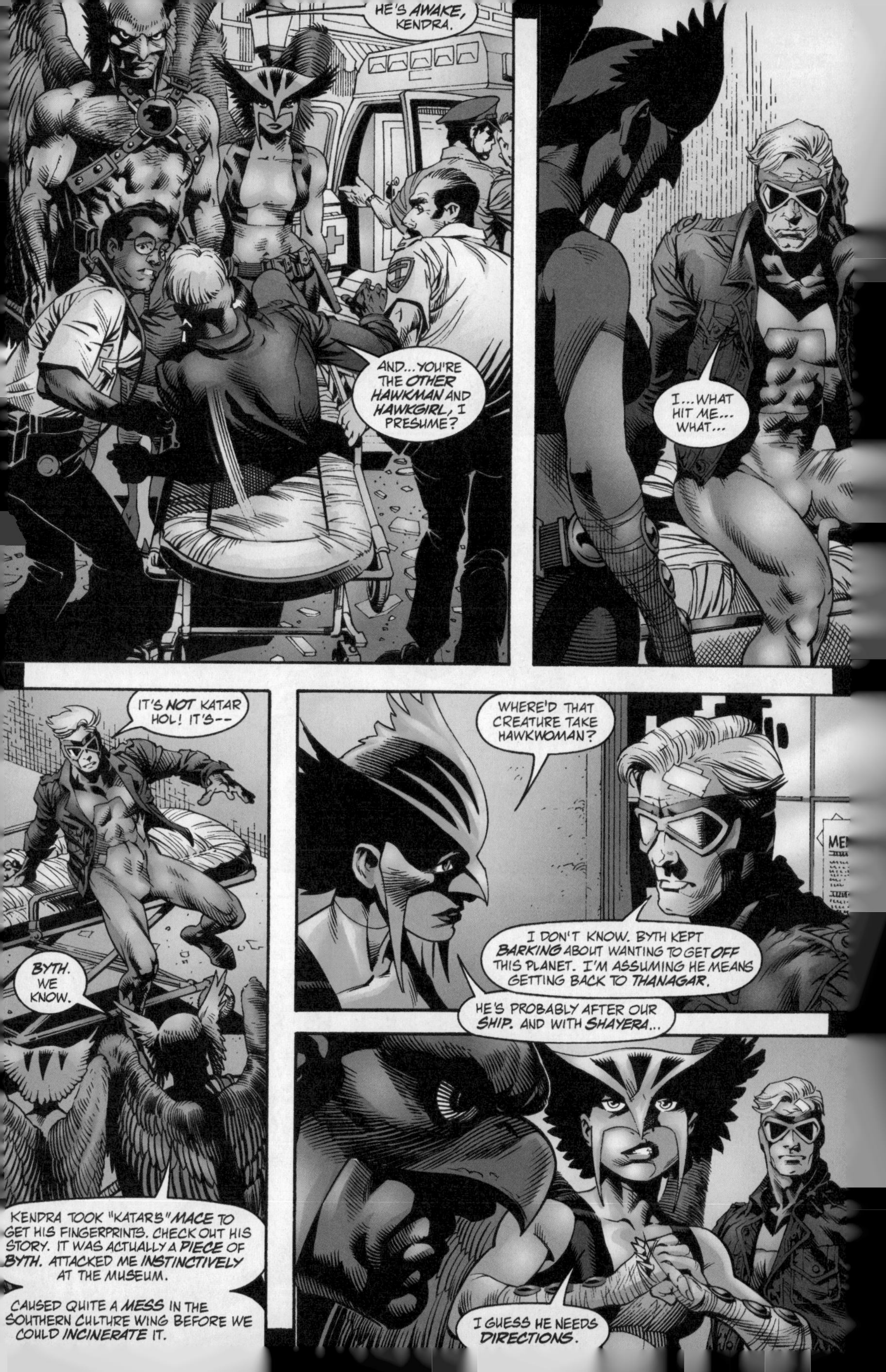
HE'S AWAKE, KENDRA.
AND... YOU'RE THE OTHER HAWKMAN AND HAWKGIRL, I PRESUME?
I... WHAT HIT ME... WHAT...
IT'S NOT KATAR HOL! IT'S--
BYTH. WE KNOW.
KENDRA TOOK "KATAR'S" MACE TO GET HIS FINGERPRINTS. CHECK OUT HIS STORY. IT WAS ACTUALLY A PIECE OF BYTH. ATTACKED ME INSTINCTIVELY AT THE MUSEUM.
CAUSED QUITE A MESS IN THE SOUTHERN CULTURE WING BEFORE WE COULD INCINERATE IT.
WHERE'D THAT CREATURE TAKE HAWKWOMAN?
I DON'T KNOW. BYTH KEPT BARKING ABOUT WANTING TO GET OFF THIS PLANET. I'M ASSUMING HE MEANS GETTING BACK TO THANAGAR.
HE'S PROBABLY AFTER OUR SHIP. AND WITH SHAYERA...
I GUESS HE NEEDS DIRECTIONS.

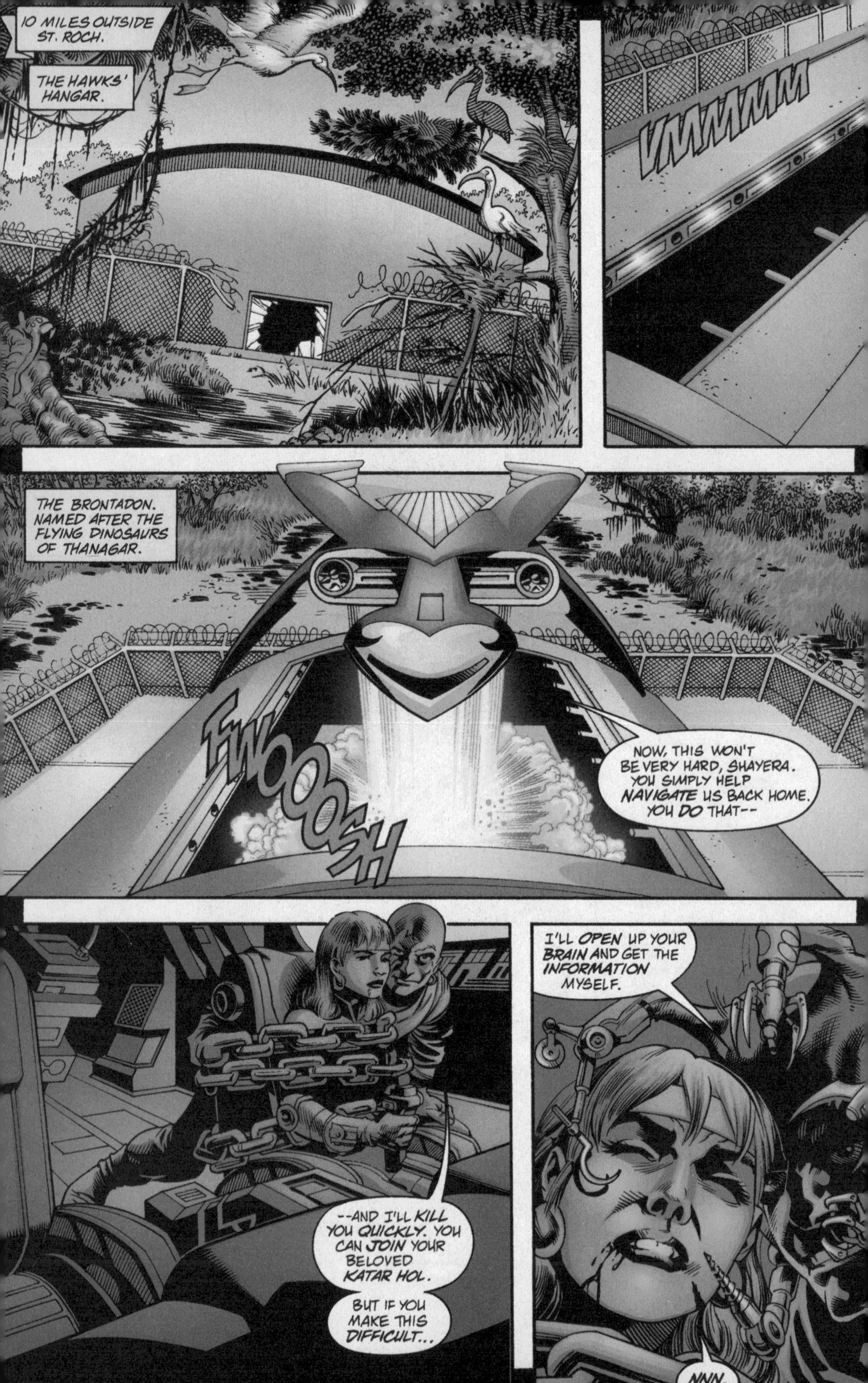

10 MILES OUTSIDE ST. ROCH.
THE HAWKS' HANGAR.
VMMMMM
THE BRONTADON. NAMED AFTER THE FLYING DINOSAURS OF THANAGAR.
FWOOOOSH
NOW, THIS WON'T BE VERY HARD, SHAYERA. YOU SIMPLY HELP NAVIGATE US BACK HOME. YOU DO THAT--
--AND I'LL KILL YOU QUICKLY. YOU CAN JOIN YOUR BELOVED KATAR HOL.
BUT IF YOU MAKE THIS DIFFICULT...
I'LL OPEN UP YOUR BRAIN AND GET THE INFORMATION MYSELF.
NNN.

YOU KNOW WHAT YOU ARE, SHAYERA THAL? WITHOUT YOUR *WINGS* AND *WEAPONS*? WITHOUT YOUR *PARTNER*?

YOU'RE. NOTHING.

I KNOW WHAT I AM, BYTH.

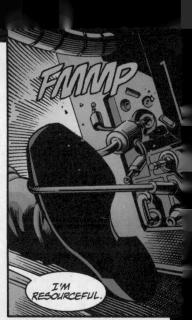

FMMP

I'M RESOURCEFUL.

VRROOOARR

HAASSSS!

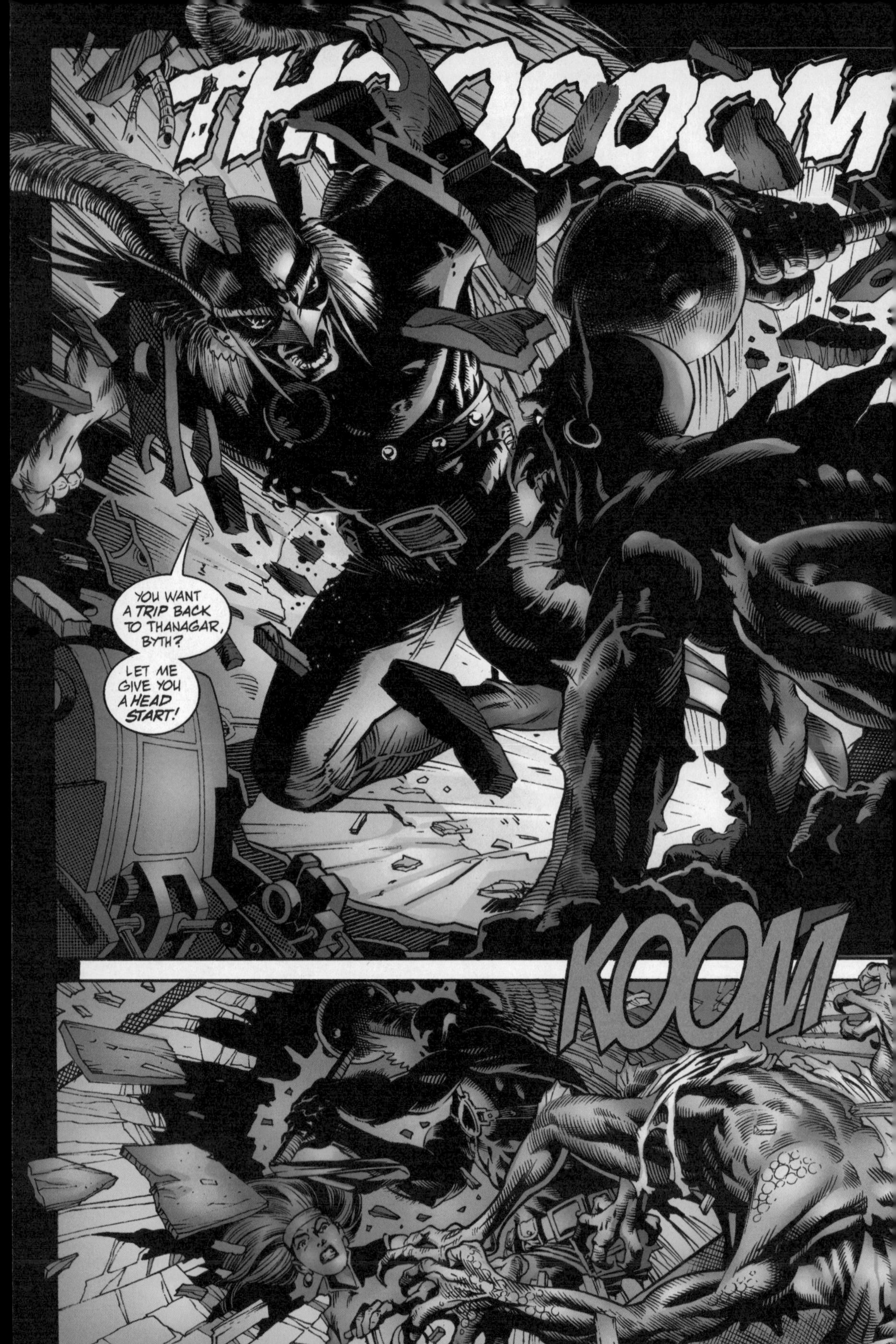
YOU WANT A TRIP BACK TO THANAGAR, BYTH?
LET ME GIVE YOU A HEAD START!
KOOM

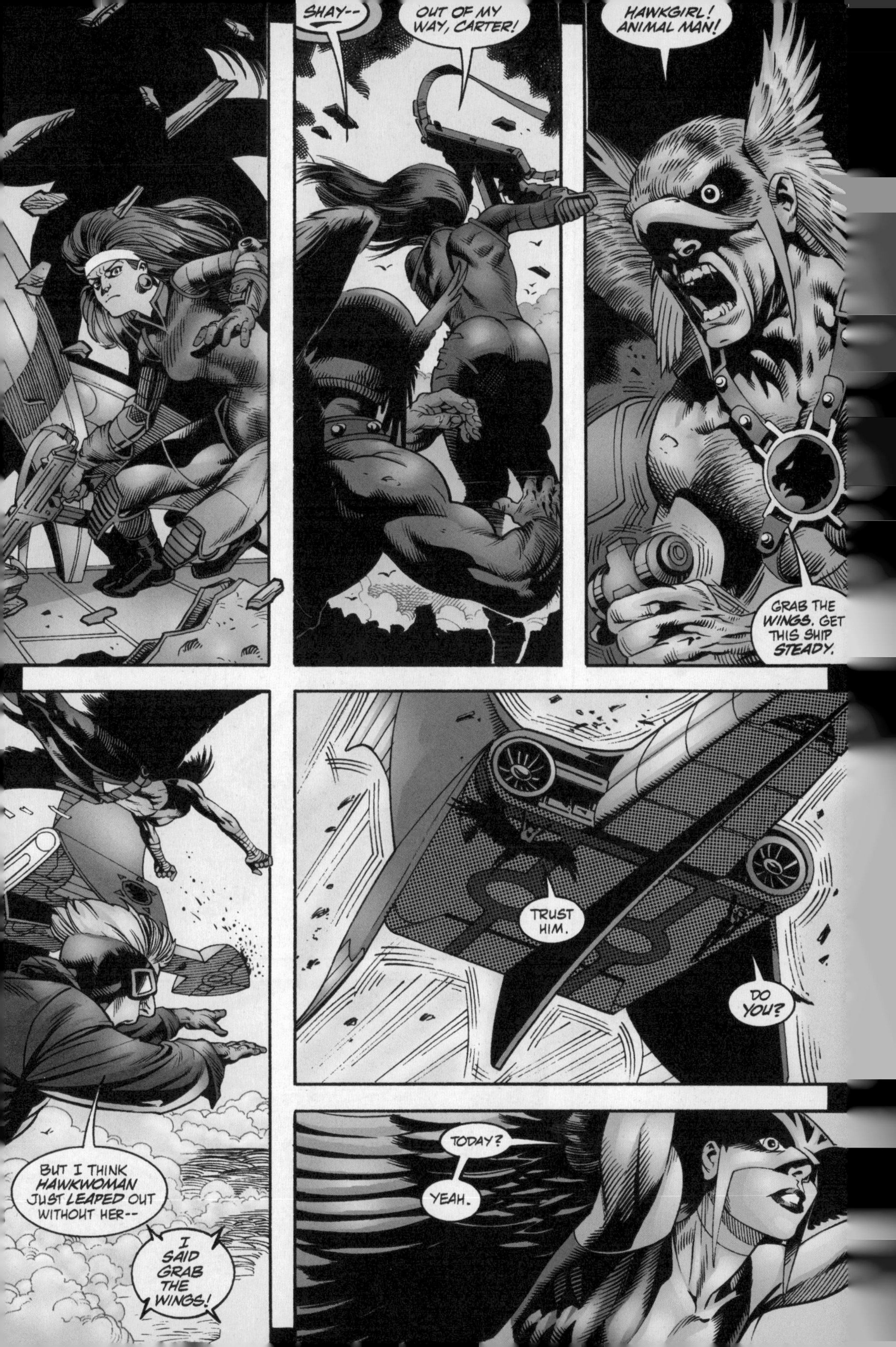
SHAY--
OUT OF MY WAY, CARTER!
HAWKGIRL! ANIMAL MAN!
GRAB THE WINGS. GET THIS SHIP STEADY.
TRUST HIM.
DO YOU?
BUT I THINK HAWKWOMAN JUST LEAPED OUT WITHOUT HER--
I SAID GRAB THE WINGS!
TODAY?
YEAH.

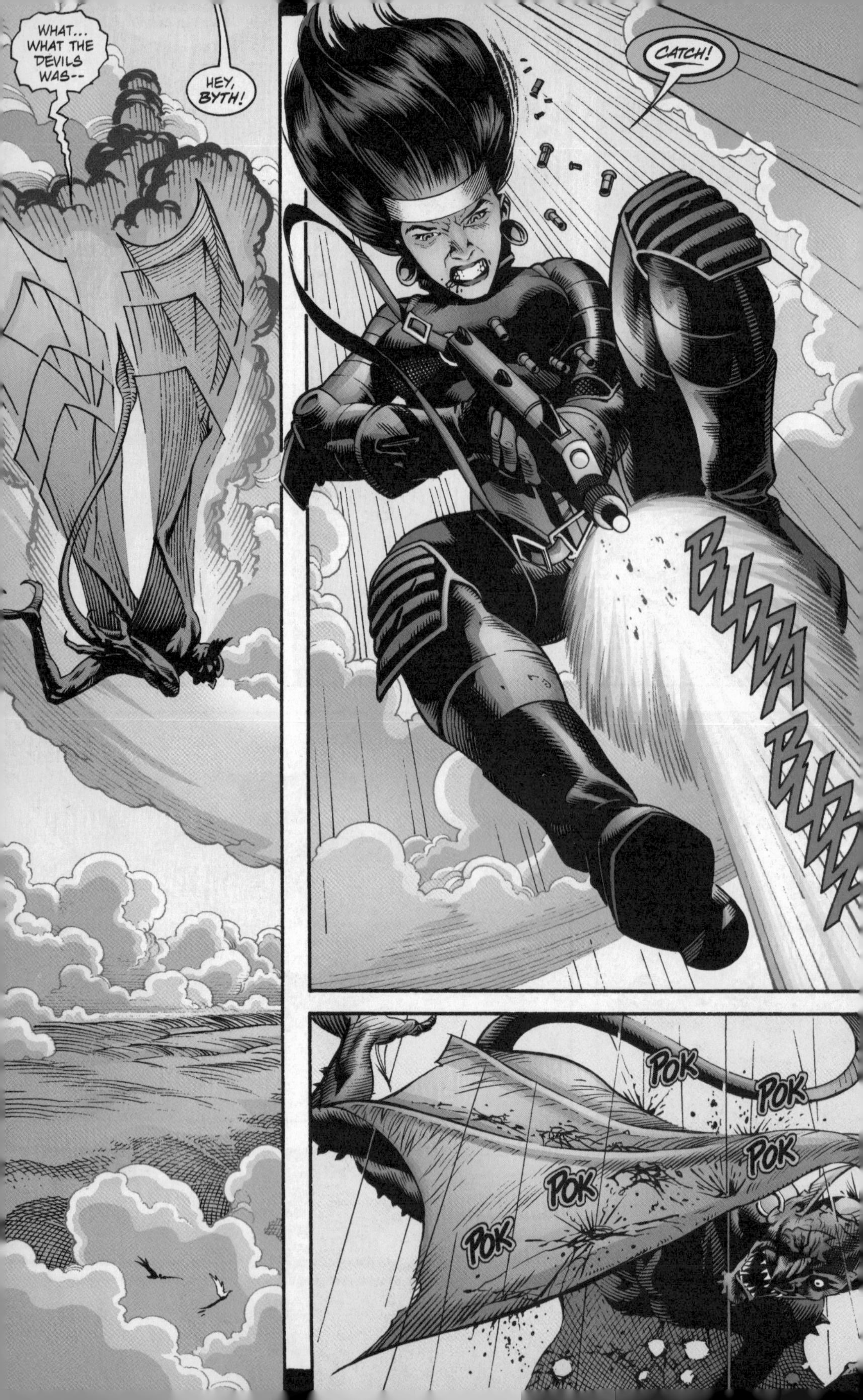

WHAT... WHAT THE DEVILS WAS--
HEY, BYTH!
CATCH!
BUDDABUDDA
POK
POK
POK
POK
POK

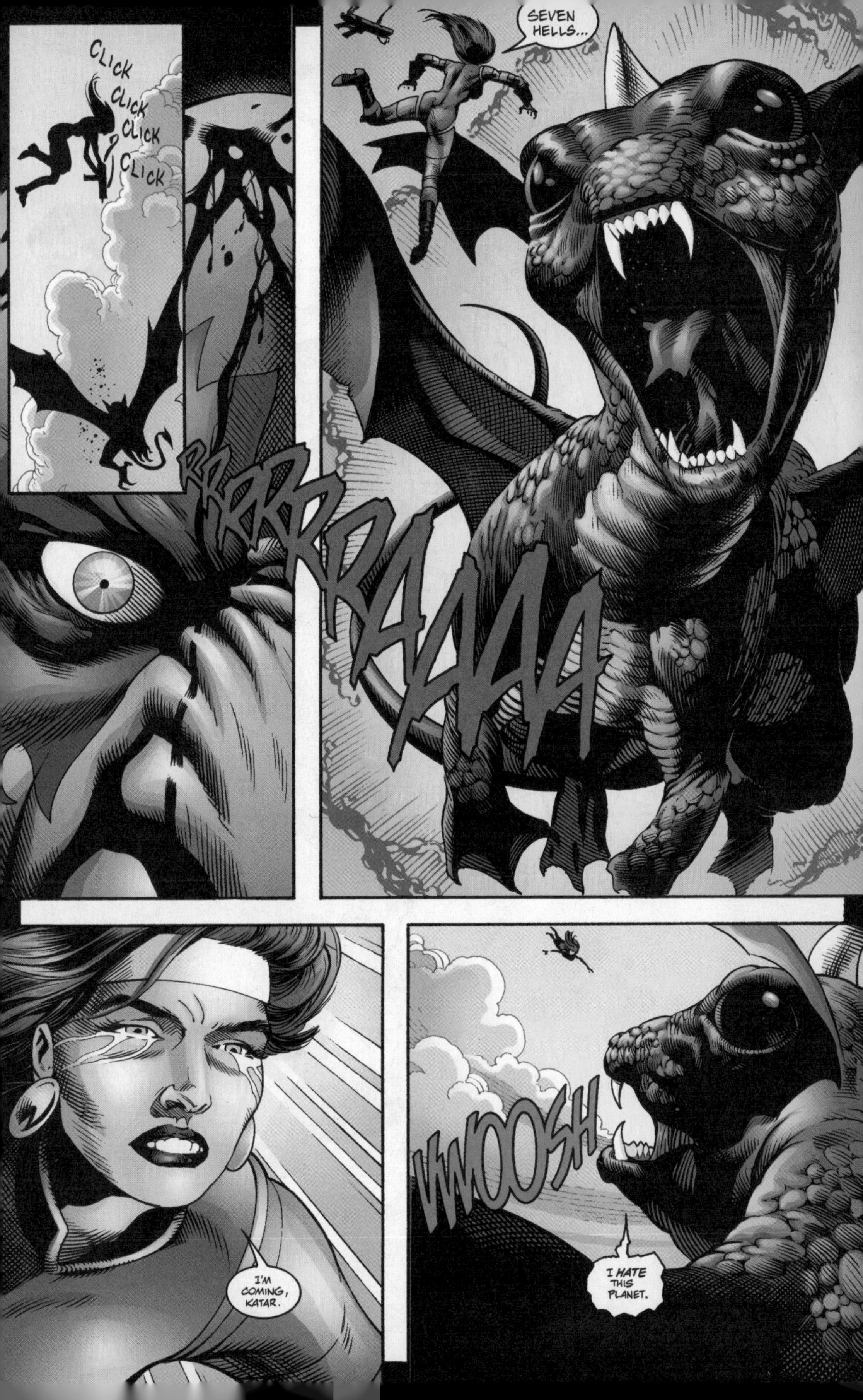
CLICK
CLICK
CLICK
CLICK
SEVEN HELLS...
RRRRRRAAAAA
I'M COMING, KATAR.
VWOOSH
I HATE THIS PLANET.

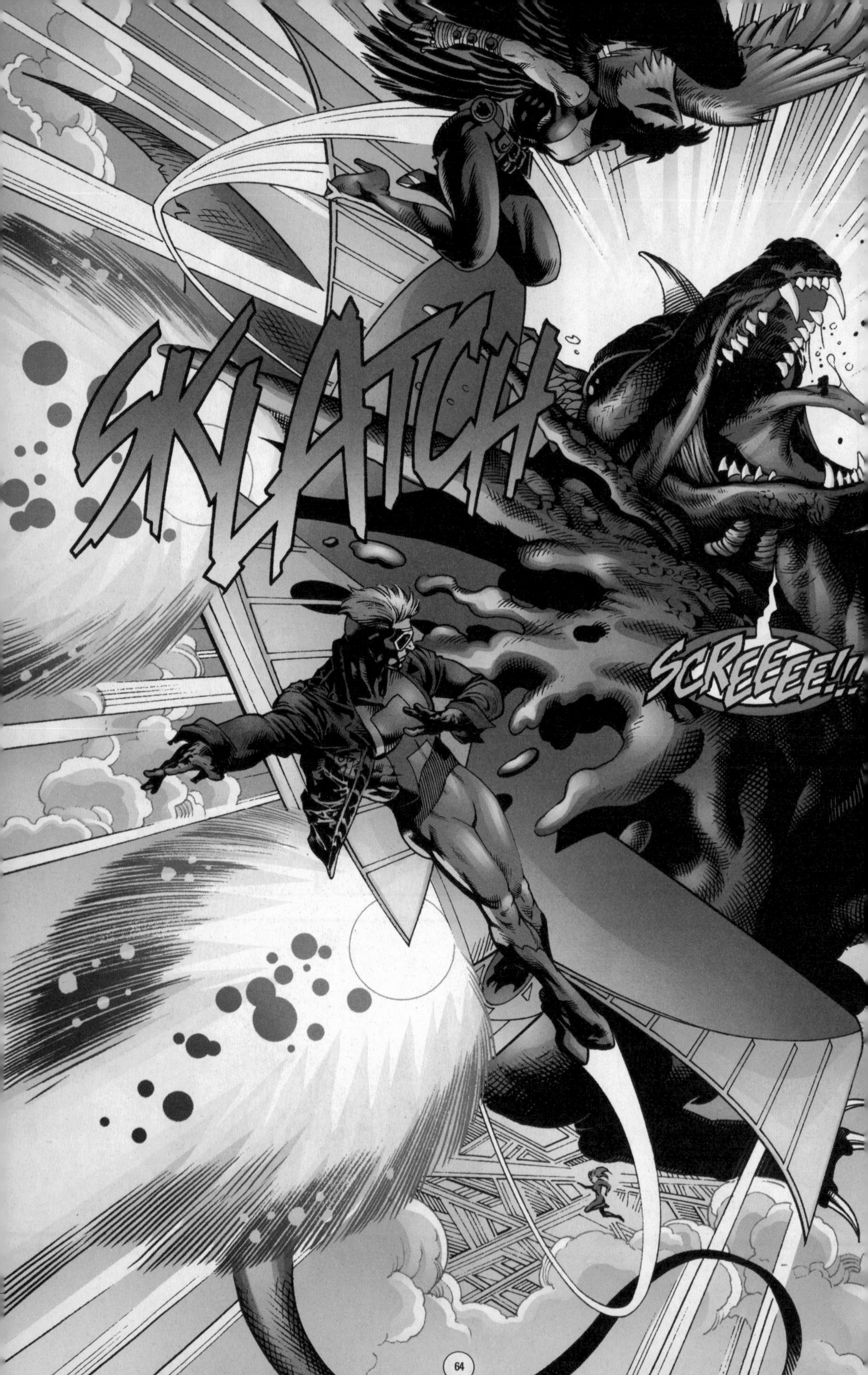
SKLATCH
SCREEEE!!!

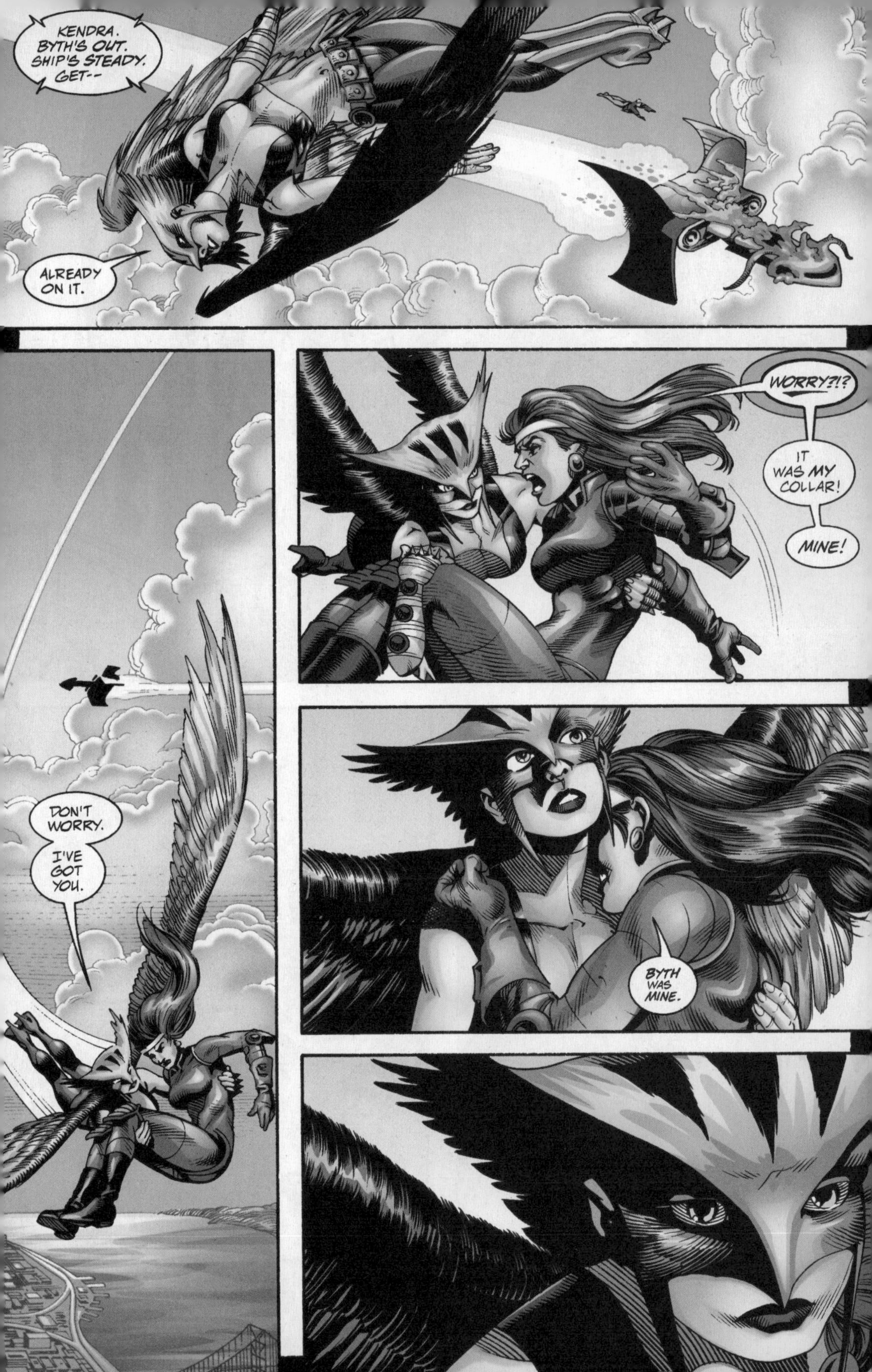
KENDRA. BYTH'S OUT. SHIP'S STEADY. GET--
ALREADY ON IT.
DON'T WORRY.
I'VE GOT YOU.
WORRY?!?
IT WAS MY COLLAR!
MINE!
BYTH WAS MINE.

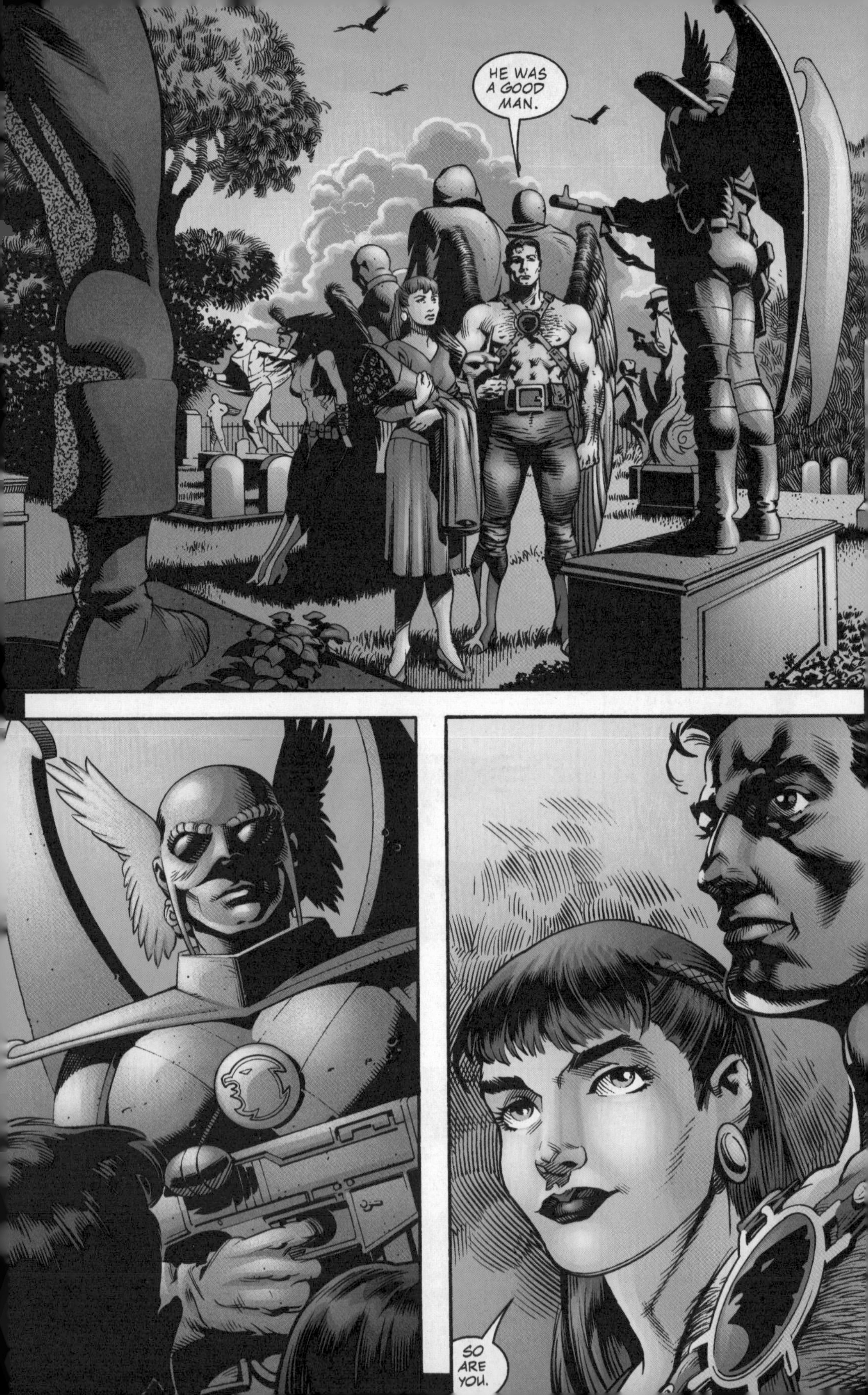
HE WAS A GOOD MAN.
SO ARE YOU.

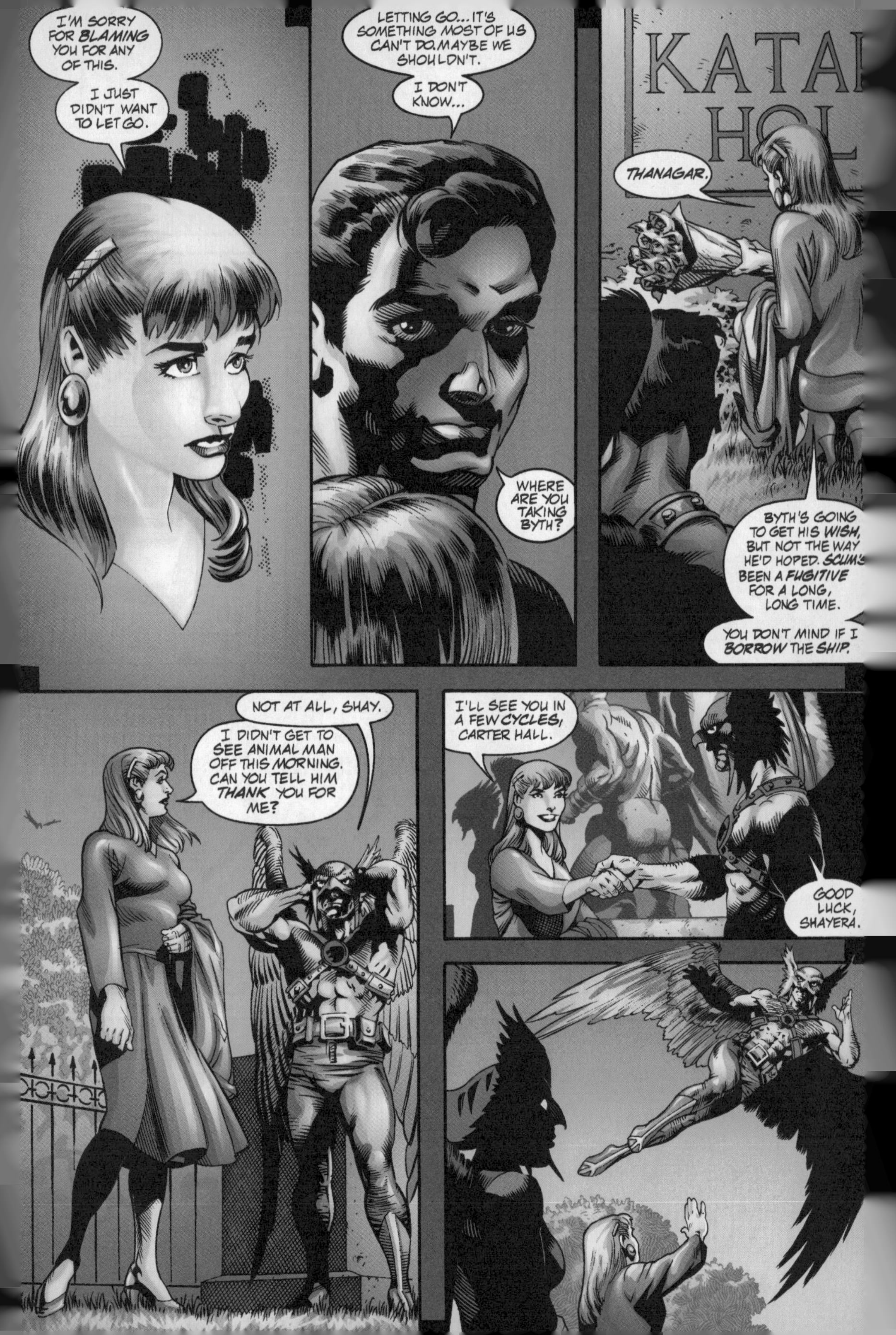

I'M SORRY FOR BLAMING YOU FOR ANY OF THIS.
I JUST DIDN'T WANT TO LET GO.
LETTING GO... IT'S SOMETHING MOST OF US CAN'T DO. MAYBE WE SHOULDN'T.
I DON'T KNOW...
WHERE ARE YOU TAKING BYTH?
THANAGAR.
BYTH'S GOING TO GET HIS WISH, BUT NOT THE WAY HE'D HOPED. SCUM'S BEEN A FUGITIVE FOR A LONG, LONG TIME.
YOU DON'T MIND IF I BORROW THE SHIP.
NOT AT ALL, SHAY.
I DIDN'T GET TO SEE ANIMAL MAN OFF THIS MORNING. CAN YOU TELL HIM THANK YOU FOR ME?
I'LL SEE YOU IN A FEW CYCLES, CARTER HALL.
GOOD LUCK, SHAYERA.

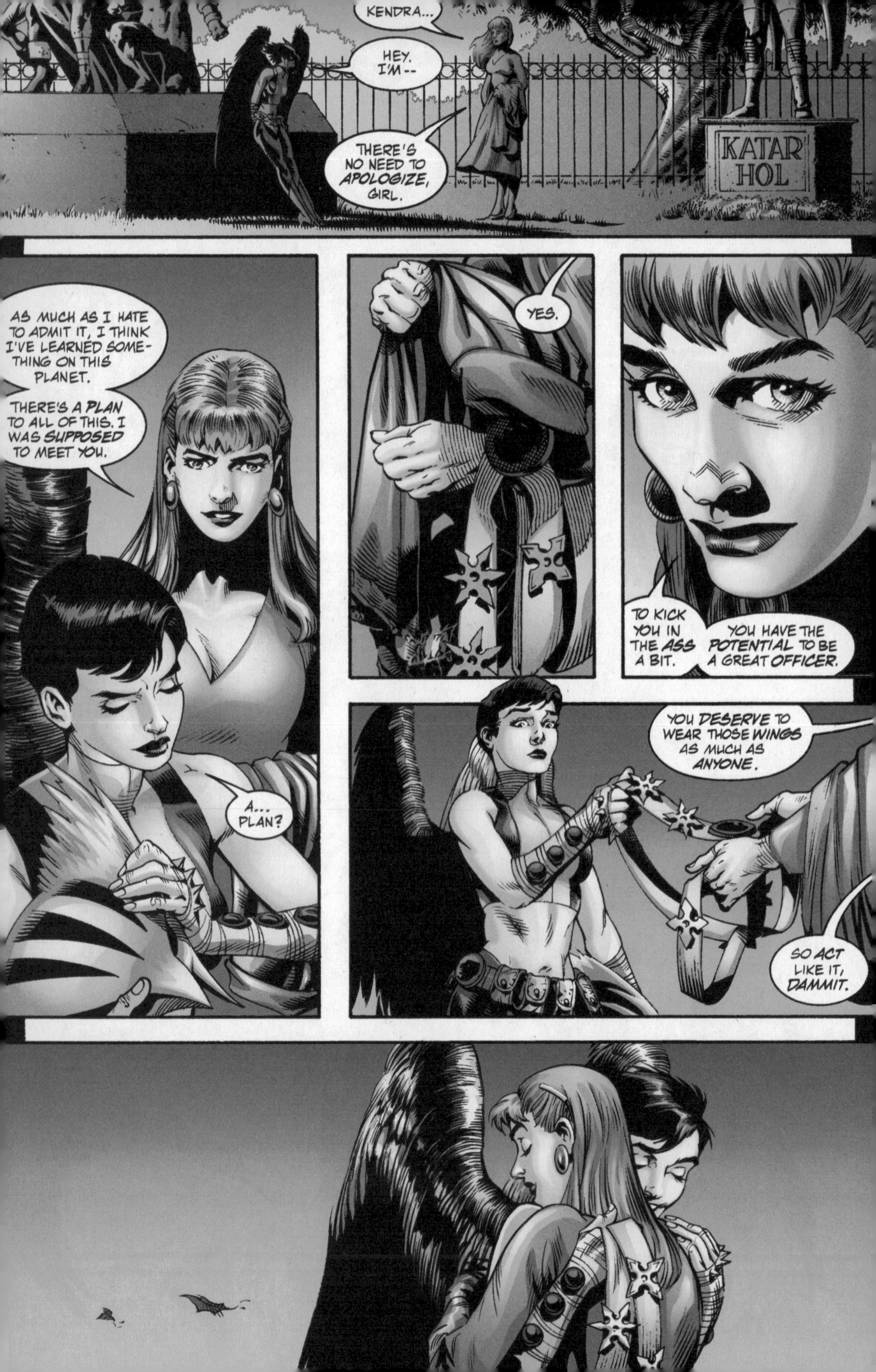
KENDRA...
HEY. I'M --
THERE'S NO NEED TO APOLOGIZE, GIRL.
KATAR HOL
AS MUCH AS I HATE TO ADMIT IT, I THINK I'VE LEARNED SOME-THING ON THIS PLANET.
THERE'S A PLAN TO ALL OF THIS. I WAS SUPPOSED TO MEET YOU.
A... PLAN?
YES.
TO KICK YOU IN THE ASS A BIT.
YOU HAVE THE POTENTIAL TO BE A GREAT OFFICER.
YOU DESERVE TO WEAR THOSE WINGS AS MUCH AS ANYONE.
SO ACT LIKE IT, DAMMIT.

IT WAS A LEARNING EXPERIENCE.

AND I KNOW I'LL BE BACK. AFTER I *HAUL* THIS *DEVIL* ACROSS SPACE...I'LL BE BACK.

BECAUSE I HAVE *FRIENDS* DOWN THERE.

KATAR.

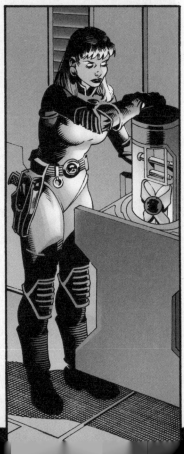

I WILL NEVER GIVE UP *HOPE* THAT WE WILL SEE EACH OTHER AGAIN.

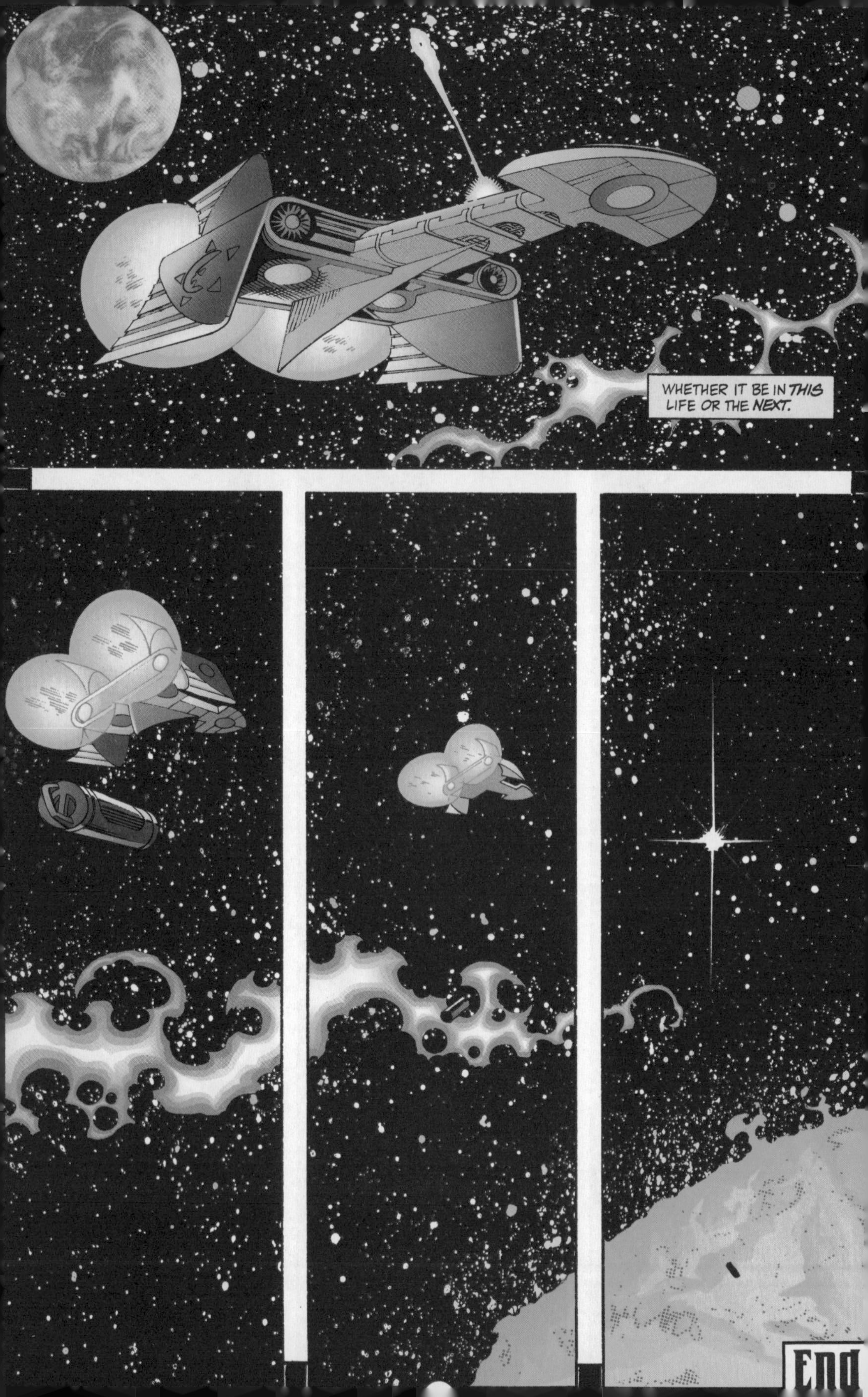
WHETHER IT BE IN THIS LIFE OR THE NEXT.
End

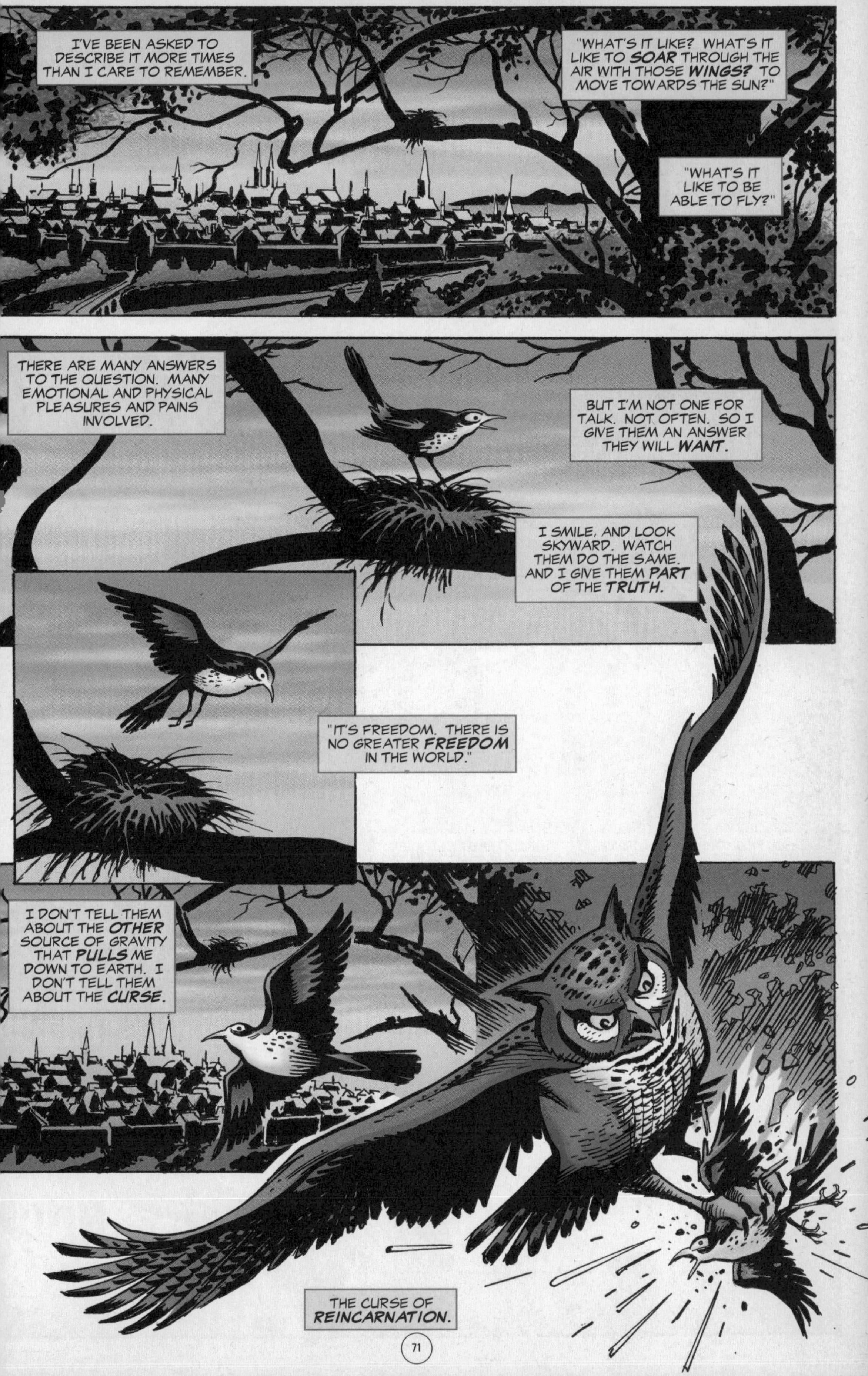
I'VE BEEN ASKED TO DESCRIBE IT MORE TIMES THAN I CARE TO REMEMBER.
"WHAT'S IT LIKE? WHAT'S IT LIKE TO SOAR THROUGH THE AIR WITH THOSE WINGS? TO MOVE TOWARDS THE SUN?"
"WHAT'S IT LIKE TO BE ABLE TO FLY?"
THERE ARE MANY ANSWERS TO THE QUESTION. MANY EMOTIONAL AND PHYSICAL PLEASURES AND PAINS INVOLVED.
BUT I'M NOT ONE FOR TALK. NOT OFTEN. SO I GIVE THEM AN ANSWER THEY WILL WANT.
I SMILE, AND LOOK SKYWARD. WATCH THEM DO THE SAME. AND I GIVE THEM PART OF THE TRUTH.
"IT'S FREEDOM. THERE IS NO GREATER FREEDOM IN THE WORLD."
I DON'T TELL THEM ABOUT THE OTHER SOURCE OF GRAVITY THAT PULLS ME DOWN TO EARTH. I DON'T TELL THEM ABOUT THE CURSE.
THE CURSE OF REINCARNATION.

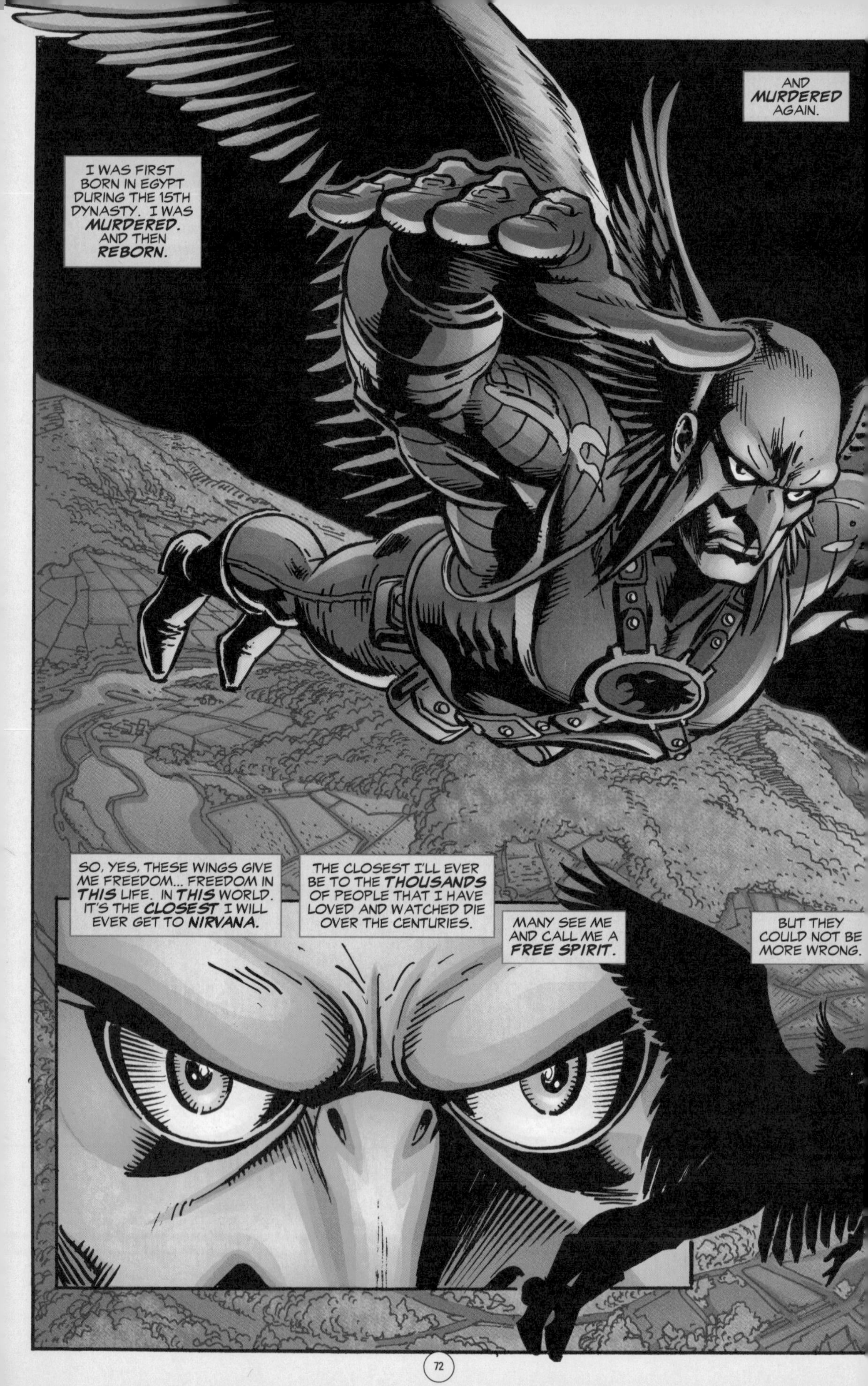
I WAS FIRST BORN IN EGYPT DURING THE 15TH DYNASTY. I WAS MURDERED. AND THEN REBORN.
AND MURDERED AGAIN.
SO, YES, THESE WINGS GIVE ME FREEDOM... FREEDOM IN THIS LIFE. IN THIS WORLD. IT'S THE CLOSEST I WILL EVER GET TO NIRVANA.
THE CLOSEST I'LL EVER BE TO THE THOUSANDS OF PEOPLE THAT I HAVE LOVED AND WATCHED DIE OVER THE CENTURIES.
MANY SEE ME AND CALL ME A FREE SPIRIT.
BUT THEY COULD NOT BE MORE WRONG.

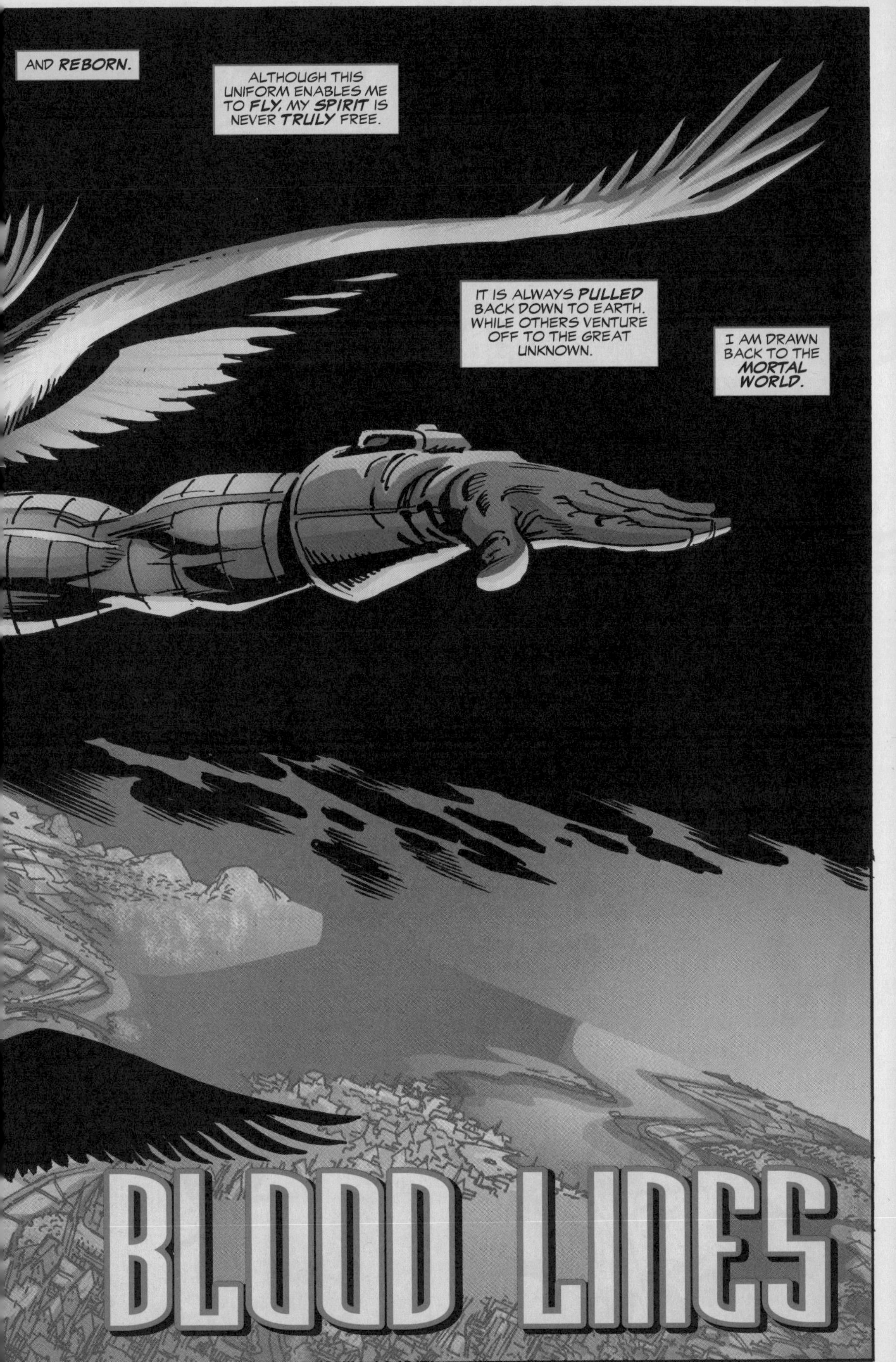
AND REBORN.
ALTHOUGH THIS UNIFORM ENABLES ME TO FLY, MY SPIRIT IS NEVER TRULY FREE.
IT IS ALWAYS PULLED BACK DOWN TO EARTH. WHILE OTHERS VENTURE OFF TO THE GREAT UNKNOWN.
I AM DRAWN BACK TO THE MORTAL WORLD.
BLOOD LINES

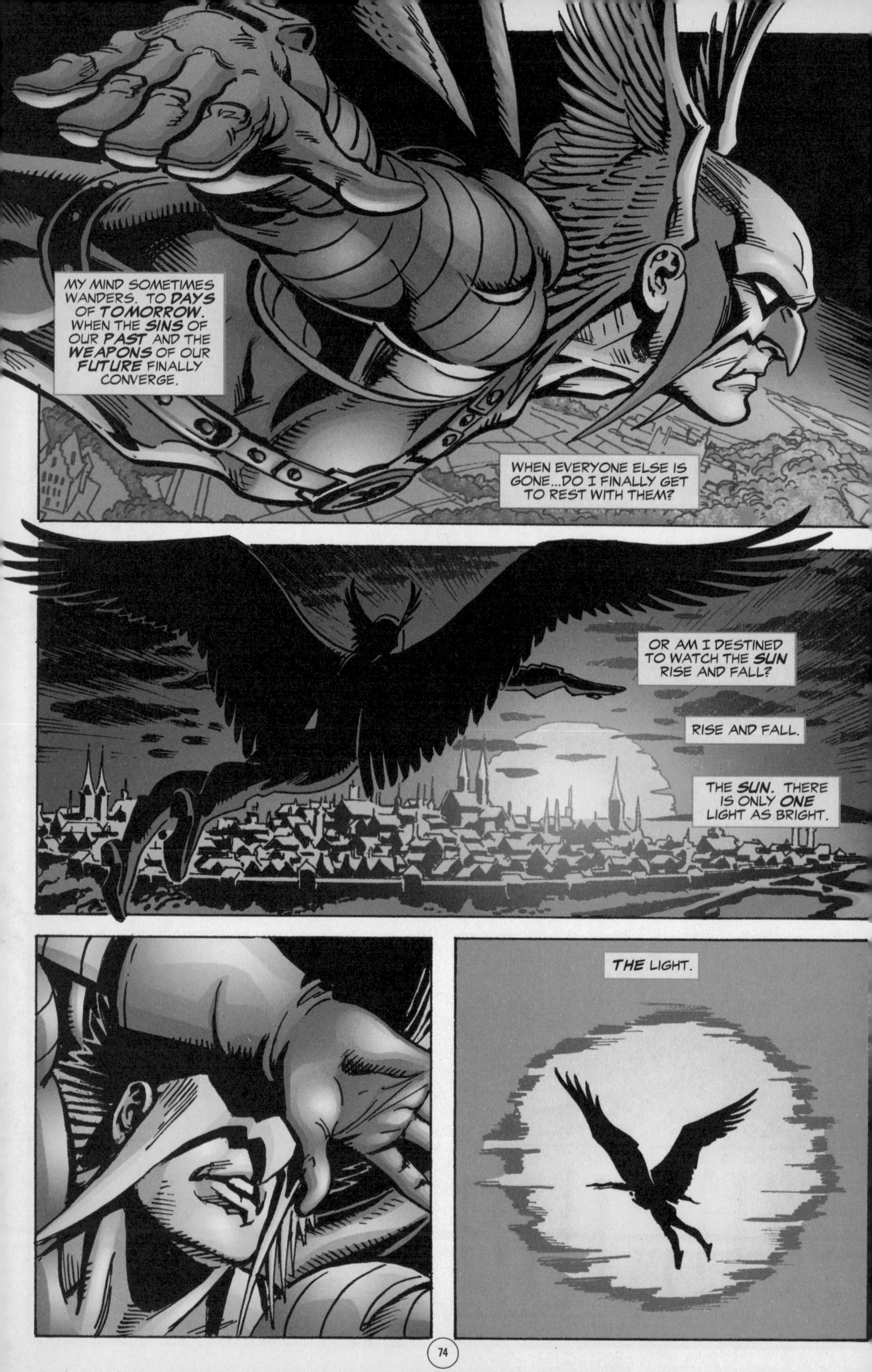
MY MIND SOMETIMES WANDERS. TO DAYS OF TOMORROW. WHEN THE SINS OF OUR PAST AND THE WEAPONS OF OUR FUTURE FINALLY CONVERGE.
WHEN EVERYONE ELSE IS GONE...DO I FINALLY GET TO REST WITH THEM?
OR AM I DESTINED TO WATCH THE SUN RISE AND FALL?
RISE AND FALL.
THE SUN. THERE IS ONLY ONE LIGHT AS BRIGHT.
THE LIGHT.

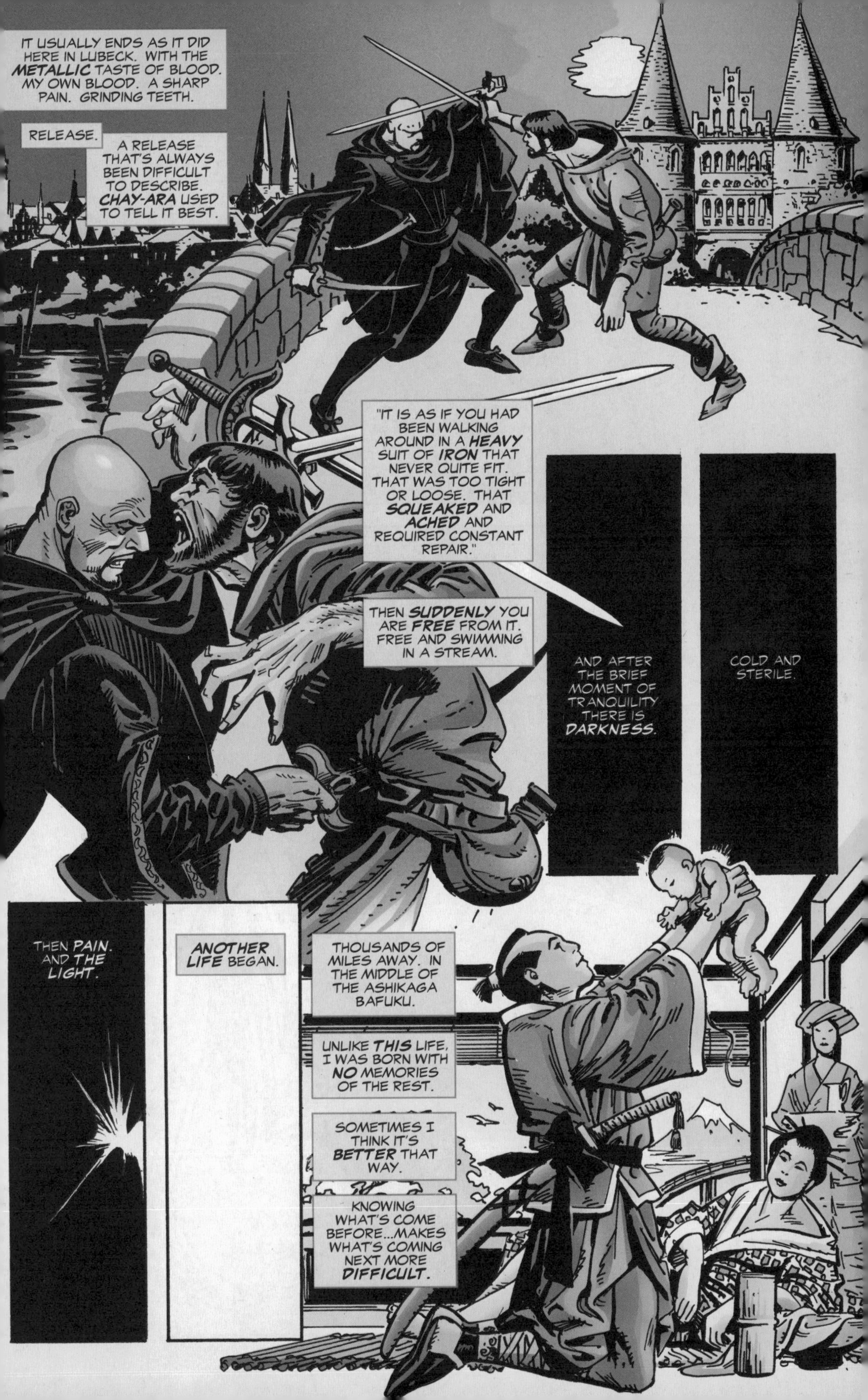
IT USUALLY ENDS AS IT DID HERE IN LUBECK. WITH THE METALLIC TASTE OF BLOOD. MY OWN BLOOD. A SHARP PAIN. GRINDING TEETH.
RELEASE.
A RELEASE THAT'S ALWAYS BEEN DIFFICULT TO DESCRIBE. CHAY-ARA USED TO TELL IT BEST.
"IT IS AS IF YOU HAD BEEN WALKING AROUND IN A HEAVY SUIT OF IRON THAT NEVER QUITE FIT. THAT WAS TOO TIGHT OR LOOSE. THAT SQUEAKED AND ACHED AND REQUIRED CONSTANT REPAIR."
THEN SUDDENLY YOU ARE FREE FROM IT. FREE AND SWIMMING IN A STREAM.
AND AFTER THE BRIEF MOMENT OF TRANQUILITY THERE IS DARKNESS.
COLD AND STERILE.
THEN PAIN. AND THE LIGHT.
ANOTHER LIFE BEGAN.
THOUSANDS OF MILES AWAY. IN THE MIDDLE OF THE ASHIKAGA BAFUKU.
UNLIKE THIS LIFE, I WAS BORN WITH NO MEMORIES OF THE REST.
SOMETIMES I THINK IT'S BETTER THAT WAY.
KNOWING WHAT'S COME BEFORE...MAKES WHAT'S COMING NEXT MORE DIFFICULT.

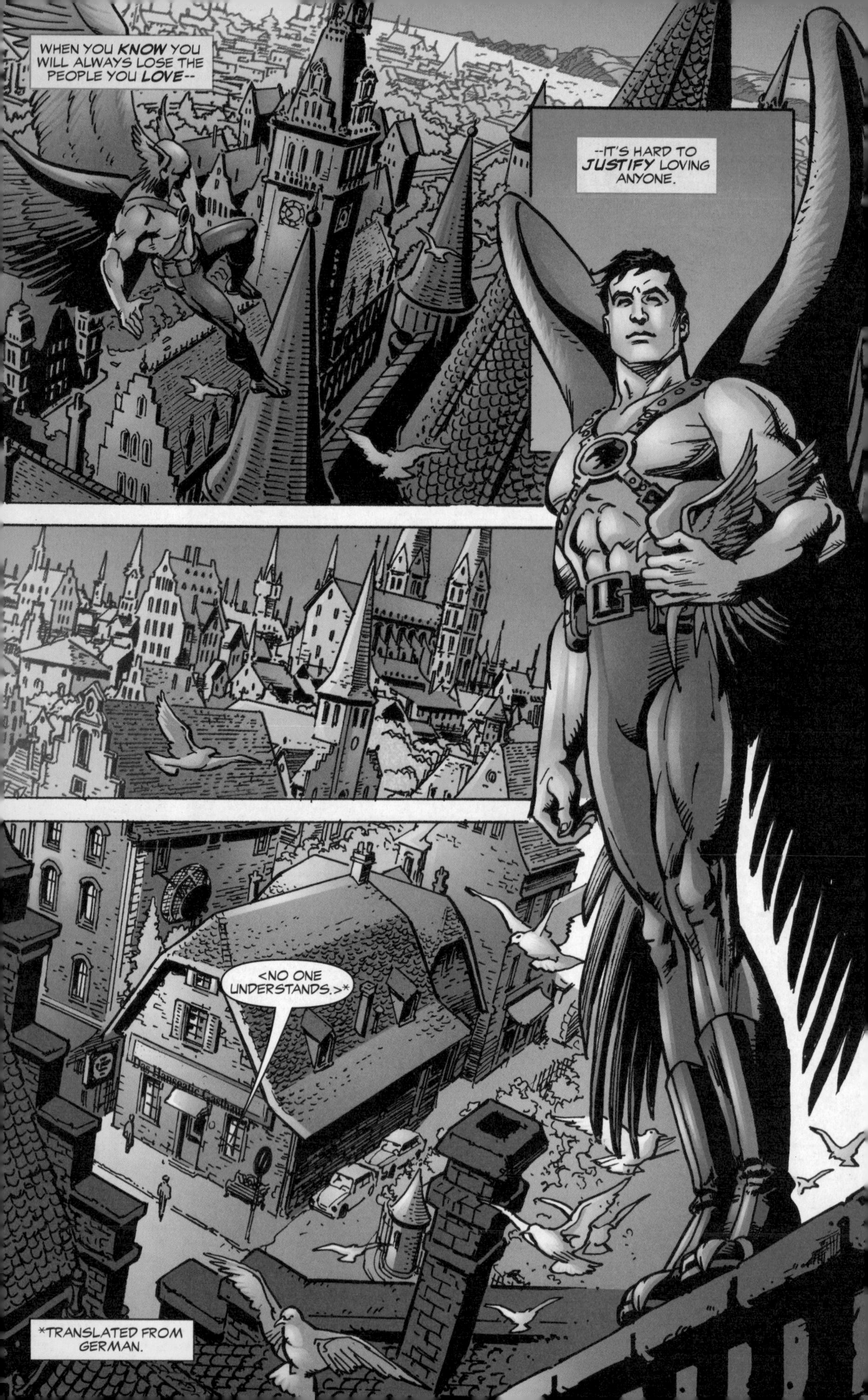
WHEN YOU KNOW YOU WILL ALWAYS LOSE THE PEOPLE YOU LOVE--
--IT'S HARD TO JUSTIFY LOVING ANYONE.
<NO ONE UNDERSTANDS.>*
*TRANSLATED FROM GERMAN.

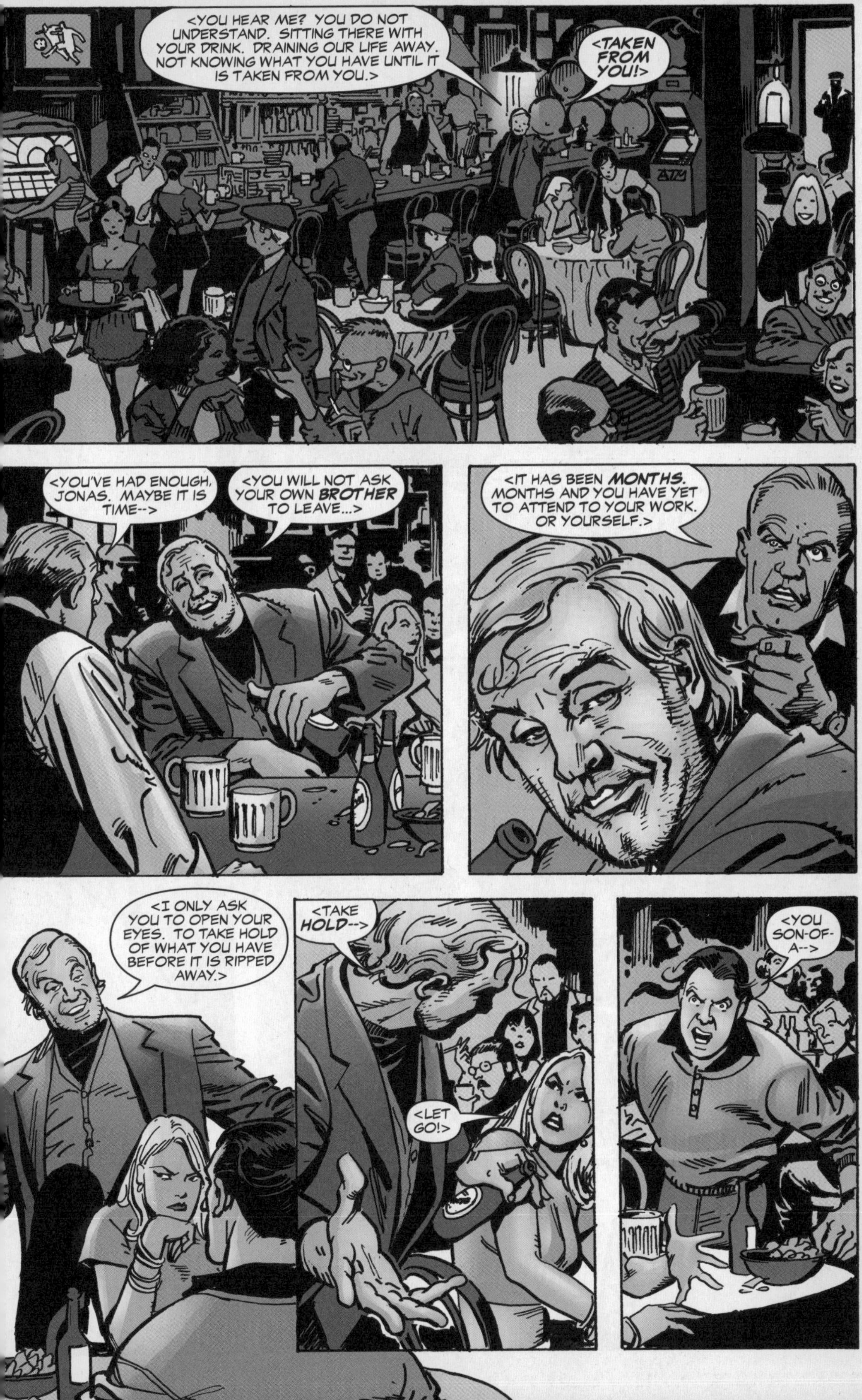

<YOU HEAR ME? YOU DO NOT UNDERSTAND. SITTING THERE WITH YOUR DRINK. DRAINING OUR LIFE AWAY. NOT KNOWING WHAT YOU HAVE UNTIL IT IS TAKEN FROM YOU.>
<TAKEN FROM YOU!>
<YOU'VE HAD ENOUGH, JONAS. MAYBE IT IS TIME-->
<YOU WILL NOT ASK YOUR OWN BROTHER TO LEAVE...>
<IT HAS BEEN MONTHS. MONTHS AND YOU HAVE YET TO ATTEND TO YOUR WORK. OR YOURSELF.>
<I ONLY ASK YOU TO OPEN YOUR EYES. TO TAKE HOLD OF WHAT YOU HAVE BEFORE IT IS RIPPED AWAY.>
<TAKE HOLD-->
<LET GO!>
<YOU SON-OF-A-->

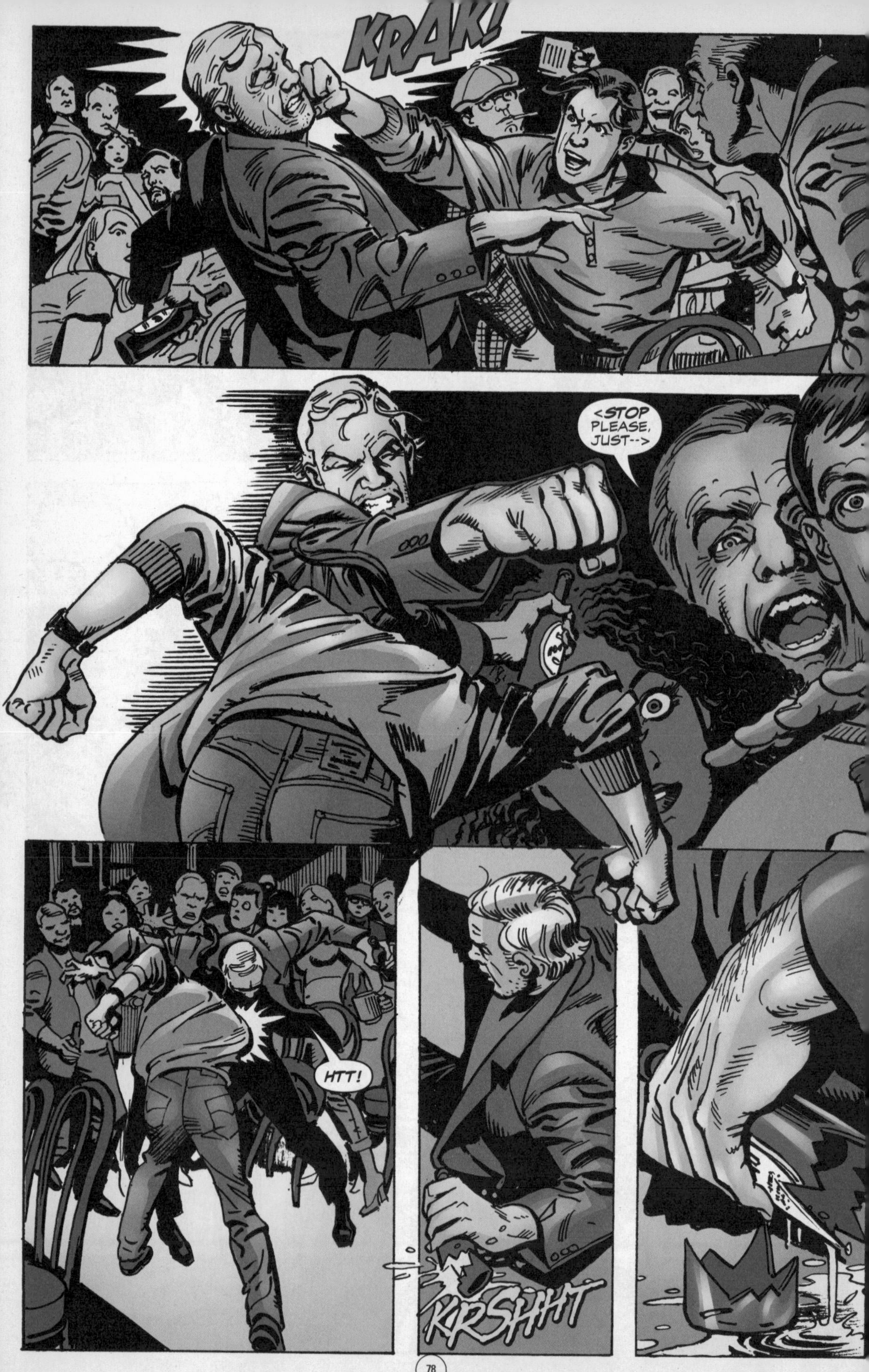
KRAK!
<STOP PLEASE, JUST-->
HTT!
KRSHHT

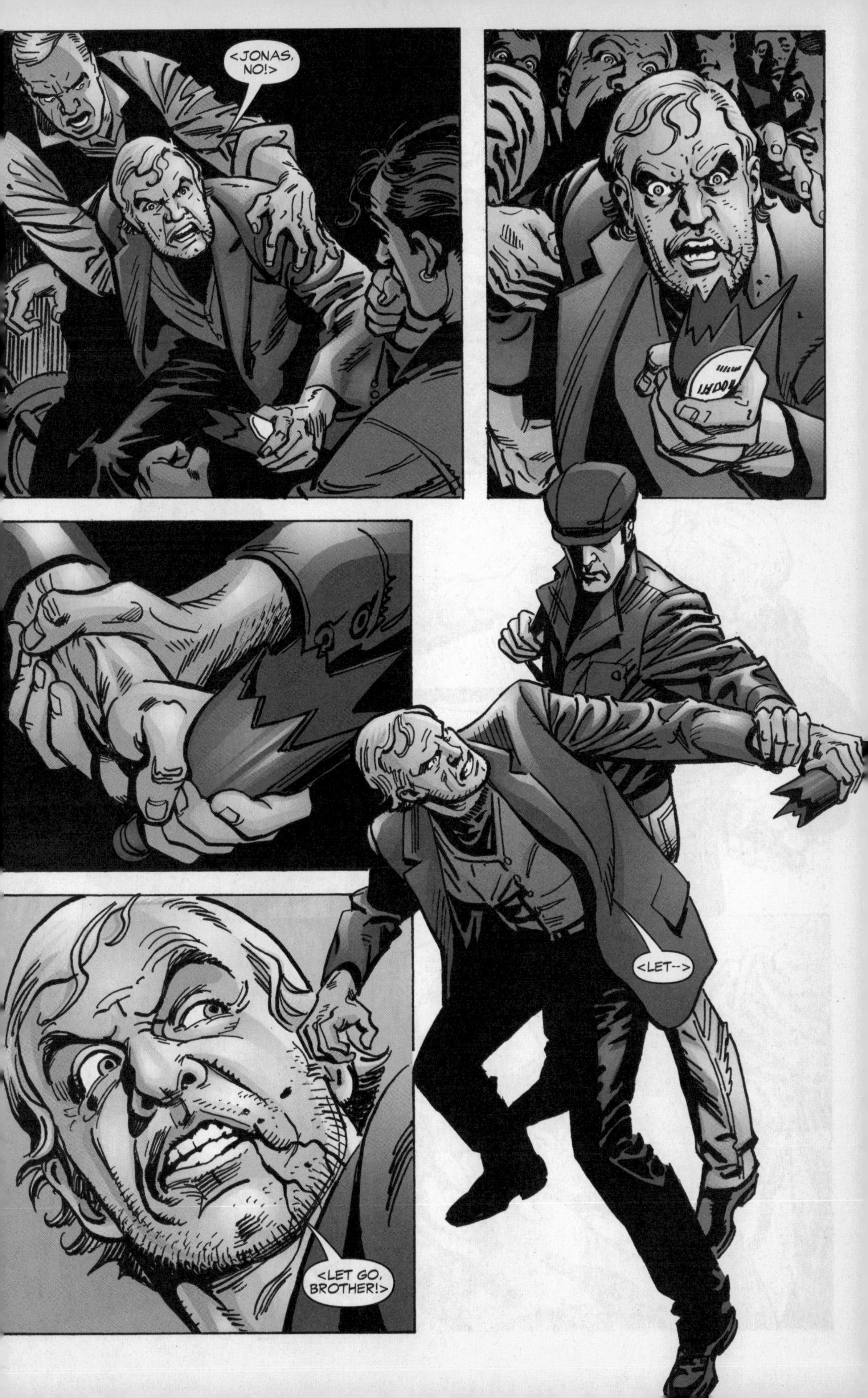
<JONAS, NO!>
<LET-->
<LET GO, BROTHER!>

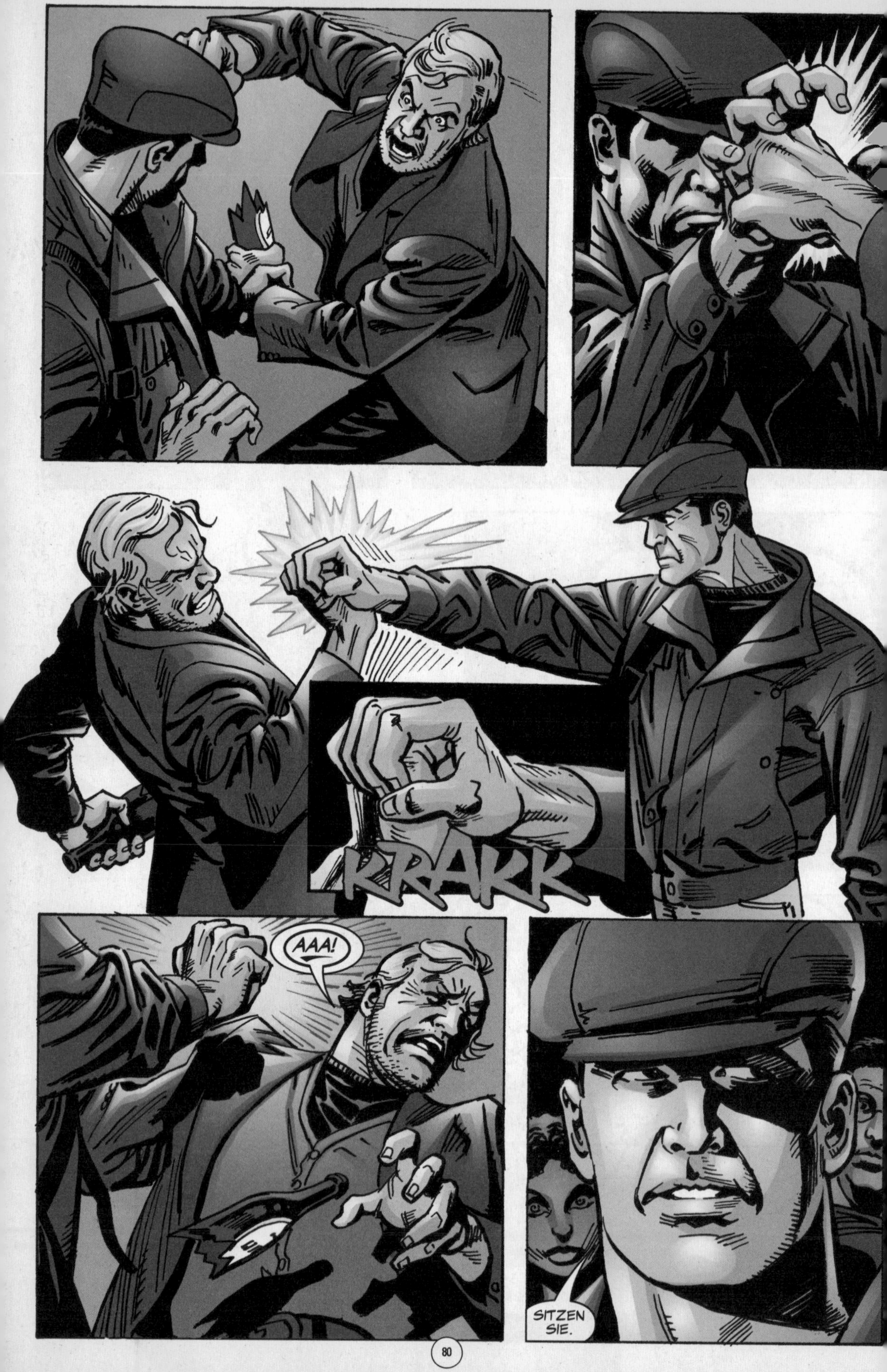
KRAKK
AAA!
SITZEN SIE.

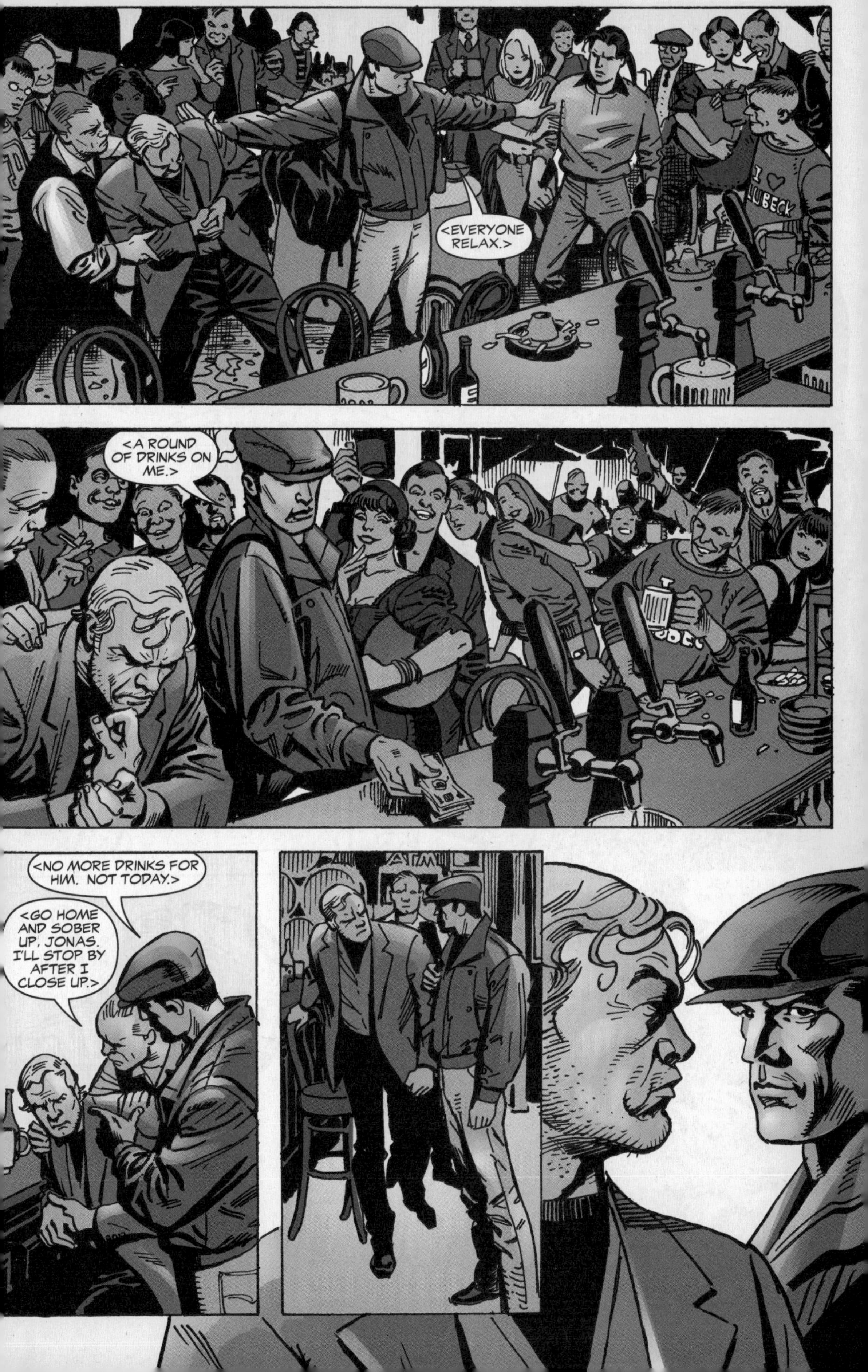
I ♥ LUBECK
<EVERYONE RELAX.>
<A ROUND OF DRINKS ON ME.>
<NO MORE DRINKS FOR HIM. NOT TODAY.>
<GO HOME AND SOBER UP, JONAS. I'LL STOP BY AFTER I CLOSE UP.>

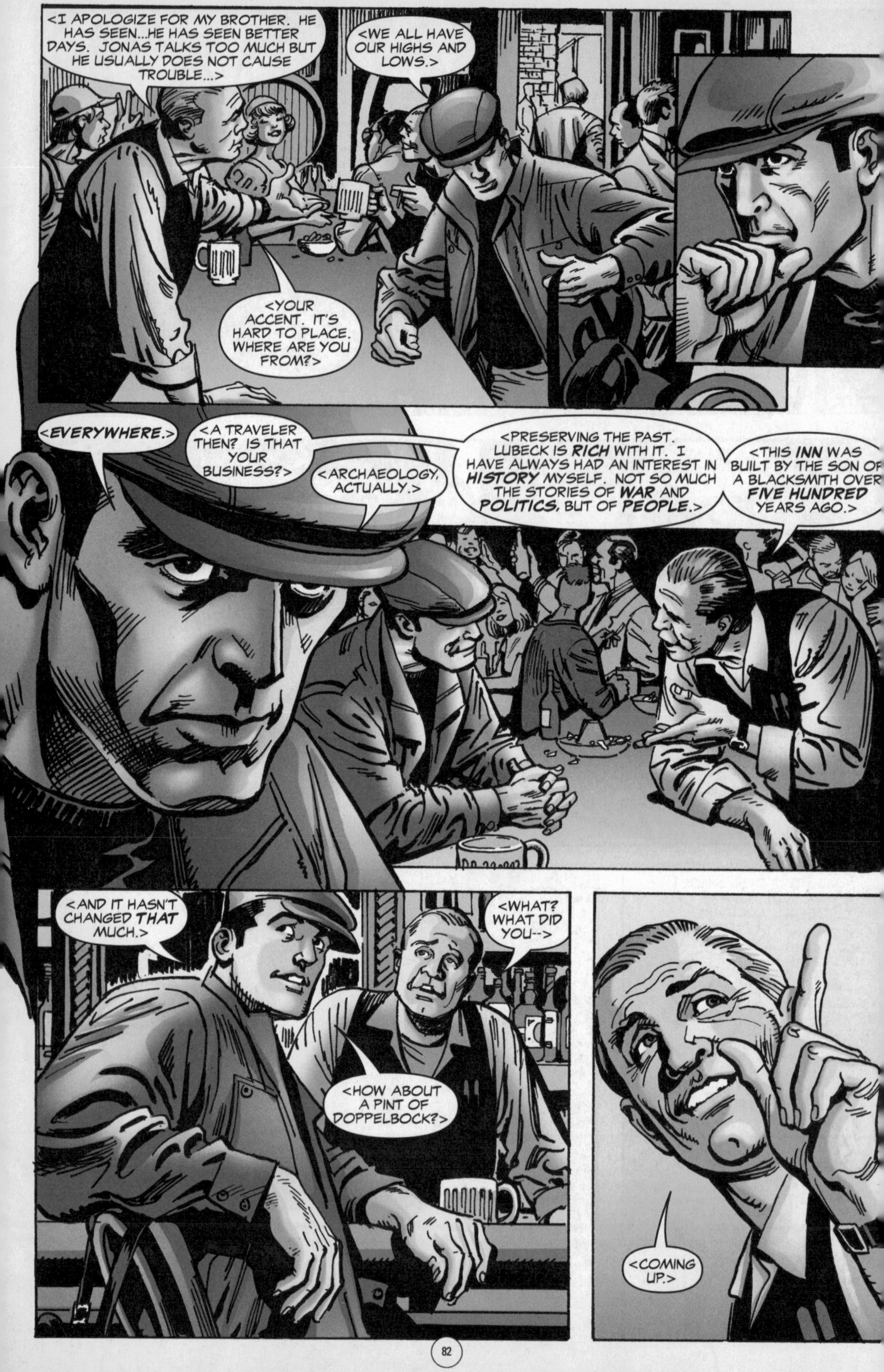

<I APOLOGIZE FOR MY BROTHER. HE HAS SEEN...HE HAS SEEN BETTER DAYS. JONAS TALKS TOO MUCH BUT HE USUALLY DOES NOT CAUSE TROUBLE...>
<WE ALL HAVE OUR HIGHS AND LOWS.>
<YOUR ACCENT. IT'S HARD TO PLACE. WHERE ARE YOU FROM?>
<EVERYWHERE.>
<A TRAVELER THEN? IS THAT YOUR BUSINESS?>
<ARCHAEOLOGY, ACTUALLY.>
<PRESERVING THE PAST. LUBECK IS RICH WITH IT. I HAVE ALWAYS HAD AN INTEREST IN HISTORY MYSELF. NOT SO MUCH THE STORIES OF WAR AND POLITICS, BUT OF PEOPLE.>
<THIS INN WAS BUILT BY THE SON OF A BLACKSMITH OVER FIVE HUNDRED YEARS AGO.>
<AND IT HASN'T CHANGED THAT MUCH.>
<WHAT? WHAT DID YOU-->
<HOW ABOUT A PINT OF DOPPELBOCK?>
<COMING UP.>

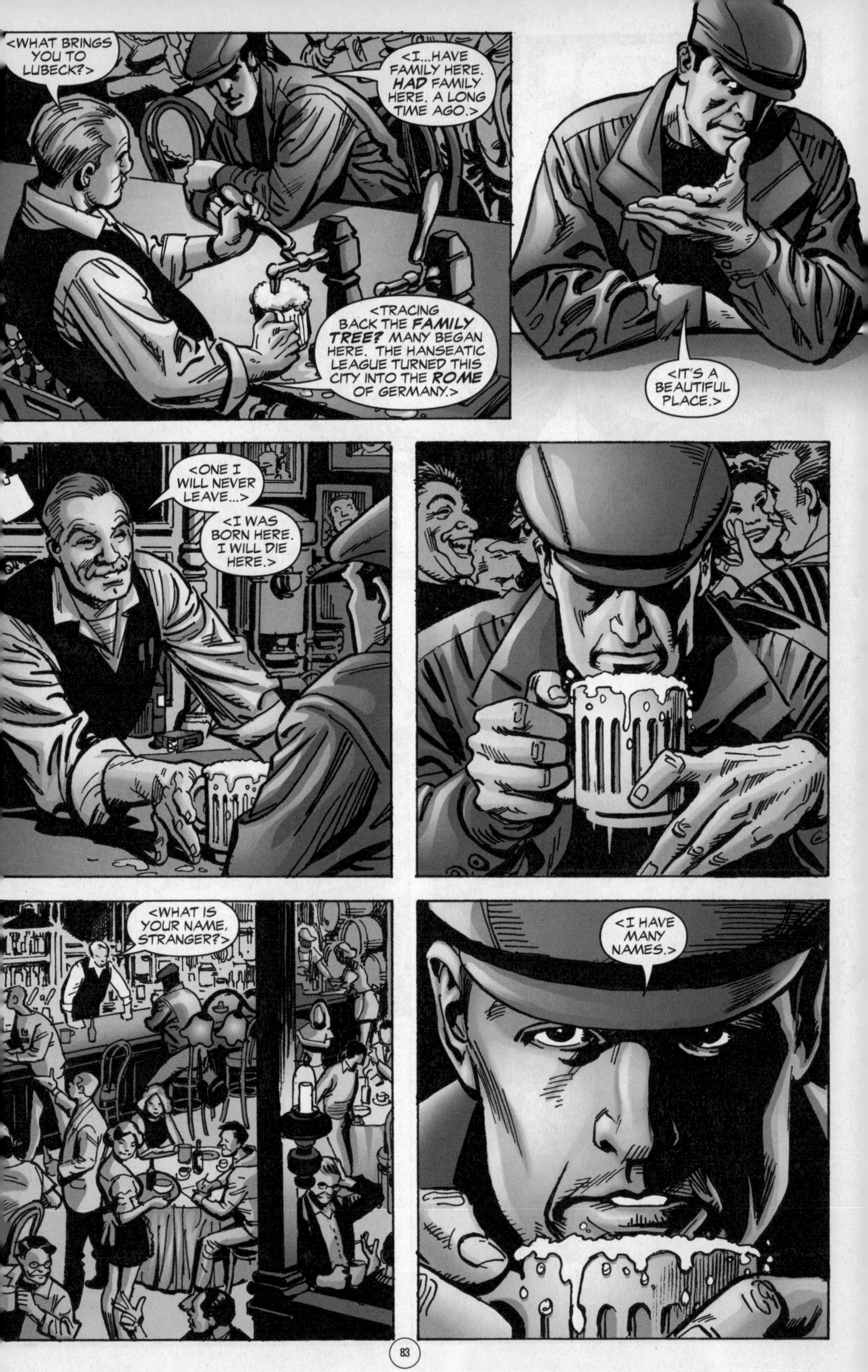

<WHAT BRINGS YOU TO LUBECK?>
<I...HAVE FAMILY HERE. HAD FAMILY HERE. A LONG TIME AGO.>
<TRACING BACK THE FAMILY TREE? MANY BEGAN HERE. THE HANSEATIC LEAGUE TURNED THIS CITY INTO THE ROME OF GERMANY.>
<IT'S A BEAUTIFUL PLACE.>
<ONE I WILL NEVER LEAVE...>
<I WAS BORN HERE. I WILL DIE HERE.>
<WHAT IS YOUR NAME, STRANGER?>
<I HAVE MANY NAMES.>

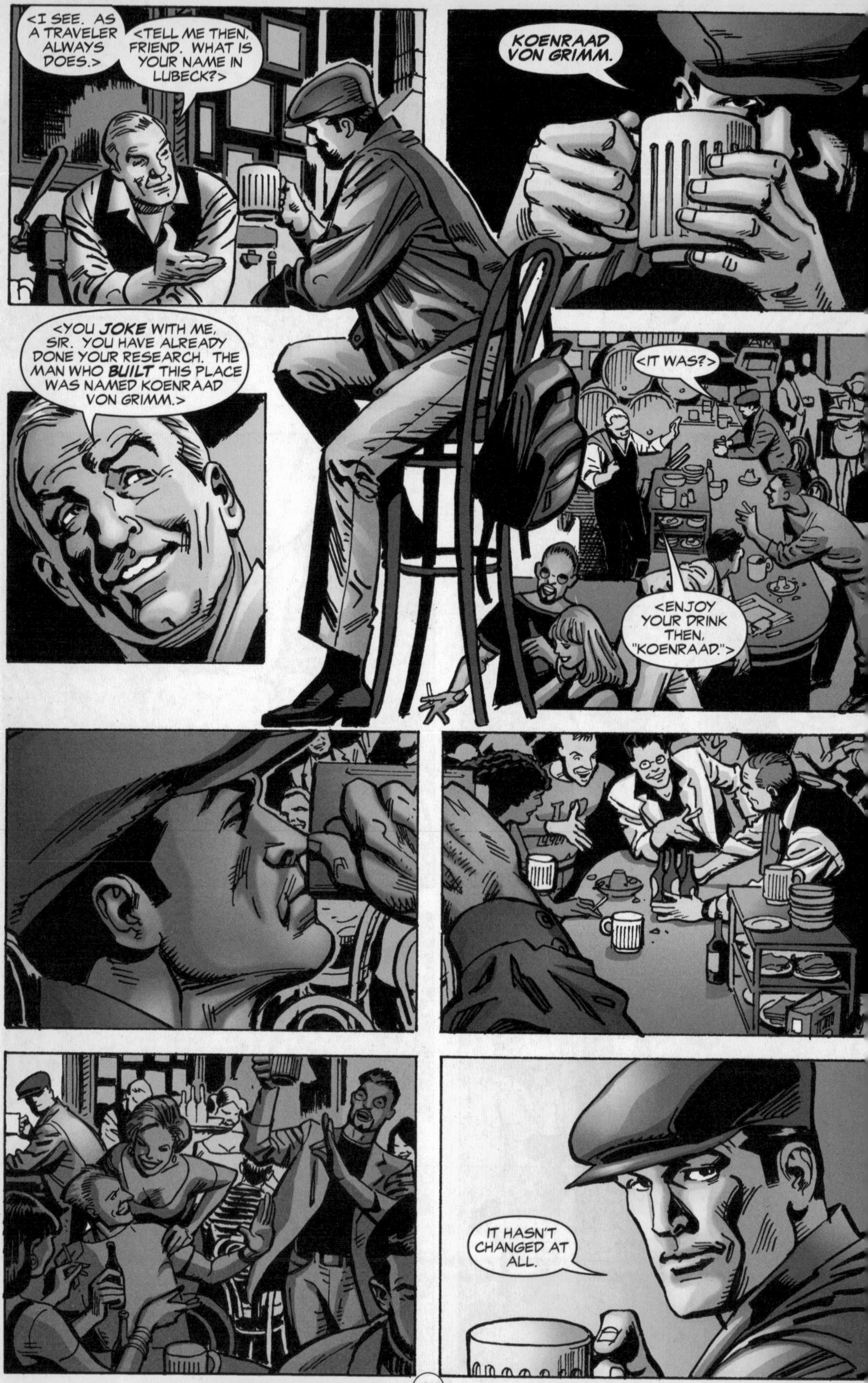
<I SEE. AS A TRAVELER ALWAYS DOES.>
<TELL ME THEN, FRIEND. WHAT IS YOUR NAME IN LUBECK?>
KOENRAAD VON GRIMM.
<YOU JOKE WITH ME, SIR. YOU HAVE ALREADY DONE YOUR RESEARCH. THE MAN WHO BUILT THIS PLACE WAS NAMED KOENRAAD VON GRIMM.>
<IT WAS?>
<ENJOY YOUR DRINK THEN, "KOENRAAD.">
IT HASN'T CHANGED AT ALL.

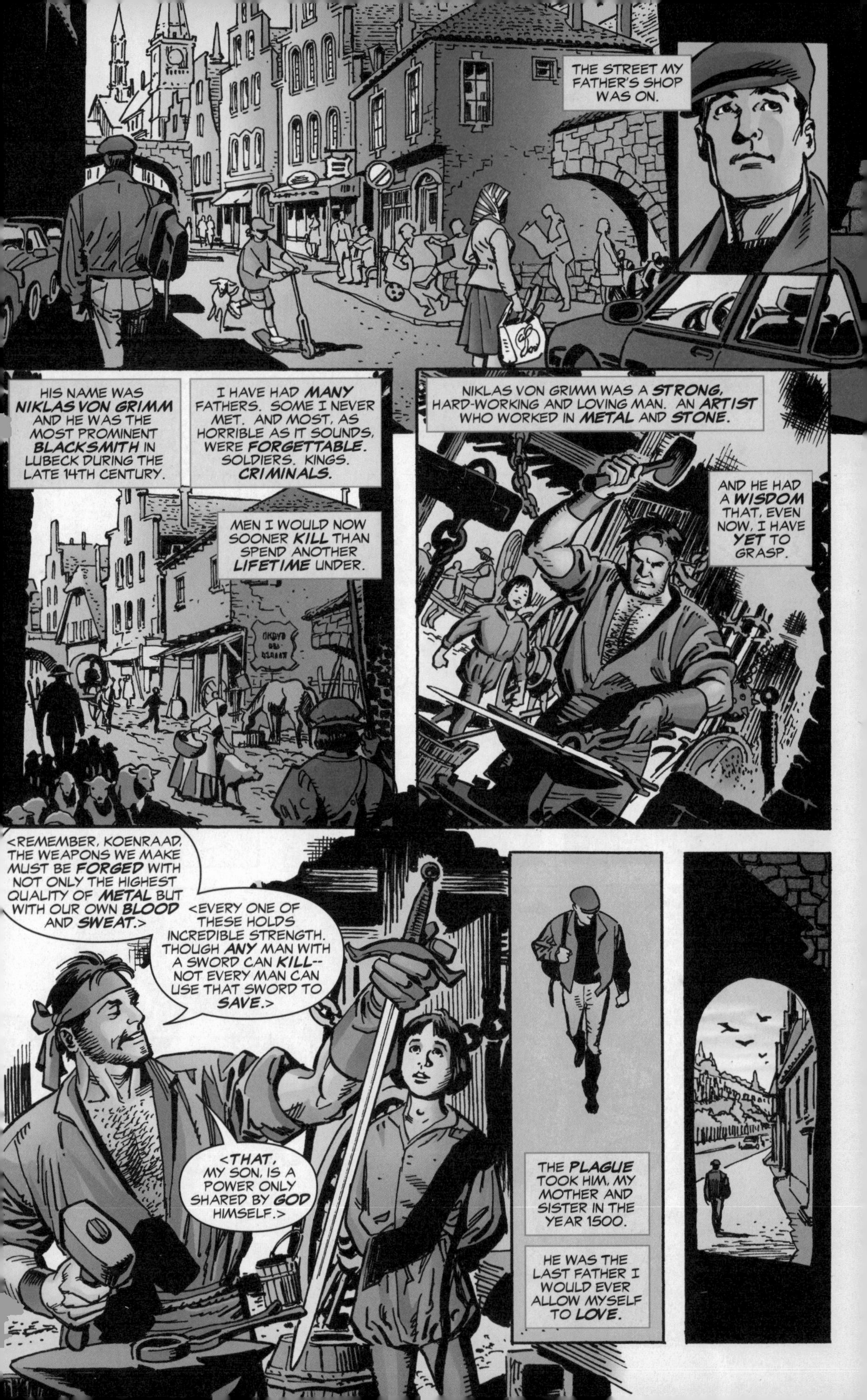
THE STREET MY FATHER'S SHOP WAS ON.
HIS NAME WAS NIKLAS VON GRIMM AND HE WAS THE MOST PROMINENT BLACKSMITH IN LUBECK DURING THE LATE 14TH CENTURY.
I HAVE HAD MANY FATHERS. SOME I NEVER MET. AND MOST, AS HORRIBLE AS IT SOUNDS, WERE FORGETTABLE. SOLDIERS. KINGS. CRIMINALS.
MEN I WOULD NOW SOONER KILL THAN SPEND ANOTHER LIFETIME UNDER.
NIKLAS VON GRIMM WAS A STRONG, HARD-WORKING AND LOVING MAN. AN ARTIST WHO WORKED IN METAL AND STONE.
AND HE HAD A WISDOM THAT, EVEN NOW, I HAVE YET TO GRASP.
<REMEMBER, KOENRAAD, THE WEAPONS WE MAKE MUST BE FORGED WITH NOT ONLY THE HIGHEST QUALITY OF METAL BUT WITH OUR OWN BLOOD AND SWEAT.>
<EVERY ONE OF THESE HOLDS INCREDIBLE STRENGTH. THOUGH ANY MAN WITH A SWORD CAN KILL-- NOT EVERY MAN CAN USE THAT SWORD TO SAVE.>
<THAT, MY SON, IS A POWER ONLY SHARED BY GOD HIMSELF.>
THE PLAGUE TOOK HIM, MY MOTHER AND SISTER IN THE YEAR 1500.
HE WAS THE LAST FATHER I WOULD EVER ALLOW MYSELF TO LOVE.

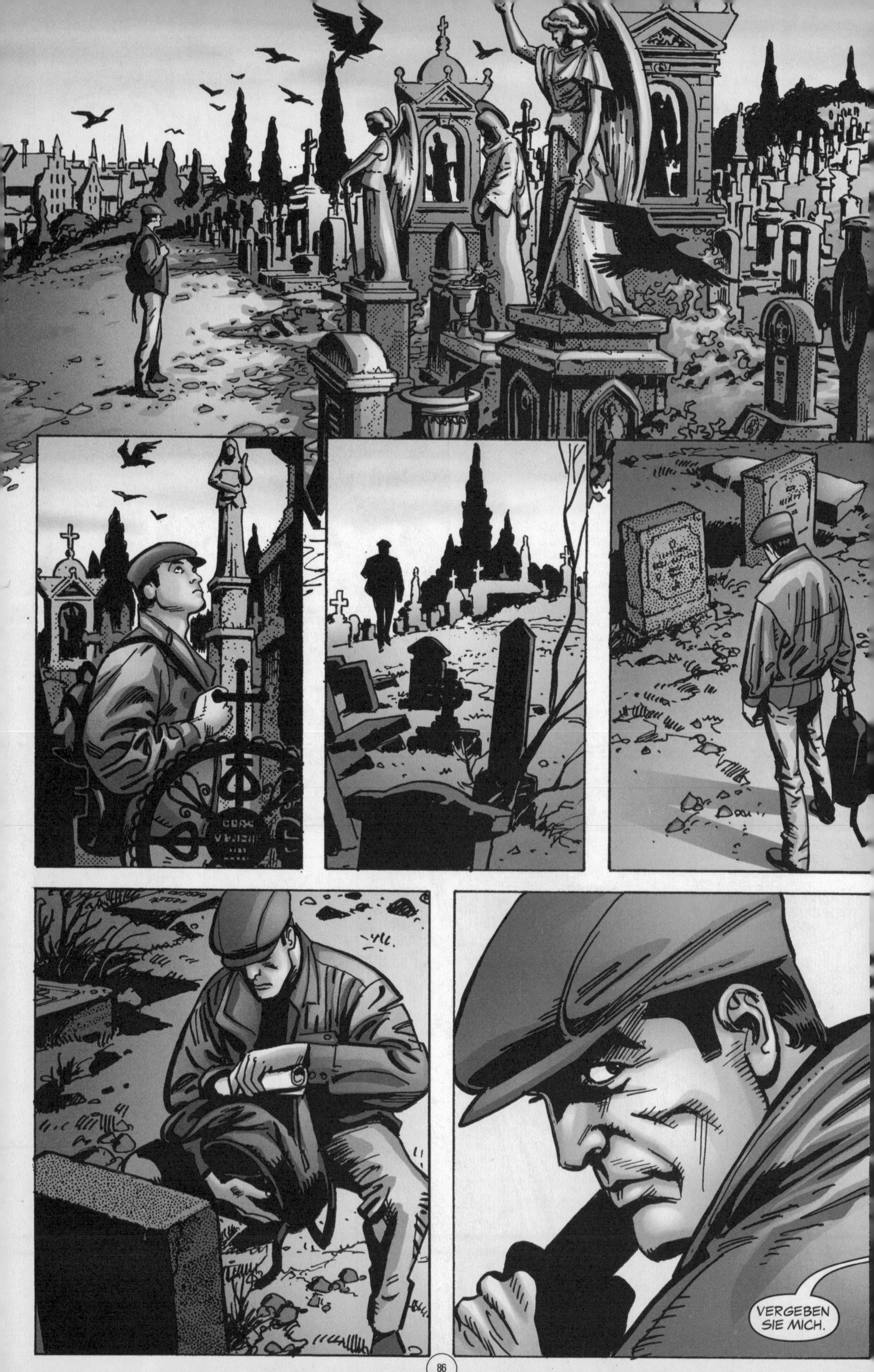
VERGEBEN SIE MICH.

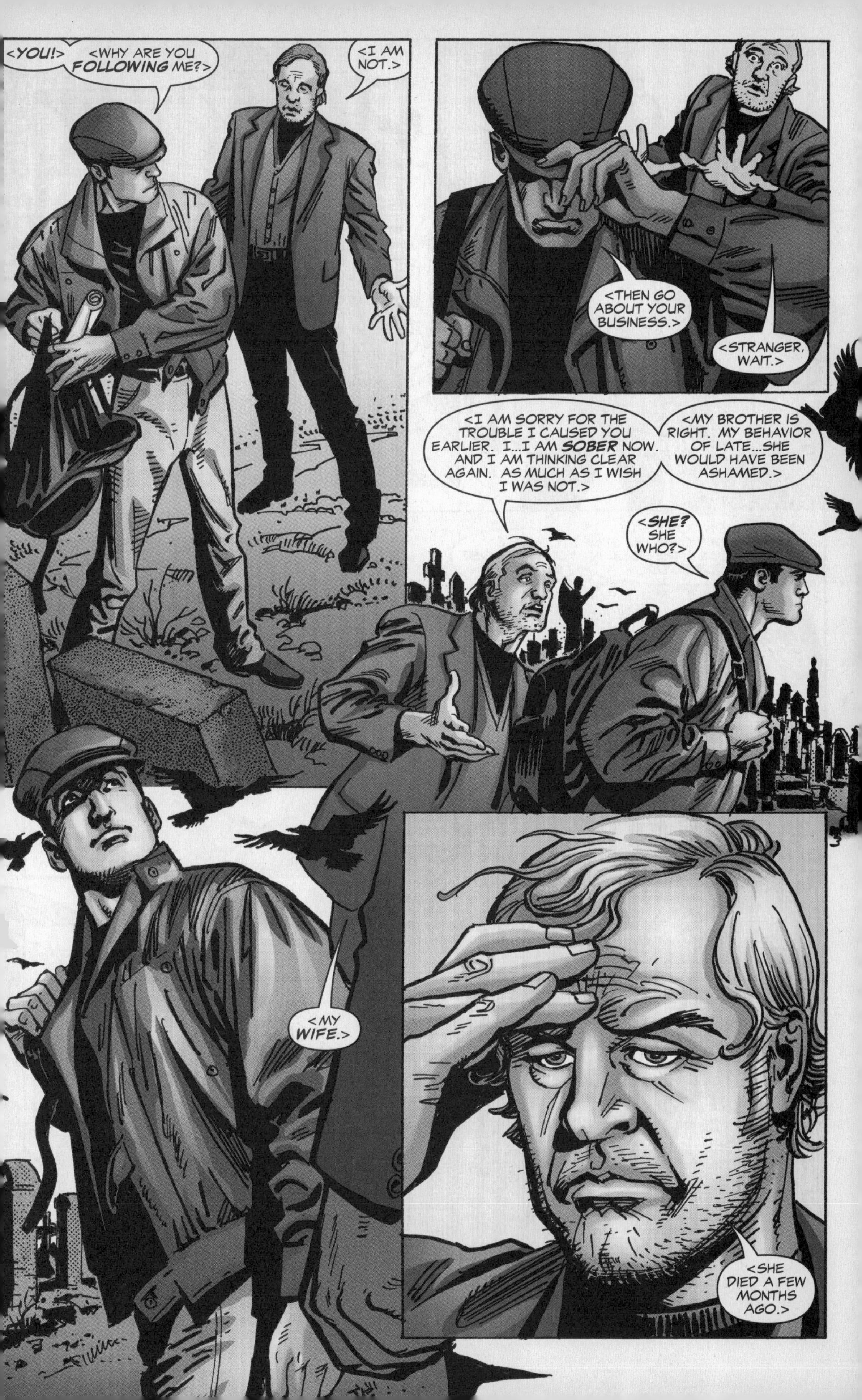

<YOU!>
<WHY ARE YOU FOLLOWING ME?>
<I AM NOT.>
<THEN GO ABOUT YOUR BUSINESS.>
<STRANGER, WAIT.>
<I AM SORRY FOR THE TROUBLE I CAUSED YOU EARLIER. I...I AM SOBER NOW. AND I AM THINKING CLEAR AGAIN. AS MUCH AS I WISH I WAS NOT.>
<MY BROTHER IS RIGHT. MY BEHAVIOR OF LATE...SHE WOULD HAVE BEEN ASHAMED.>
<SHE? SHE WHO?>
<MY WIFE.>
<SHE DIED A FEW MONTHS AGO.>

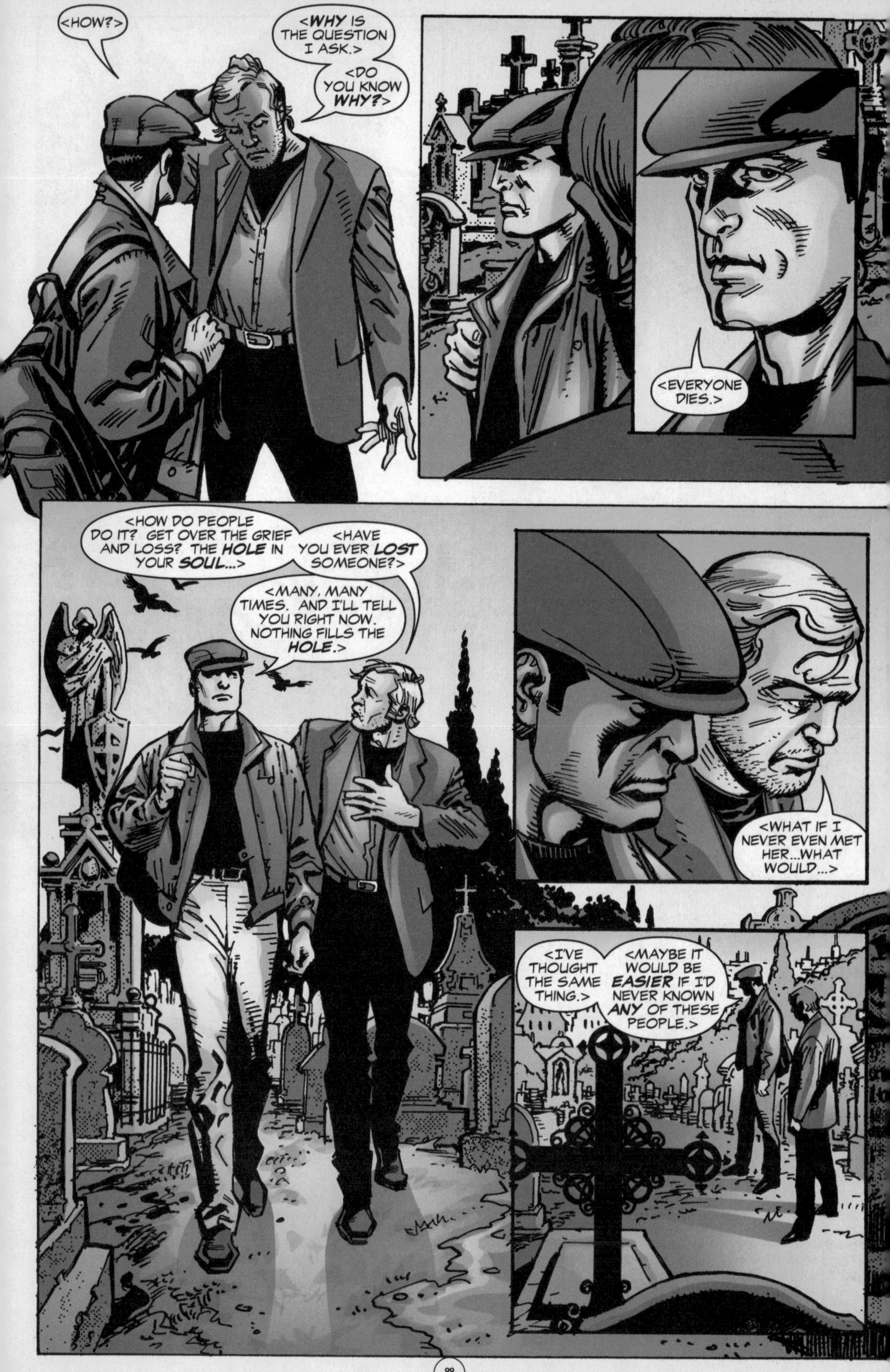
<HOW?>
<WHY IS THE QUESTION I ASK.>
<DO YOU KNOW WHY?>
<EVERYONE DIES.>
<HOW DO PEOPLE DO IT? GET OVER THE GRIEF AND LOSS? THE HOLE IN YOUR SOUL...>
<HAVE YOU EVER LOST SOMEONE?>
<MANY, MANY TIMES. AND I'LL TELL YOU RIGHT NOW. NOTHING FILLS THE HOLE.>
<WHAT IF I NEVER EVEN MET HER...WHAT WOULD...>
<I'VE THOUGHT THE SAME THING.>
<MAYBE IT WOULD BE EASIER IF I'D NEVER KNOWN ANY OF THESE PEOPLE.>

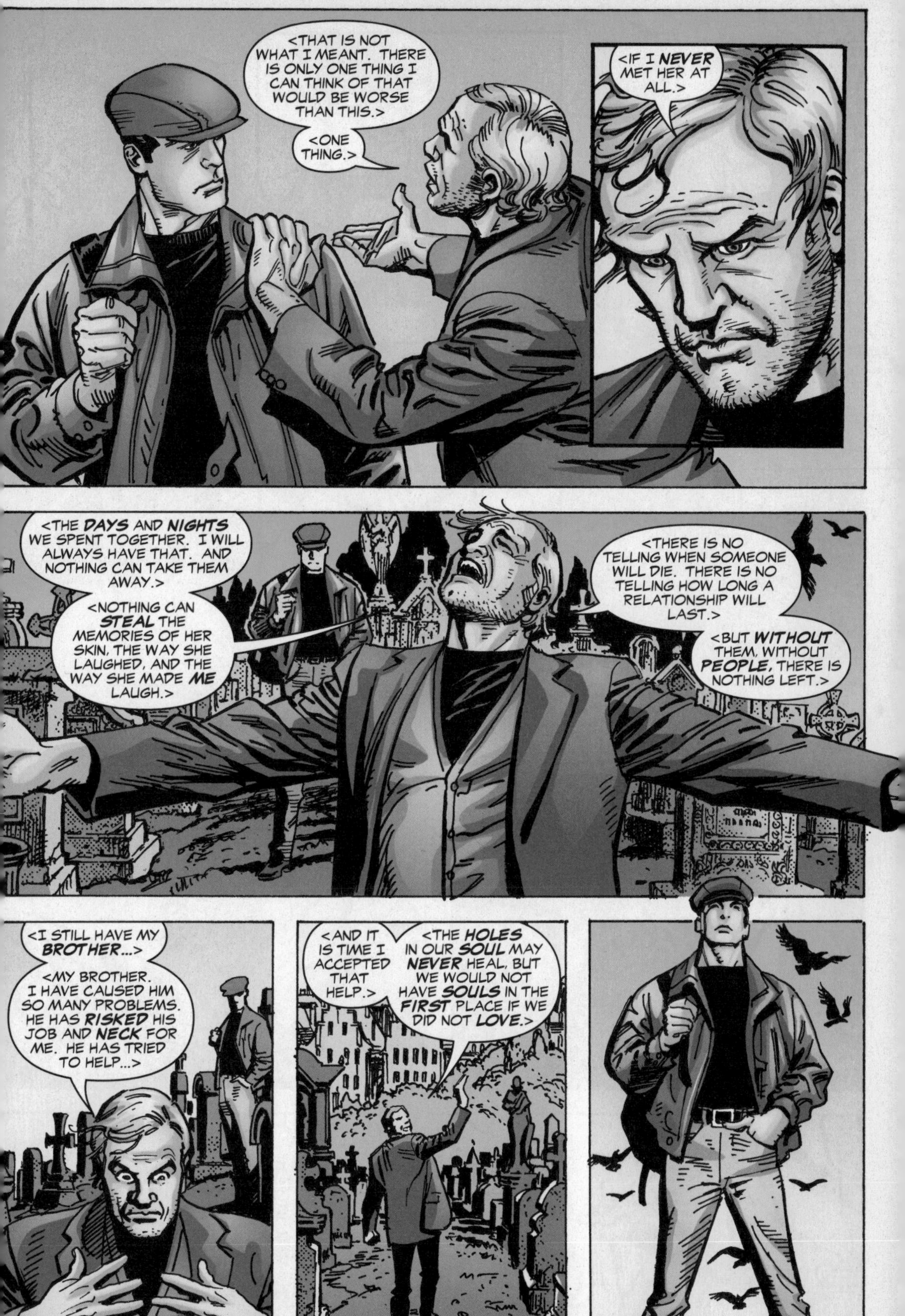
<THAT IS NOT WHAT I MEANT. THERE IS ONLY ONE THING I CAN THINK OF THAT WOULD BE WORSE THAN THIS.>
<ONE THING.>
<IF I NEVER MET HER AT ALL.>
<THE DAYS AND NIGHTS WE SPENT TOGETHER. I WILL ALWAYS HAVE THAT. AND NOTHING CAN TAKE THEM AWAY.>
<NOTHING CAN STEAL THE MEMORIES OF HER SKIN, THE WAY SHE LAUGHED, AND THE WAY SHE MADE ME LAUGH.>
<THERE IS NO TELLING WHEN SOMEONE WILL DIE. THERE IS NO TELLING HOW LONG A RELATIONSHIP WILL LAST.>
<BUT WITHOUT THEM, WITHOUT PEOPLE, THERE IS NOTHING LEFT.>
<I STILL HAVE MY BROTHER...>
<MY BROTHER. I HAVE CAUSED HIM SO MANY PROBLEMS. HE HAS RISKED HIS JOB AND NECK FOR ME. HE HAS TRIED TO HELP...>
<AND IT IS TIME I ACCEPTED THAT HELP.>
<THE HOLES IN OUR SOUL MAY NEVER HEAL, BUT WE WOULD NOT HAVE SOULS IN THE FIRST PLACE IF WE DID NOT LOVE.>

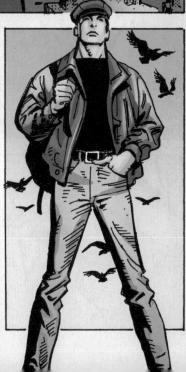

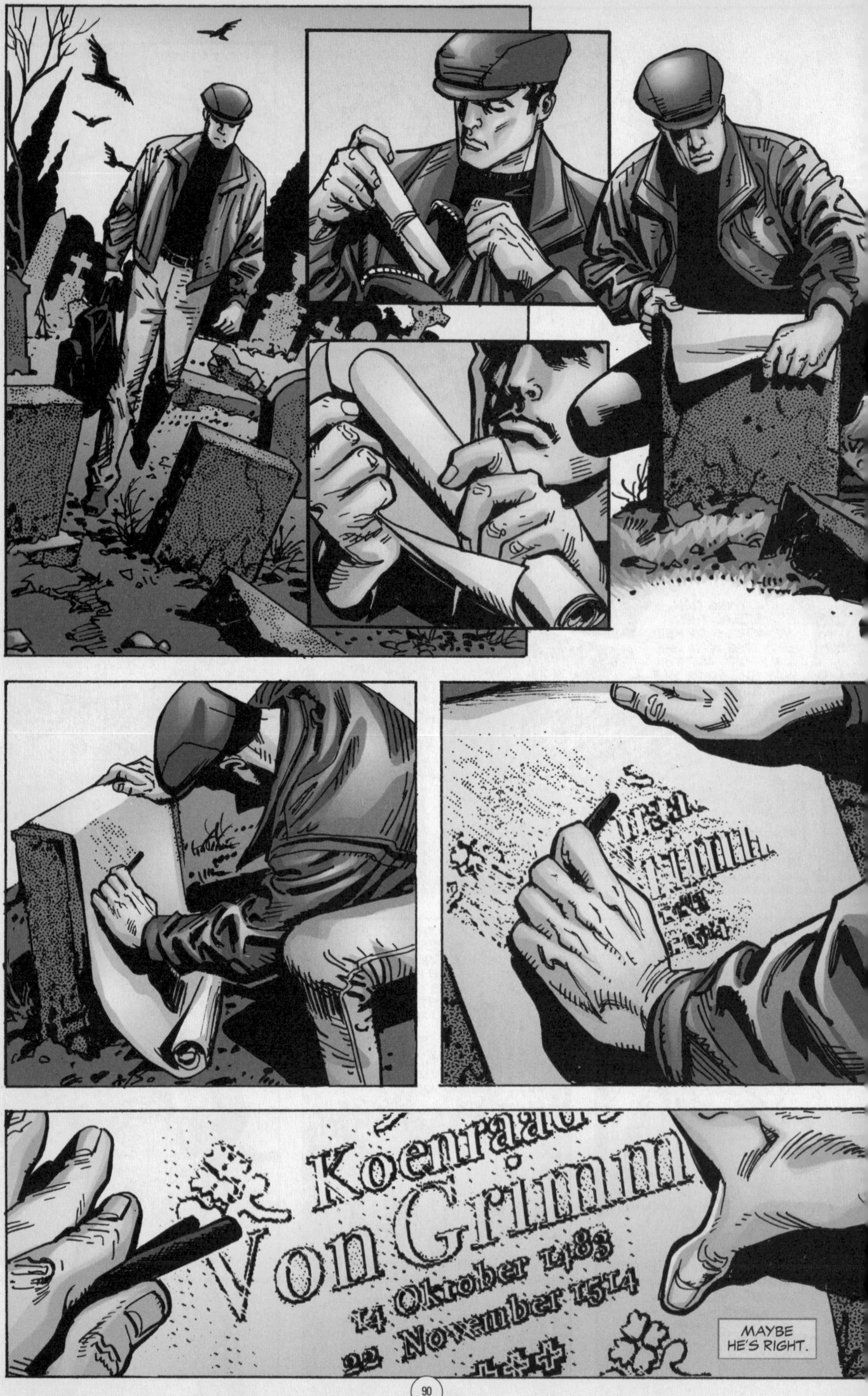
Koenraad
Von Grimm
14 Oktober 1483
22 November 1514
MAYBE HE'S RIGHT.

I HAVE LIVED MANY LIVES. I HAVE LOVED MANY PEOPLE.

I HAVE BEEN CALLED MANY NAMES.

Captain JOHN SMITH

April 3, 1519
June 22, 1691

Hannibal Hawkes

HUNDREDS OF NAMES.

EACH ONE HAD A LIFE WORTH *LIVING*. EACH PERSON WORTH *REMEMBERING*.

RRING RRING

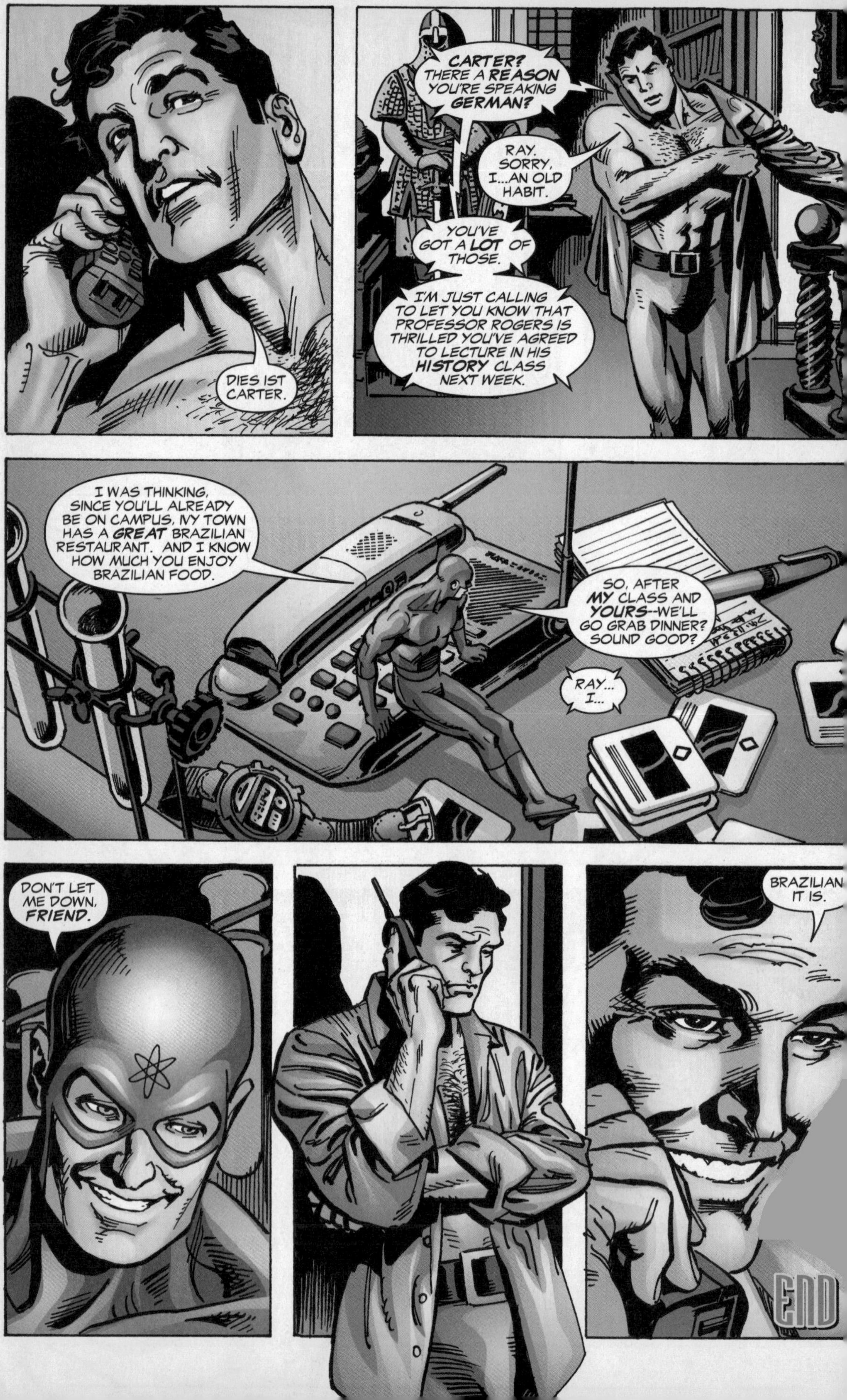
DIES IST CARTER.
CARTER? THERE A REASON YOU'RE SPEAKING GERMAN?
RAY. SORRY, I...AN OLD HABIT.
YOU'VE GOT A LOT OF THOSE.
I'M JUST CALLING TO LET YOU KNOW THAT PROFESSOR ROGERS IS THRILLED YOU'VE AGREED TO LECTURE IN HIS HISTORY CLASS NEXT WEEK.
I WAS THINKING, SINCE YOU'LL ALREADY BE ON CAMPUS, IVY TOWN HAS A GREAT BRAZILIAN RESTAURANT. AND I KNOW HOW MUCH YOU ENJOY BRAZILIAN FOOD.
SO, AFTER MY CLASS AND YOURS--WE'LL GO GRAB DINNER? SOUND GOOD?
RAY... I...
DON'T LET ME DOWN, FRIEND.
BRAZILIAN IT IS.
END

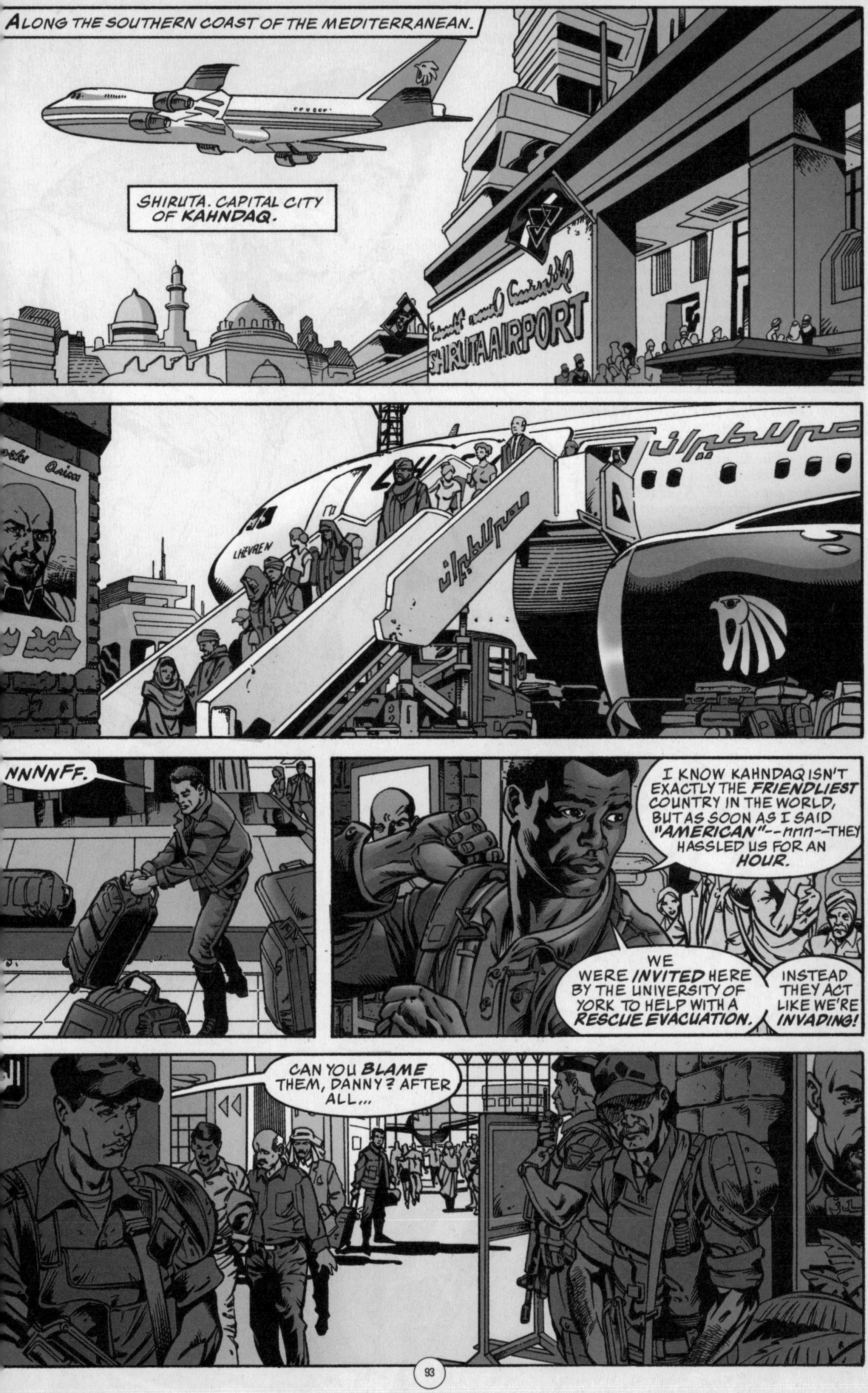

ALONG THE SOUTHERN COAST OF THE MEDITERRANEAN.
SHIRUTA. CAPITAL CITY OF KAHNDAQ.
SHIRUTA AIRPORT
NNNNFF.
I KNOW KAHNDAQ ISN'T EXACTLY THE FRIENDLIEST COUNTRY IN THE WORLD, BUT AS SOON AS I SAID "AMERICAN"--nnn--THEY HASSLED US FOR AN HOUR.
WE WERE INVITED HERE BY THE UNIVERSITY OF YORK TO HELP WITH A RESCUE EVACUATION.
INSTEAD THEY ACT LIKE WE'RE INVADING!
CAN YOU BLAME THEM, DANNY? AFTER ALL...

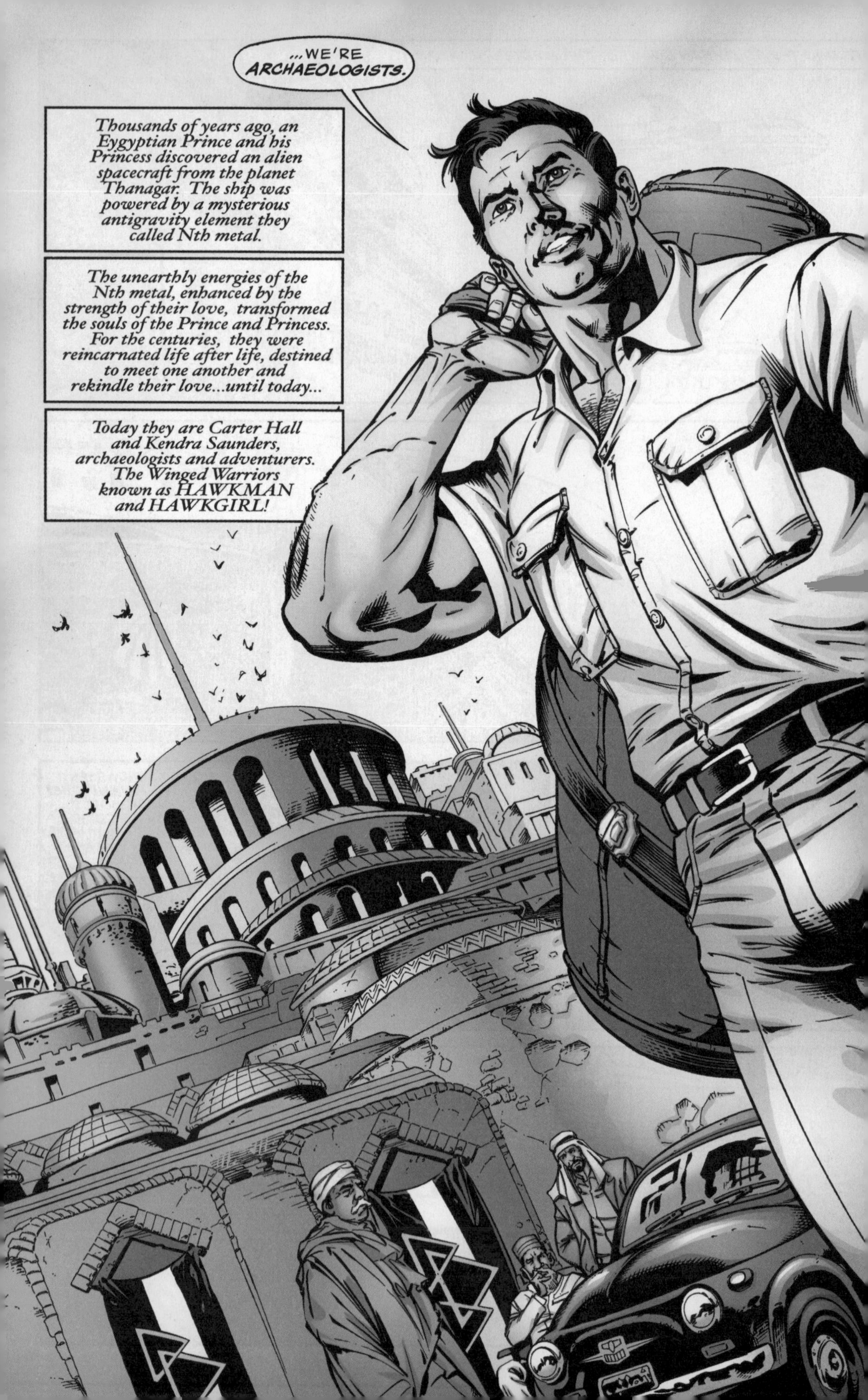
...WE'RE ARCHAEOLOGISTS.
Thousands of years ago, an Eygyptian Prince and his Princess discovered an alien spacecraft from the planet Thanagar. The ship was powered by a mysterious antigravity element they called Nth metal.
The unearthly energies of the Nth metal, enhanced by the strength of their love, transformed the souls of the Prince and Princess. For the centuries, they were reincarnated life after life, destined to meet one another and rekindle their love...until today...
Today they are Carter Hall and Kendra Saunders, archaeologists and adventurers. The Winged Warriors known as HAWKMAN and HAWKGIRL!

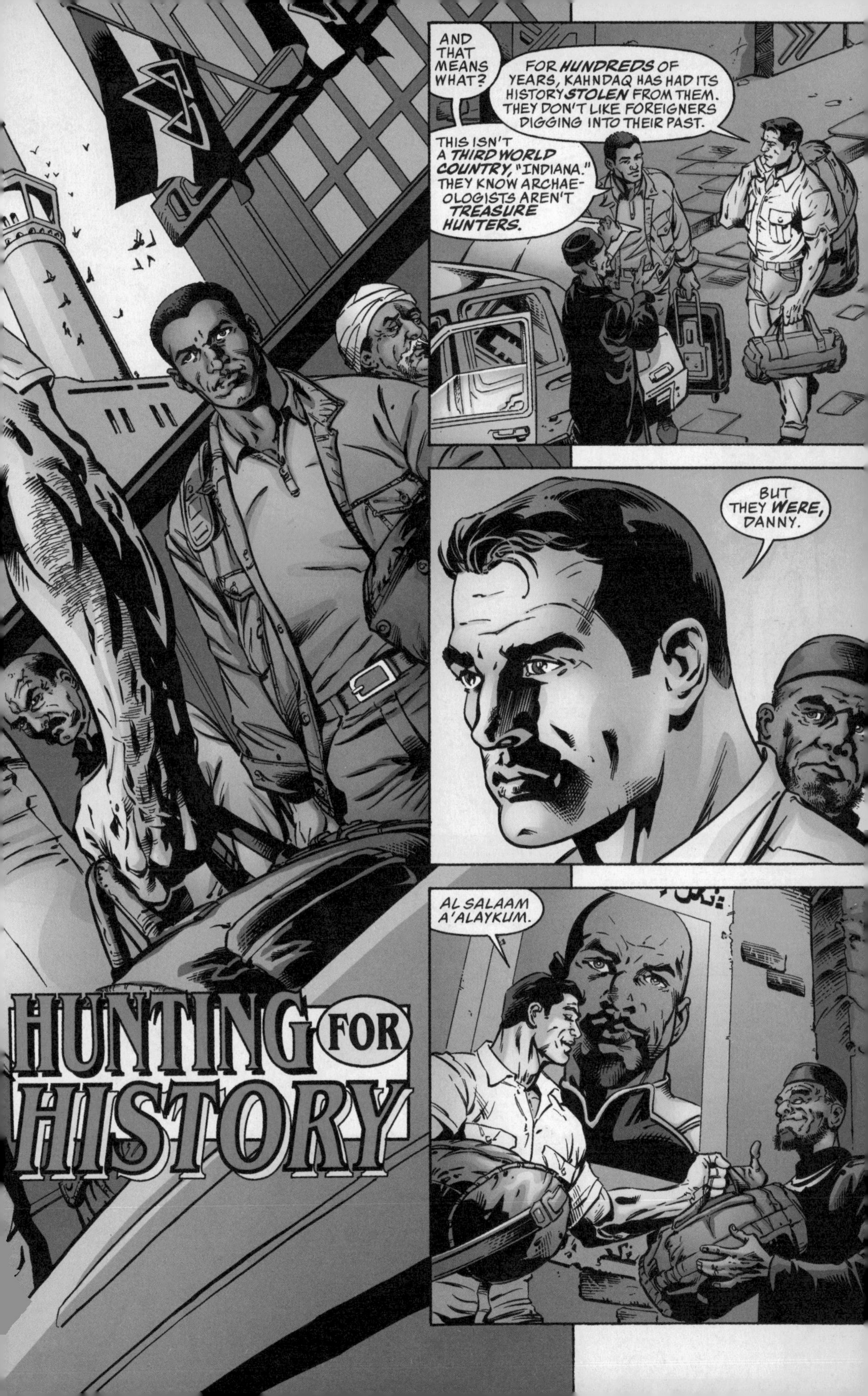
HUNTING FOR HISTORY
AND THAT MEANS WHAT?
FOR HUNDREDS OF YEARS, KAHNDAQ HAS HAD ITS HISTORY STOLEN FROM THEM. THEY DON'T LIKE FOREIGNERS DIGGING INTO THEIR PAST.
THIS ISN'T A THIRD WORLD COUNTRY, "INDIANA." THEY KNOW ARCHAEOLOGISTS AREN'T TREASURE HUNTERS.
BUT THEY WERE, DANNY.
AL SALAAM A'ALAYKUM.

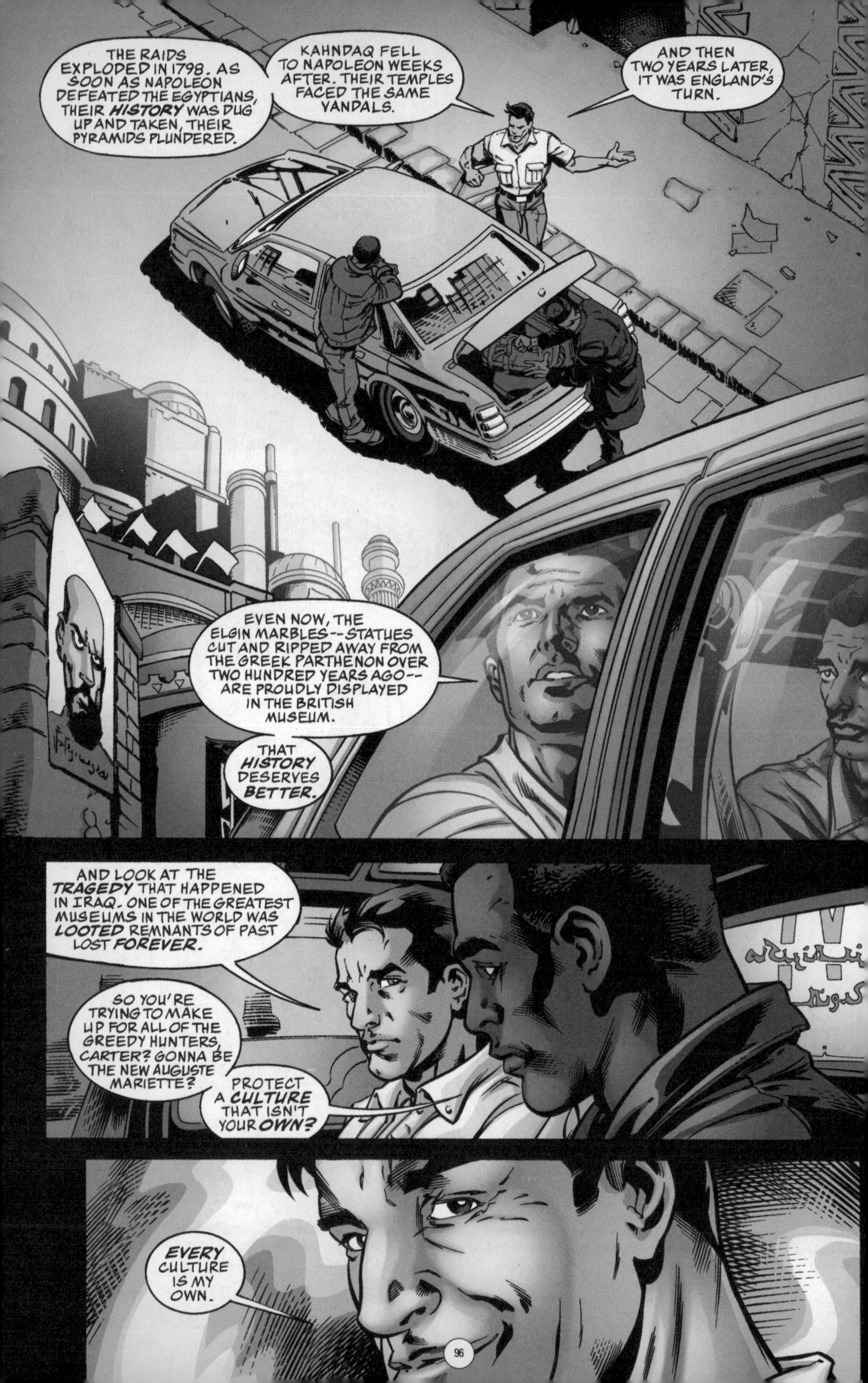
THE RAIDS EXPLODED IN 1798. AS SOON AS NAPOLEON DEFEATED THE EGYPTIANS, THEIR HISTORY WAS DUG UP AND TAKEN, THEIR PYRAMIDS PLUNDERED.
KAHNDAQ FELL TO NAPOLEON WEEKS AFTER. THEIR TEMPLES FACED THE SAME VANDALS.
AND THEN TWO YEARS LATER, IT WAS ENGLAND'S TURN.
EVEN NOW, THE ELGIN MARBLES--STATUES CUT AND RIPPED AWAY FROM THE GREEK PARTHENON OVER TWO HUNDRED YEARS AGO--ARE PROUDLY DISPLAYED IN THE BRITISH MUSEUM.
THAT HISTORY DESERVES BETTER.
AND LOOK AT THE TRAGEDY THAT HAPPENED IN IRAQ. ONE OF THE GREATEST MUSEUMS IN THE WORLD WAS LOOTED REMNANTS OF PAST LOST FOREVER.
SO YOU'RE TRYING TO MAKE UP FOR ALL OF THE GREEDY HUNTERS, CARTER? GONNA BE THE NEW AUGUSTE MARIETTE?
PROTECT A CULTURE THAT ISN'T YOUR OWN?
EVERY CULTURE IS MY OWN.

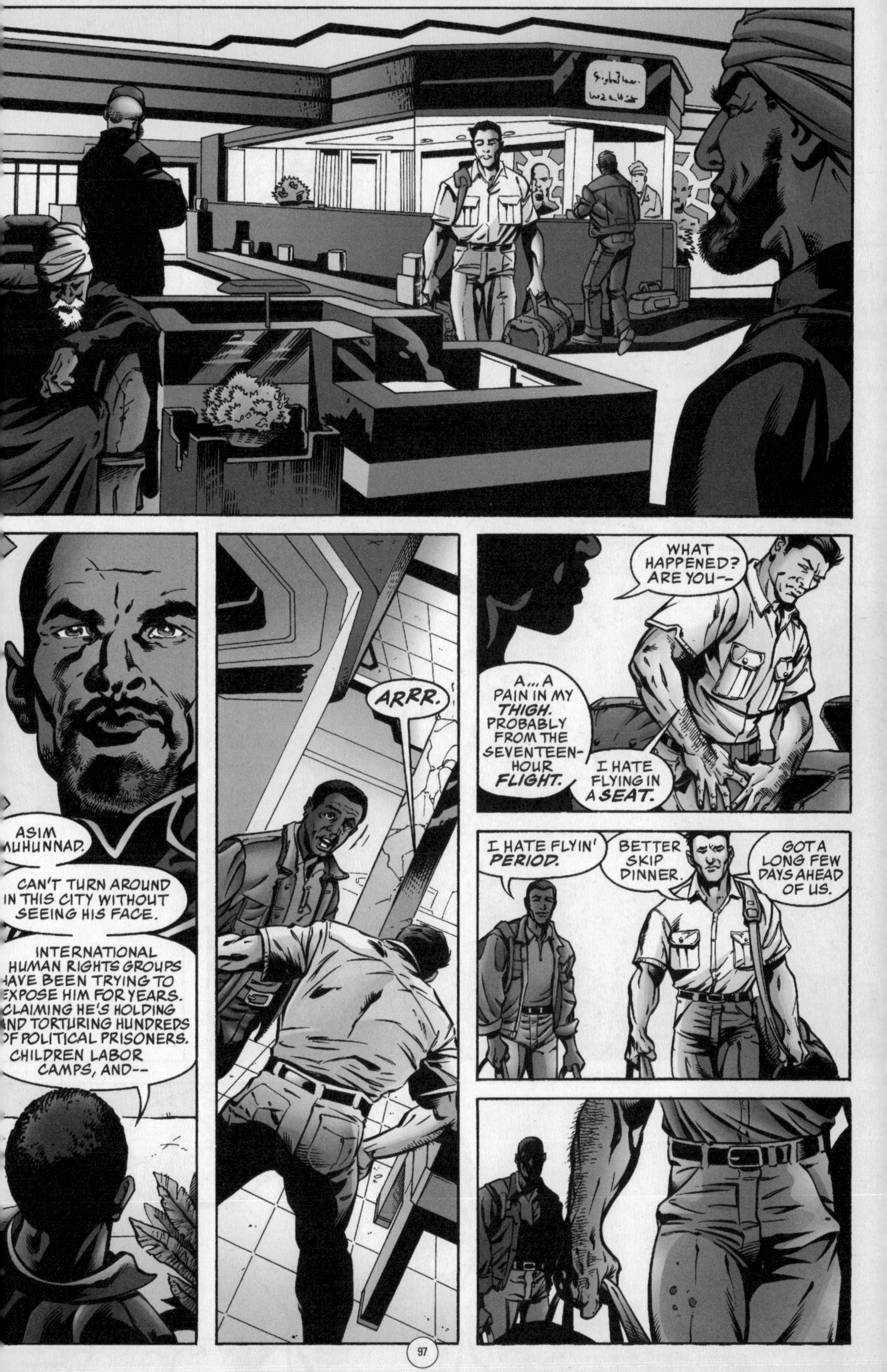
ASIM MUHUNNAD.
CAN'T TURN AROUND IN THIS CITY WITHOUT SEEING HIS FACE.
INTERNATIONAL HUMAN RIGHTS GROUPS HAVE BEEN TRYING TO EXPOSE HIM FOR YEARS. CLAIMING HE'S HOLDING AND TORTURING HUNDREDS OF POLITICAL PRISONERS. CHILDREN LABOR CAMPS, AND--
ARRR.
WHAT HAPPENED? ARE YOU--
A... A PAIN IN MY THIGH. PROBABLY FROM THE SEVENTEEN-HOUR FLIGHT.
I HATE FLYING IN A SEAT.
I HATE FLYIN' PERIOD.
BETTER SKIP DINNER.
GOT A LONG FEW DAYS AHEAD OF US.

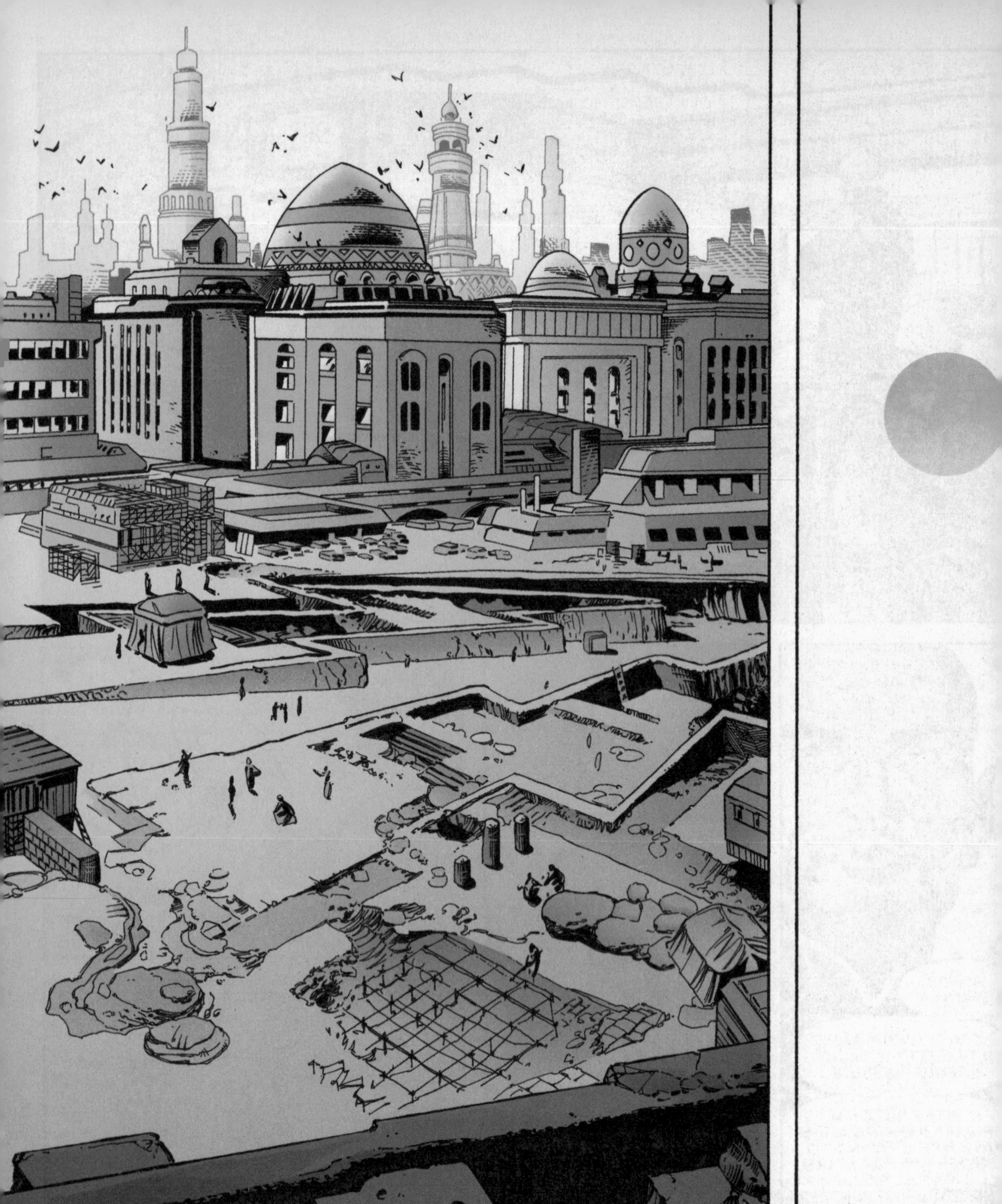

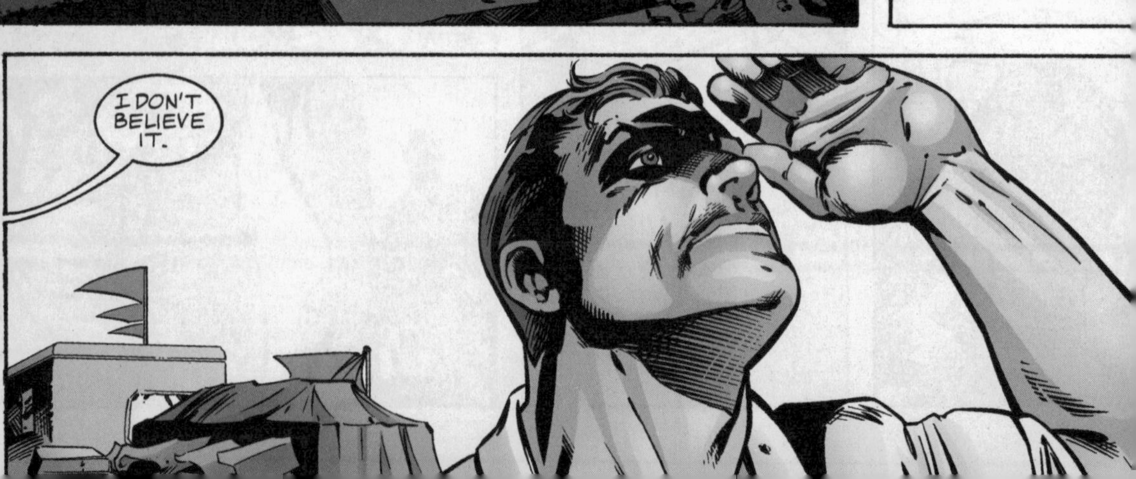
I DON'T BELIEVE IT.

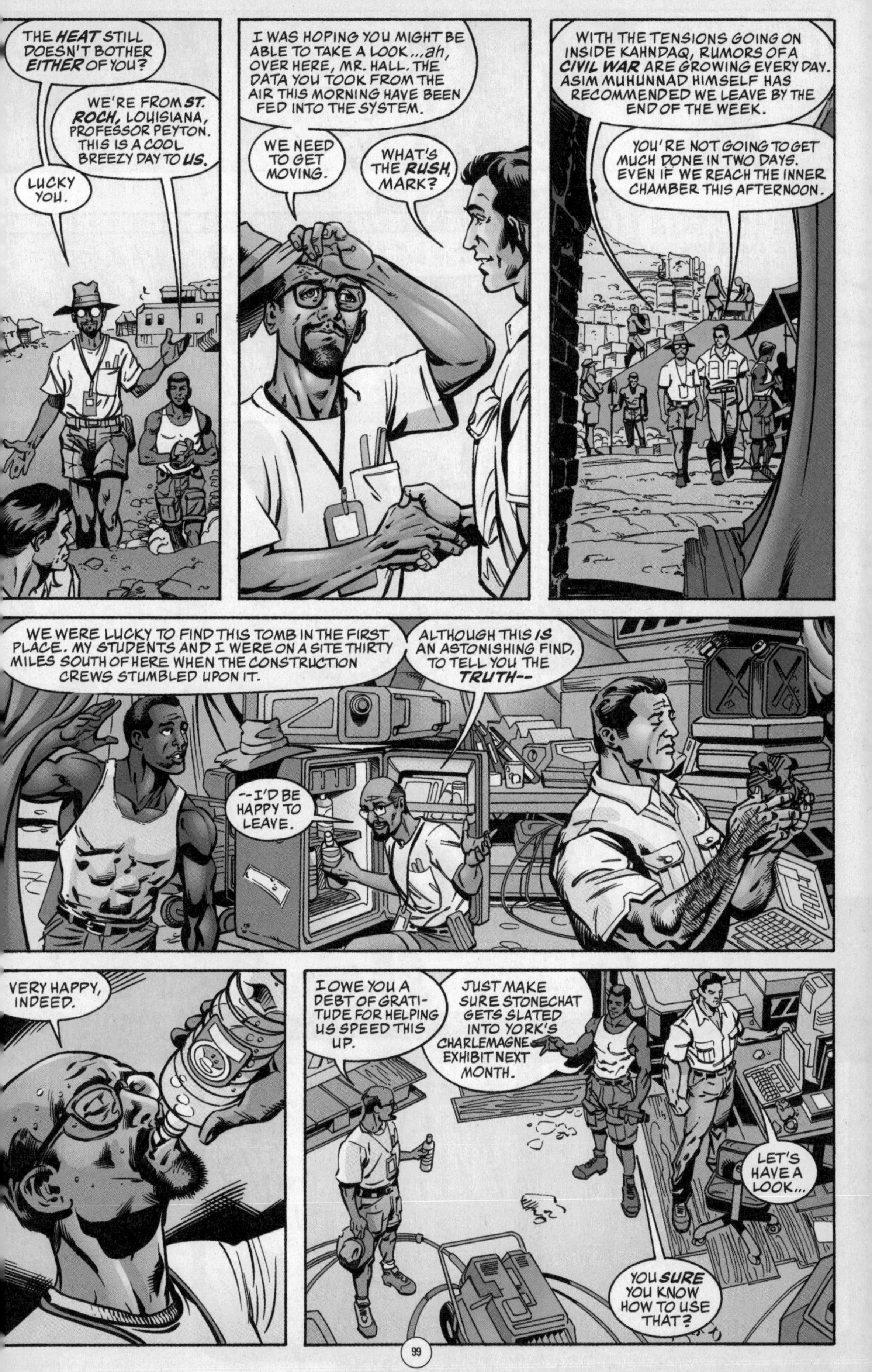
THE HEAT STILL DOESN'T BOTHER EITHER OF YOU?
WE'RE FROM ST. ROCH, LOUISIANA, PROFESSOR PEYTON. THIS IS A COOL BREEZY DAY TO US.
LUCKY YOU.
I WAS HOPING YOU MIGHT BE ABLE TO TAKE A LOOK ...ah, OVER HERE, MR. HALL. THE DATA YOU TOOK FROM THE AIR THIS MORNING HAVE BEEN FED INTO THE SYSTEM.
WE NEED TO GET MOVING.
WHAT'S THE RUSH, MARK?
WITH THE TENSIONS GOING ON INSIDE KAHNDAQ, RUMORS OF A CIVIL WAR ARE GROWING EVERY DAY. ASIM MUHUNNAD HIMSELF HAS RECOMMENDED WE LEAVE BY THE END OF THE WEEK.
YOU'RE NOT GOING TO GET MUCH DONE IN TWO DAYS. EVEN IF WE REACH THE INNER CHAMBER THIS AFTERNOON.
WE WERE LUCKY TO FIND THIS TOMB IN THE FIRST PLACE. MY STUDENTS AND I WERE ON A SITE THIRTY MILES SOUTH OF HERE WHEN THE CONSTRUCTION CREWS STUMBLED UPON IT.
ALTHOUGH THIS IS AN ASTONISHING FIND, TO TELL YOU THE TRUTH--
--I'D BE HAPPY TO LEAVE.
VERY HAPPY, INDEED.
I OWE YOU A DEBT OF GRATITUDE FOR HELPING US SPEED THIS UP.
JUST MAKE SURE STONECHAT GETS SLATED INTO YORK'S CHARLEMAGNE EXHIBIT NEXT MONTH.
LET'S HAVE A LOOK...
YOU SURE YOU KNOW HOW TO USE THAT?

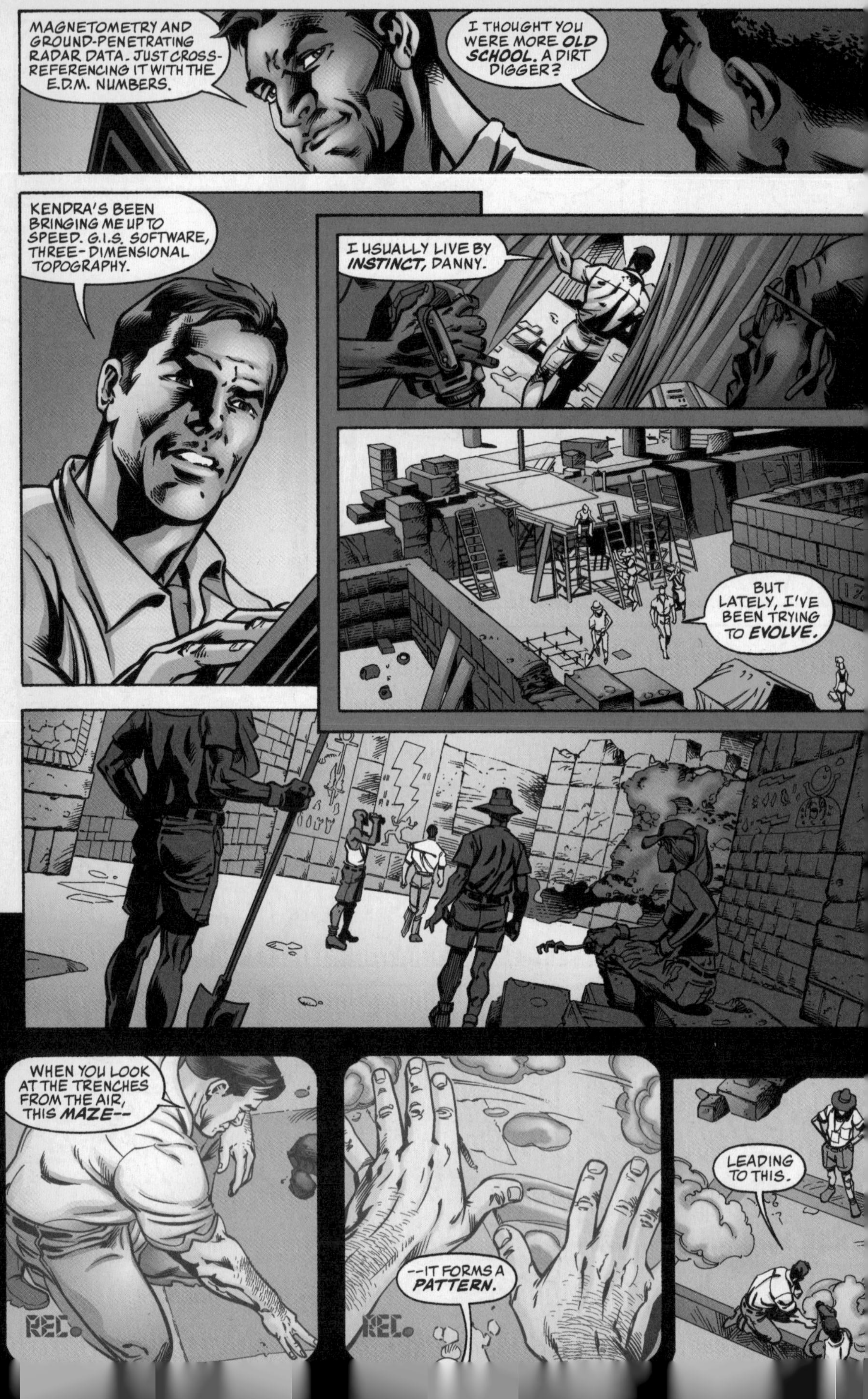
MAGNETOMETRY AND GROUND-PENETRATING RADAR DATA. JUST CROSS-REFERENCING IT WITH THE E.D.M. NUMBERS.
I THOUGHT YOU WERE MORE OLD SCHOOL. A DIRT DIGGER?
KENDRA'S BEEN BRINGING ME UP TO SPEED. G.I.S. SOFTWARE, THREE-DIMENSIONAL TOPOGRAPHY.
I USUALLY LIVE BY INSTINCT, DANNY.
BUT LATELY, I'VE BEEN TRYING TO EVOLVE.
WHEN YOU LOOK AT THE TRENCHES FROM THE AIR, THIS MAZE--
REC.
--IT FORMS A PATTERN.
REC.
LEADING TO THIS.

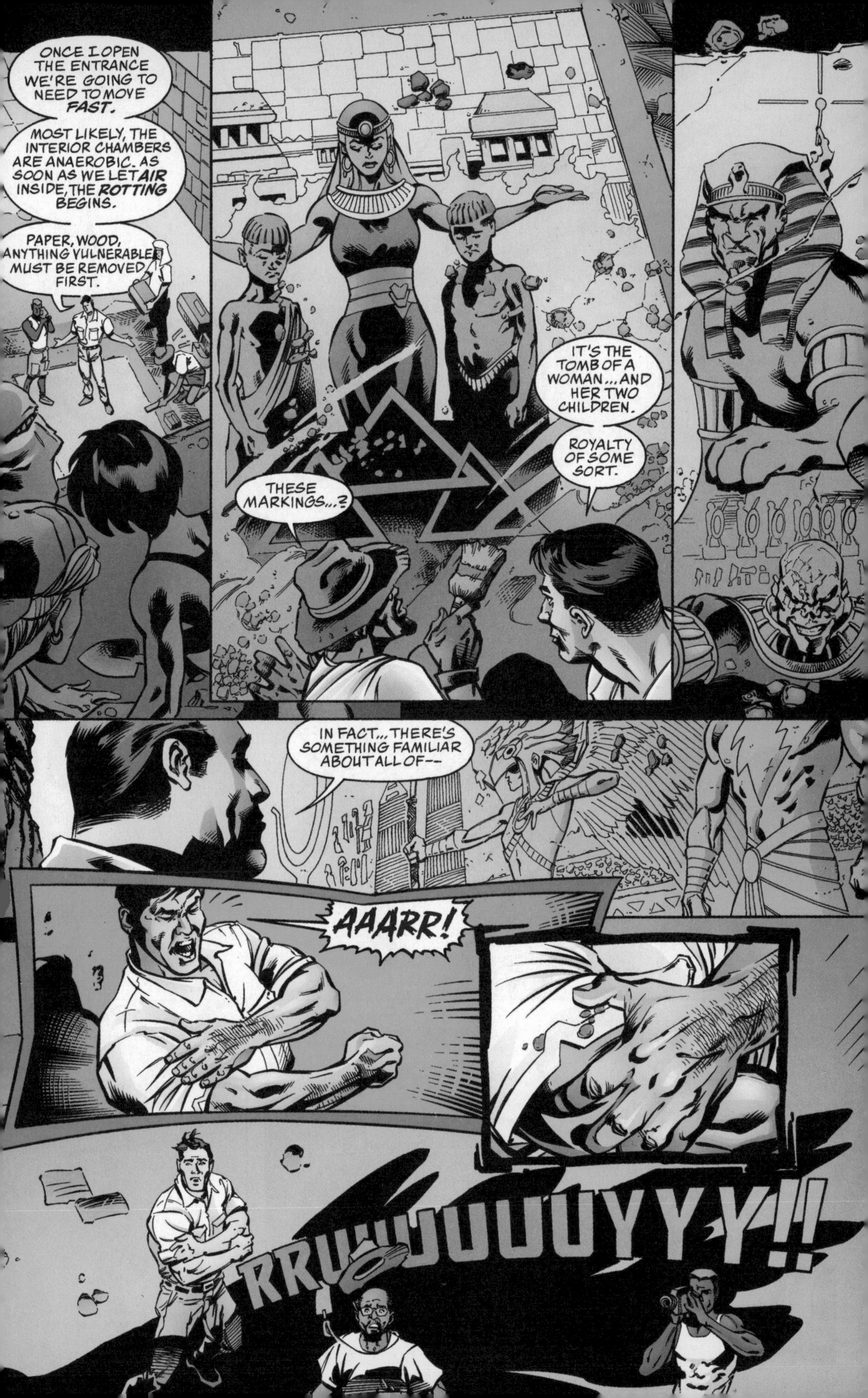
ONCE I OPEN THE ENTRANCE WE'RE GOING TO NEED TO MOVE FAST.
MOST LIKELY, THE INTERIOR CHAMBERS ARE ANAEROBIC. AS SOON AS WE LET AIR INSIDE, THE ROTTING BEGINS.
PAPER, WOOD, ANYTHING VULNERABLE MUST BE REMOVED FIRST.
THESE MARKINGS...?
IT'S THE TOMB OF A WOMAN... AND HER TWO CHILDREN.
ROYALTY OF SOME SORT.
IN FACT... THERE'S SOMETHING FAMILIAR ABOUT ALL OF--
AAARR!
RRUUUUUUYYY!!

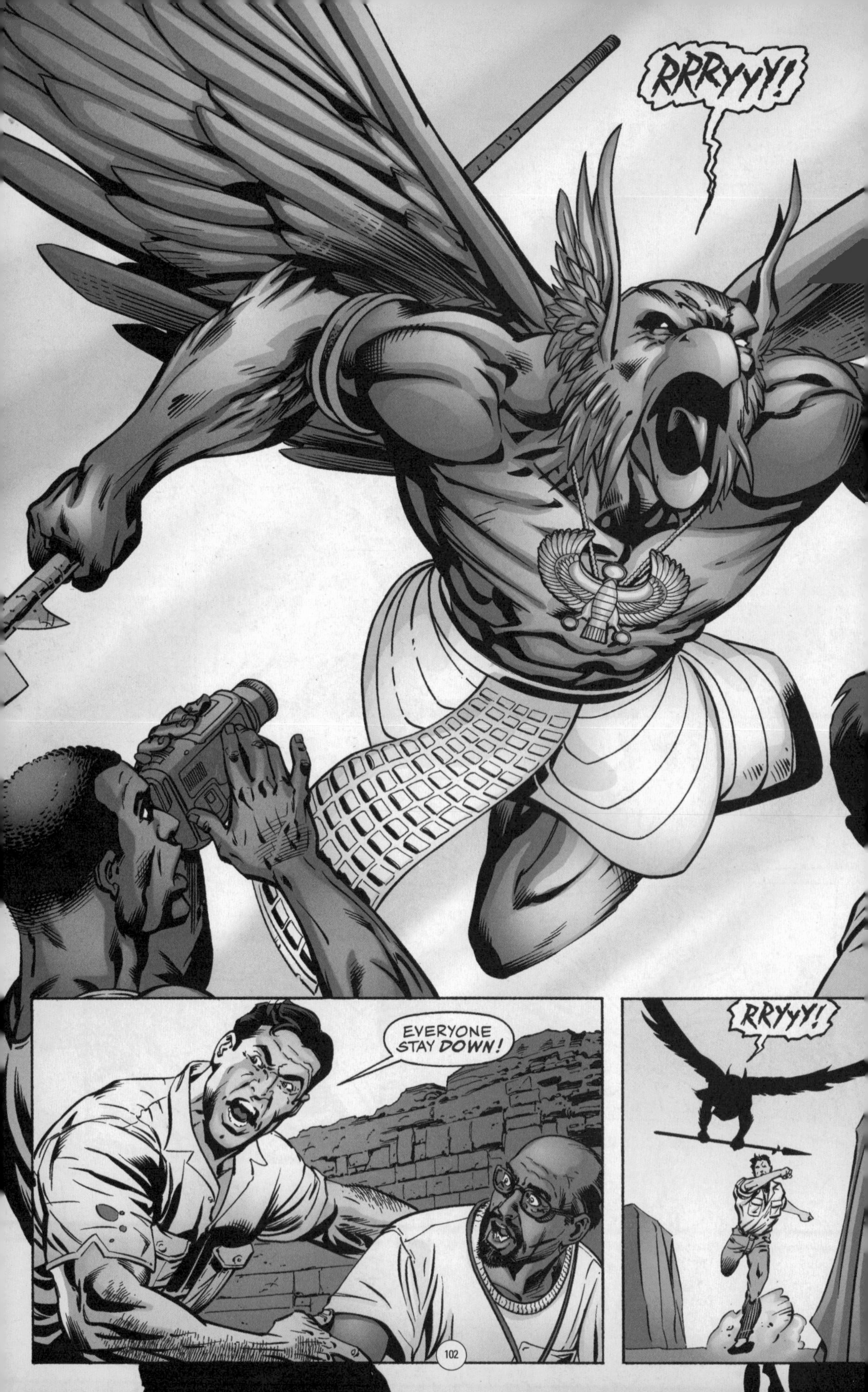
RRRYYY!
EVERYONE STAY DOWN!
RRYYY!

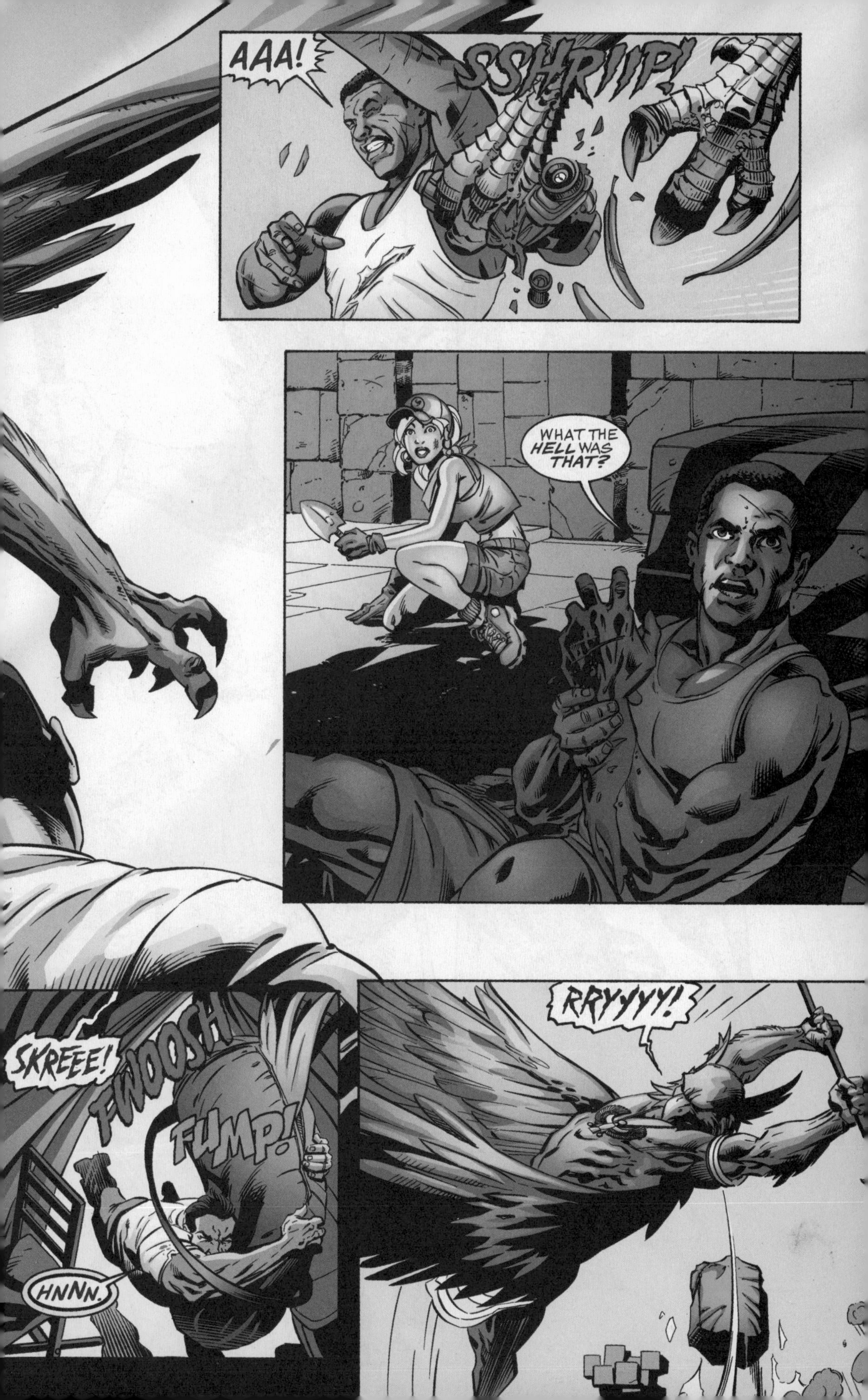
AAA!
SSHRIIP!
WHAT THE HELL WAS THAT?
SKREEE!
FWOOSH
FUMP!
HNNN.
RRYYYY!

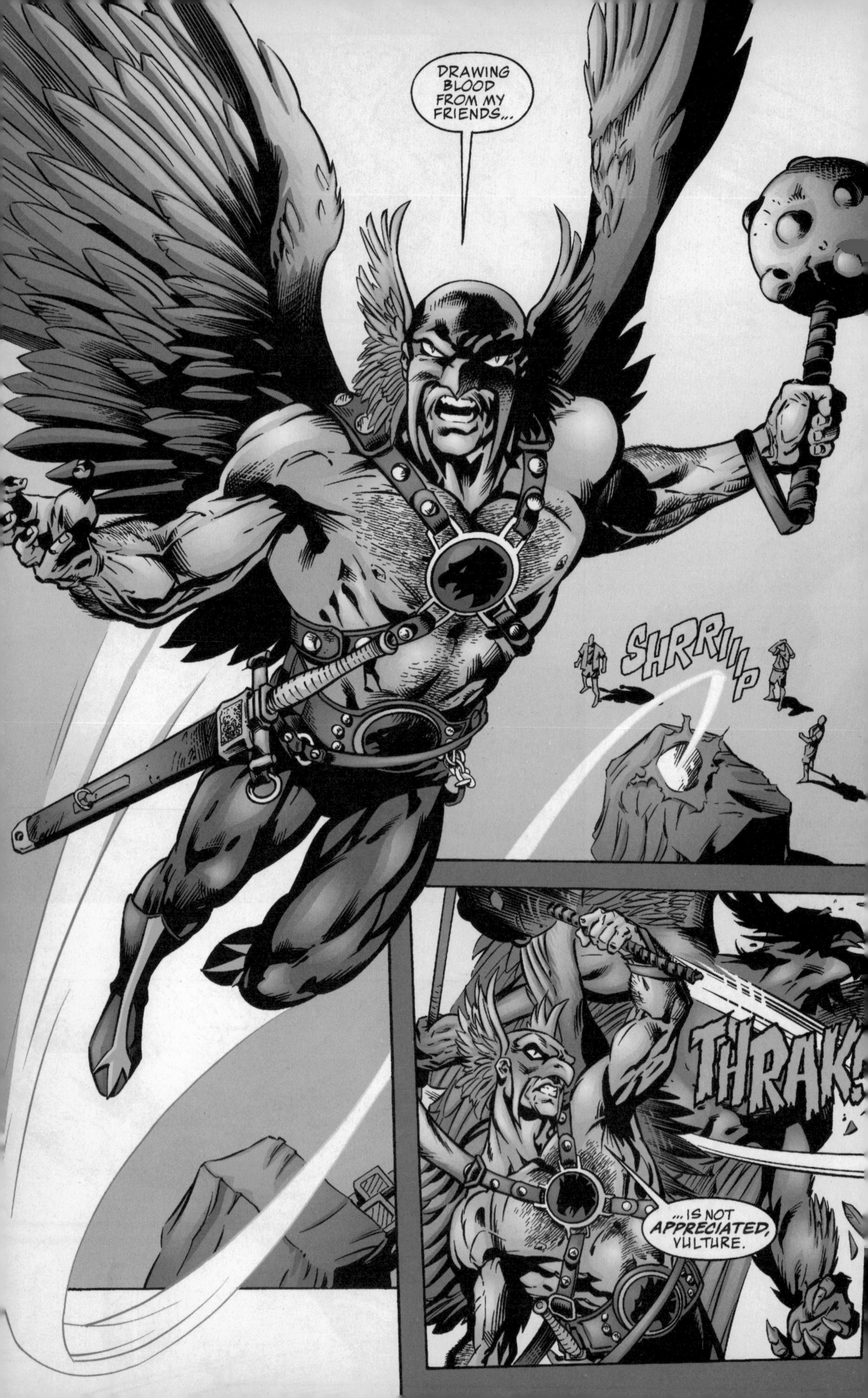
DRAWING BLOOD FROM MY FRIENDS...
SHRRIIIP
THRAK!
...IS NOT APPRECIATED, VULTURE.

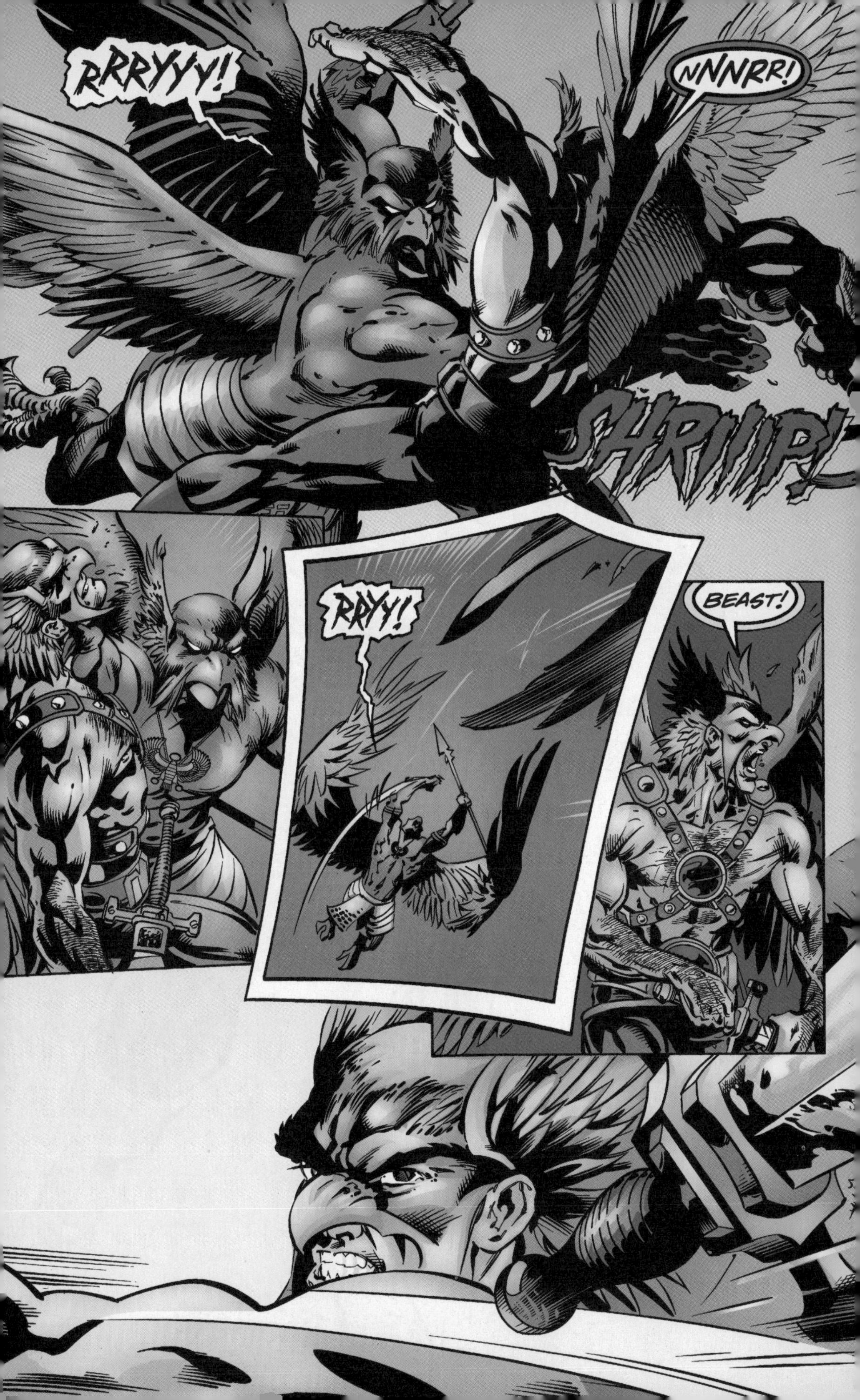
RRRYYY!
NNNRR!
SHRIIIP!
RRYY!
BEAST!

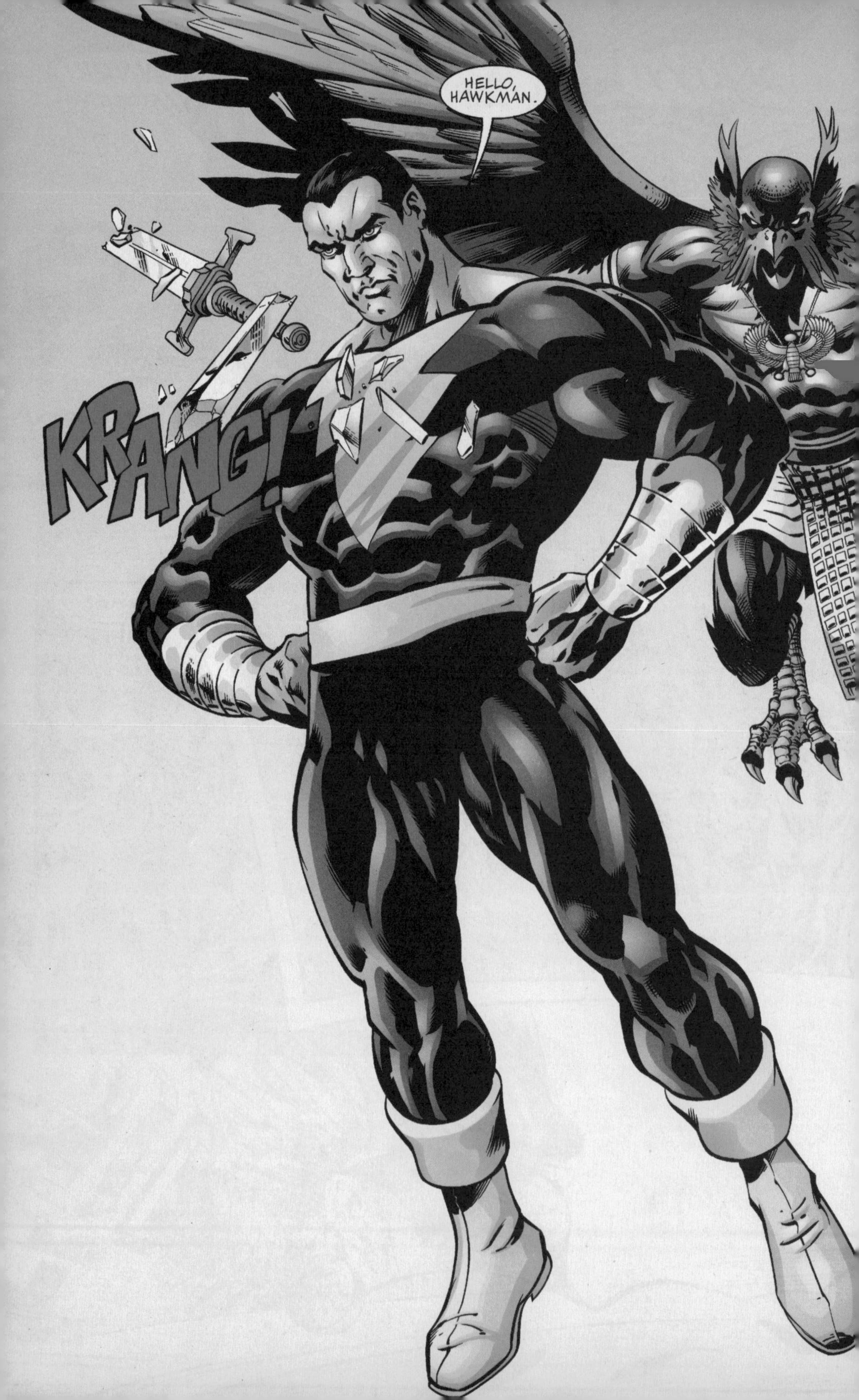

HELLO, HAWKMAN.
KRANG!

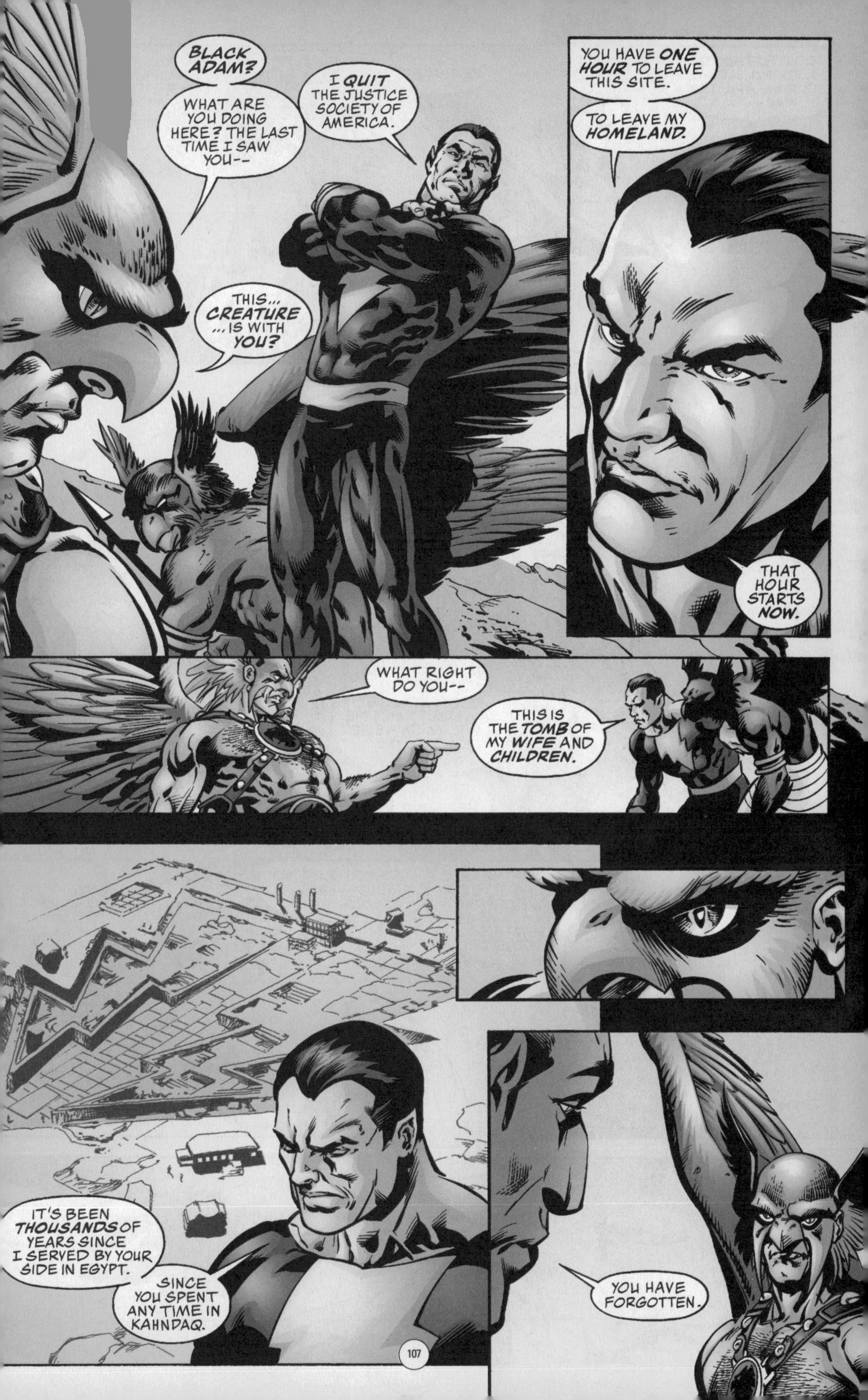

BLACK ADAM?
WHAT ARE YOU DOING HERE? THE LAST TIME I SAW YOU--
I QUIT THE JUSTICE SOCIETY OF AMERICA.
THIS... CREATURE ...IS WITH YOU?
YOU HAVE ONE HOUR TO LEAVE THIS SITE.
TO LEAVE MY HOMELAND.
THAT HOUR STARTS NOW.
WHAT RIGHT DO YOU--
THIS IS THE TOMB OF MY WIFE AND CHILDREN.
IT'S BEEN THOUSANDS OF YEARS SINCE I SERVED BY YOUR SIDE IN EGYPT.
SINCE YOU SPENT ANY TIME IN KAHNDAQ.
YOU HAVE FORGOTTEN.

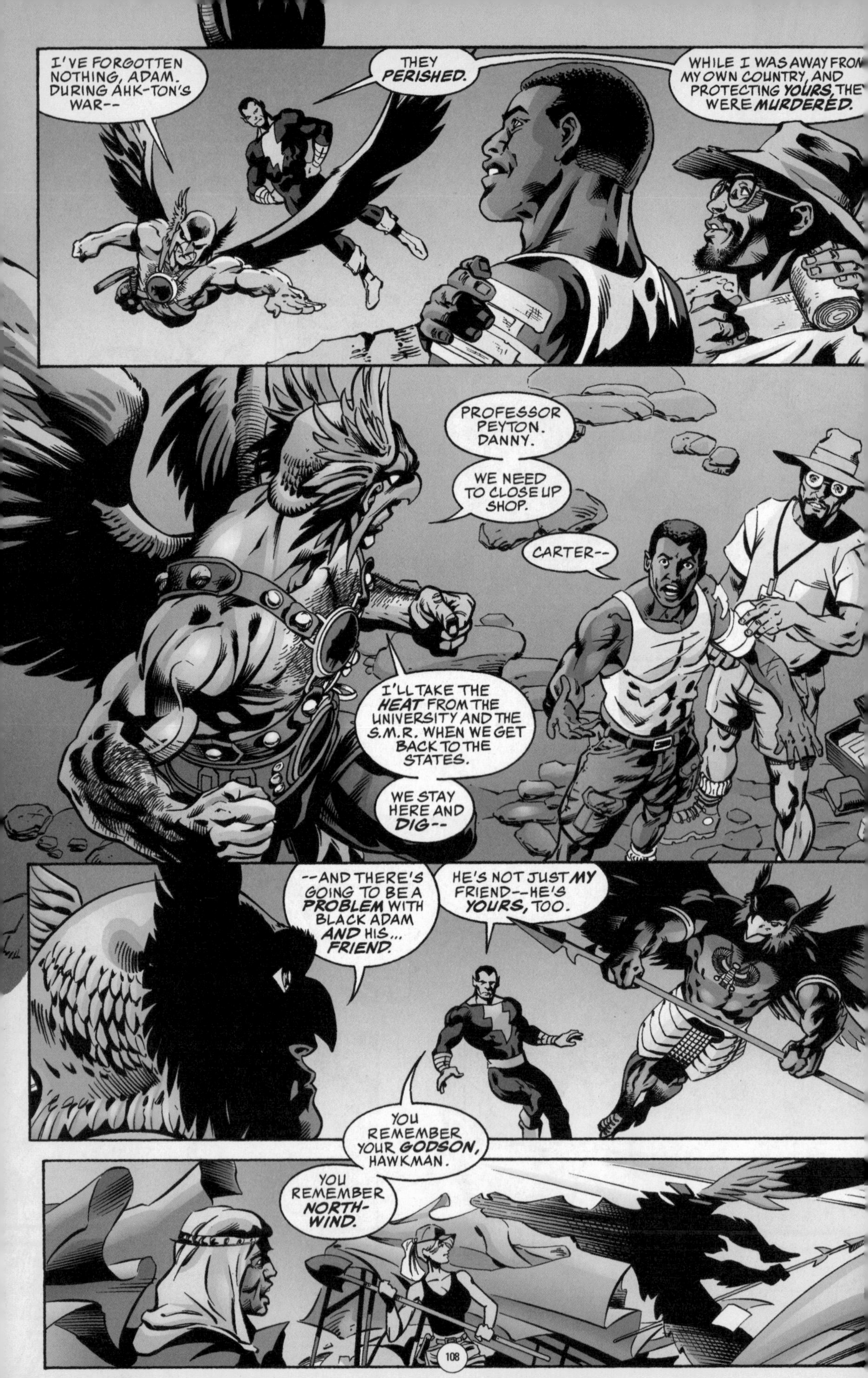
I'VE FORGOTTEN NOTHING, ADAM. DURING AHK-TON'S WAR--
THEY PERISHED.
WHILE I WAS AWAY FROM MY OWN COUNTRY, AND PROTECTING YOURS, THEY WERE MURDERED.
PROFESSOR PEYTON. DANNY.
WE NEED TO CLOSE UP SHOP.
CARTER--
I'LL TAKE THE HEAT FROM THE UNIVERSITY AND THE S.M.R. WHEN WE GET BACK TO THE STATES.
WE STAY HERE AND DIG--
--AND THERE'S GOING TO BE A PROBLEM WITH BLACK ADAM AND HIS... FRIEND.
HE'S NOT JUST MY FRIEND--HE'S YOURS, TOO.
YOU REMEMBER YOUR GODSON, HAWKMAN.
YOU REMEMBER NORTH-WIND.

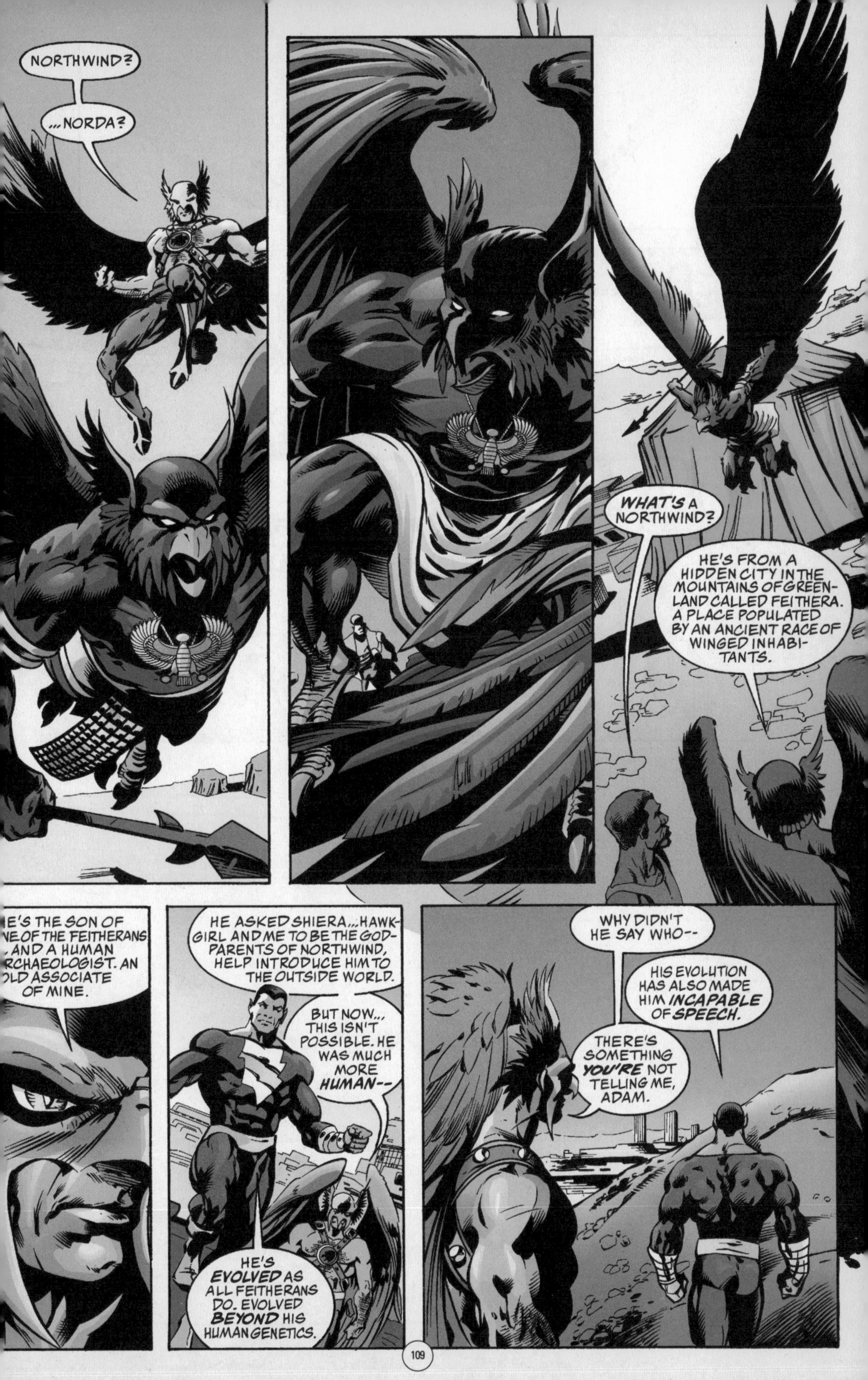
NORTHWIND?
...NORDA?
WHAT'S A NORTHWIND?
HE'S FROM A HIDDEN CITY IN THE MOUNTAINS OF GREENLAND CALLED FEITHERA. A PLACE POPULATED BY AN ANCIENT RACE OF WINGED INHABITANTS.
E'S THE SON OF NE OF THE FEITHERANS AND A HUMAN RCHAEOLOGIST. AN LD ASSOCIATE OF MINE.
HE ASKED SHIERA... HAWKGIRL AND ME TO BE THE GODPARENTS OF NORTHWIND, HELP INTRODUCE HIM TO THE OUTSIDE WORLD.
BUT NOW... THIS ISN'T POSSIBLE. HE WAS MUCH MORE HUMAN--
HE'S EVOLVED AS ALL FEITHERANS DO. EVOLVED BEYOND HIS HUMAN GENETICS.
WHY DIDN'T HE SAY WHO--
HIS EVOLUTION HAS ALSO MADE HIM INCAPABLE OF SPEECH.
THERE'S SOMETHING YOU'RE NOT TELLING ME, ADAM.

BOOOOOOMM!

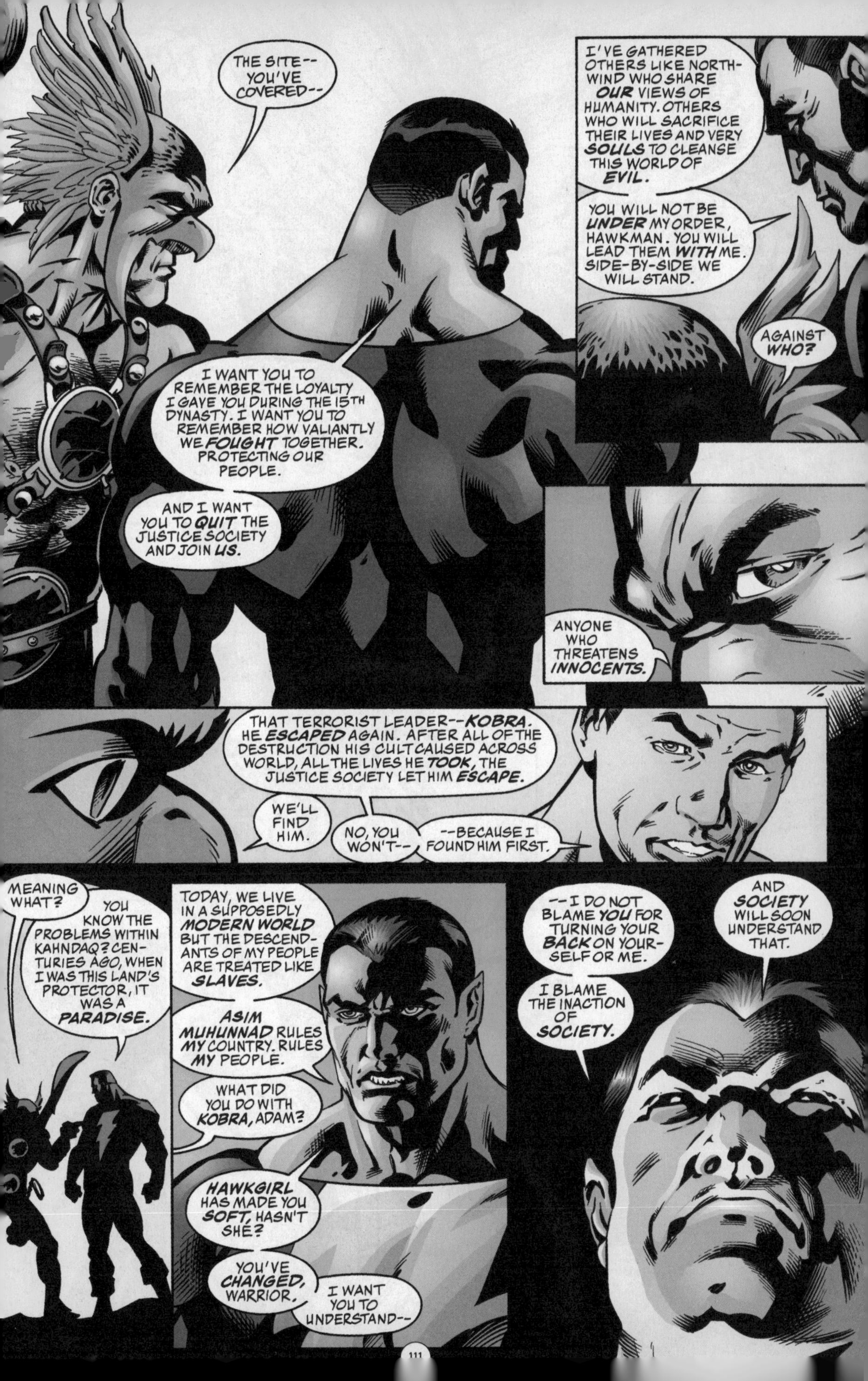
THE SITE-- YOU'VE COVERED--
I WANT YOU TO REMEMBER THE LOYALTY I GAVE YOU DURING THE 15TH DYNASTY. I WANT YOU TO REMEMBER HOW VALIANTLY WE FOUGHT TOGETHER. PROTECTING OUR PEOPLE.
AND I WANT YOU TO QUIT THE JUSTICE SOCIETY AND JOIN US.
I'VE GATHERED OTHERS LIKE NORTH-WIND WHO SHARE OUR VIEWS OF HUMANITY. OTHERS WHO WILL SACRIFICE THEIR LIVES AND VERY SOULS TO CLEANSE THIS WORLD OF EVIL.
YOU WILL NOT BE UNDER MY ORDER, HAWKMAN. YOU WILL LEAD THEM WITH ME. SIDE-BY-SIDE WE WILL STAND.
AGAINST WHO?
ANYONE WHO THREATENS INNOCENTS.
THAT TERRORIST LEADER--KOBRA. HE ESCAPED AGAIN. AFTER ALL OF THE DESTRUCTION HIS CULT CAUSED ACROSS WORLD, ALL THE LIVES HE TOOK, THE JUSTICE SOCIETY LET HIM ESCAPE.
WE'LL FIND HIM.
NO, YOU WON'T--
--BECAUSE I FOUND HIM FIRST.
MEANING WHAT?
YOU KNOW THE PROBLEMS WITHIN KAHNDAQ? CENTURIES AGO, WHEN I WAS THIS LAND'S PROTECTOR, IT WAS A PARADISE.
TODAY, WE LIVE IN A SUPPOSEDLY MODERN WORLD BUT THE DESCENDANTS OF MY PEOPLE ARE TREATED LIKE SLAVES.
ASIM MUHUNNAD RULES MY COUNTRY. RULES MY PEOPLE.
WHAT DID YOU DO WITH KOBRA, ADAM?
HAWKGIRL HAS MADE YOU SOFT, HASN'T SHE?
YOU'VE CHANGED, WARRIOR.
I WANT YOU TO UNDERSTAND--
--I DO NOT BLAME YOU FOR TURNING YOUR BACK ON YOURSELF OR ME.
I BLAME THE INACTION OF SOCIETY.
AND SOCIETY WILL SOON UNDERSTAND THAT.

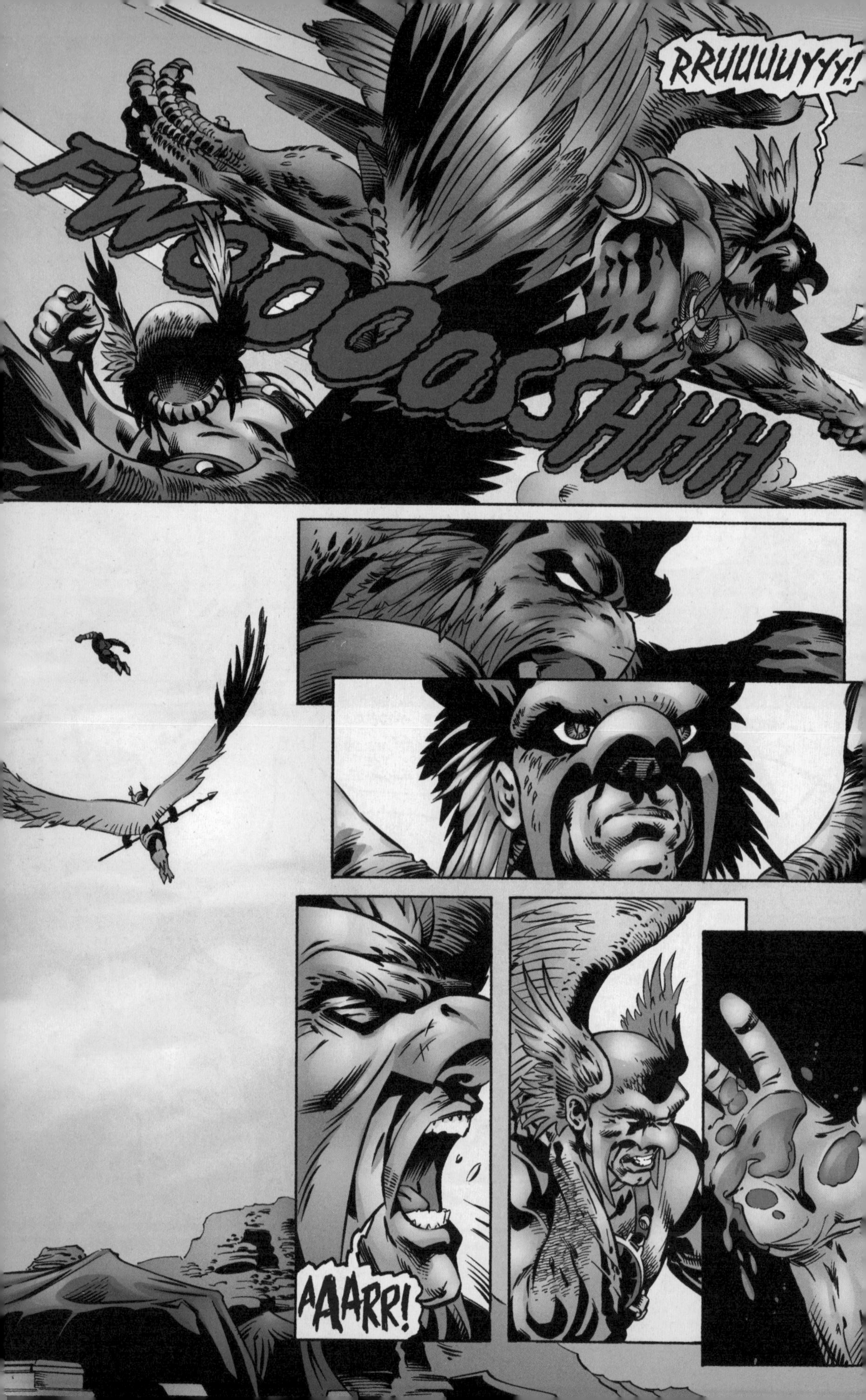
RRUUUUUYYY!
FWOOOOOSHHH
AAARR!

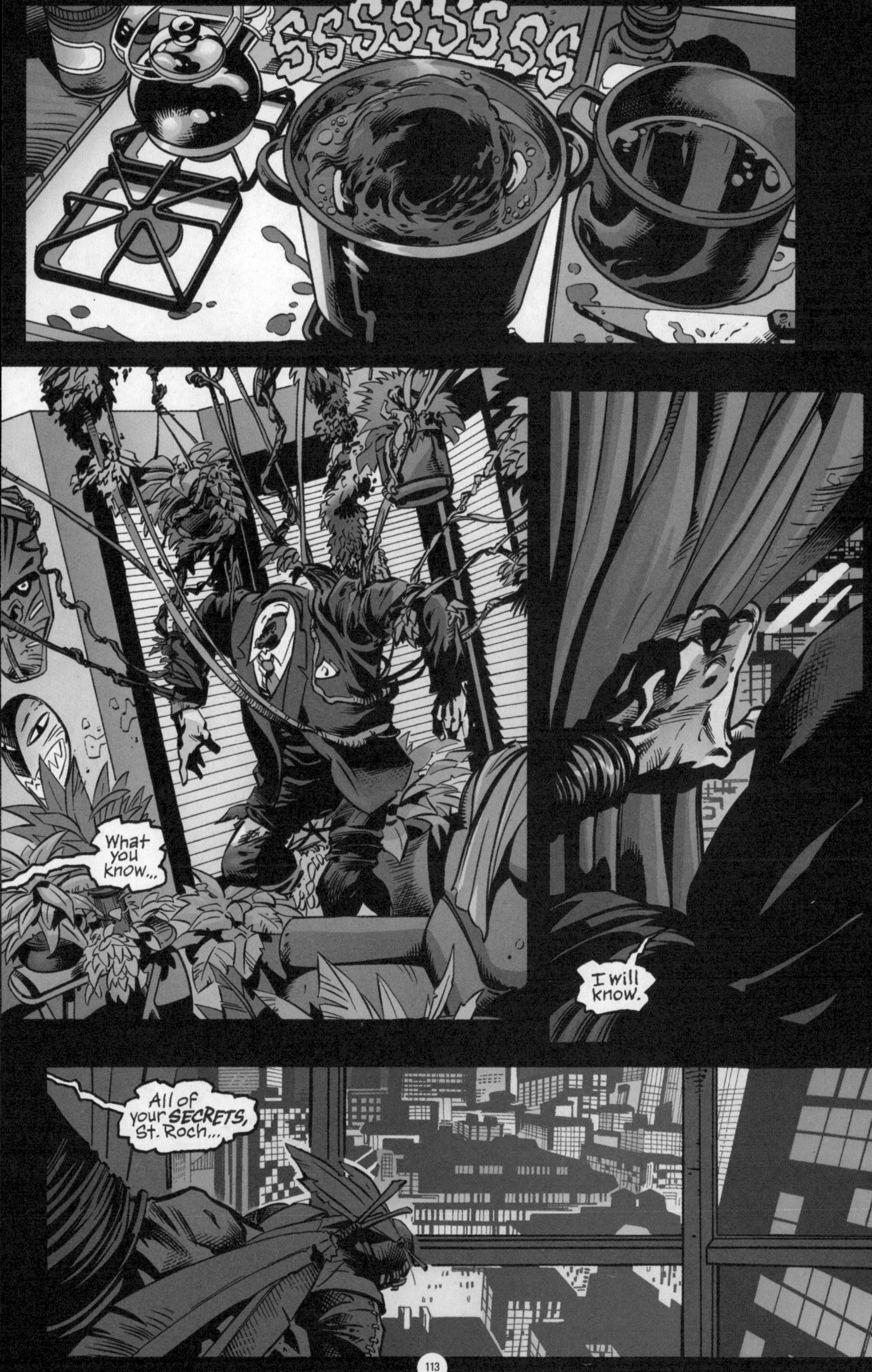
SSSSSSSSS
What you know...
I will know.
All of your SECRETS, St. Roch...

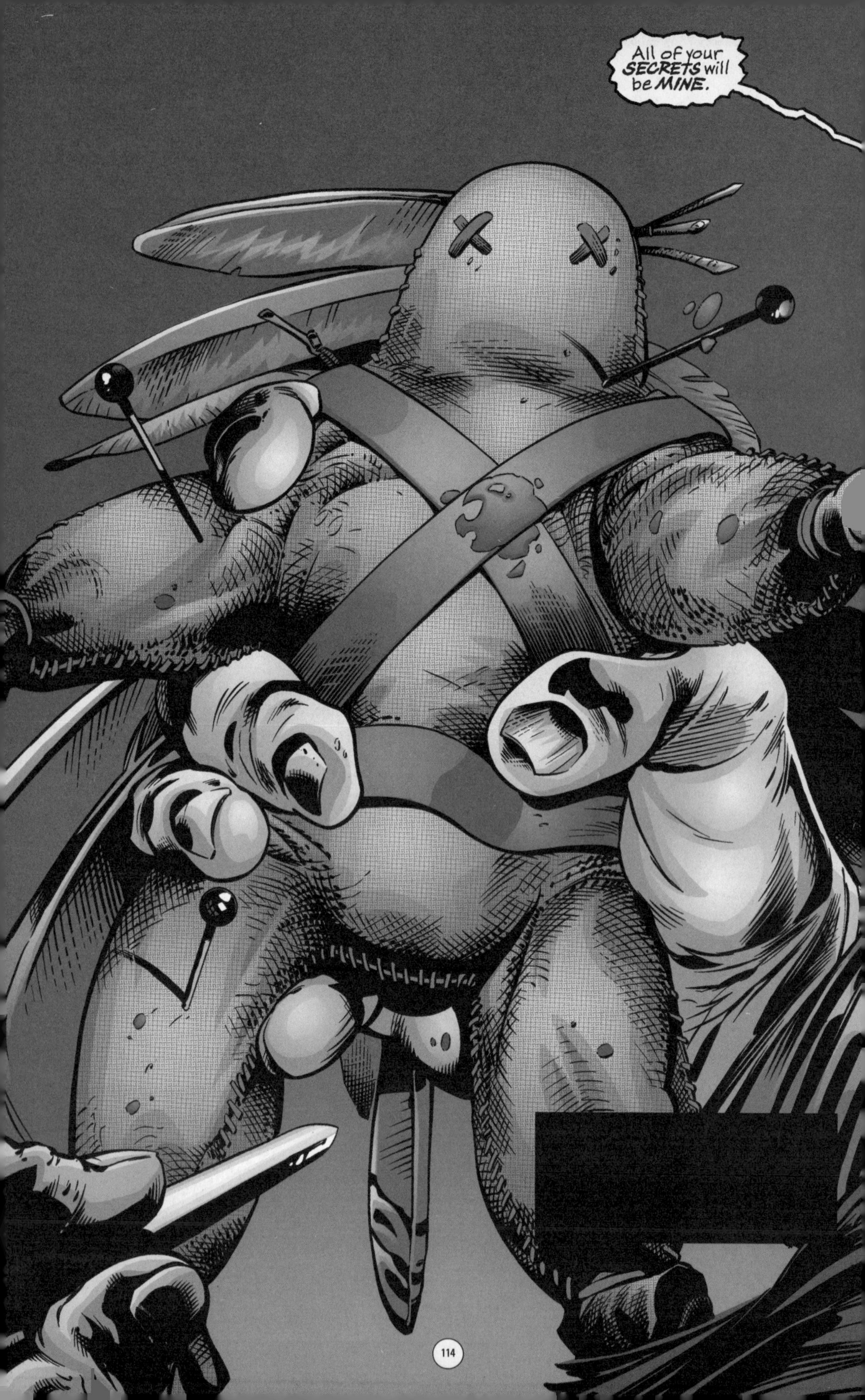
All of your SECRETS will be MINE.
[redacted]

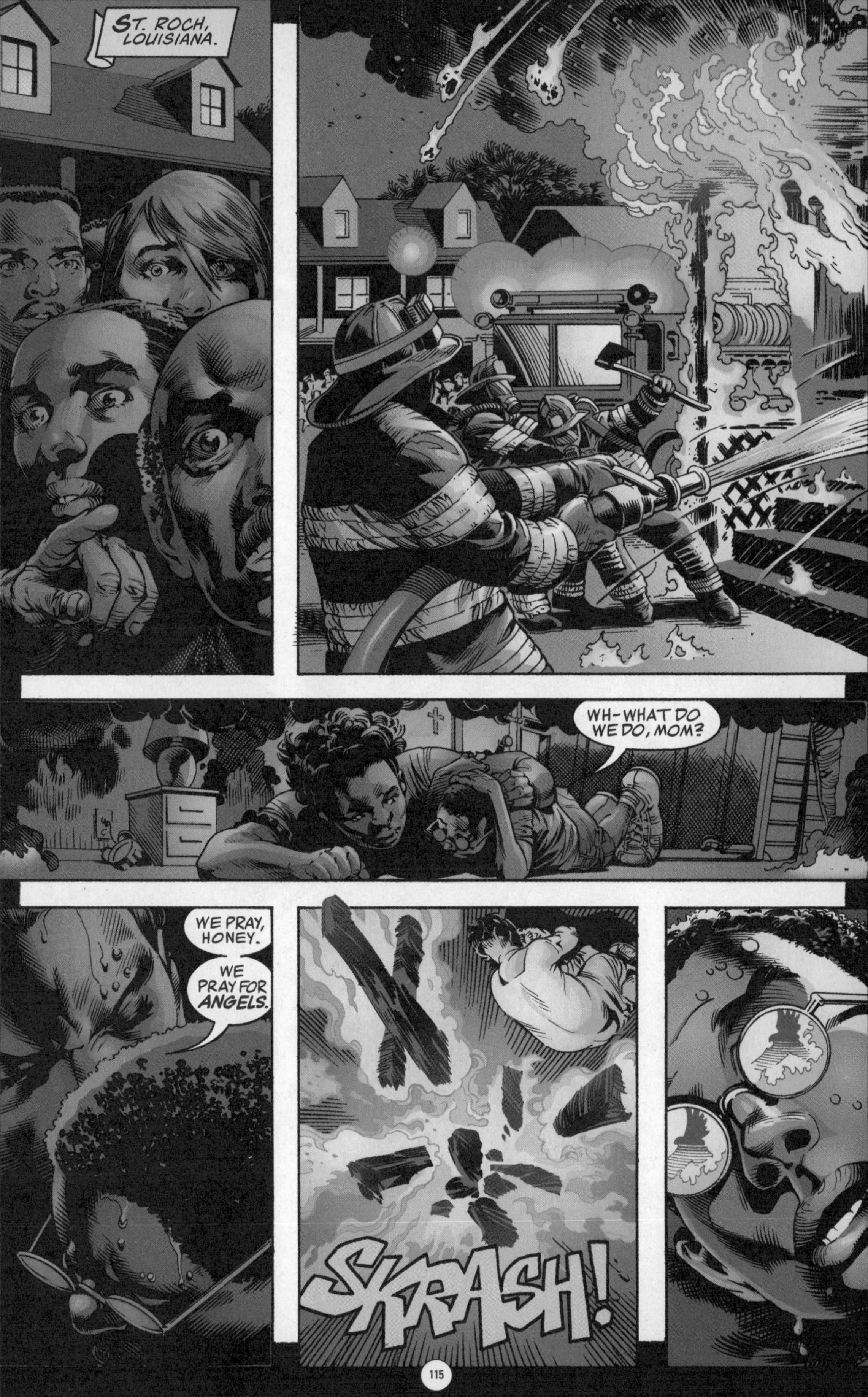
ST. ROCH, LOUISIANA.
WH-WHAT DO WE DO, MOM?
WE PRAY, HONEY.
WE PRAY FOR ANGELS.
SKRASH!

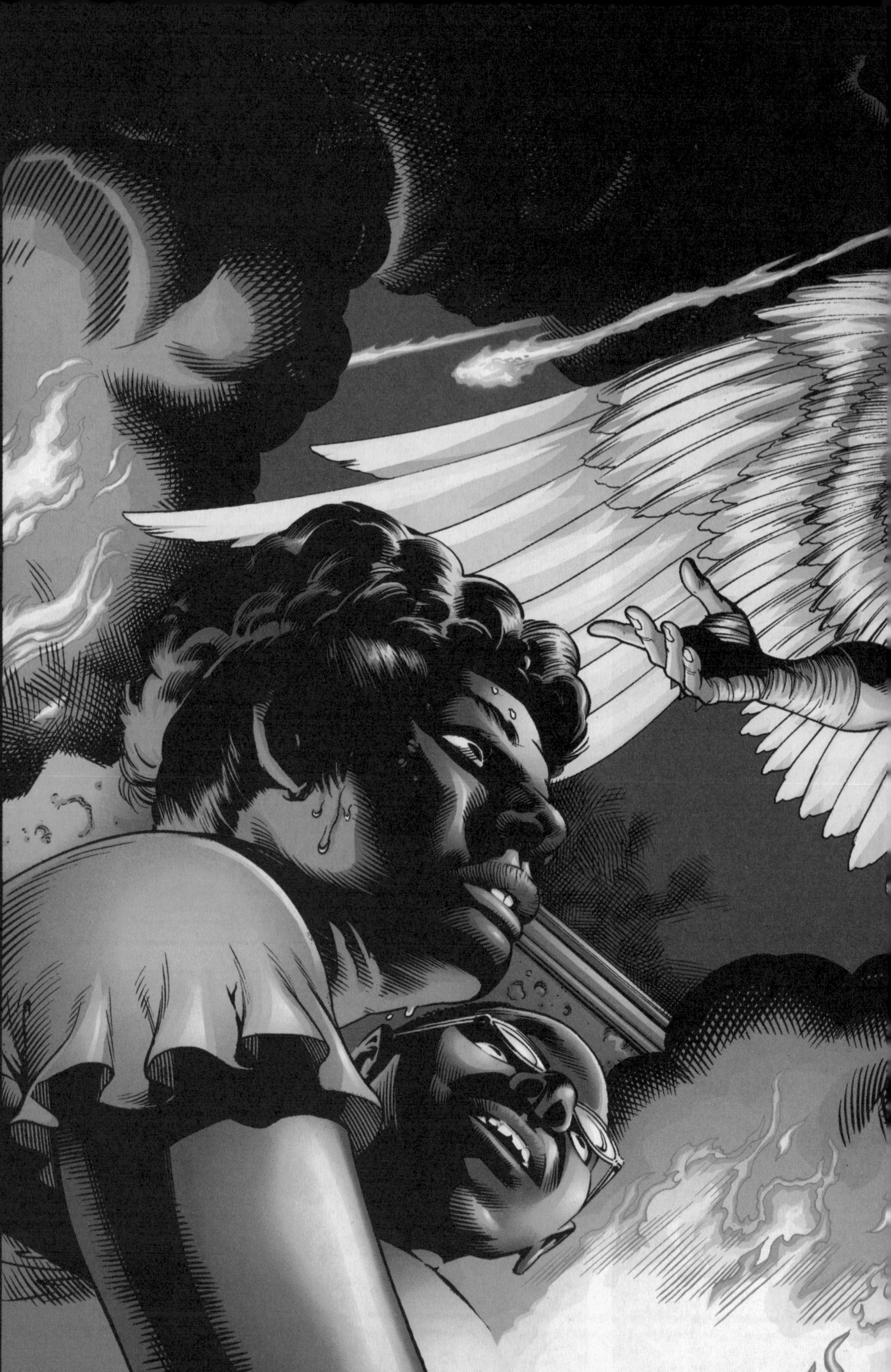

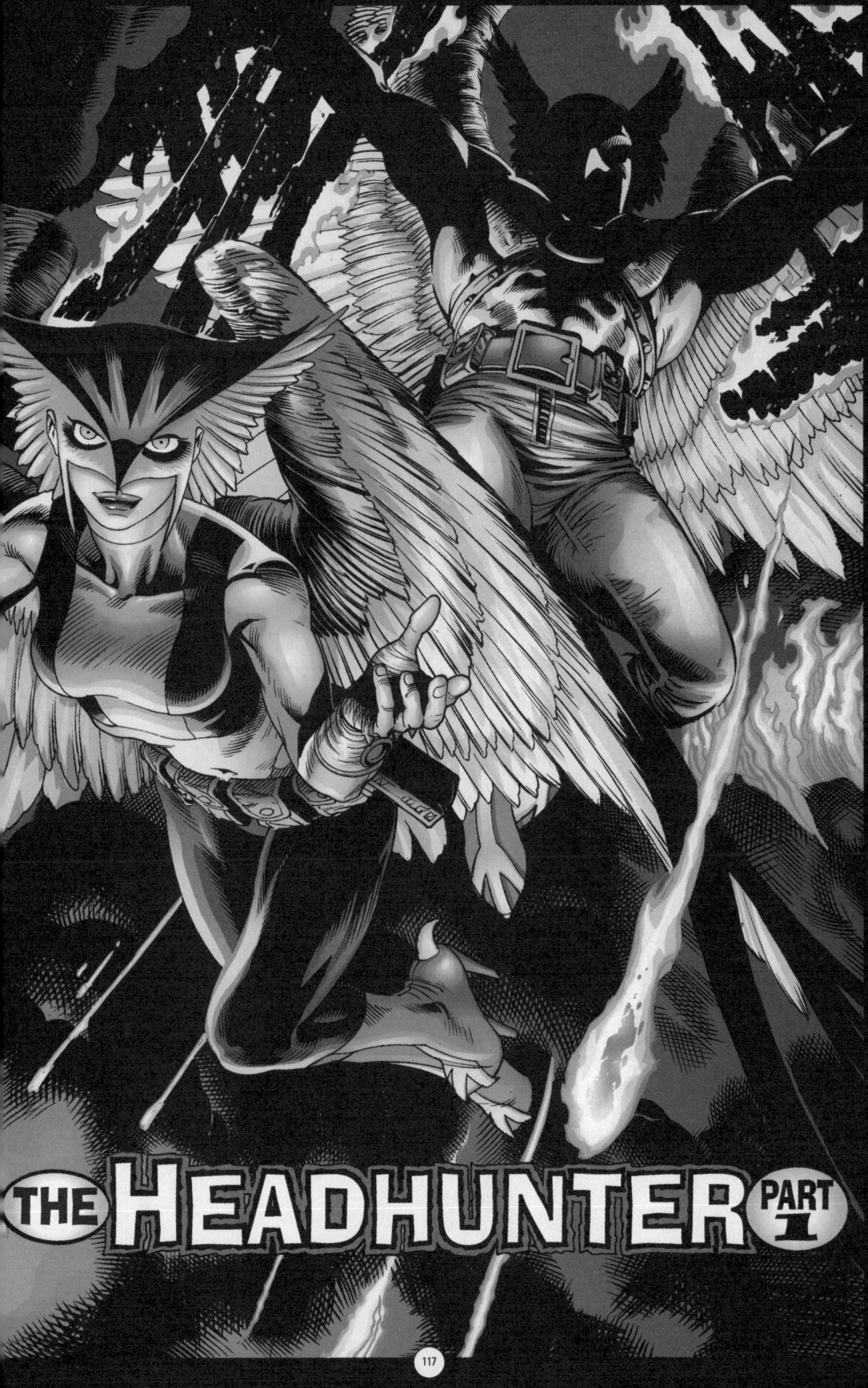
THE HEADHUNTER PART 1

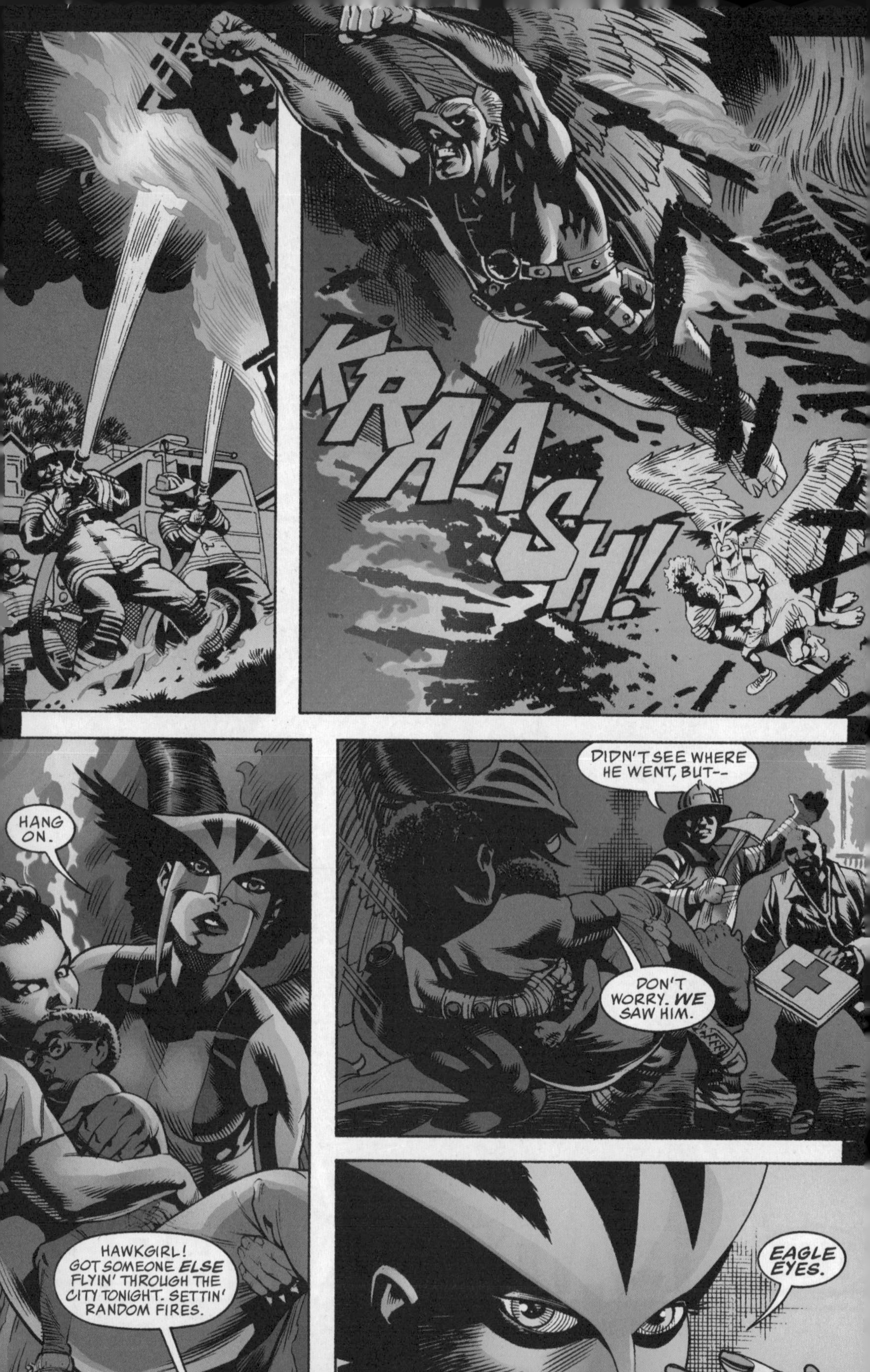
KRAASH!
HANG ON.
HAWKGIRL! GOT SOMEONE ELSE FLYIN' THROUGH THE CITY TONIGHT. SETTIN' RANDOM FIRES.
DIDN'T SEE WHERE HE WENT, BUT--
DON'T WORRY. WE SAW HIM.
EAGLE EYES.

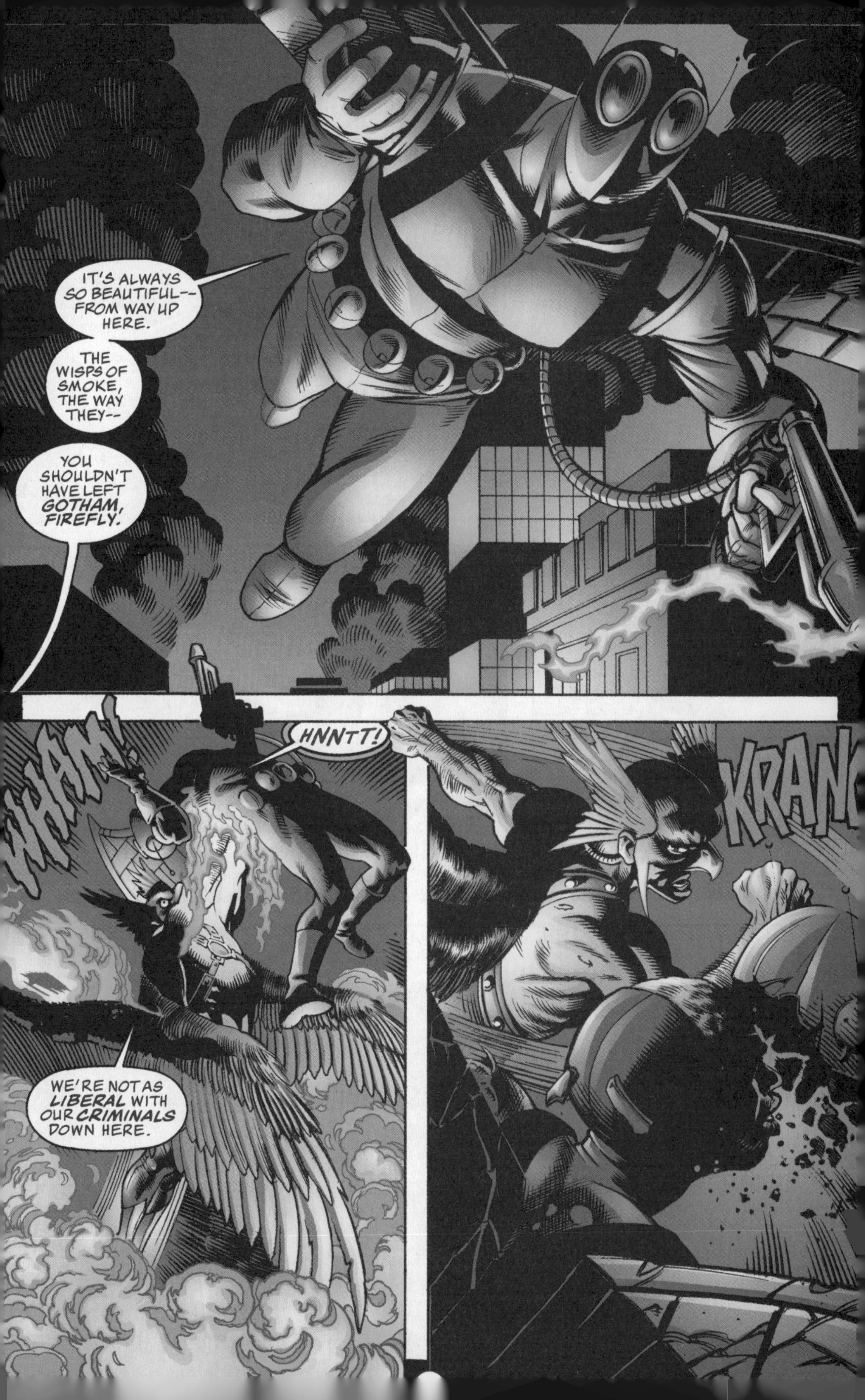
IT'S ALWAYS SO BEAUTIFUL-- FROM WAY UP HERE.
THE WISPS OF SMOKE, THE WAY THEY--
YOU SHOULDN'T HAVE LEFT GOTHAM, FIREFLY.
WHAM!
HNNTT!
WE'RE NOT AS LIBERAL WITH OUR CRIMINALS DOWN HERE.
KRANG

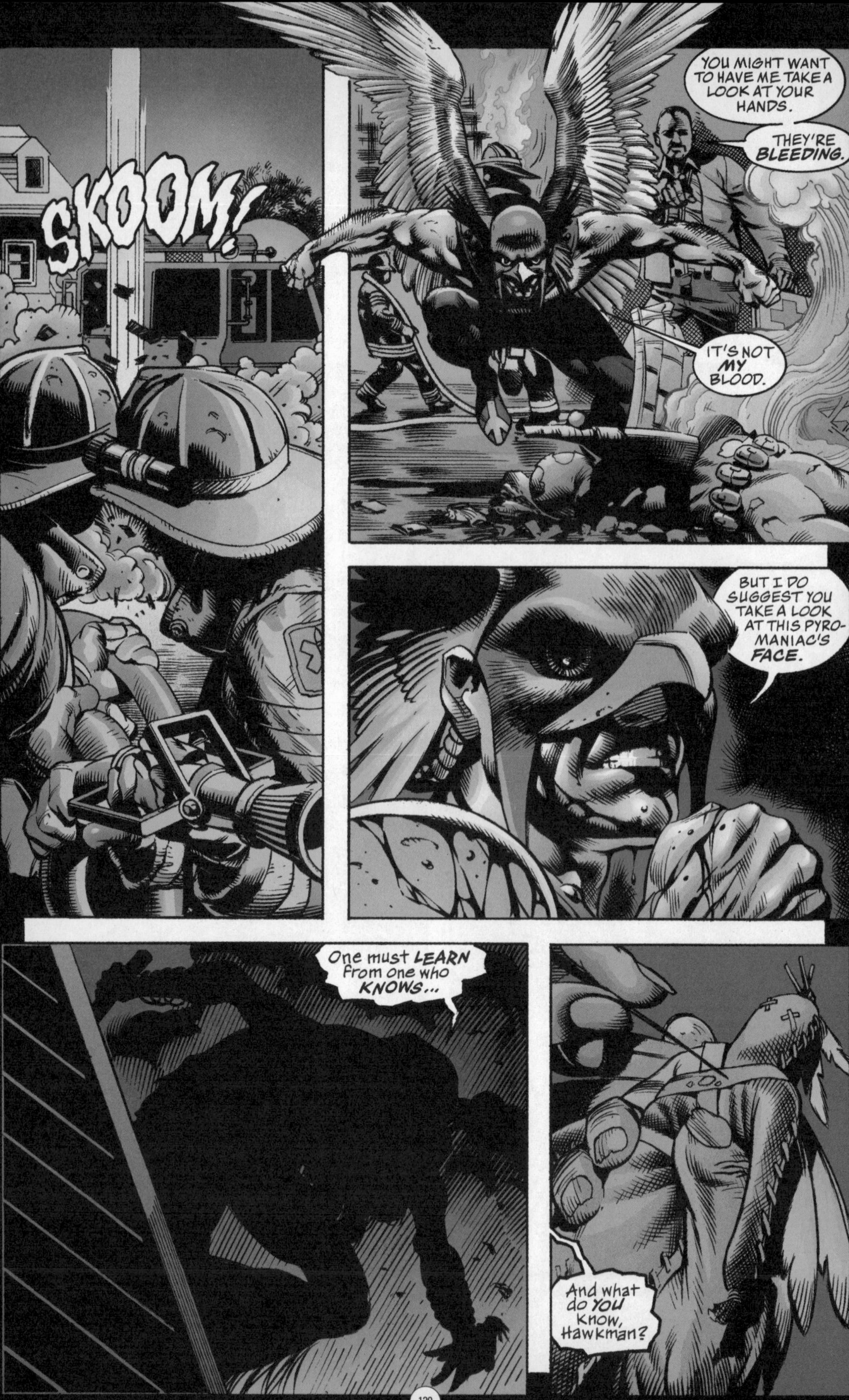

SKOOM!
YOU MIGHT WANT TO HAVE ME TAKE A LOOK AT YOUR HANDS.
THEY'RE BLEEDING.
IT'S NOT MY BLOOD.
BUT I DO SUGGEST YOU TAKE A LOOK AT THIS PYRO-MANIAC'S FACE.
One must LEARN from one who KNOWS...
And what do YOU know, Hawkman?

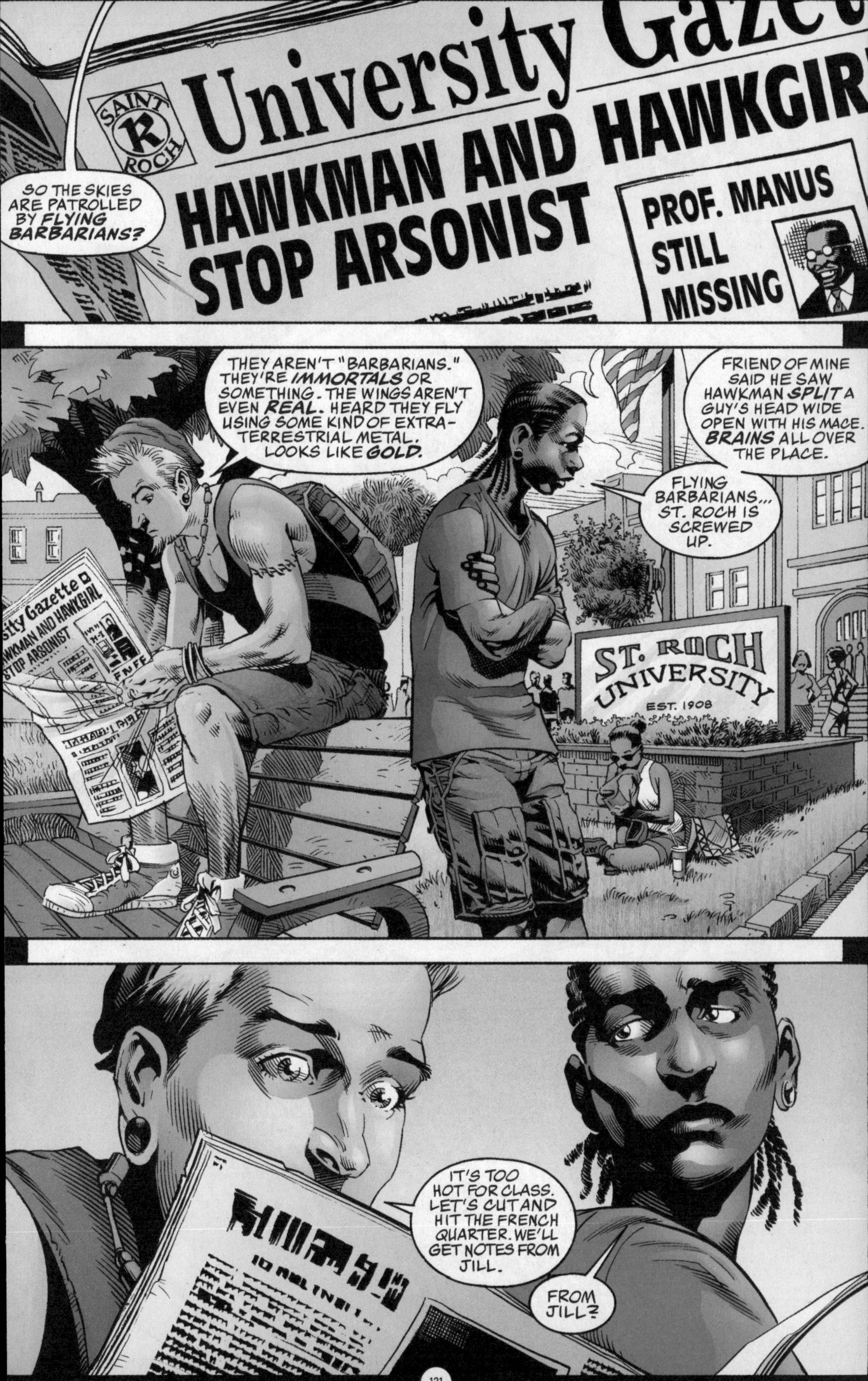

University Gazette
SAINT R ROCH
HAWKMAN AND HAWKGIRL
STOP ARSONIST
PROF. MANUS STILL MISSING
SO THE SKIES ARE PATROLLED BY FLYING BARBARIANS?
THEY AREN'T "BARBARIANS." THEY'RE IMMORTALS OR SOMETHING. THE WINGS AREN'T EVEN REAL. HEARD THEY FLY USING SOME KIND OF EXTRA-TERRESTRIAL METAL. LOOKS LIKE GOLD.
FRIEND OF MINE SAID HE SAW HAWKMAN SPLIT A GUY'S HEAD WIDE OPEN WITH HIS MACE. BRAINS ALL OVER THE PLACE.
FLYING BARBARIANS... ST. ROCH IS SCREWED UP.
ST. ROCH UNIVERSITY EST. 1908
IT'S TOO HOT FOR CLASS. LET'S CUT AND HIT THE FRENCH QUARTER. WE'LL GET NOTES FROM JILL.
FROM JILL?

"JILL *NEVER* PAYS ATTENTION IN CLASS."

--JIVAROS WERE THE ONLY PEOPLE OF THE ECUADORIAN AMAZON THAT MANAGED TO FIGHT OFF THE SPANISH EMPIRE.

IN FACT, THEY SLAUGHTERED OVER *TWENTY-FIVE THOUSAND* WHITE INVADERS IN 1599. KILLING THE MEN AND CHILDREN AND ABSORBING THE WOMEN INTO THEIR TRIBES.

AND EVEN AFTER THE TRADING ROUTES BEGAN, THE JIVAROS DEALT WITH THEIR COMPETITORS IN RATHER *UNIQUE* AND *EXTREME* WAYS.

A GOVERNOR TAXING THEM ON THEIR GOLD-TRADE WAS PINNED DOWN WHILE THE JIVAROS POURED MOLTEN GOLD INTO HIS THROAT.

THEY DIDN'T STOP UNTIL HIS *BOWELS* EXPLODED.

EVEN TODAY, THE JIVAROS REMAIN RELATIVELY UNCHANGED. AND SINCE THEIR TERRITORIES ARE SO IN-ACCESSIBLE, THE ECUADORIAN LAWS DON'T REALLY APPLY. THEIR WARS OVER POLYGAMY AND THEIR PRIMITIVE FORMS OF JUSTICE CARRY ON.

S. American Hist
Mr. Hall
JIVARO TRIBES
① Ashuar
② Aquaruna
③ Huambisa
④ Shuar

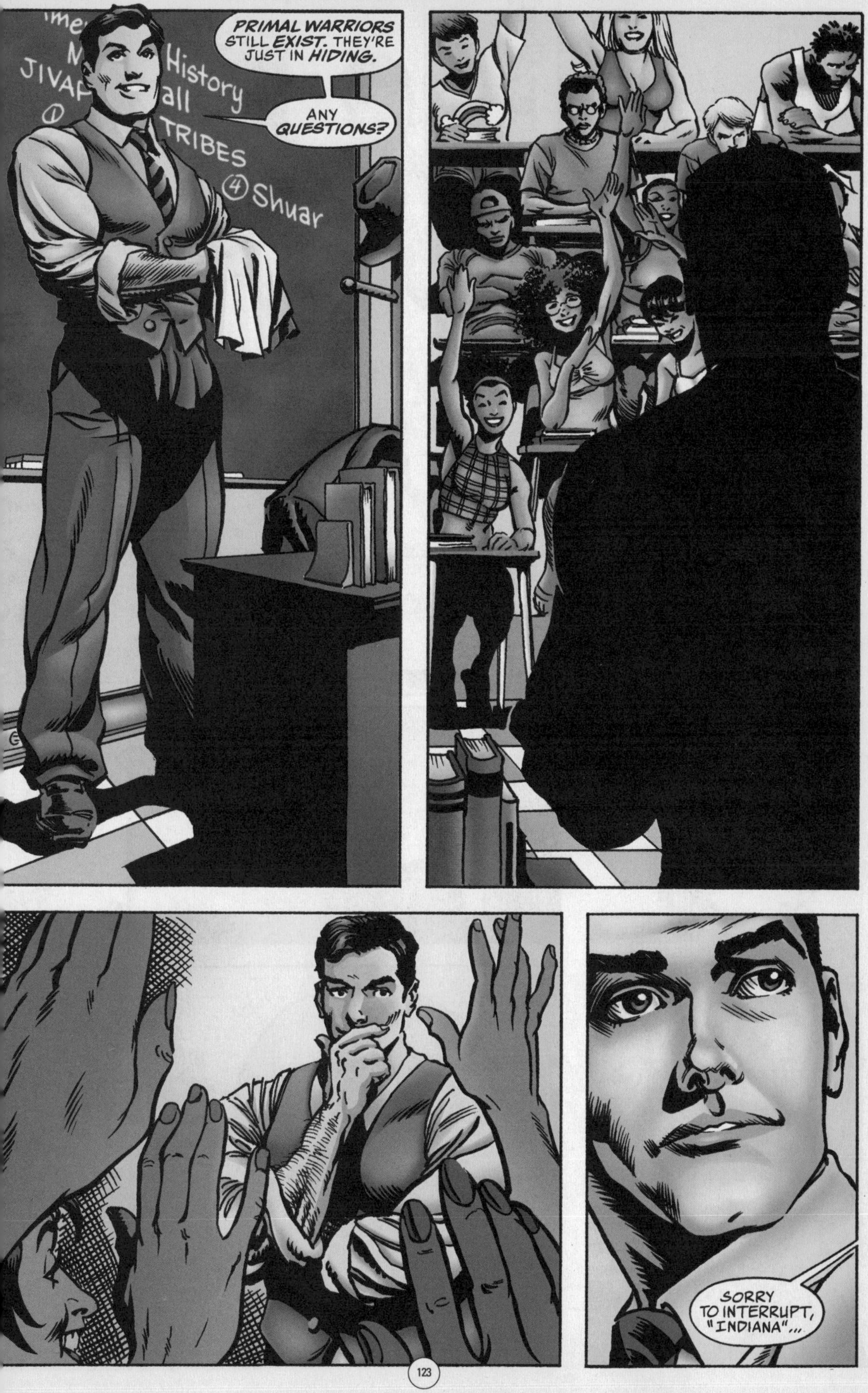
PRIMAL WARRIORS STILL EXIST. THEY'RE JUST IN HIDING.
History
TRIBES
Shuar
ANY QUESTIONS?
SORRY TO INTERRUPT, "INDIANA"....

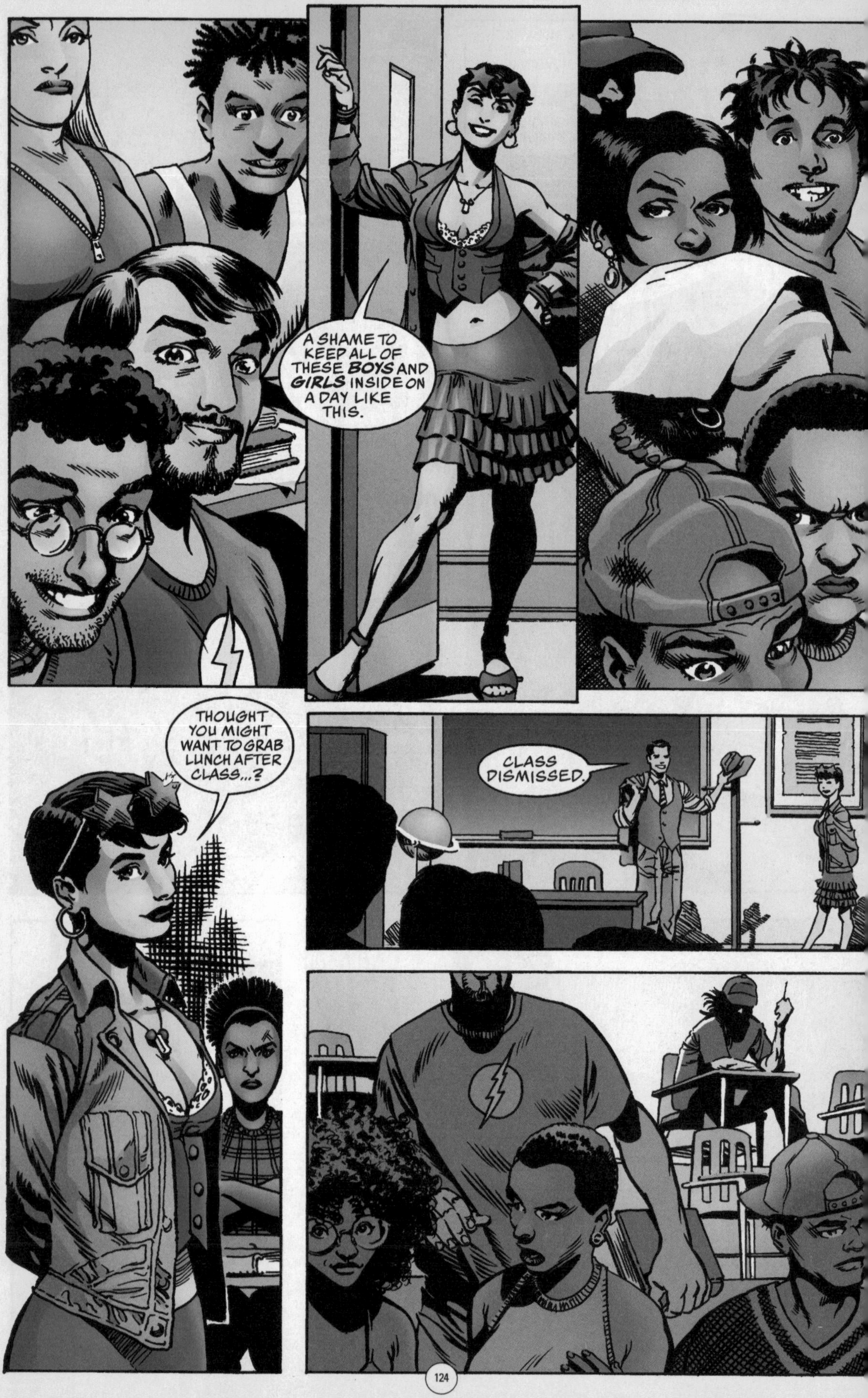
A SHAME TO KEEP ALL OF THESE BOYS AND GIRLS INSIDE ON A DAY LIKE THIS.
THOUGHT YOU MIGHT WANT TO GRAB LUNCH AFTER CLASS...?
CLASS DISMISSED.

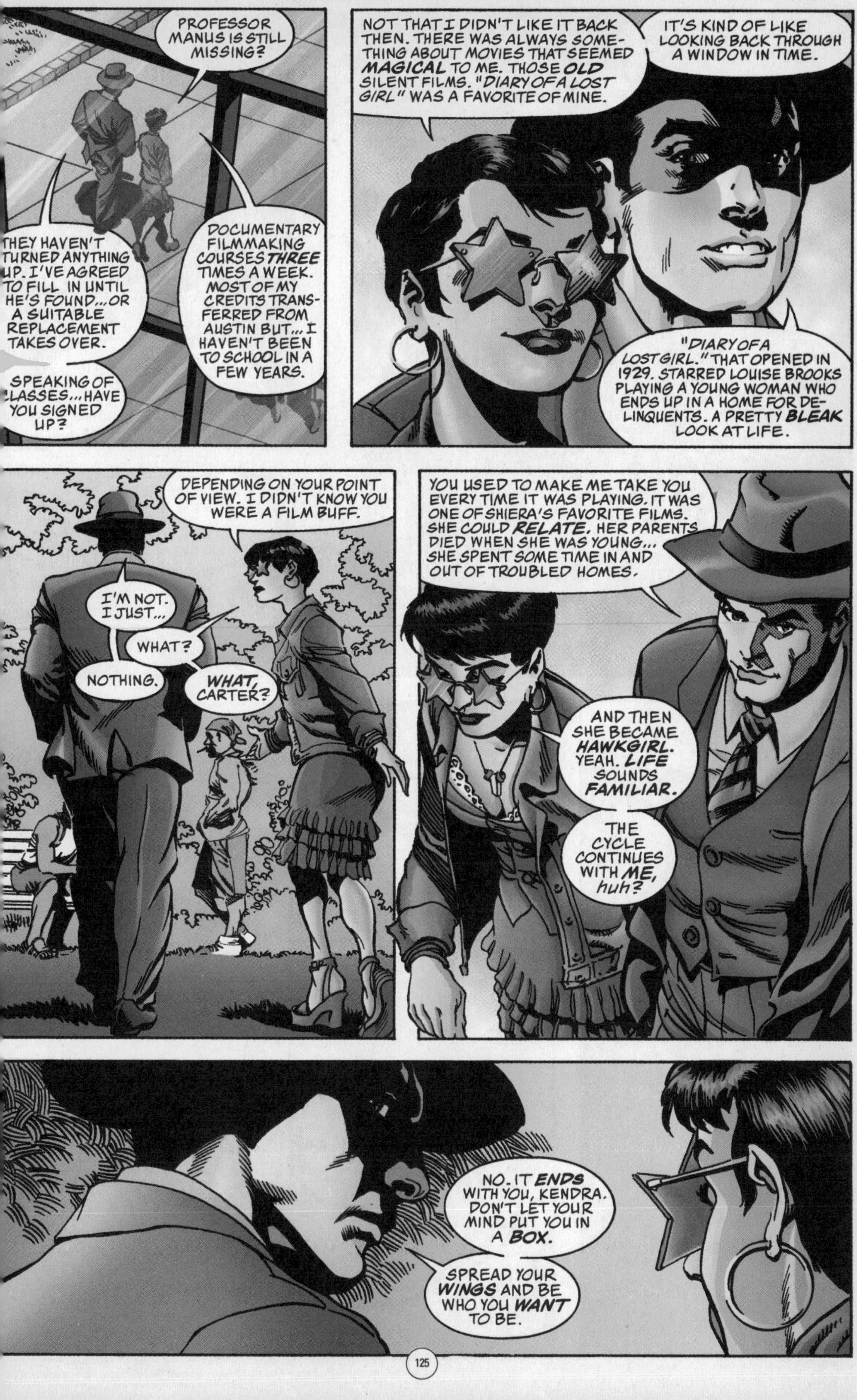
PROFESSOR MANUS IS STILL MISSING?
THEY HAVEN'T TURNED ANYTHING UP. I'VE AGREED TO FILL IN UNTIL HE'S FOUND...OR A SUITABLE REPLACEMENT TAKES OVER.
DOCUMENTARY FILMMAKING COURSES THREE TIMES A WEEK. MOST OF MY CREDITS TRANSFERRED FROM AUSTIN BUT... I HAVEN'T BEEN TO SCHOOL IN A FEW YEARS.
SPEAKING OF CLASSES... HAVE YOU SIGNED UP?
NOT THAT I DIDN'T LIKE IT BACK THEN. THERE WAS ALWAYS SOMETHING ABOUT MOVIES THAT SEEMED MAGICAL TO ME. THOSE OLD SILENT FILMS. "DIARY OF A LOST GIRL" WAS A FAVORITE OF MINE.
IT'S KIND OF LIKE LOOKING BACK THROUGH A WINDOW IN TIME.
"DIARY OF A LOST GIRL." THAT OPENED IN 1929. STARRED LOUISE BROOKS PLAYING A YOUNG WOMAN WHO ENDS UP IN A HOME FOR DELINQUENTS. A PRETTY BLEAK LOOK AT LIFE.
DEPENDING ON YOUR POINT OF VIEW. I DIDN'T KNOW YOU WERE A FILM BUFF.
I'M NOT. I JUST...
WHAT?
NOTHING.
WHAT, CARTER?
YOU USED TO MAKE ME TAKE YOU EVERY TIME IT WAS PLAYING. IT WAS ONE OF SHIERA'S FAVORITE FILMS. SHE COULD RELATE. HER PARENTS DIED WHEN SHE WAS YOUNG... SHE SPENT SOME TIME IN AND OUT OF TROUBLED HOMES.
AND THEN SHE BECAME HAWKGIRL. YEAH. LIFE SOUNDS FAMILIAR.
THE CYCLE CONTINUES WITH ME, huh?
NO. IT ENDS WITH YOU, KENDRA. DON'T LET YOUR MIND PUT YOU IN A BOX.
SPREAD YOUR WINGS AND BE WHO YOU WANT TO BE.

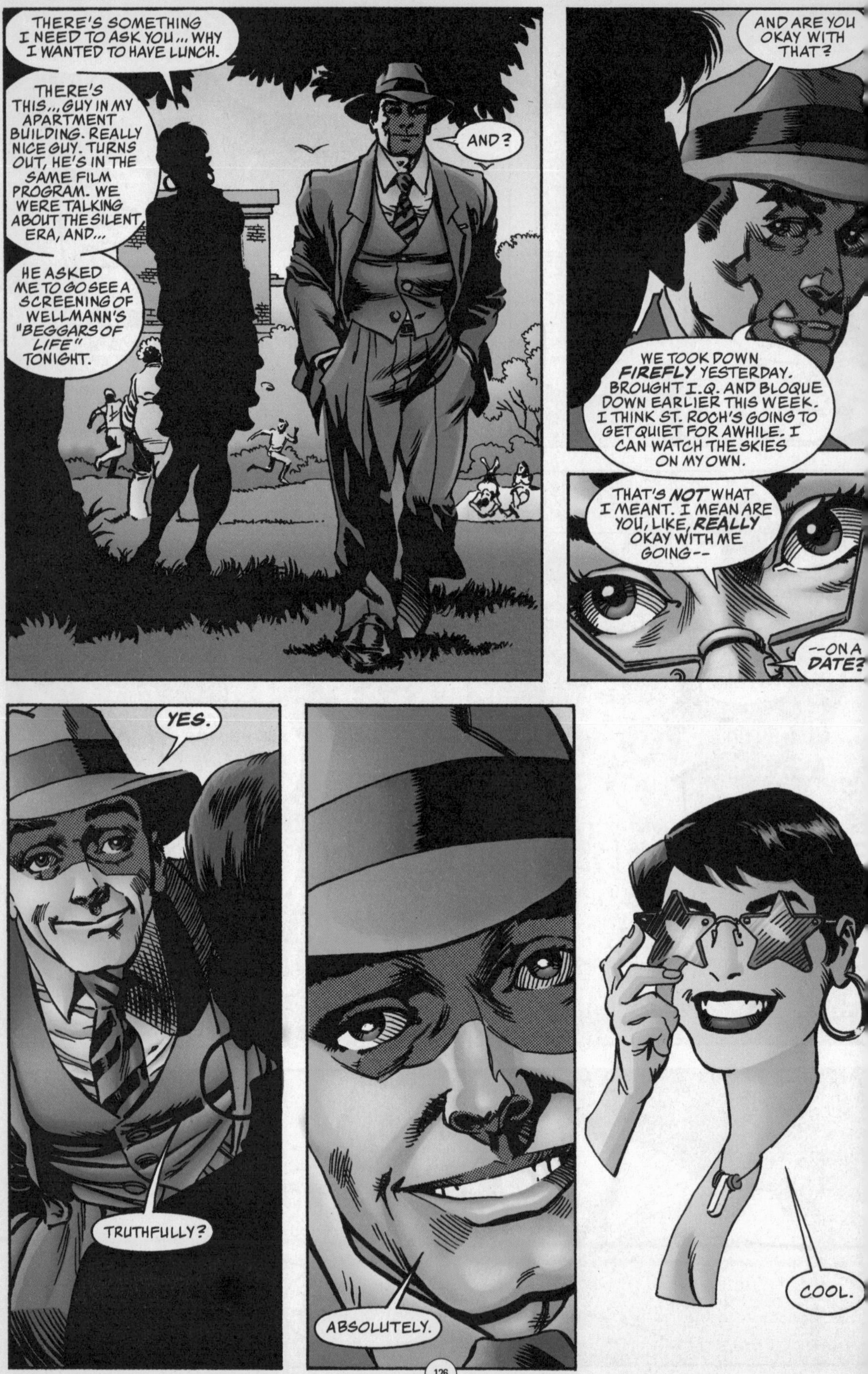
THERE'S SOMETHING I NEED TO ASK YOU... WHY I WANTED TO HAVE LUNCH.
THERE'S THIS... GUY IN MY APARTMENT BUILDING. REALLY NICE GUY. TURNS OUT, HE'S IN THE SAME FILM PROGRAM. WE WERE TALKING ABOUT THE SILENT ERA, AND...
HE ASKED ME TO GO SEE A SCREENING OF WELLMANN'S "BEGGARS OF LIFE" TONIGHT.
AND?
AND ARE YOU OKAY WITH THAT?
WE TOOK DOWN FIREFLY YESTERDAY. BROUGHT I.Q. AND BLOQUE DOWN EARLIER THIS WEEK. I THINK ST. ROCH'S GOING TO GET QUIET FOR AWHILE. I CAN WATCH THE SKIES ON MY OWN.
THAT'S NOT WHAT I MEANT. I MEAN ARE YOU, LIKE, REALLY OKAY WITH ME GOING--
--ON A DATE?
YES.
TRUTHFULLY?
ABSOLUTELY.
COOL.

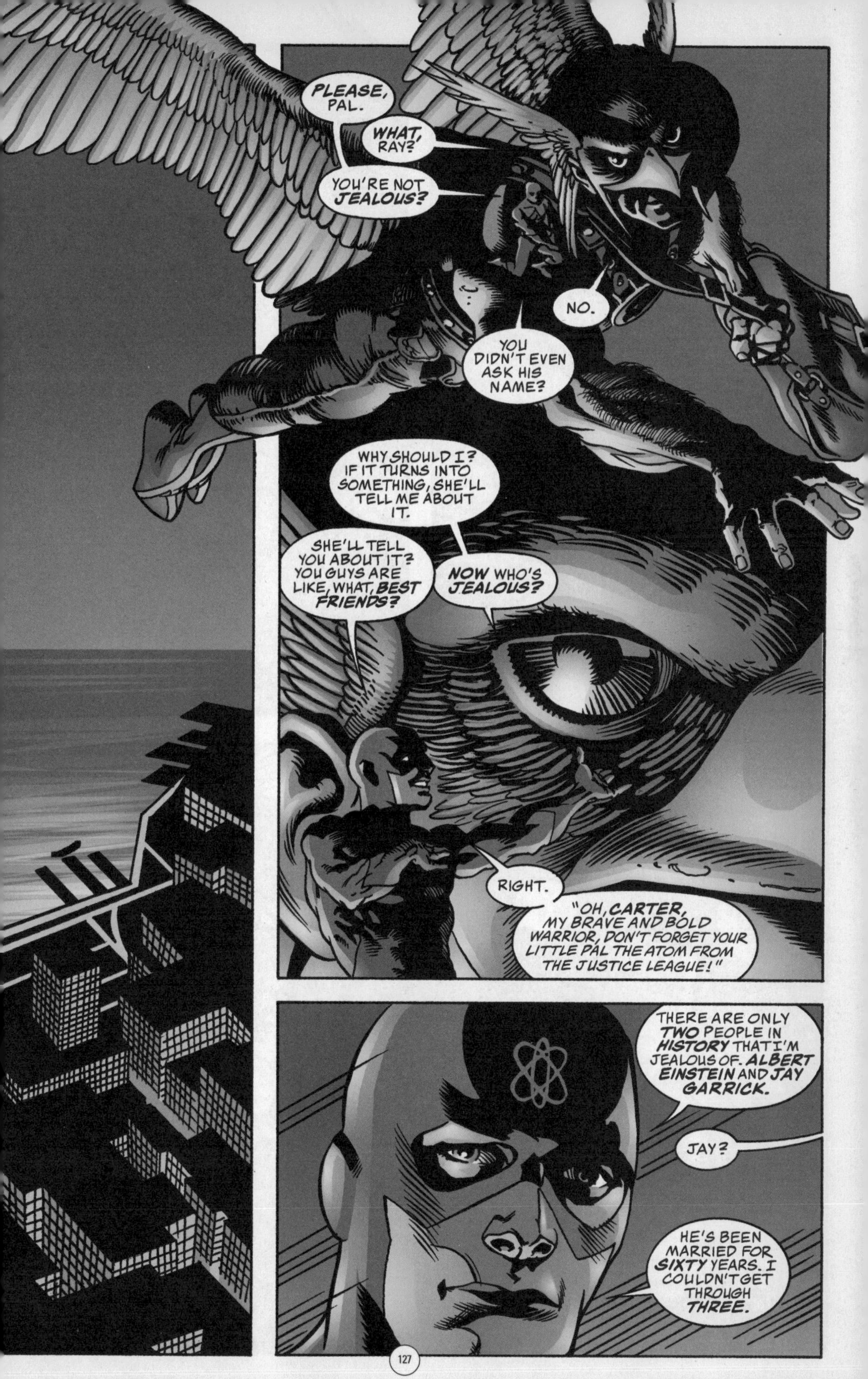

PLEASE, PAL.
WHAT, RAY?
YOU'RE NOT JEALOUS?
NO.
YOU DIDN'T EVEN ASK HIS NAME?
WHY SHOULD I? IF IT TURNS INTO SOMETHING, SHE'LL TELL ME ABOUT IT.
SHE'LL TELL YOU ABOUT IT? YOU GUYS ARE LIKE, WHAT, BEST FRIENDS?
NOW WHO'S JEALOUS?
RIGHT.
"OH, CARTER, MY BRAVE AND BOLD WARRIOR, DON'T FORGET YOUR LITTLE PAL THE ATOM FROM THE JUSTICE LEAGUE!"
THERE ARE ONLY TWO PEOPLE IN HISTORY THAT I'M JEALOUS OF. ALBERT EINSTEIN AND JAY GARRICK.
JAY?
HE'S BEEN MARRIED FOR SIXTY YEARS. I COULDN'T GET THROUGH THREE.

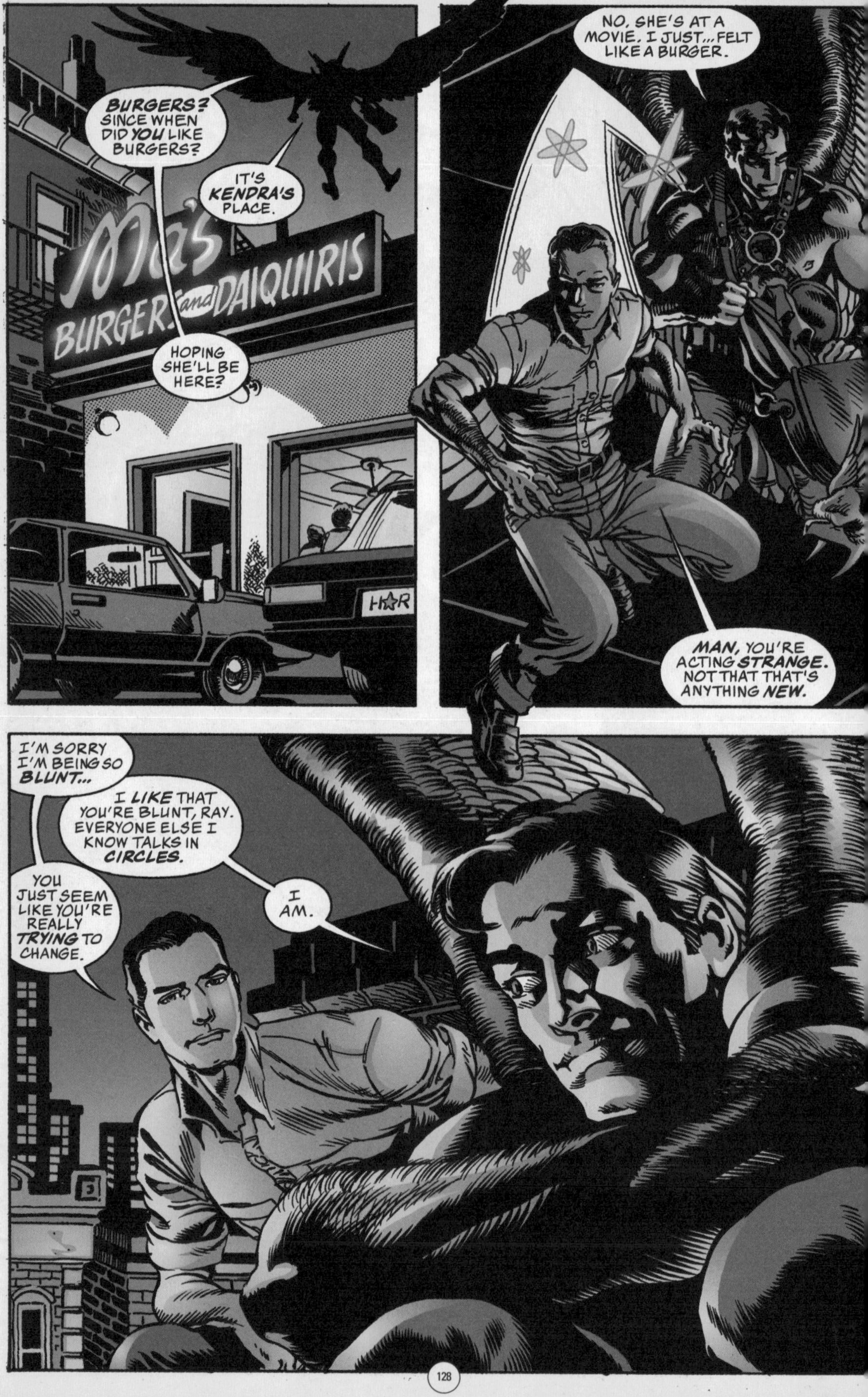
BURGERS? SINCE WHEN DID YOU LIKE BURGERS?
IT'S KENDRA'S PLACE.
HOPING SHE'LL BE HERE?
Ma's BURGERS and DAIQUIRIS
H★R
NO, SHE'S AT A MOVIE. I JUST... FELT LIKE A BURGER.
MAN, YOU'RE ACTING STRANGE. NOT THAT THAT'S ANYTHING NEW.
I'M SORRY I'M BEING SO BLUNT...
I LIKE THAT YOU'RE BLUNT, RAY. EVERYONE ELSE I KNOW TALKS IN CIRCLES.
YOU JUST SEEM LIKE YOU'RE REALLY TRYING TO CHANGE.
I AM.

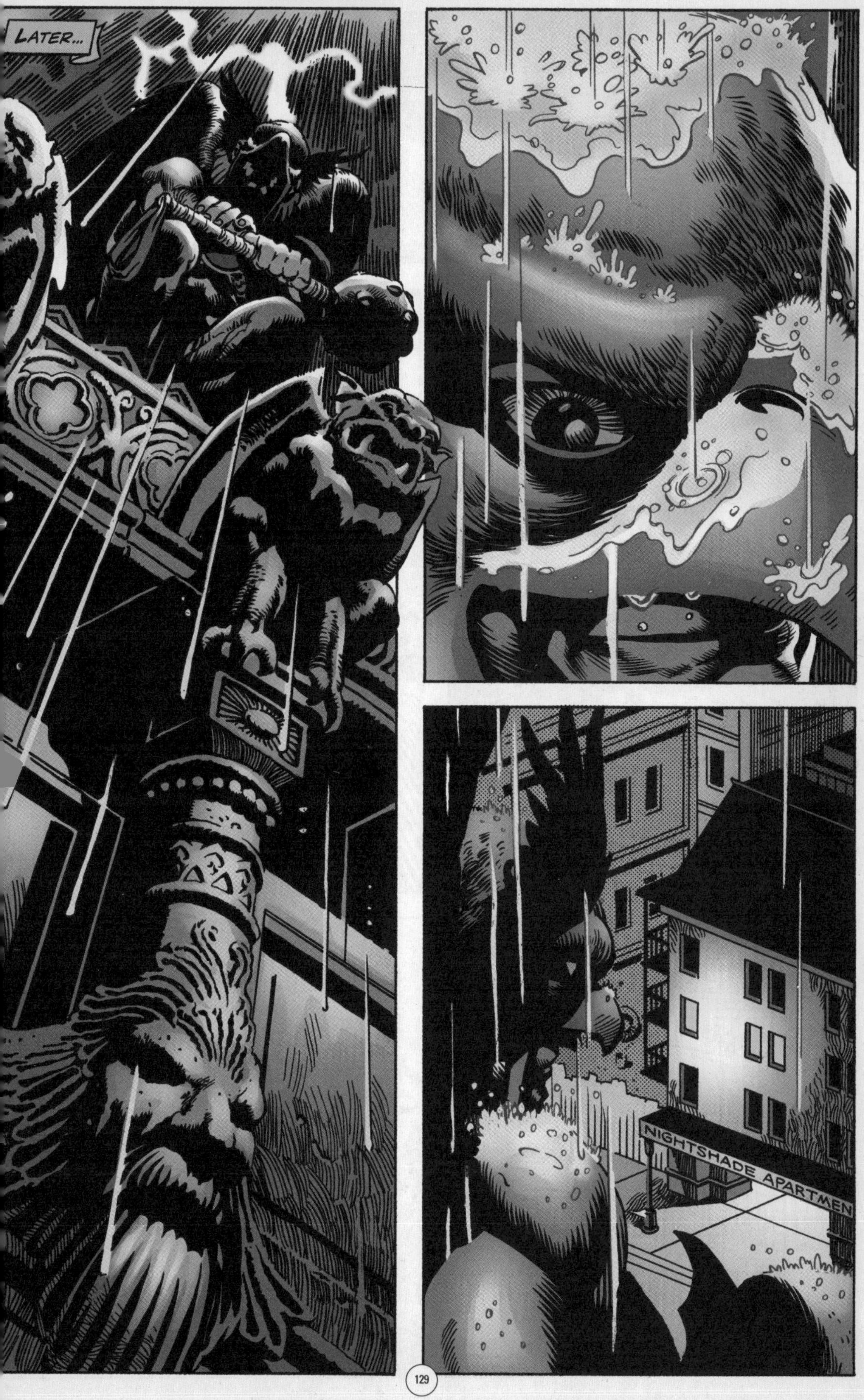
LATER...
NIGHTSHADE APARTMEN

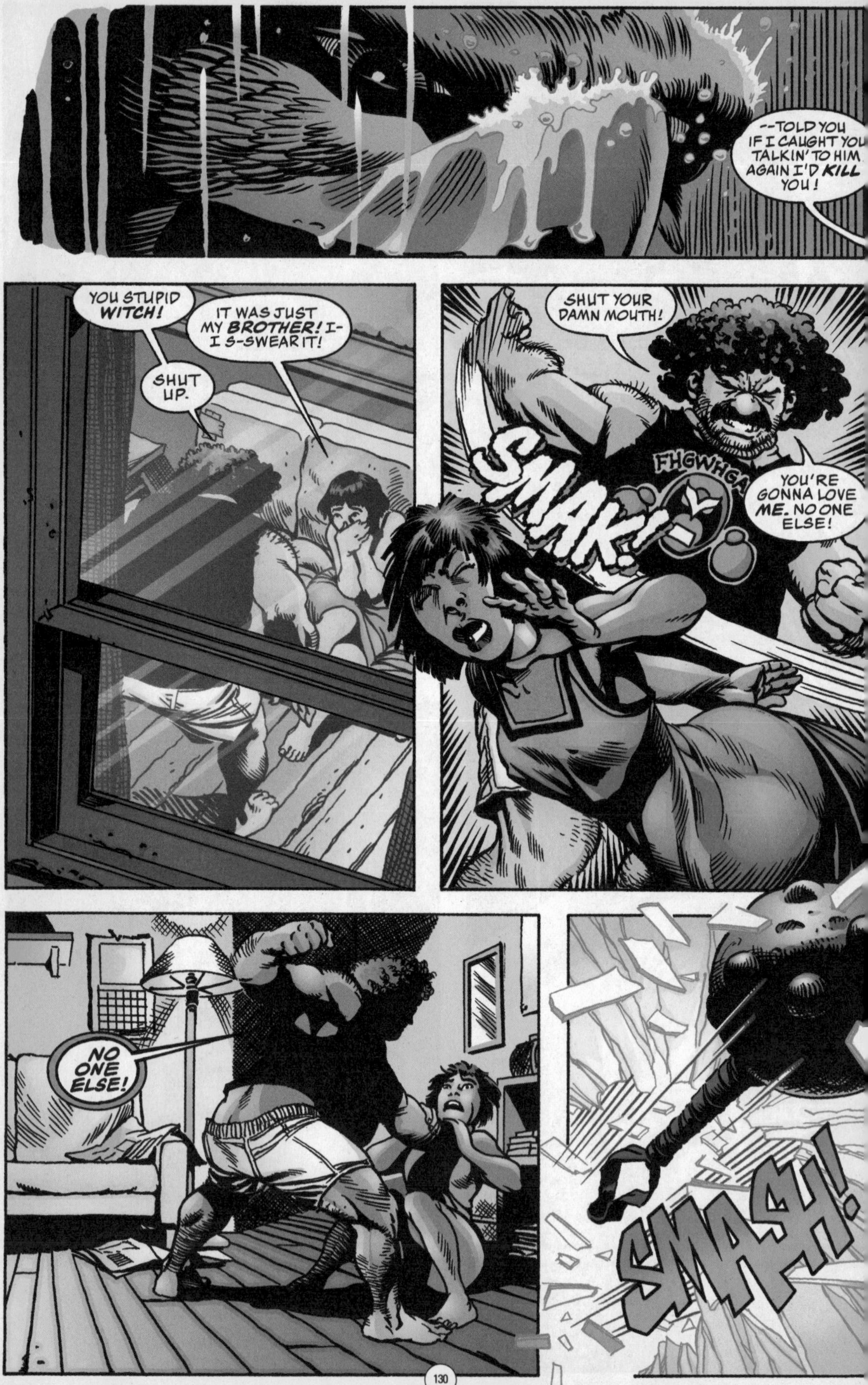
--TOLD YOU IF I CAUGHT YOU TALKIN' TO HIM AGAIN I'D KILL YOU!
YOU STUPID WITCH!
IT WAS JUST MY BROTHER! I-I S-SWEAR IT!
SHUT UP.
SHUT YOUR DAMN MOUTH!
SMAK!
FHGWHGA
YOU'RE GONNA LOVE ME. NO ONE ELSE!
NO ONE ELSE!
SMASH!

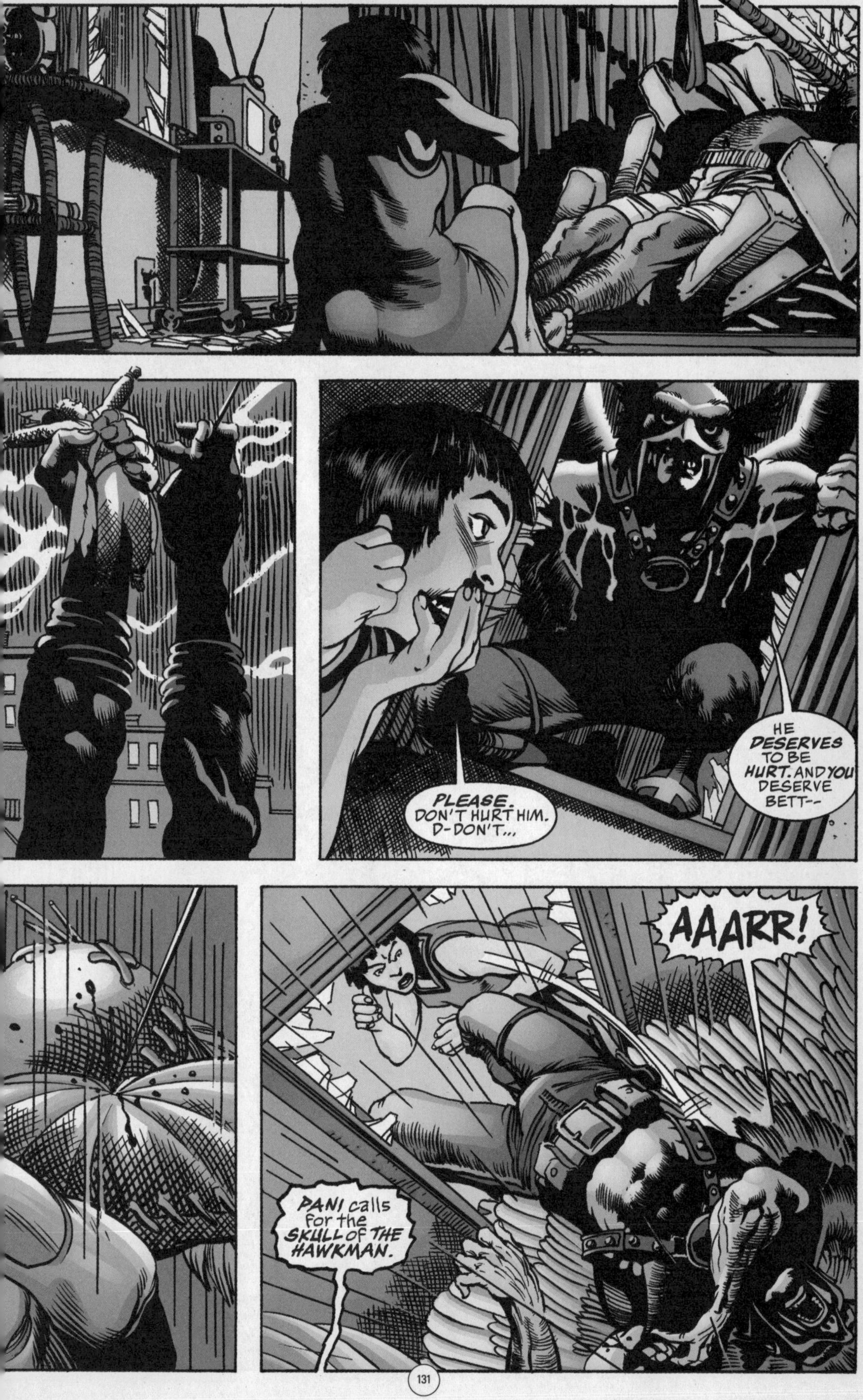
PLEASE. DON'T HURT HIM. D-DON'T...
HE DESERVES TO BE HURT. AND YOU DESERVE BETT--
AAARR!
PANI calls for the SKULL OF THE HAWKMAN.

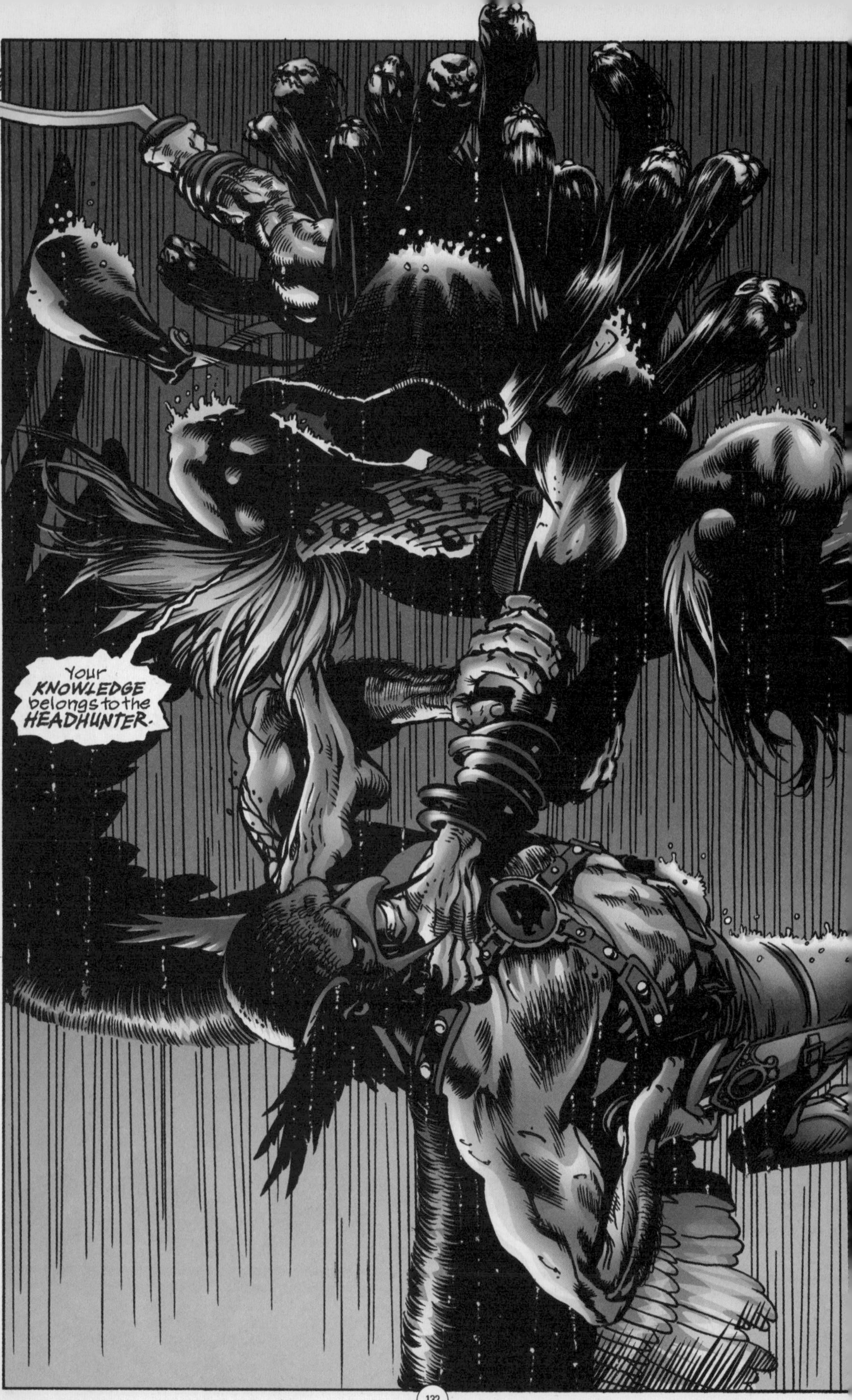
Your KNOWLEDGE belongs to the HEADHUNTER.

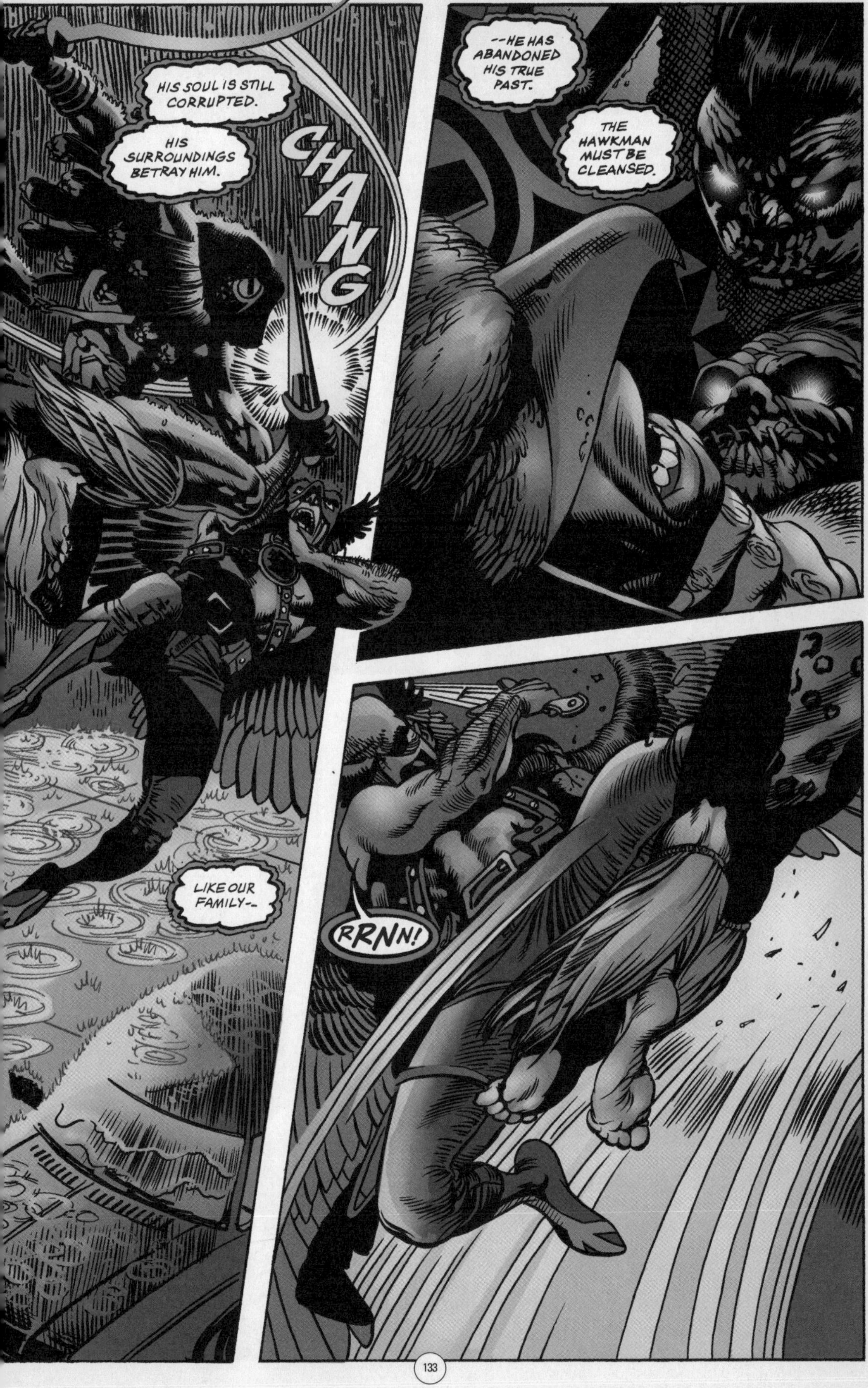

HIS SOUL IS STILL CORRUPTED.
HIS SURROUNDINGS BETRAY HIM.
CHANG
LIKE OUR FAMILY--
--HE HAS ABANDONED HIS TRUE PAST.
THE HAWKMAN MUST BE CLEANSED.
RRNN!

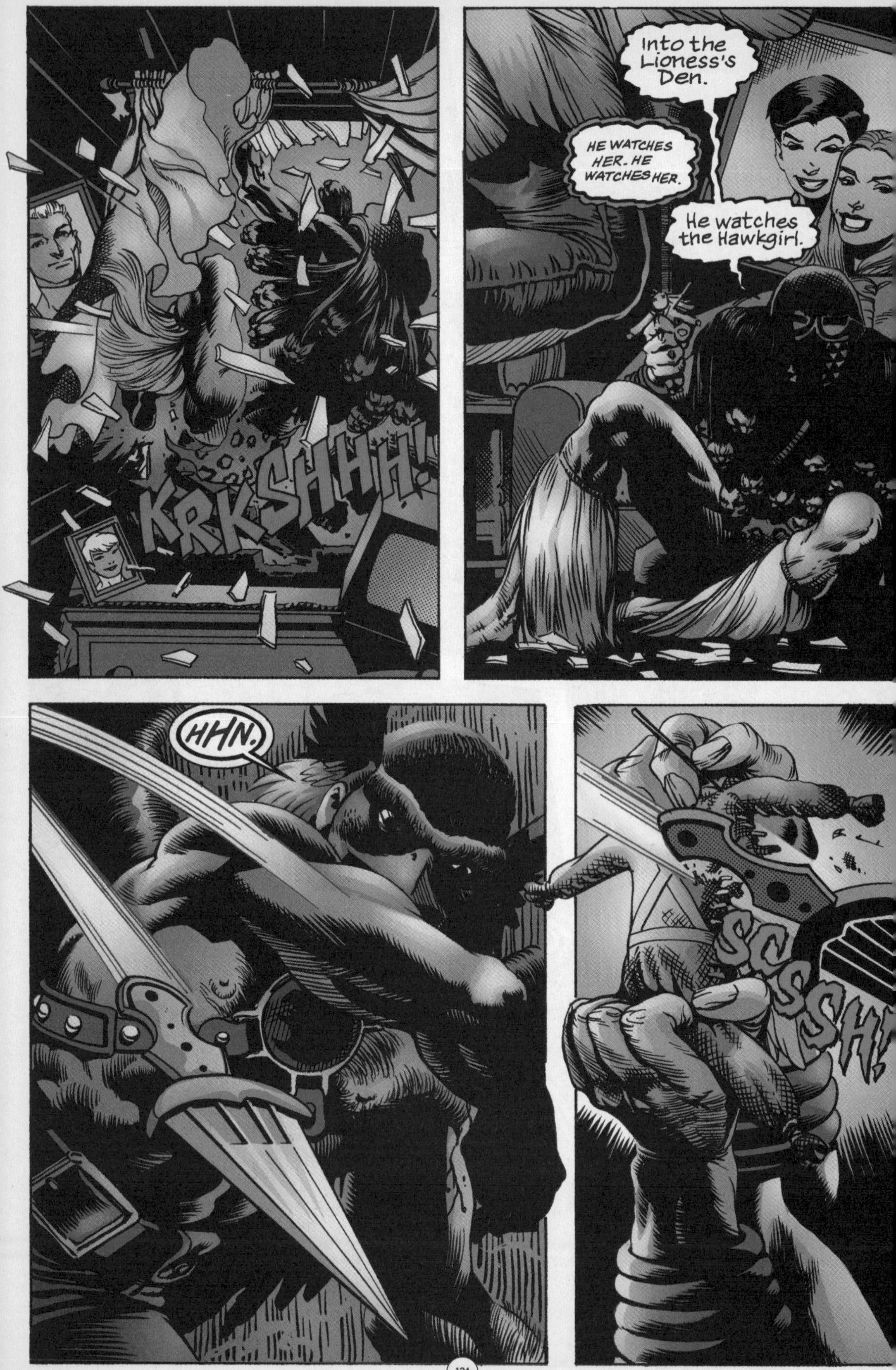
KRKSHHH!
Into the Lioness's Den.
HE WATCHES HER. HE WATCHES HER.
He watches the Hawkgirl.
HHN.
SCSSH!

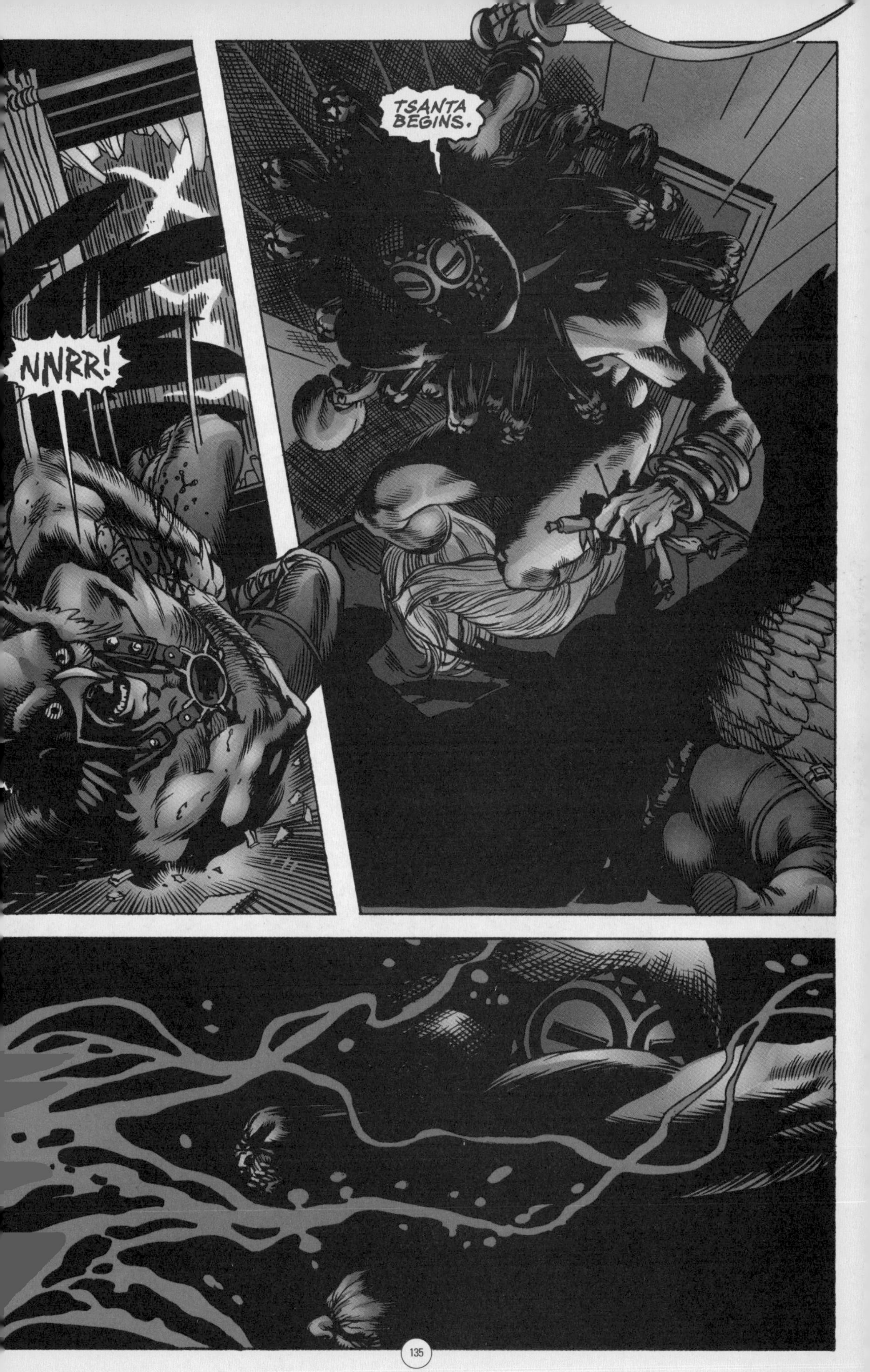
NNRR!
TSANTA BEGINS.

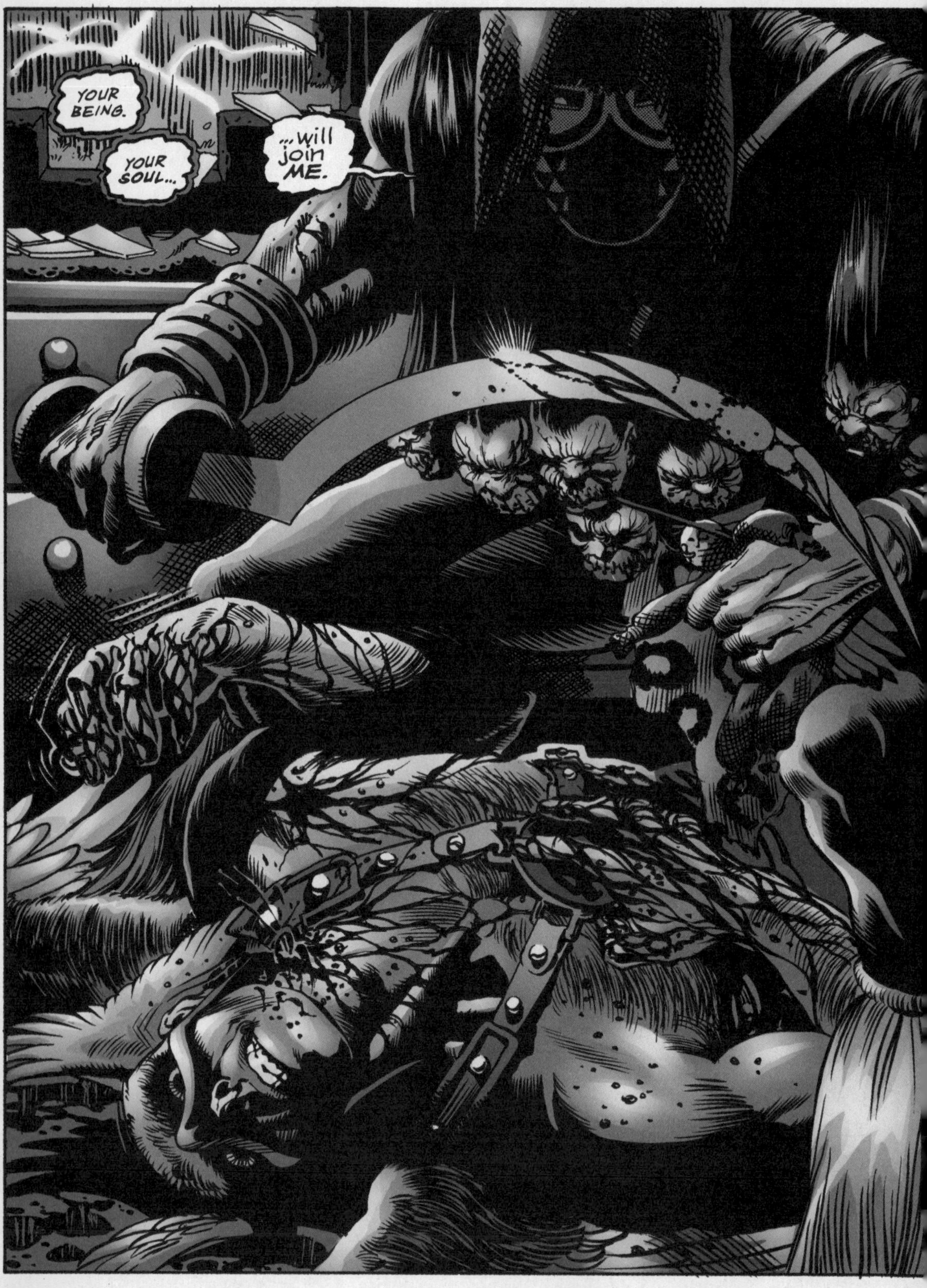
YOUR BEING.
YOUR SOUL...
...will join ME.

ST. ROCH
Filmhouse

"THE CAMERAMAN"
w/ BUSTER KEATON
"BEGGARS OF LIFE"
w/ LOUISE BROOKS

Le Maison de RUMEURS

ST. ROCH, LOUISIANA.

THAT WAS **HILARIOUS**.

I'M SURPRISED YOU OPTED TO GO SEE *THE CAMERAMAN*. YOU SAID LOUISE BROOKS IS ONE OF YOUR FAVORITE ACTRESSES.

SHE IS, MARK--

--BUT I'VE SEEN THAT FILM **ENOUGH**, AND I HAVEN'T LAUGHED LIKE THAT IN A **LONG** TIME.

MY GRANDFATHER USED TO ALWAYS BRING ME TO THE MOVIE THEATER WHENEVER WE WERE GOING THROUGH HARD TIMES. HE USED TO SAY--

--**LAUGHTER** HEALS ALL **WOUNDS**. LAUGHTER AND A SHOT OF **SCOTCH**.

'COURSE HE NEVER GAVE ME THE **SCOTCH**.

LAUGHTER AND SCOTCH HEAL *ALL* WOUNDS?

WELL--

--I'M SURE THEY **HELP**.

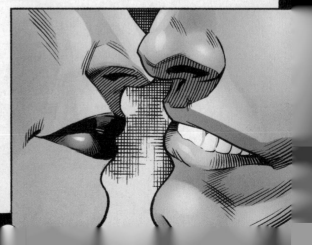

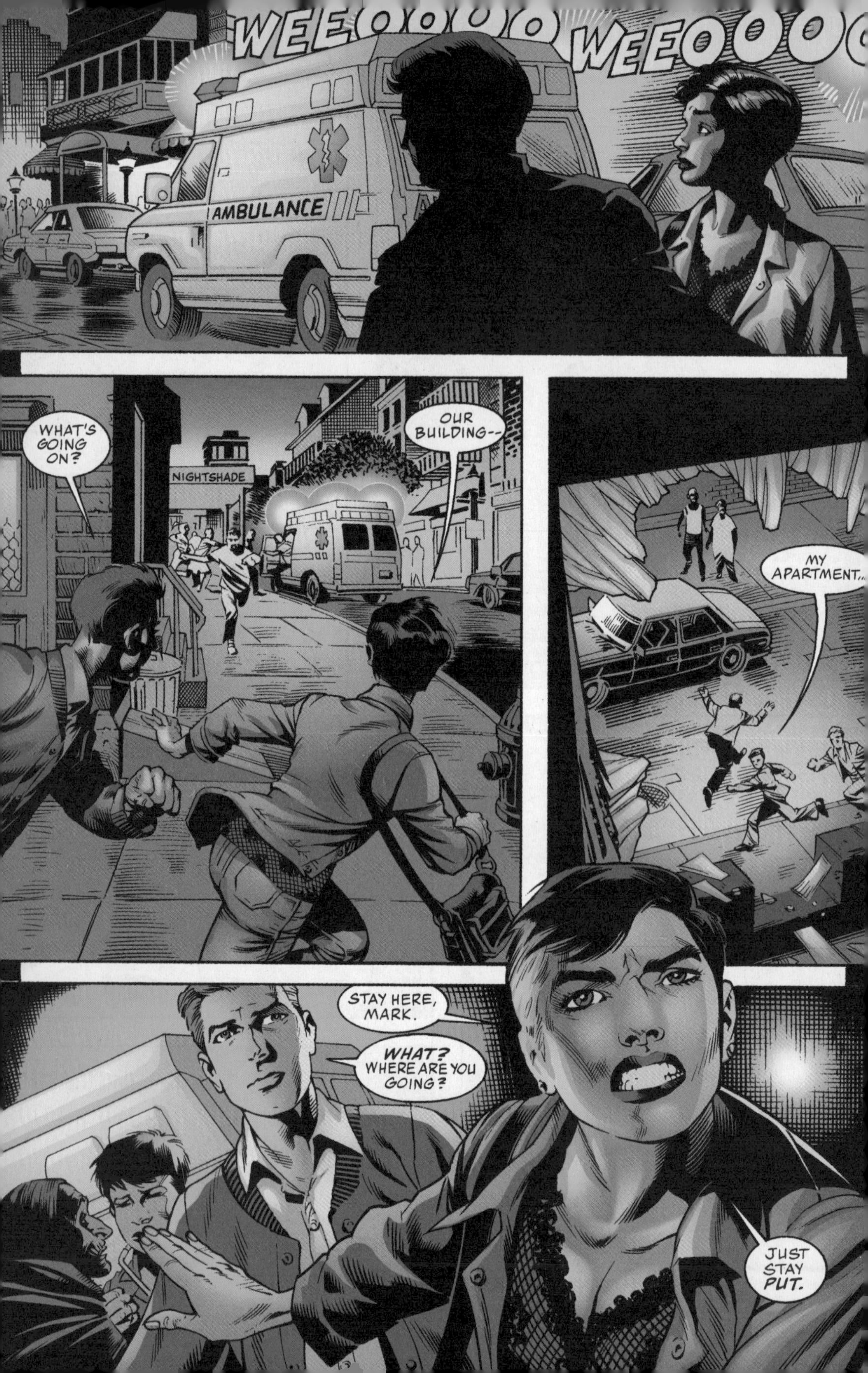
WEEOOOOO WEEOOOO
AMBULANCE
WHAT'S GOING ON?
NIGHTSHADE
OUR BUILDING--
MY APARTMENT...
STAY HERE, MARK.
WHAT? WHERE ARE YOU GOING?
JUST STAY PUT.

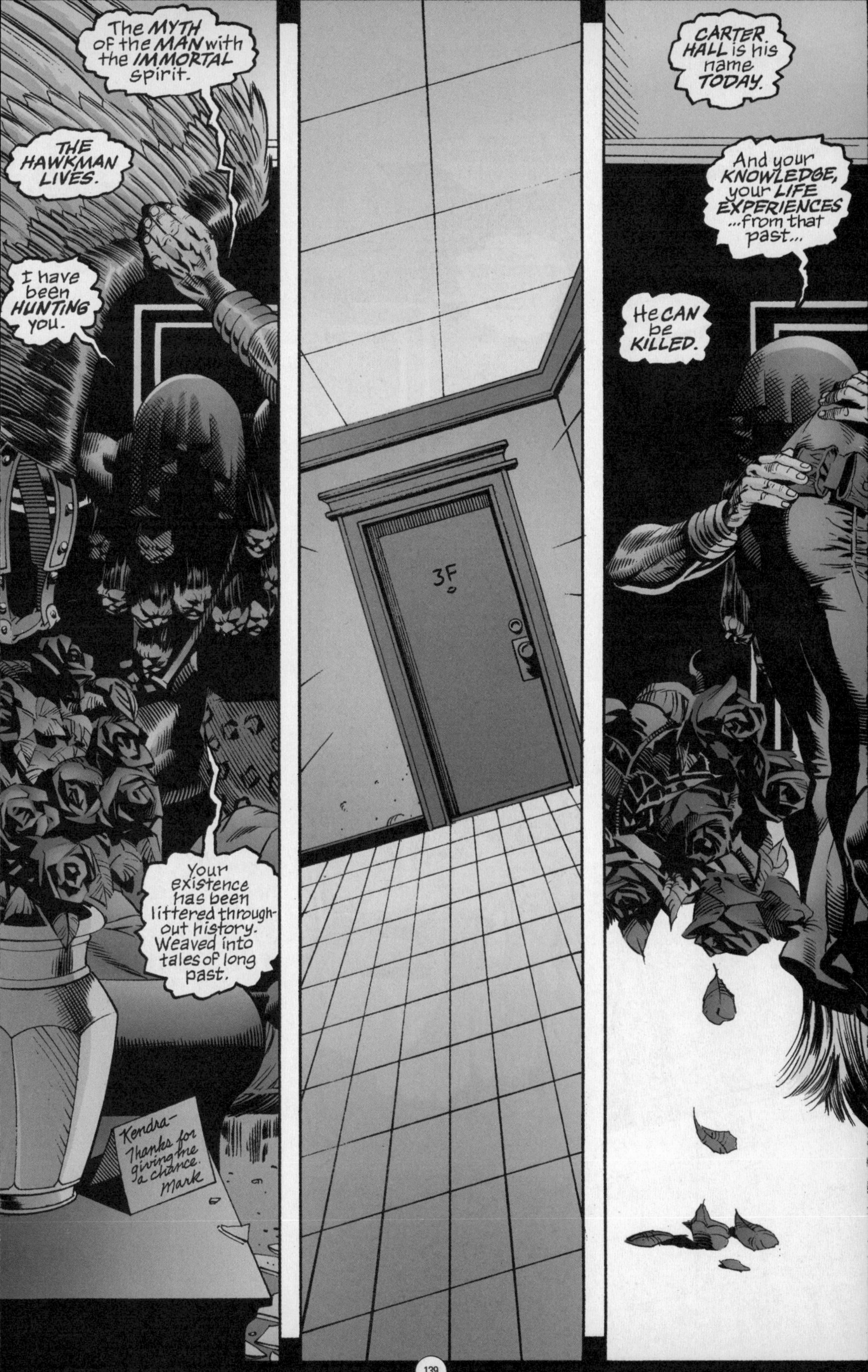
The MYTH of the MAN with the IMMORTAL spirit.
THE HAWKMAN LIVES.
I have been HUNTING you.
Your existence has been littered through-out history. Weaved into tales of long past.
Kendra- Thanks for giving me a chance. Mark
3F
CARTER HALL is his name TODAY.
And your KNOWLEDGE, your LIFE EXPERIENCES ...from that past...
He CAN be KILLED.

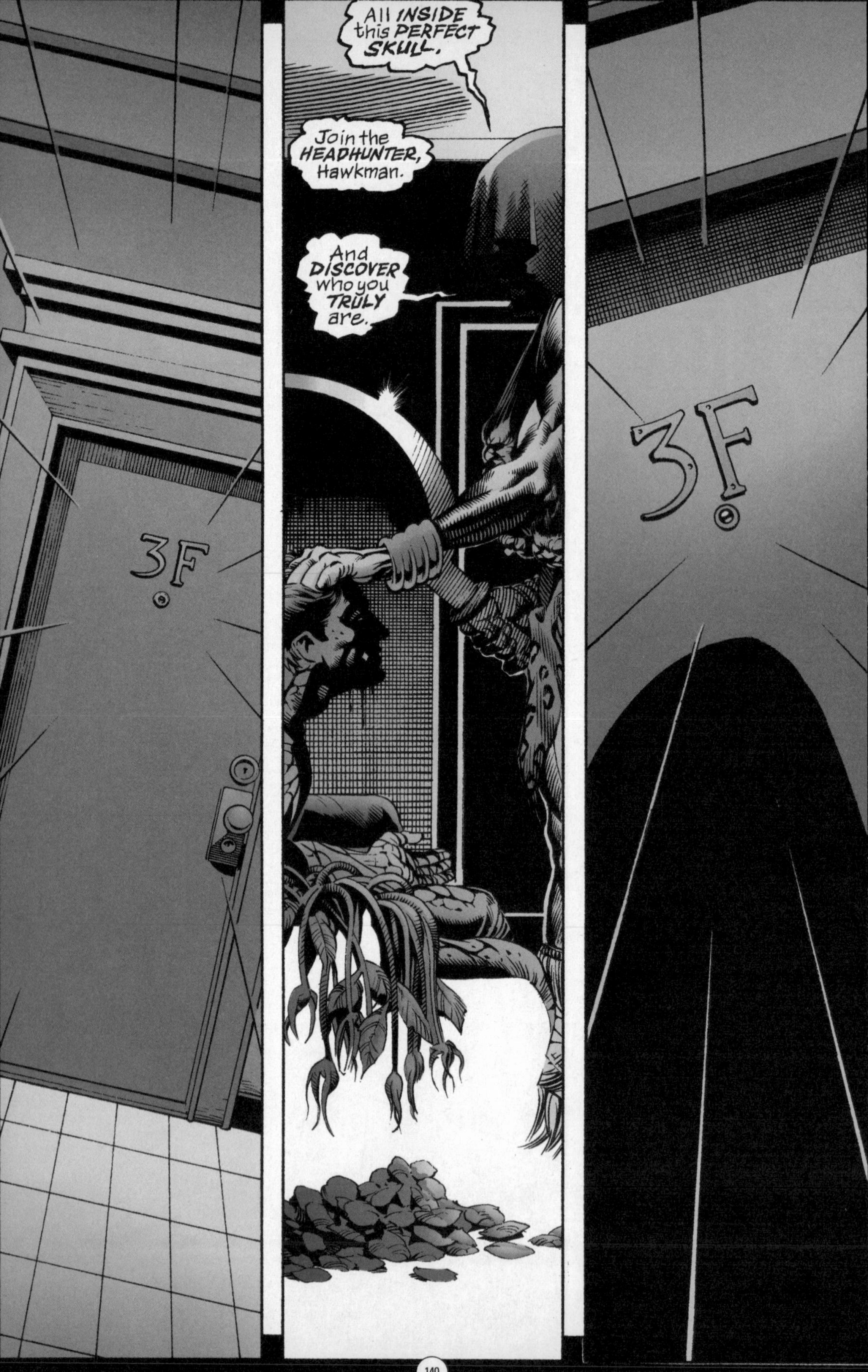
All INSIDE this PERFECT SKULL.
Join the HEADHUNTER, Hawkman.
And DISCOVER who you TRULY are.
3F
3F

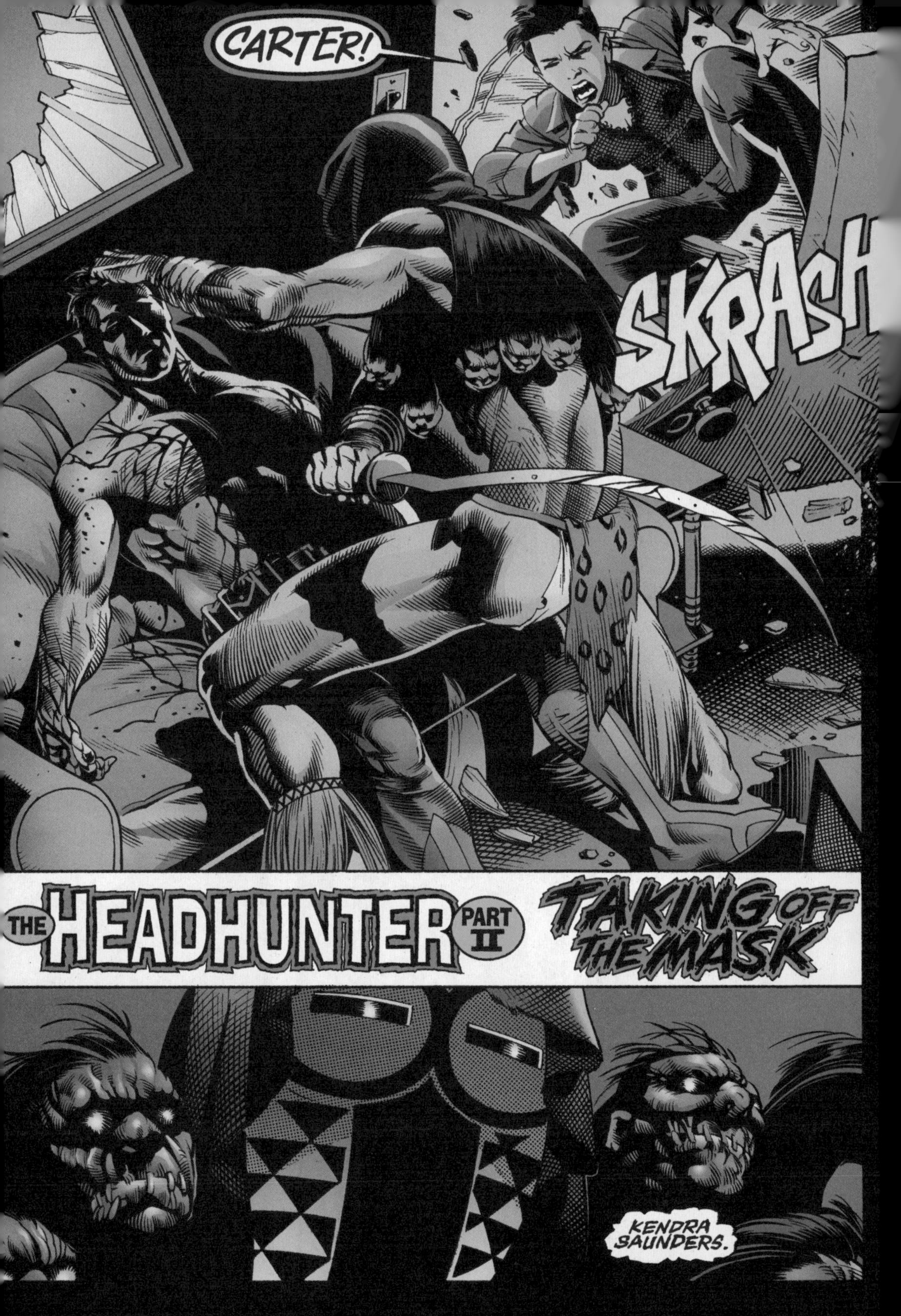
CARTER!
SKRASH
THE HEADHUNTER PART II
TAKING OFF THE MASK
KENDRA SAUNDERS.

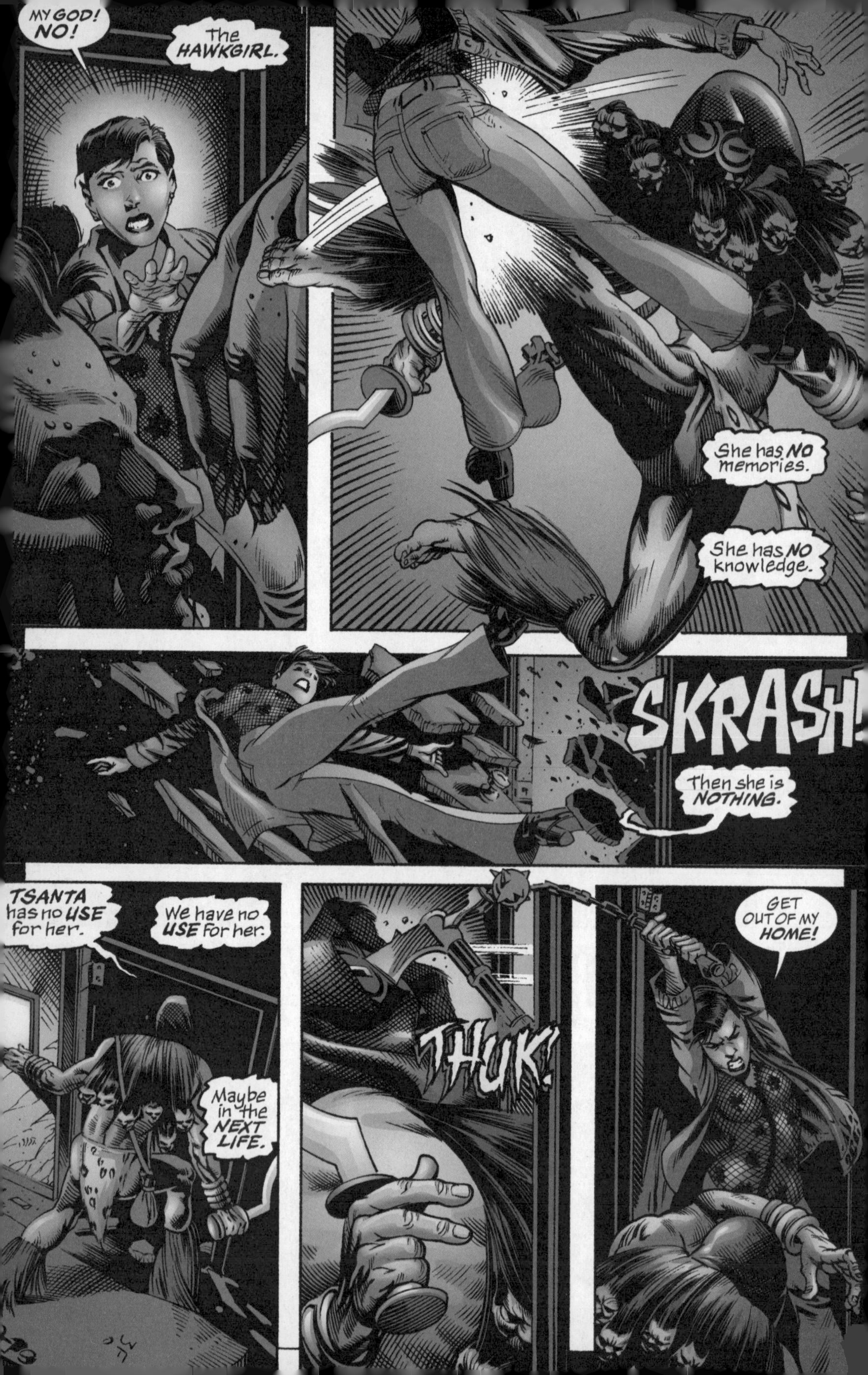
MY GOD! NO!
The HAWKGIRL.
She has NO memories.
She has NO knowledge.
SKRASH!
Then she is NOTHING.
TSANTA has no USE for her.
We have no USE for her.
Maybe in the NEXT LIFE.
THUK!
GET OUT OF MY HOME!

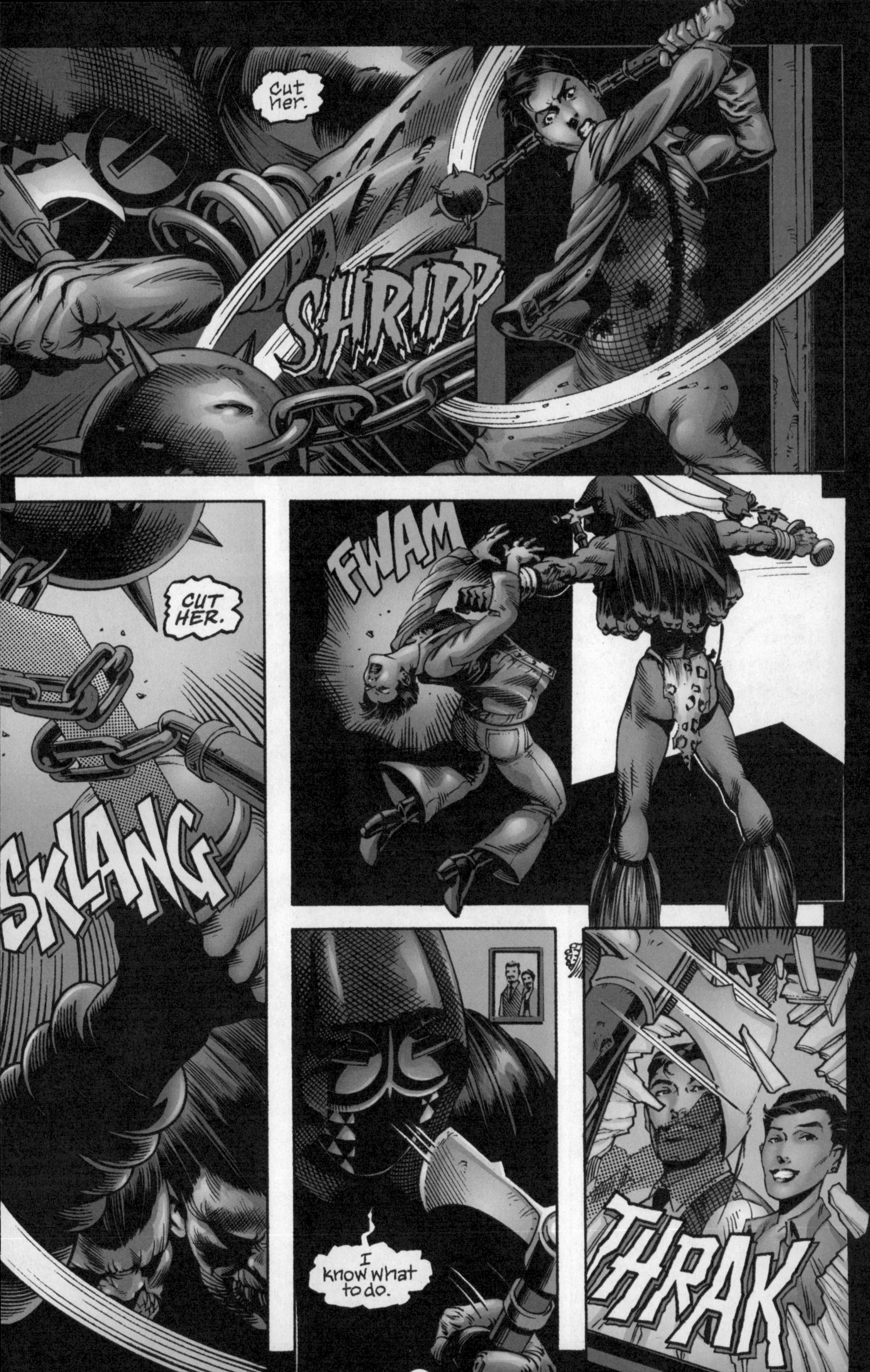
Cut her.
SHRIPP
CUT HER.
SKLANG
FWAM
I know what to do.
THRAK

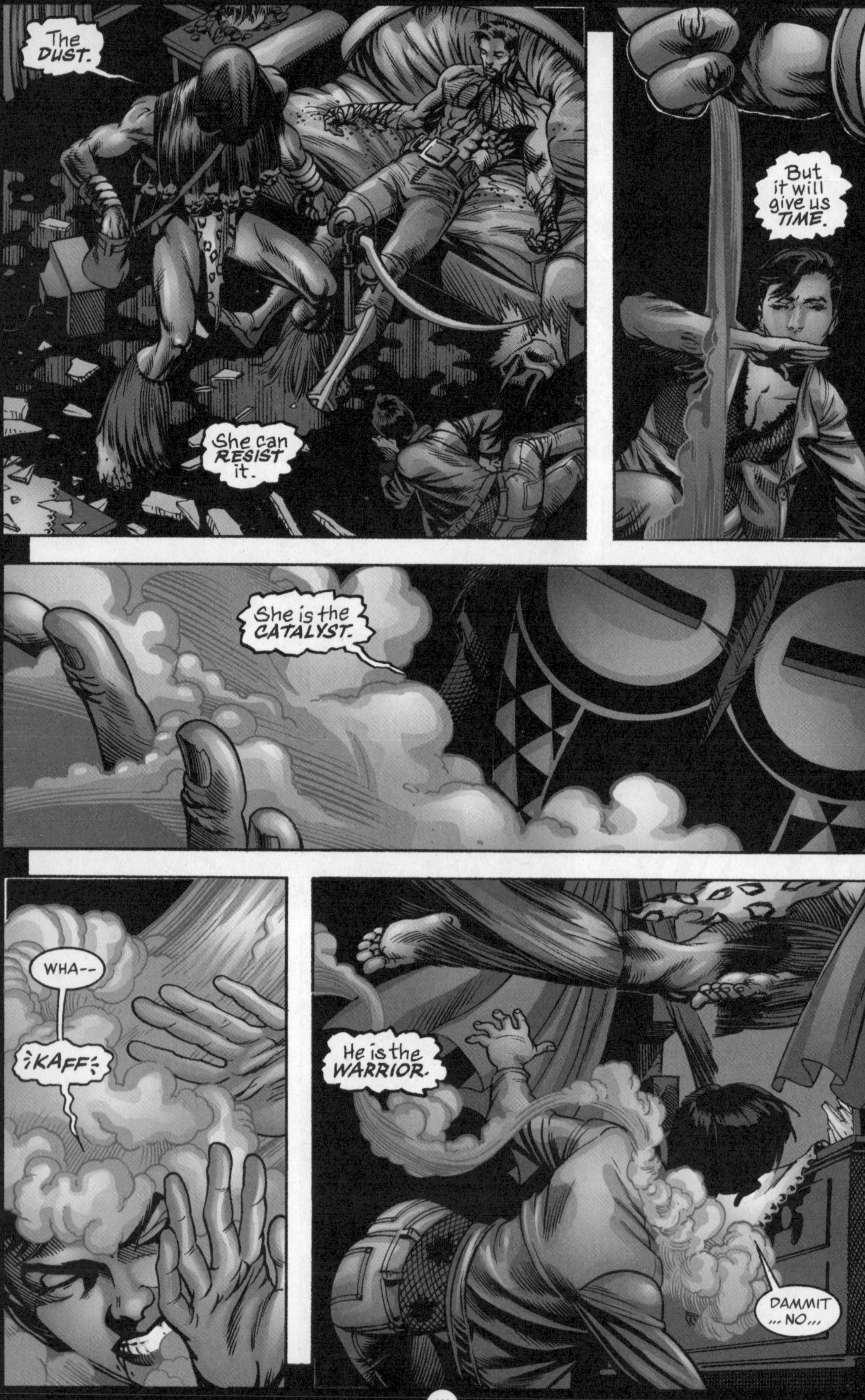
The DUST.
She can RESIST it.
But it will give us TIME.
She is the CATALYST.
WHA--
KAFF
He is the WARRIOR.
DAMMIT ... NO...

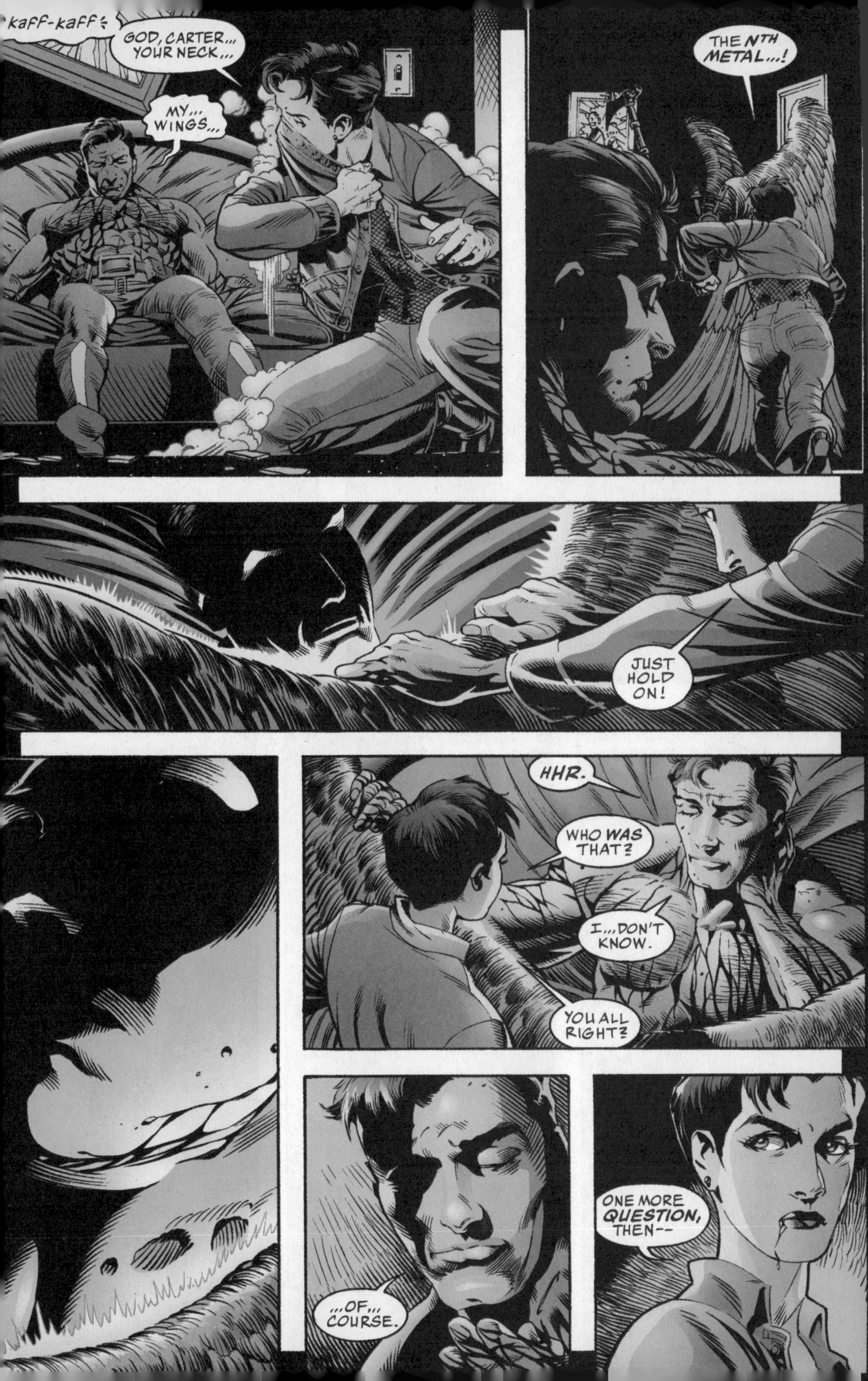
kaff-kaff
GOD, CARTER... YOUR NECK...
MY... WINGS...
THE NTH METAL...!
JUST HOLD ON!
HHR.
WHO WAS THAT?
I... DON'T KNOW.
YOU ALL RIGHT?
...OF... COURSE.
ONE MORE QUESTION, THEN--

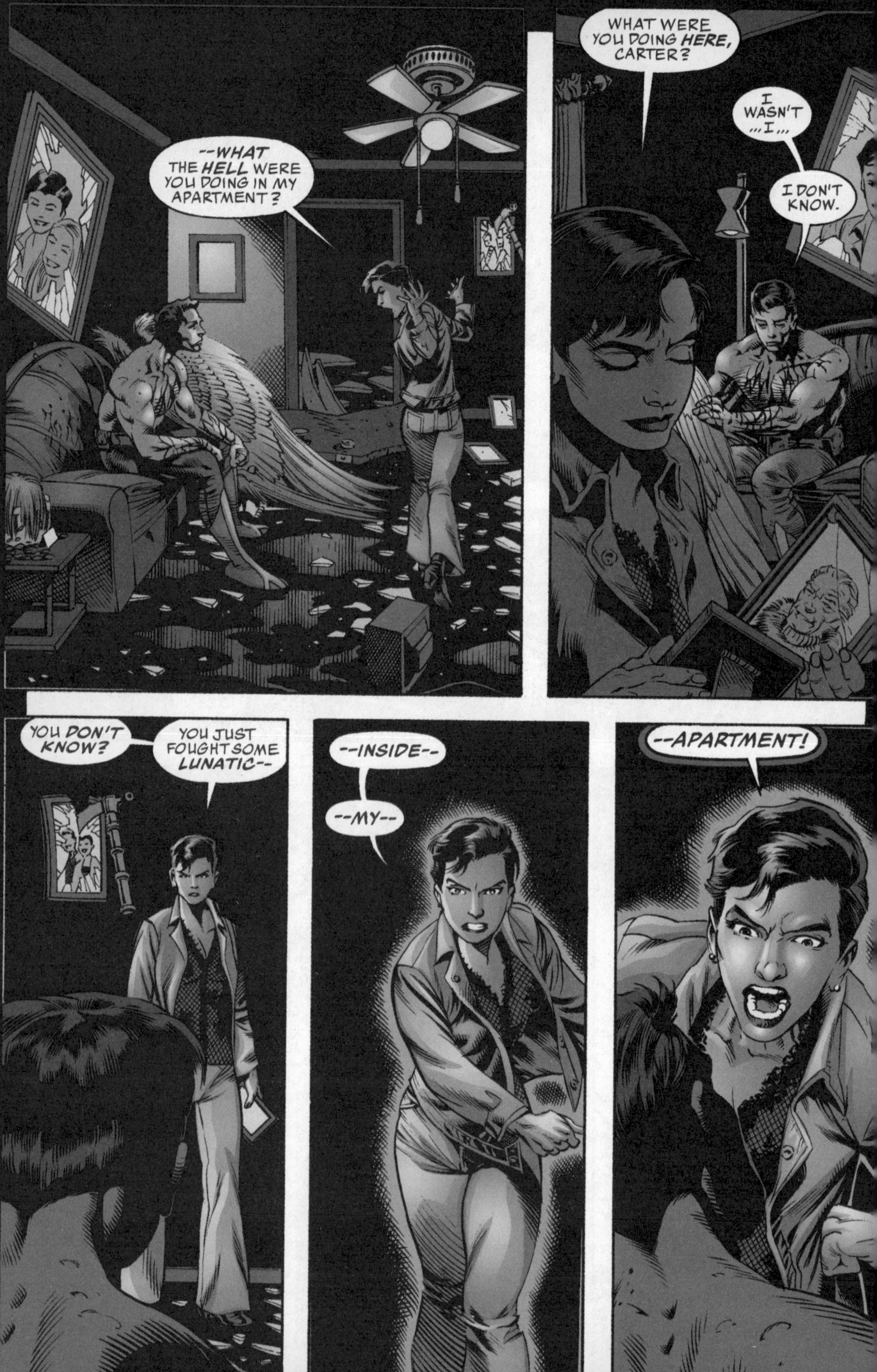
--WHAT THE HELL WERE YOU DOING IN MY APARTMENT?
WHAT WERE YOU DOING HERE, CARTER?
I WASN'T ...I...
I DON'T KNOW.
YOU DON'T KNOW?
YOU JUST FOUGHT SOME LUNATIC--
--INSIDE--
--MY--
--APARTMENT!

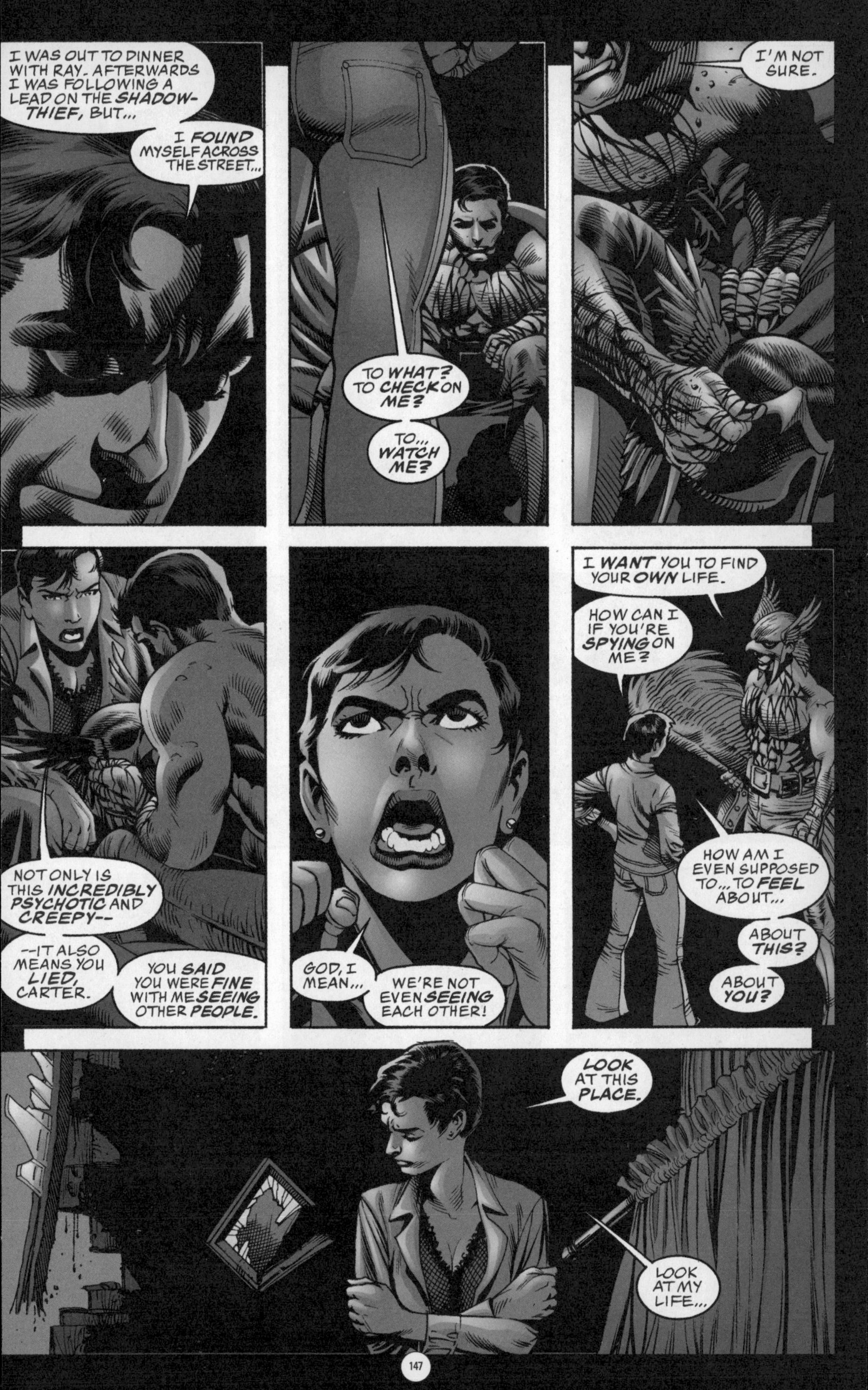
I WAS OUT TO DINNER WITH RAY. AFTERWARDS I WAS FOLLOWING A LEAD ON THE SHADOW-THIEF, BUT...
I FOUND MYSELF ACROSS THE STREET...
TO WHAT? TO CHECK ON ME?
TO... WATCH ME?
I'M NOT SURE.
NOT ONLY IS THIS INCREDIBLY PSYCHOTIC AND CREEPY--
--IT ALSO MEANS YOU LIED, CARTER.
YOU SAID YOU WERE FINE WITH ME SEEING OTHER PEOPLE.
GOD, I MEAN...
WE'RE NOT EVEN SEEING EACH OTHER!
I WANT YOU TO FIND YOUR OWN LIFE.
HOW CAN I IF YOU'RE SPYING ON ME?
HOW AM I EVEN SUPPOSED TO... TO FEEL ABOUT...
ABOUT THIS?
ABOUT YOU?
LOOK AT THIS PLACE.
LOOK AT MY LIFE...

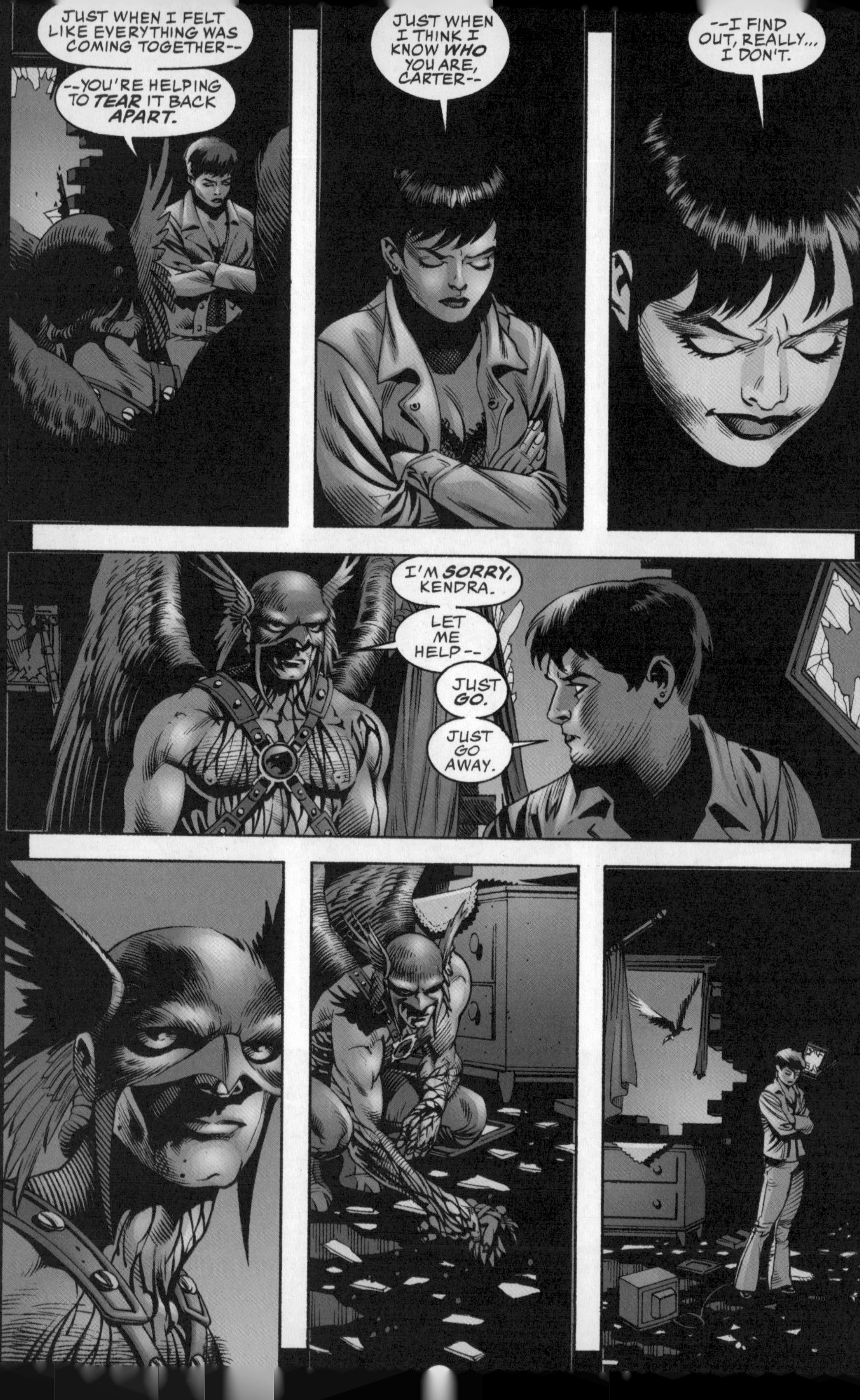
JUST WHEN I FELT LIKE EVERYTHING WAS COMING TOGETHER--
--YOU'RE HELPING TO TEAR IT BACK APART.
JUST WHEN I THINK I KNOW WHO YOU ARE, CARTER--
--I FIND OUT, REALLY... I DON'T.
I'M SORRY, KENDRA.
LET ME HELP--
JUST GO.
JUST GO AWAY.

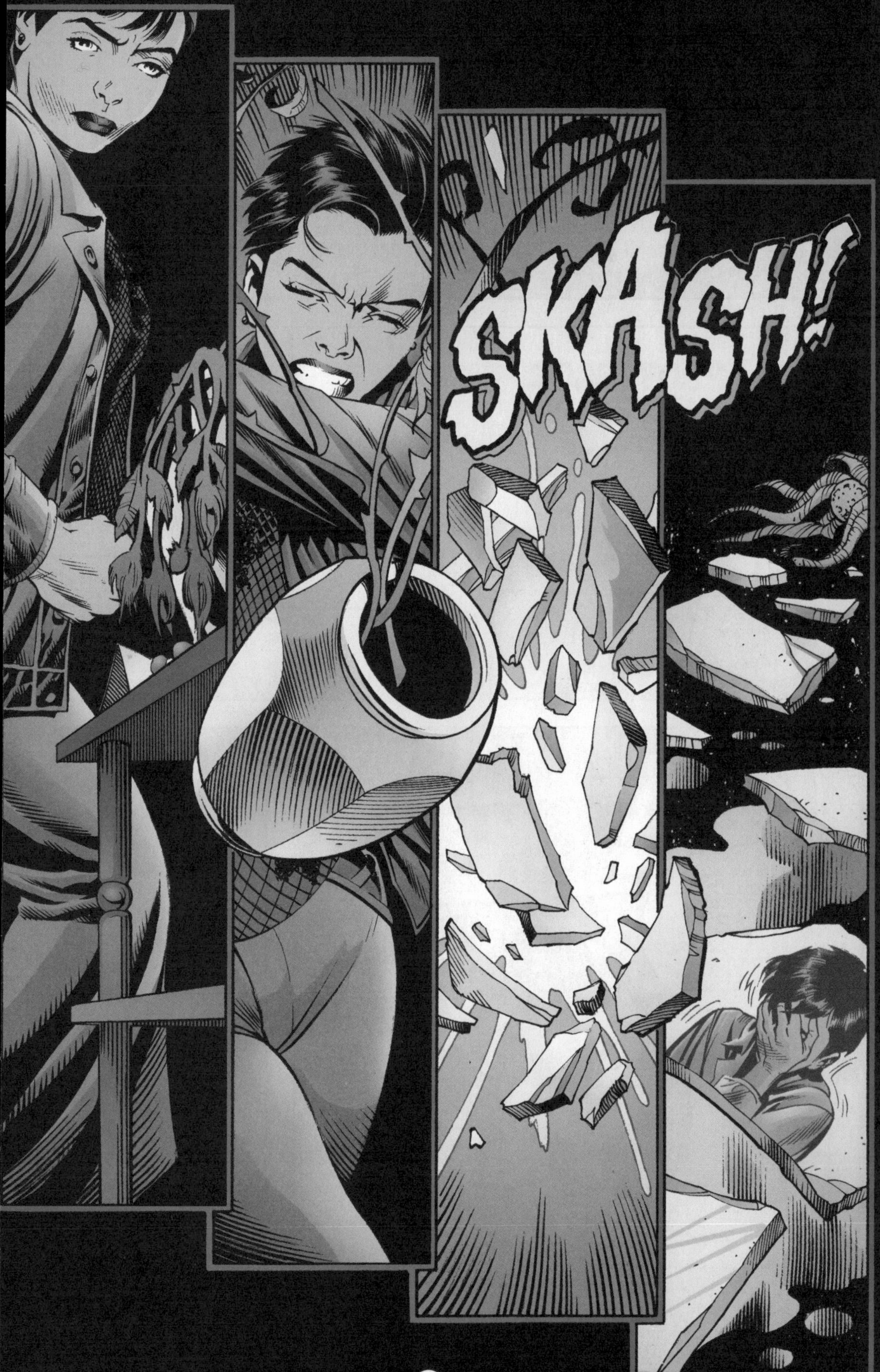
SKASH!

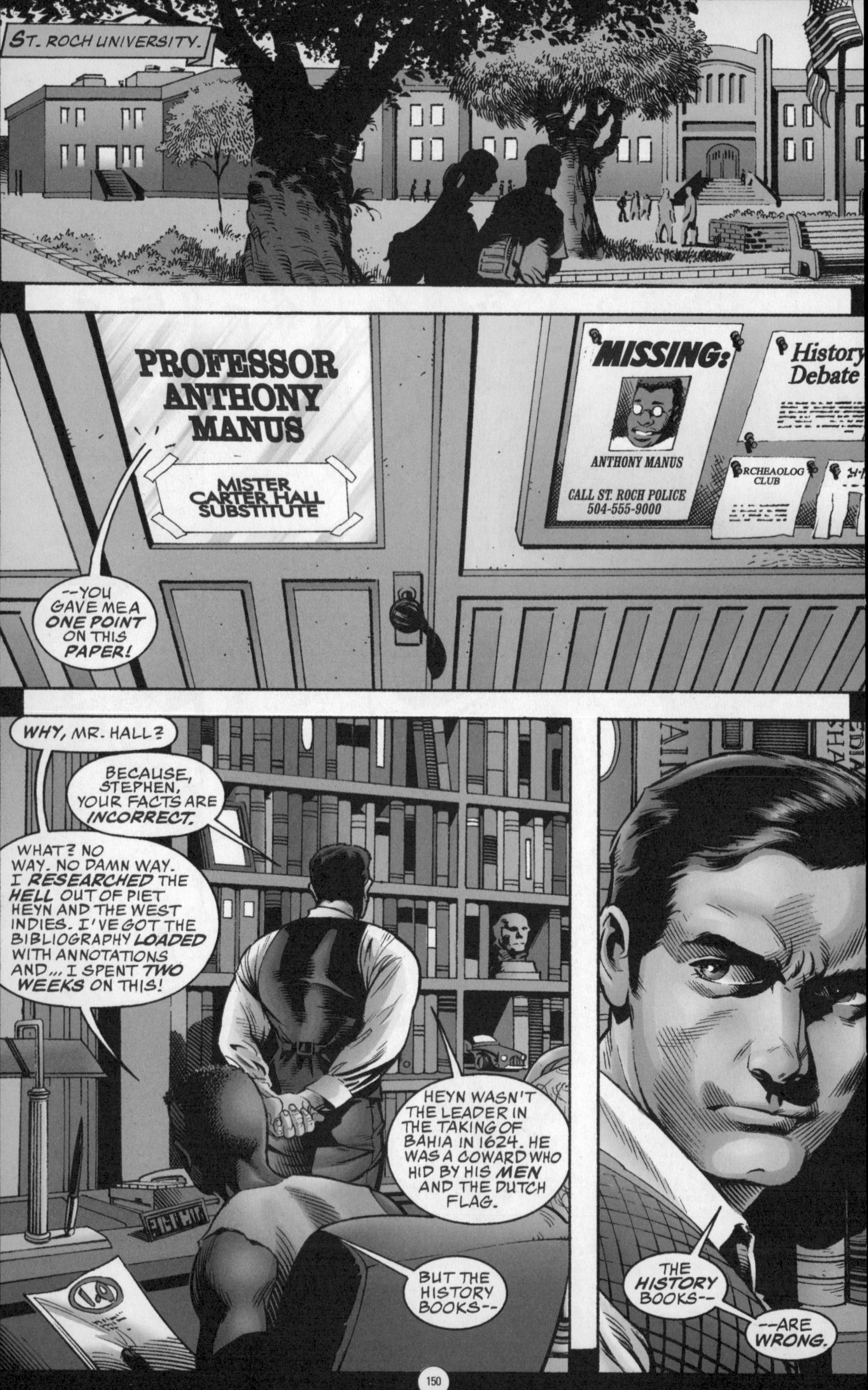

ST. ROCH UNIVERSITY.
PROFESSOR ANTHONY MANUS
MISTER CARTER HALL SUBSTITUTE
MISSING:
ANTHONY MANUS
CALL ST. ROCH POLICE 504-555-9000
History Debate
RCHEAOLOG CLUB
--YOU GAVE ME A ONE POINT ON THIS PAPER!
WHY, MR. HALL?
BECAUSE, STEPHEN, YOUR FACTS ARE INCORRECT.
WHAT? NO WAY. NO DAMN WAY. I RESEARCHED THE HELL OUT OF PIET HEYN AND THE WEST INDIES. I'VE GOT THE BIBLIOGRAPHY LOADED WITH ANNOTATIONS AND... I SPENT TWO WEEKS ON THIS!
HEYN WASN'T THE LEADER IN THE TAKING OF BAHIA IN 1624. HE WAS A COWARD WHO HID BY HIS MEN AND THE DUTCH FLAG.
BUT THE HISTORY BOOKS--
THE HISTORY BOOKS--
--ARE WRONG.

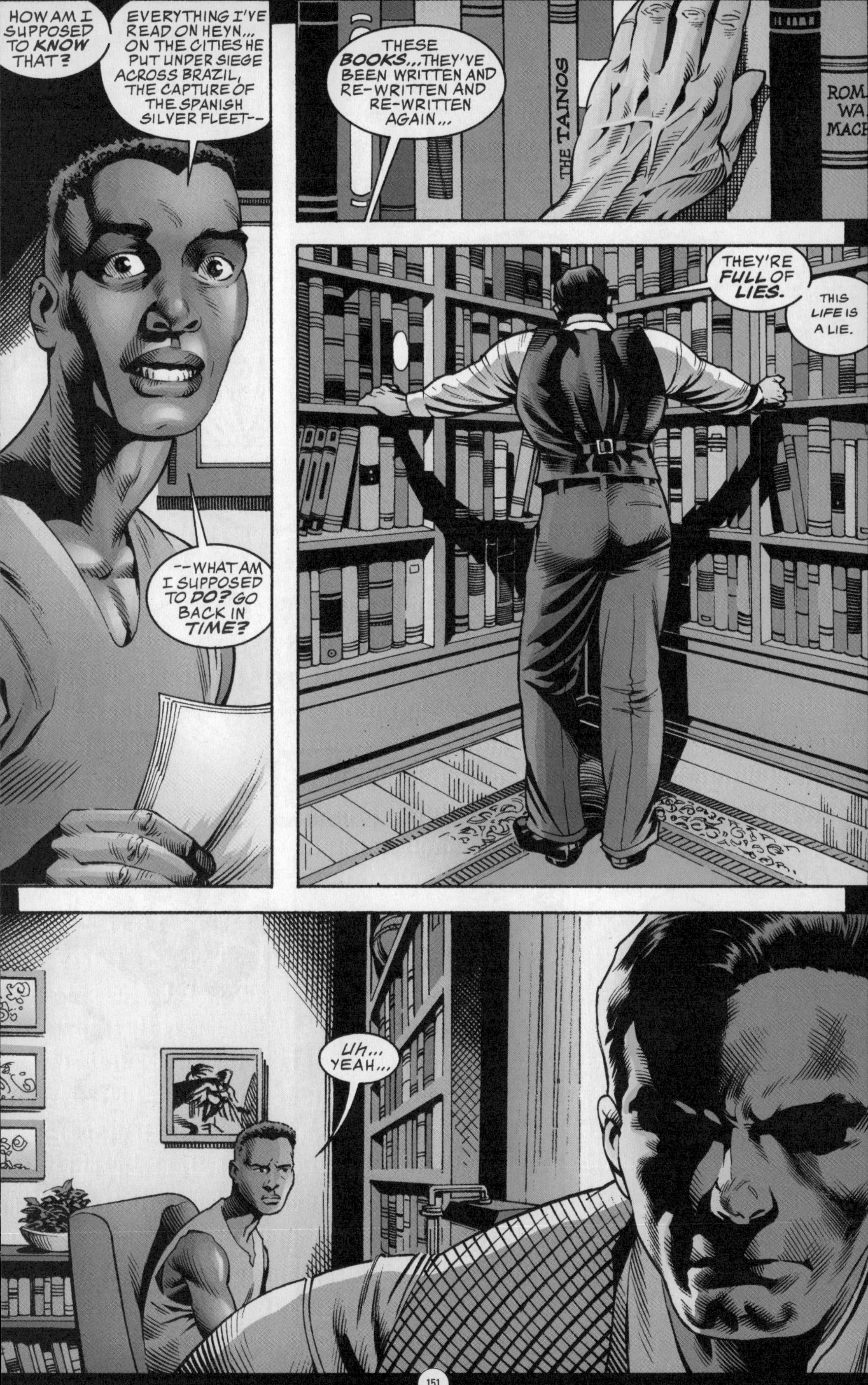

HOW AM I SUPPOSED TO KNOW THAT?
EVERYTHING I'VE READ ON HEYN... ON THE CITIES HE PUT UNDER SIEGE ACROSS BRAZIL, THE CAPTURE OF THE SPANISH SILVER FLEET--
--WHAT AM I SUPPOSED TO DO? GO BACK IN TIME?
THESE BOOKS... THEY'VE BEEN WRITTEN AND RE-WRITTEN AND RE-WRITTEN AGAIN...
THE TAINOS
THEY'RE FULL OF LIES.
THIS LIFE IS A LIE.
UH... YEAH...

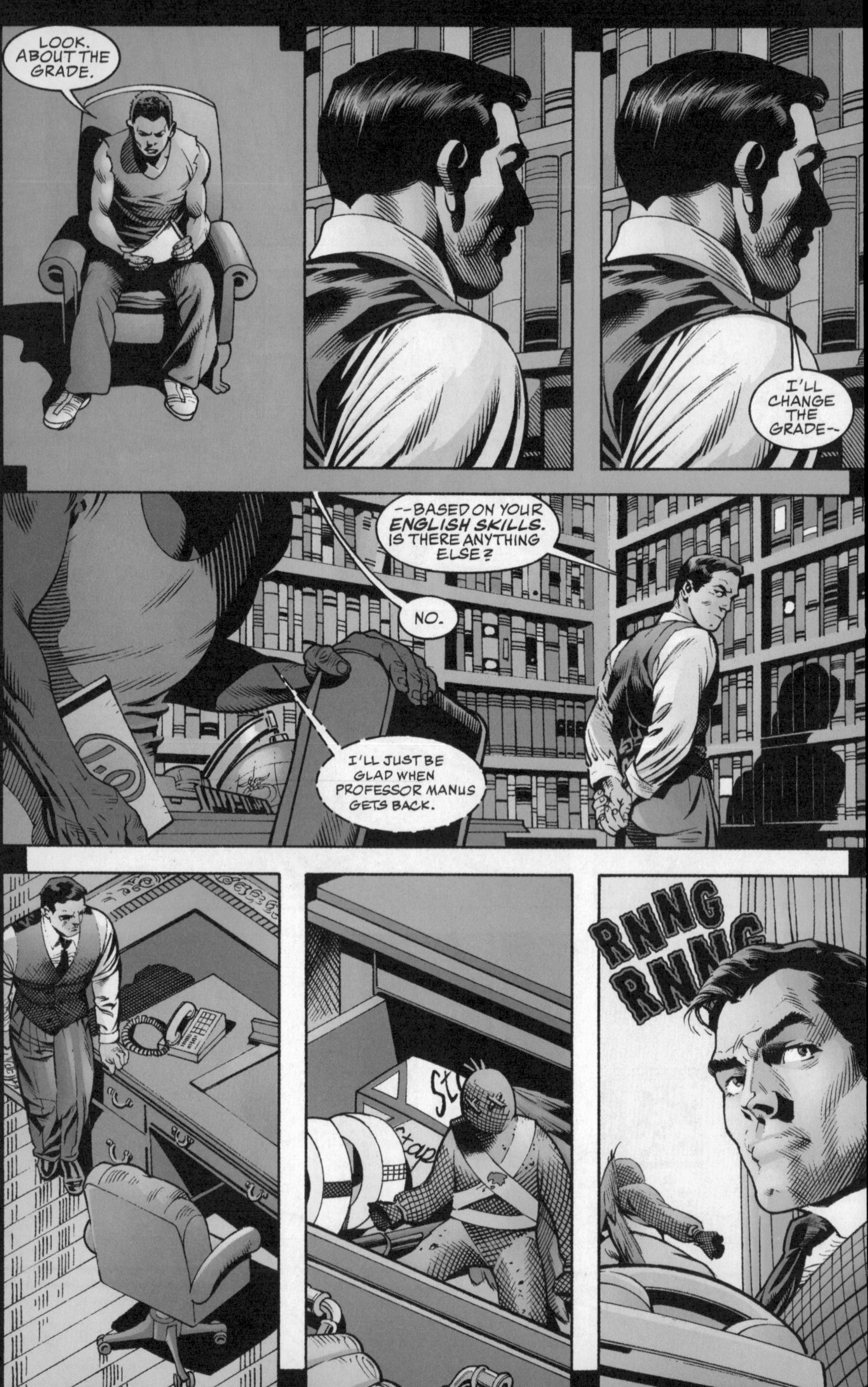
LOOK. ABOUT THE GRADE.
I'LL CHANGE THE GRADE--
--BASED ON YOUR ENGLISH SKILLS. IS THERE ANYTHING ELSE?
NO.
I'LL JUST BE GLAD WHEN PROFESSOR MANUS GETS BACK.
RNNG
RNNG

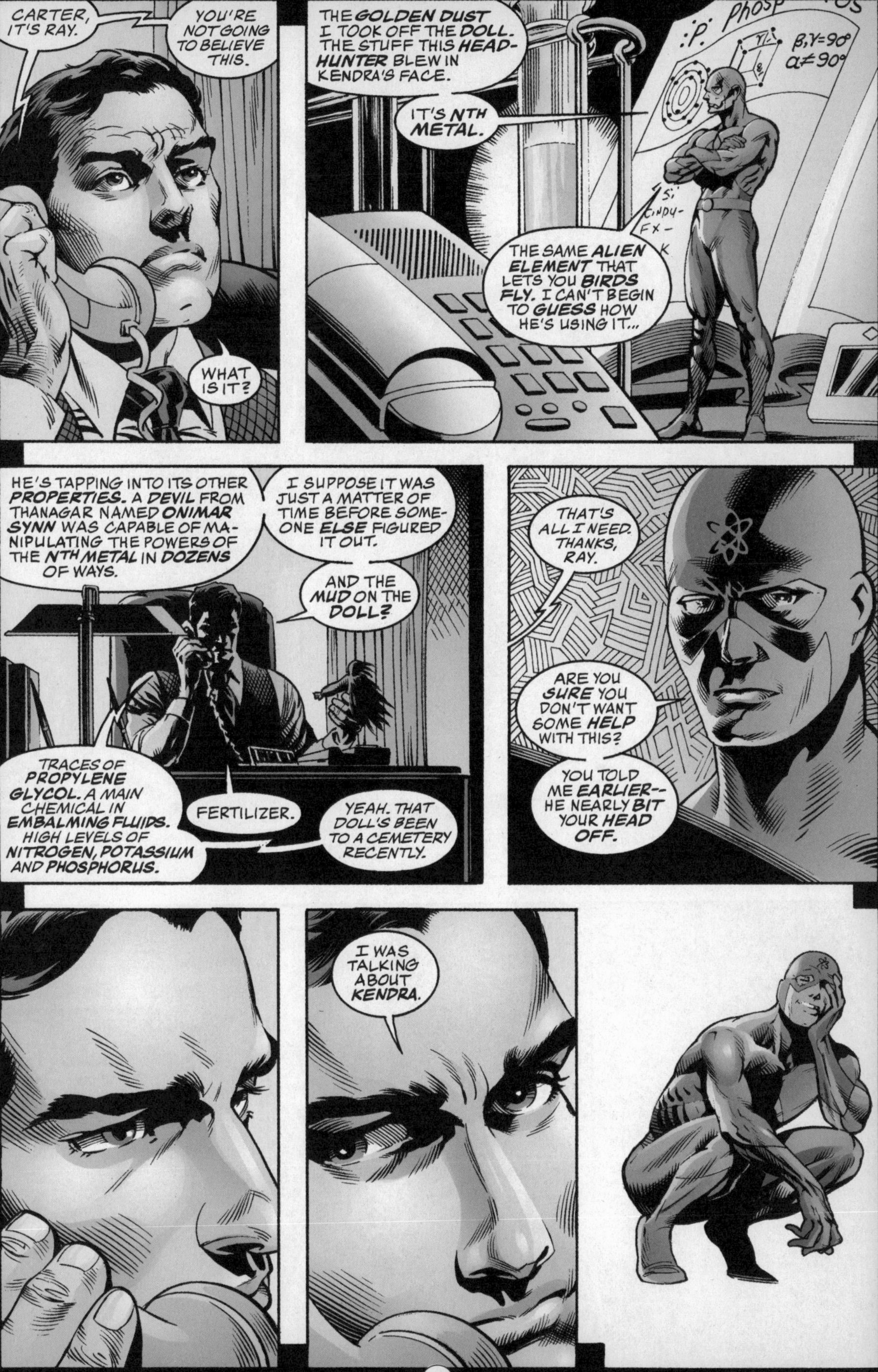
CARTER, IT'S RAY.
YOU'RE NOT GOING TO BELIEVE THIS.
WHAT IS IT?
THE GOLDEN DUST I TOOK OFF THE DOLL. THE STUFF THIS HEAD-HUNTER BLEW IN KENDRA'S FACE.
IT'S NTH METAL.
THE SAME ALIEN ELEMENT THAT LETS YOU BIRDS FLY. I CAN'T BEGIN TO GUESS HOW HE'S USING IT...
HE'S TAPPING INTO ITS OTHER PROPERTIES. A DEVIL FROM THANAGAR NAMED ONIMAR SYNN WAS CAPABLE OF MA-NIPULATING THE POWERS OF THE NTH METAL IN DOZENS OF WAYS.
I SUPPOSE IT WAS JUST A MATTER OF TIME BEFORE SOME-ONE ELSE FIGURED IT OUT.
AND THE MUD ON THE DOLL?
TRACES OF PROPYLENE GLYCOL. A MAIN CHEMICAL IN EMBALMING FLUIDS. HIGH LEVELS OF NITROGEN, POTASSIUM AND PHOSPHORUS.
FERTILIZER.
YEAH. THAT DOLL'S BEEN TO A CEMETERY RECENTLY.
THAT'S ALL I NEED. THANKS, RAY.
ARE YOU SURE YOU DON'T WANT SOME HELP WITH THIS?
YOU TOLD ME EARLIER--HE NEARLY BIT YOUR HEAD OFF.
I WAS TALKING ABOUT KENDRA.

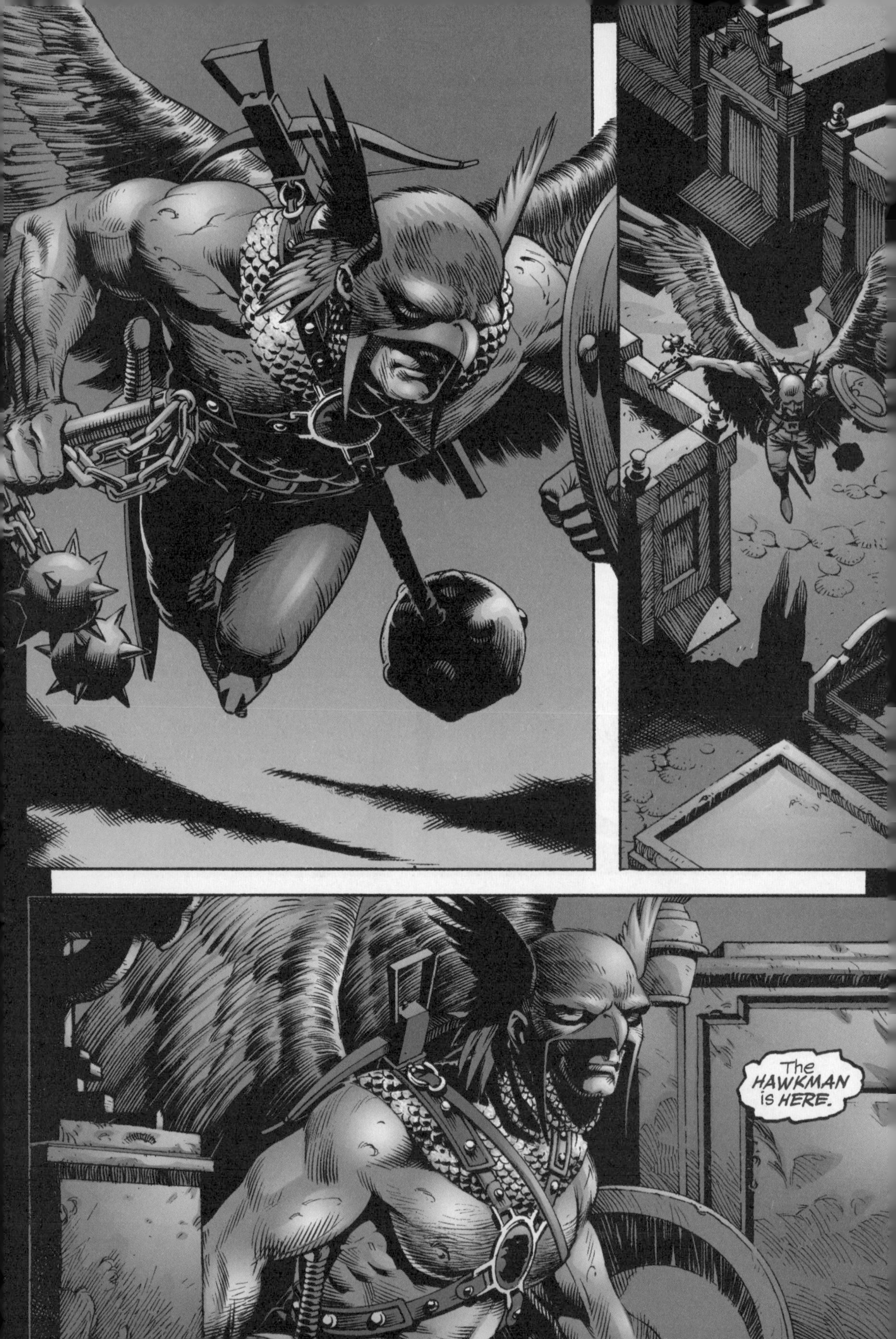
The HAWKMAN is HERE.

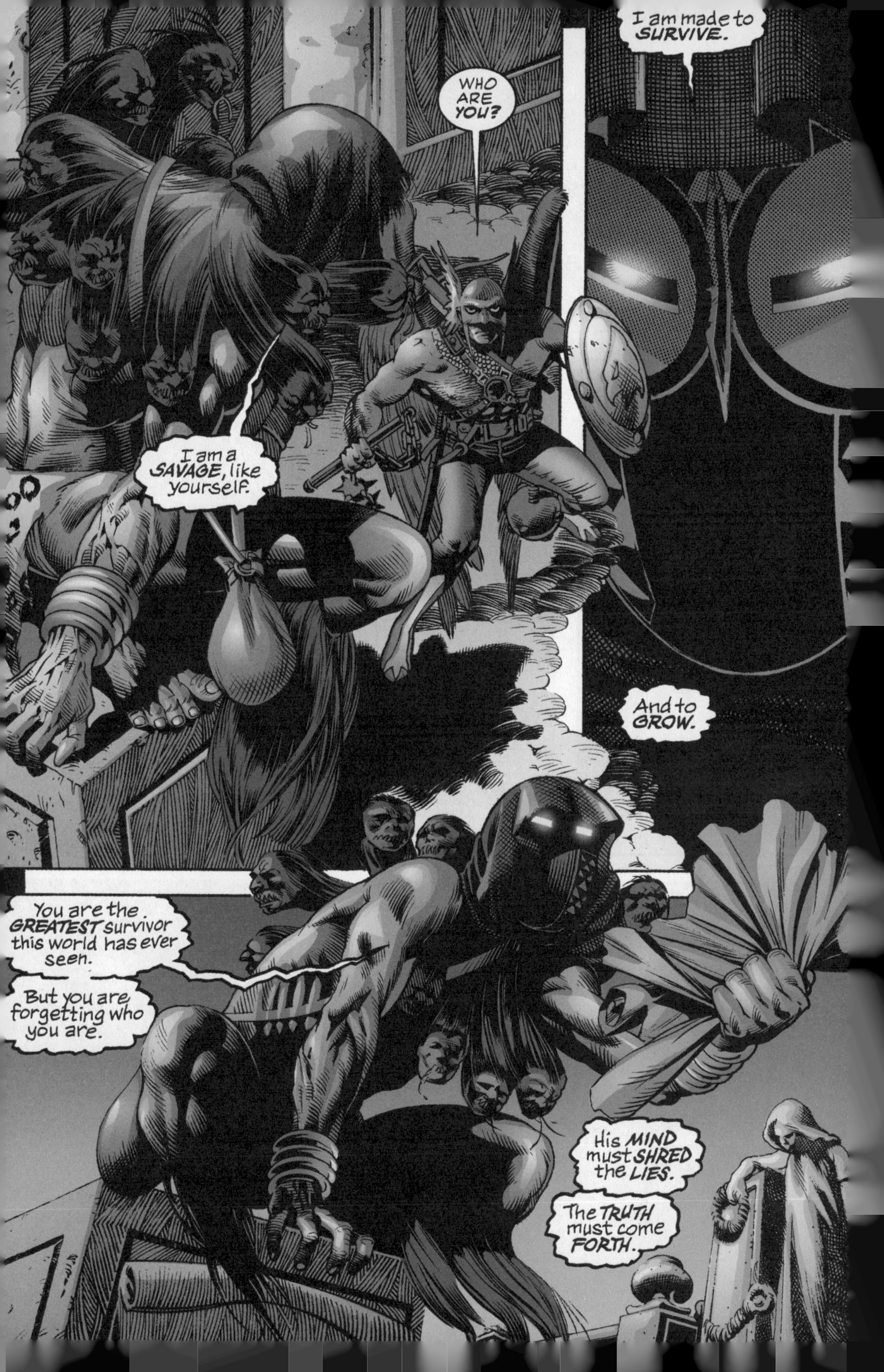
I am made to SURVIVE.
WHO ARE YOU?
I am a SAVAGE, like yourself.
And to GROW.
You are the GREATEST survivor this world has ever seen.
But you are forgetting who you are.
His MIND must SHRED the LIES.
The TRUTH must come FORTH.

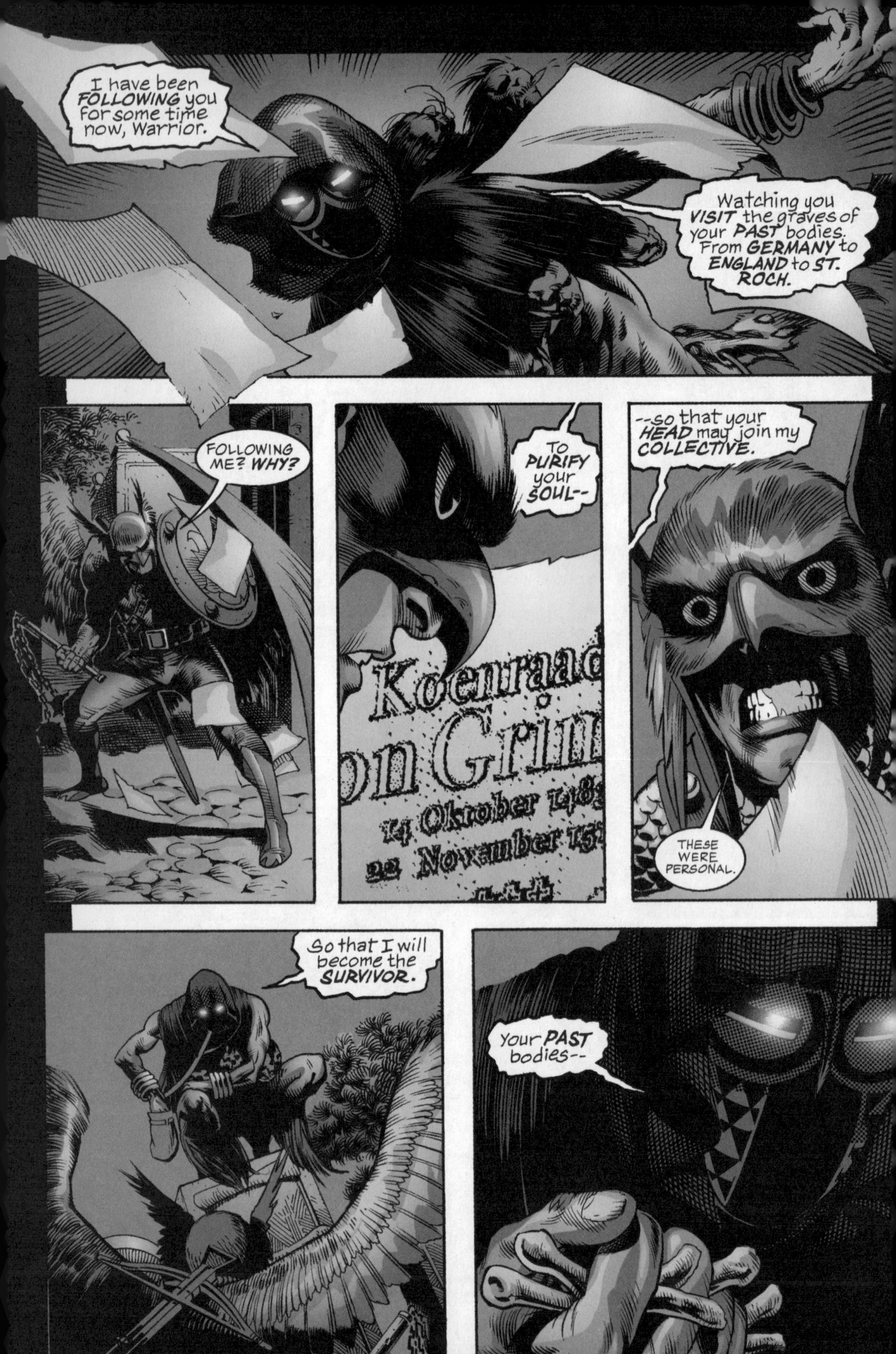
I have been FOLLOWING you for some time now, Warrior.
Watching you VISIT the graves of your PAST bodies. From GERMANY to ENGLAND to ST. ROCH.
FOLLOWING ME? WHY?
TO PURIFY your SOUL--
14 Oktober
22 November
--so that your HEAD may join my COLLECTIVE.
THESE WERE PERSONAL.
So that I will become the SURVIVOR.
Your PAST bodies--

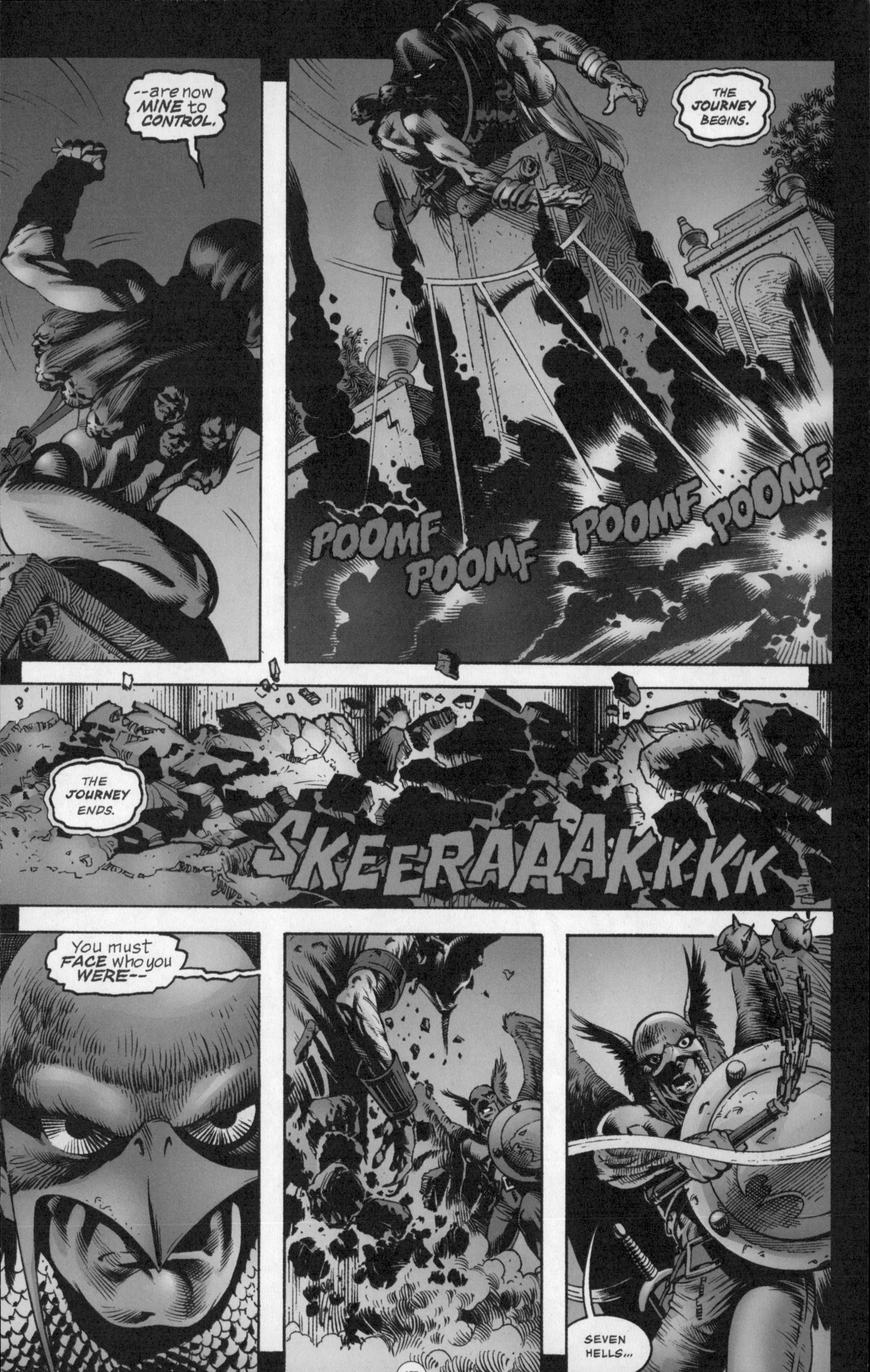
--are now MINE to CONTROL.
THE JOURNEY BEGINS.
POOMF
POOMF
POOMF
POOMF
THE JOURNEY ENDS.
SKEERAAAKKKK
You must FACE who you WERE--
SEVEN HELLS...

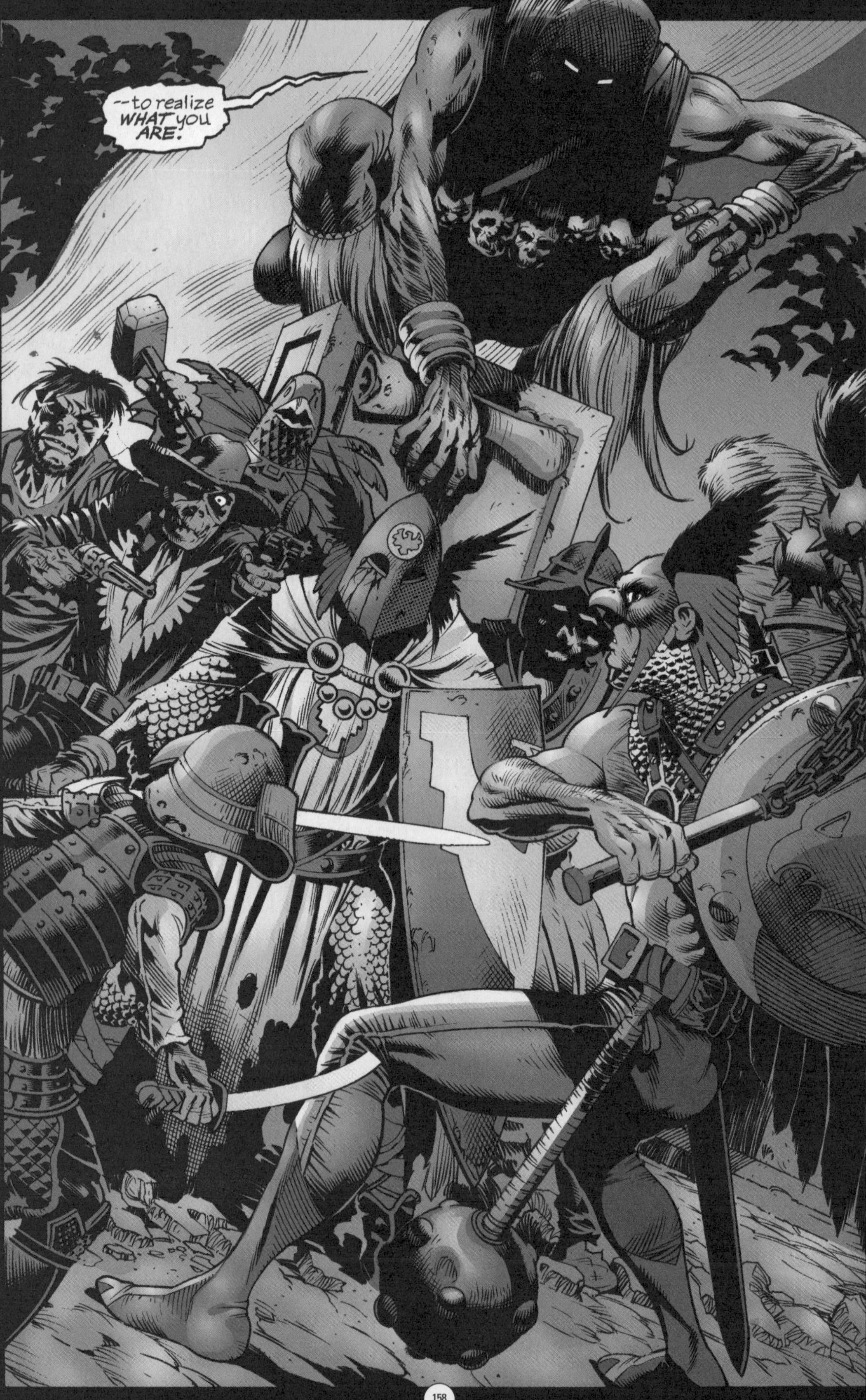
--to realize WHAT you ARE.

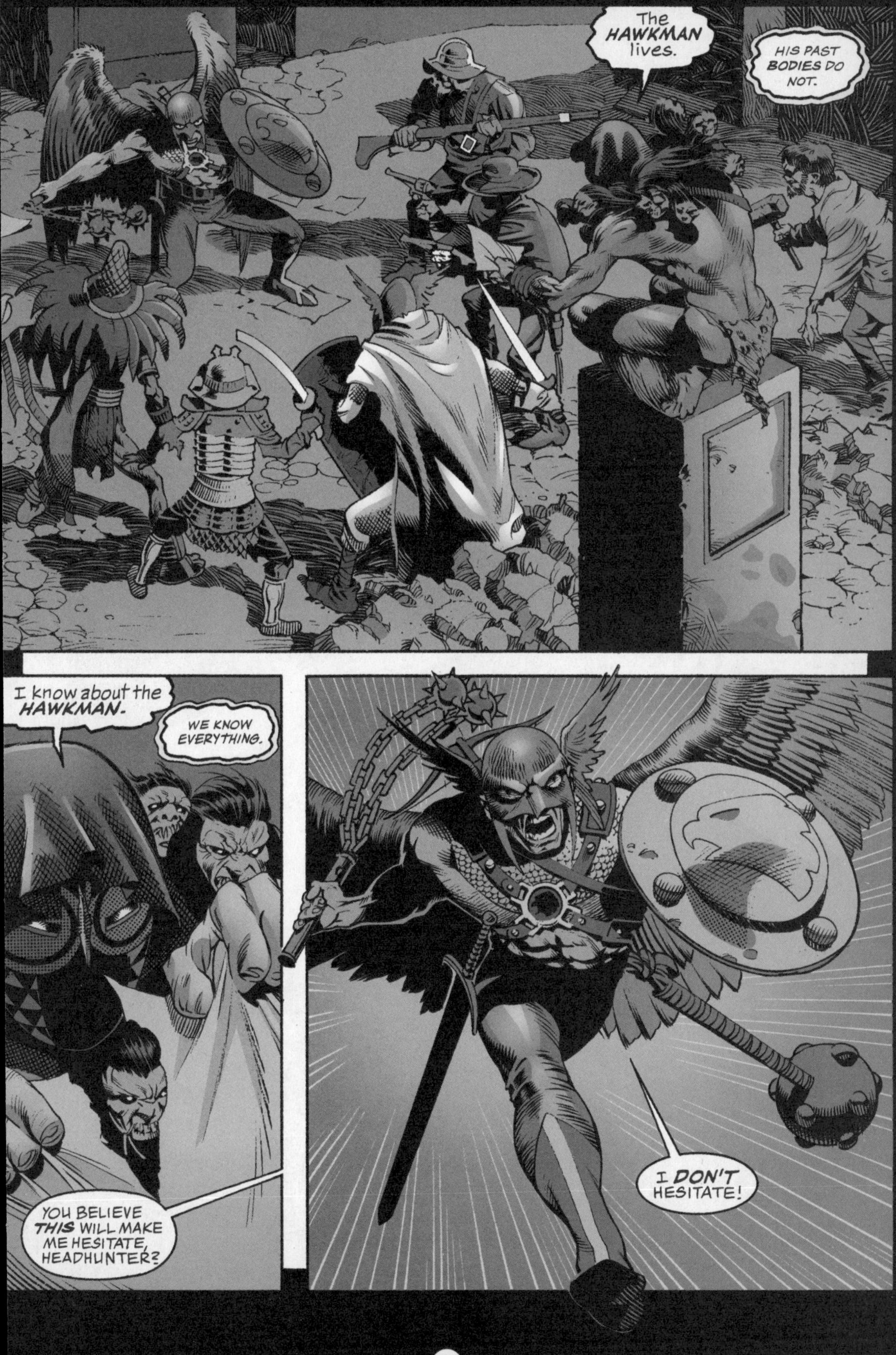
The HAWKMAN lives.
HIS PAST BODIES DO NOT.
I know about the HAWKMAN-
WE KNOW EVERYTHING.
YOU BELIEVE THIS WILL MAKE ME HESITATE, HEADHUNTER?
I DON'T HESITATE!

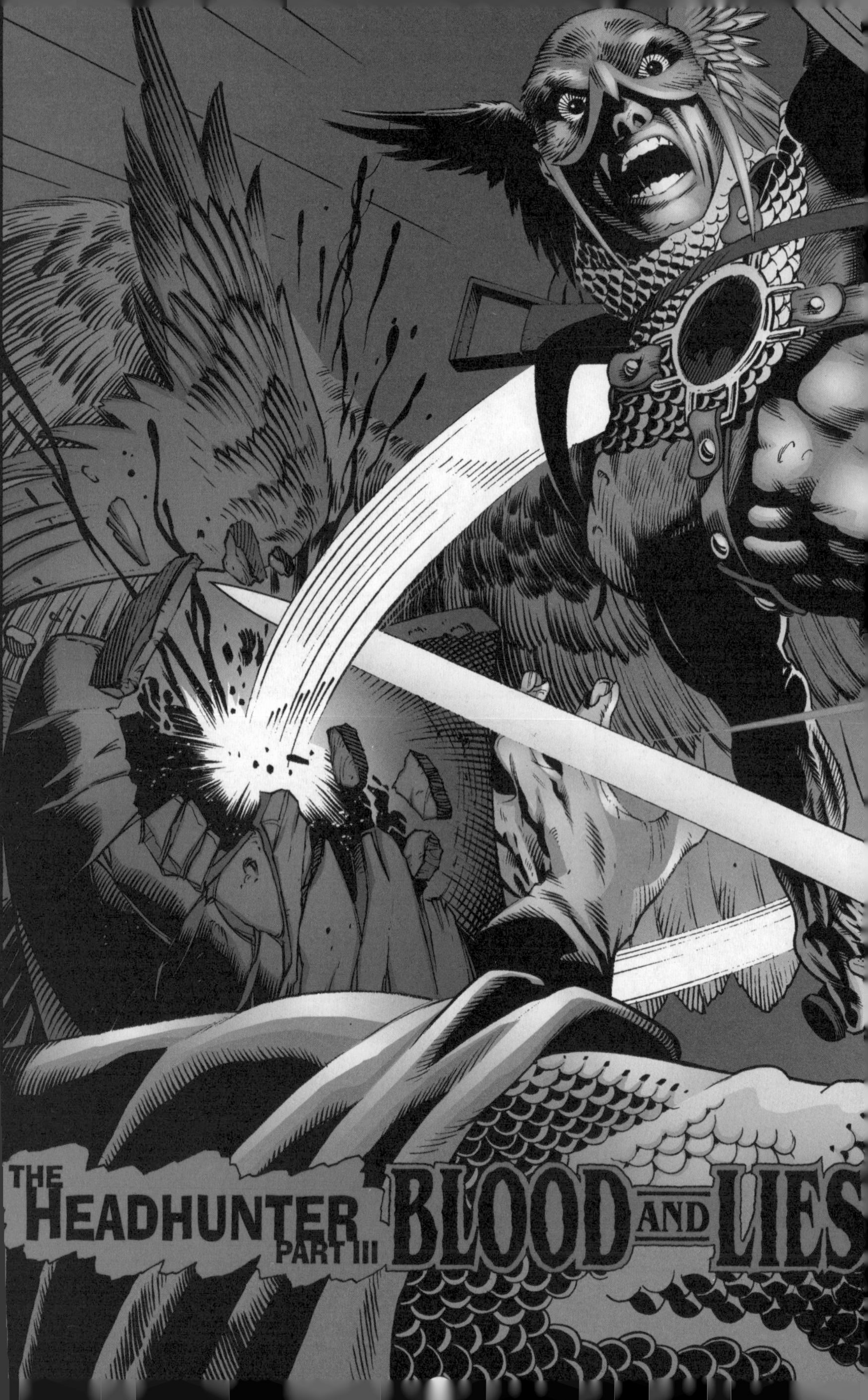
THE HEADHUNTER PART III
BLOOD AND LIES

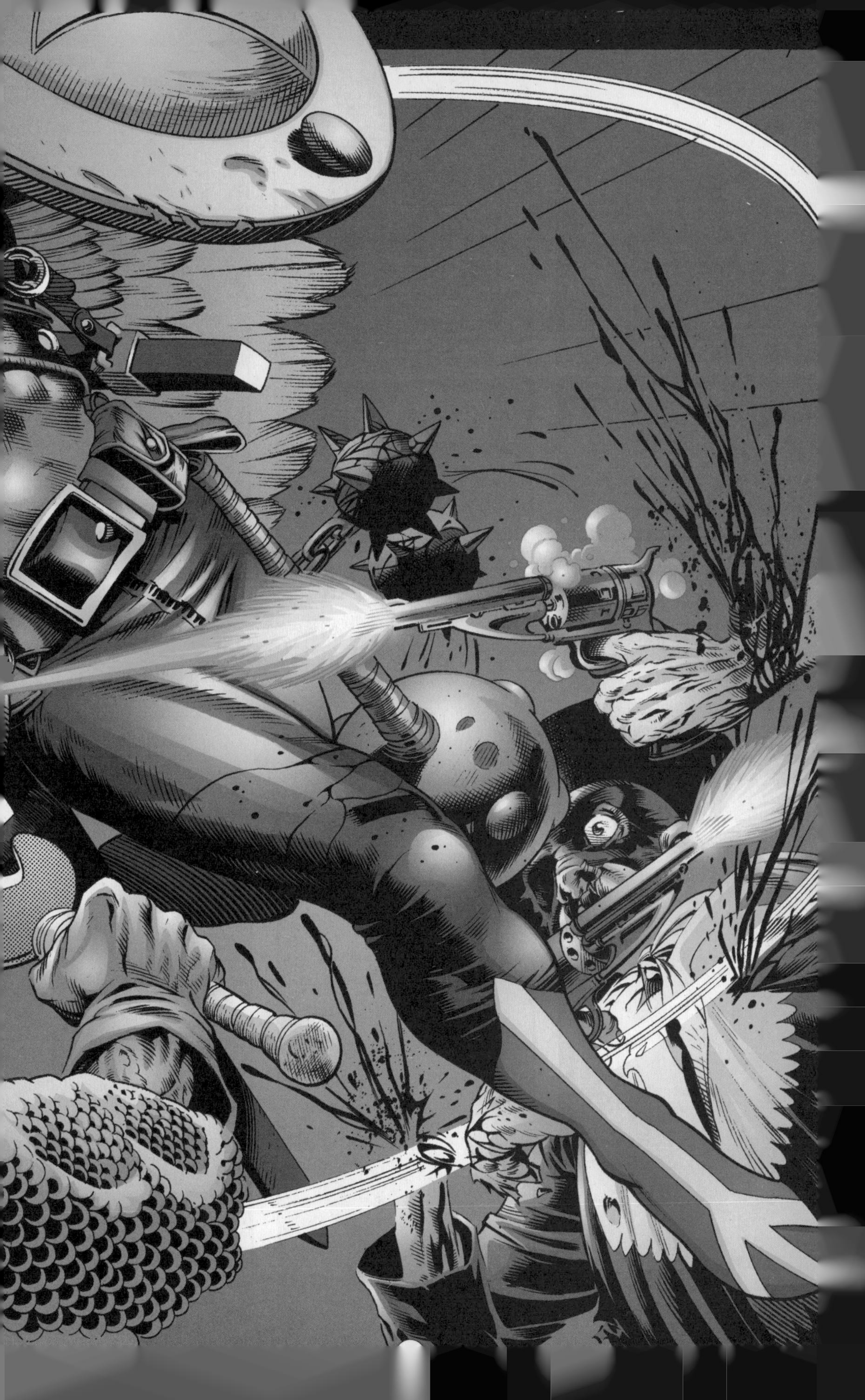

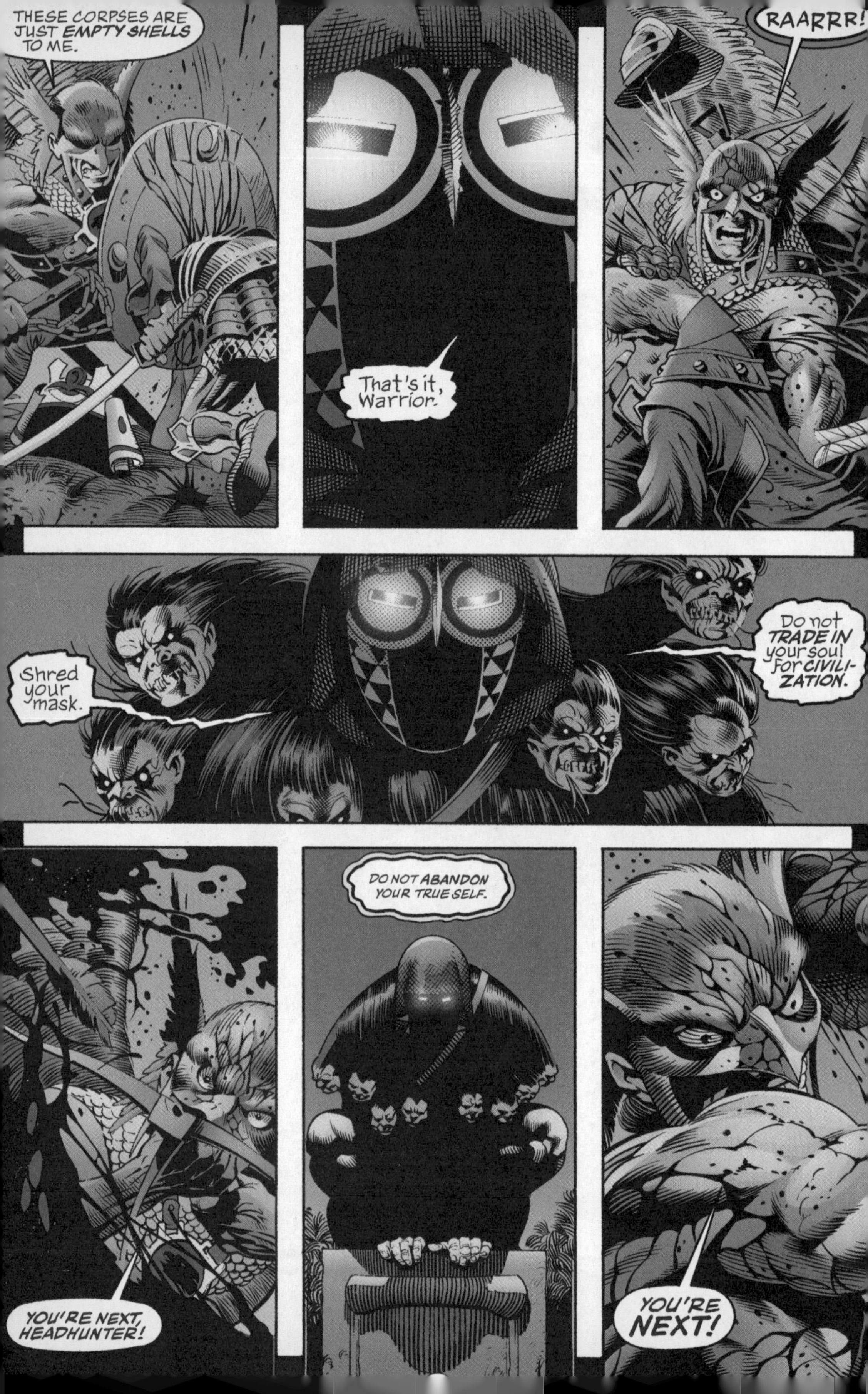
THESE CORPSES ARE JUST EMPTY SHELLS TO ME.
That's it, Warrior.
RAARRR!
Shred your mask.
Do not TRADE IN your soul for CIVILIZATION.
YOU'RE NEXT, HEADHUNTER!
DO NOT ABANDON YOUR TRUE SELF.
YOU'RE NEXT!

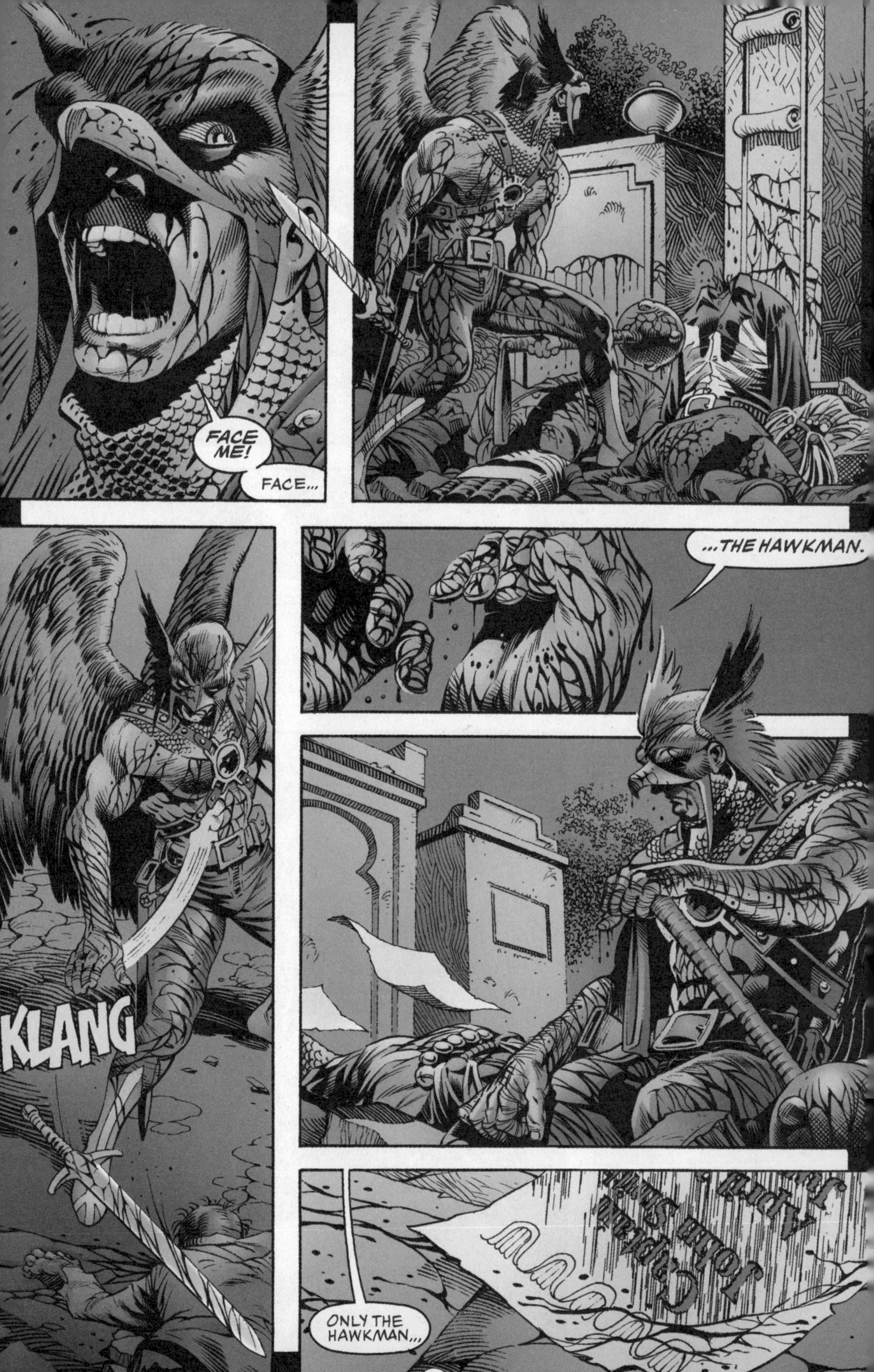
FACE ME!
FACE...
...THE HAWKMAN.
KLANG
ONLY THE HAWKMAN...

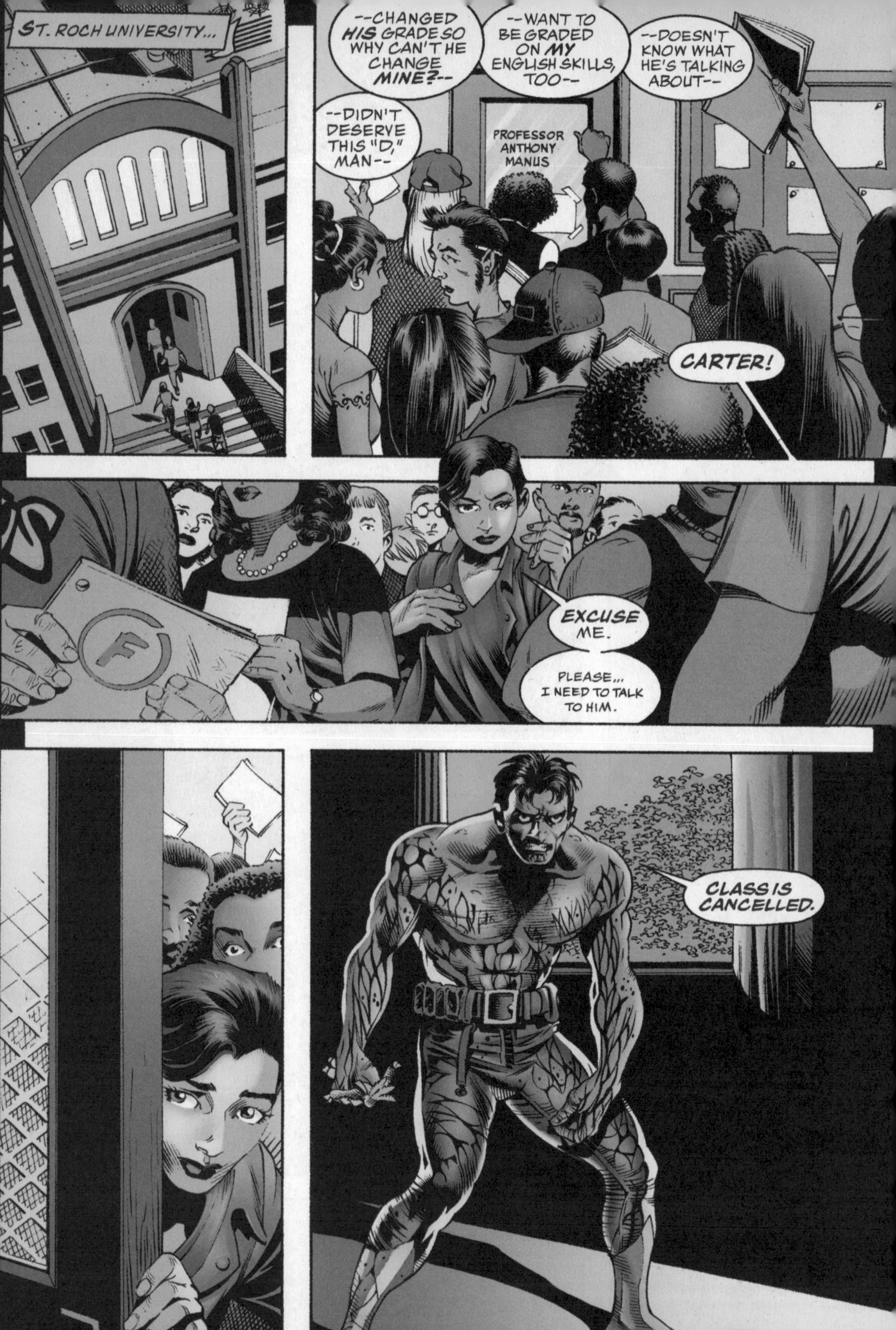
ST. ROCH UNIVERSITY...
--CHANGED HIS GRADE SO WHY CAN'T HE CHANGE MINE?--
--WANT TO BE GRADED ON MY ENGLISH SKILLS, TOO--
--DOESN'T KNOW WHAT HE'S TALKING ABOUT--
--DIDN'T DESERVE THIS "D," MAN--
PROFESSOR ANTHONY MANUS
CARTER!
EXCUSE ME.
PLEASE... I NEED TO TALK TO HIM.
CLASS IS CANCELLED.

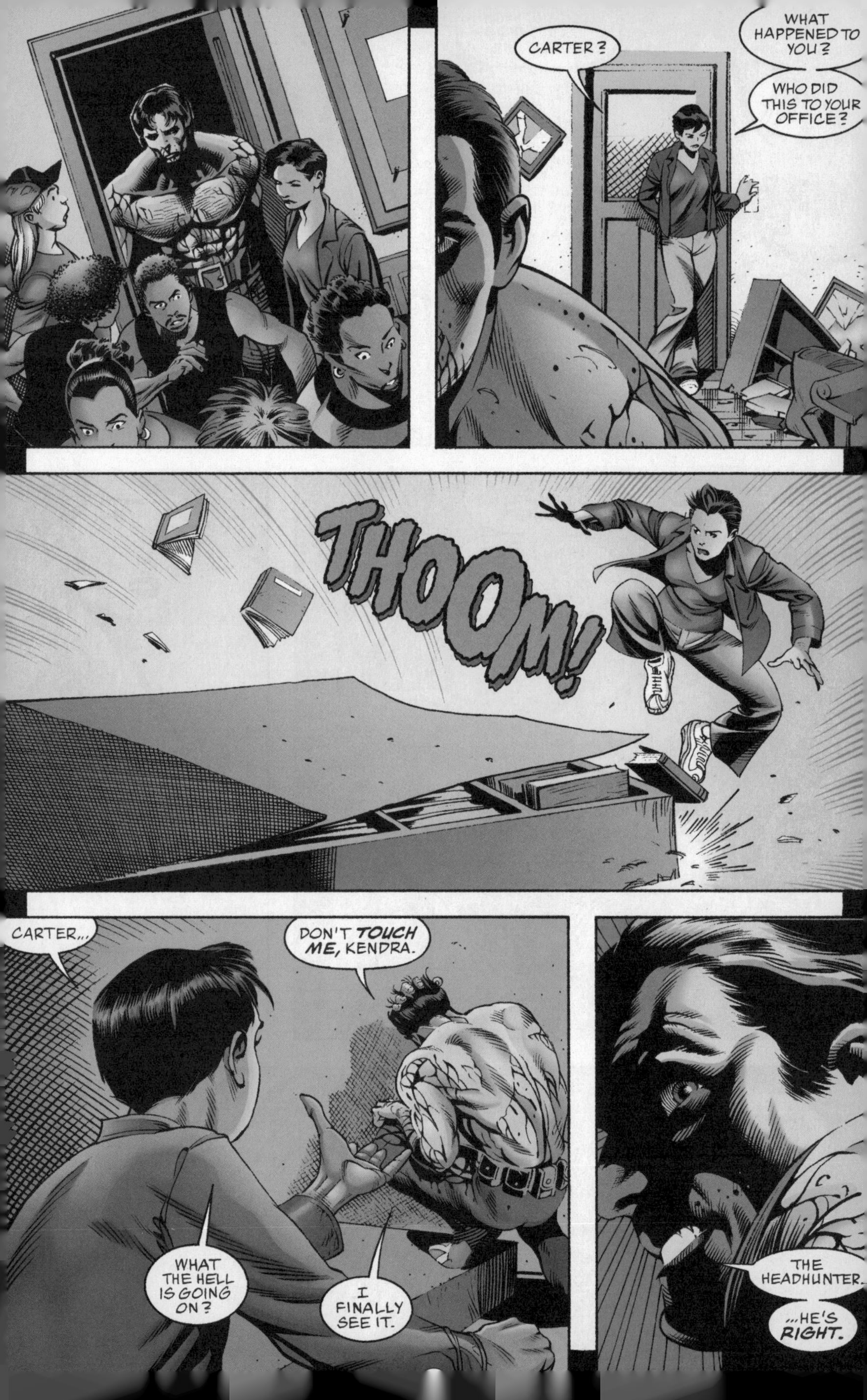
CARTER?
WHAT HAPPENED TO YOU?
WHO DID THIS TO YOUR OFFICE?
THOOM!
CARTER...
DON'T TOUCH ME, KENDRA.
WHAT THE HELL IS GOING ON?
I FINALLY SEE IT.
THE HEADHUNTER.
...HE'S RIGHT.

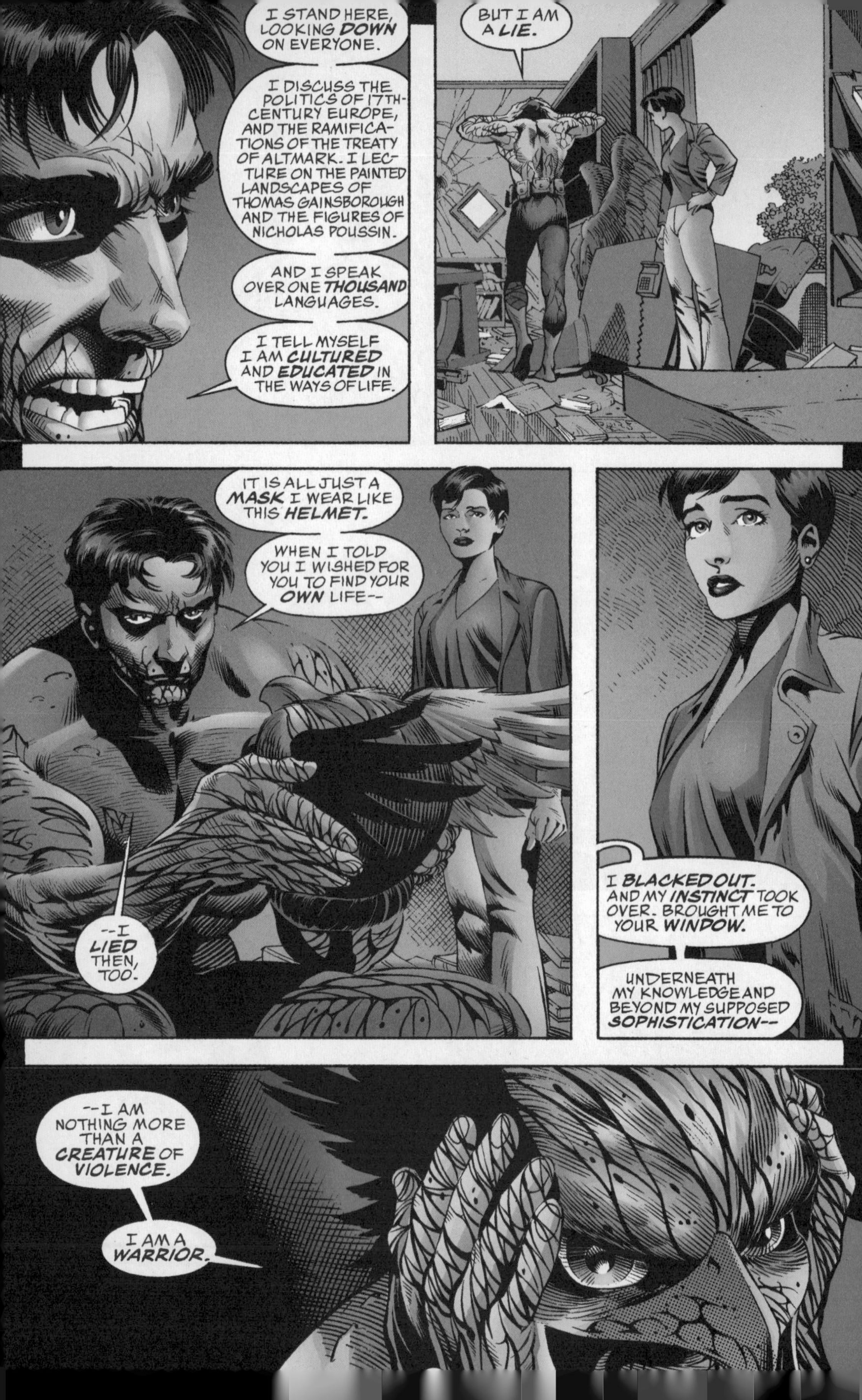
I STAND HERE, LOOKING DOWN ON EVERYONE.
I DISCUSS THE POLITICS OF 17TH-CENTURY EUROPE, AND THE RAMIFICATIONS OF THE TREATY OF ALTMARK. I LECTURE ON THE PAINTED LANDSCAPES OF THOMAS GAINSBOROUGH AND THE FIGURES OF NICHOLAS POUSSIN.
AND I SPEAK OVER ONE THOUSAND LANGUAGES.
I TELL MYSELF I AM CULTURED AND EDUCATED IN THE WAYS OF LIFE.
BUT I AM A LIE.
IT IS ALL JUST A MASK I WEAR LIKE THIS HELMET.
WHEN I TOLD YOU I WISHED FOR YOU TO FIND YOUR OWN LIFE--
--I LIED THEN, TOO.
I BLACKED OUT. AND MY INSTINCT TOOK OVER. BROUGHT ME TO YOUR WINDOW.
UNDERNEATH MY KNOWLEDGE AND BEYOND MY SUPPOSED SOPHISTICATION--
--I AM NOTHING MORE THAN A CREATURE OF VIOLENCE.
I AM A WARRIOR.

YOU JUST NEED TO SIT DOWN AND CLEAR YOUR HEAD FOR A MINUTE.

I KNOW I WAS HARD ON YOU, BUT YOU HAVE TO UNDER-STAND. I WASN'T CALLING YOU A... MONSTER OR ANY-THING... WE--

NO. THIS IS NOT ABOUT US, KENDRA.

FOR THE FIRST TIME IN A LONG TIME, I AM SIMPLY AWAKE.

FOR THE FIRST TIME IN FOREVER, I FINALLY REALIZE NOT WHO I AM--

--BUT WHAT I AM. I BELONG IN A DIFFERENT TIME. A HARDER TIME.

WAIT--!

FOR WHAT?

I'M DESTROY-ING YOUR LIFE. YOU SAID THAT YOURSELF.

I WAS MAD.

YOU SHOULD'VE BEEN.

YOU'RE MY FRIEND, CARTER. YOU ARE. AND I'M NOT GOING TO JUST TURN MY BACK ON YOU. I'M NOT GOING TO LET YOU DO WHAT I DID WHEN MY PARENTS WERE MURDER-ED. I BECAME A BIG BALL OF ANGER. I RESENTED THE WORLD. HATED EVERYONE IN IT. AND I HAVE NO DOUBT. NO DOUBT AT ALL THAT I WOULD BE DEAD IF I DIDN'T HAVE SOMEONE THERE THAT CARED ABOUT ME.

MY GRANDFATHER NEVER LEFT MY SIDE.

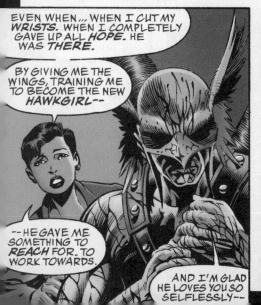

EVEN WHEN... WHEN I CUT MY WRISTS. WHEN I COMPLETELY GAVE UP ALL HOPE. HE WAS THERE.

BY GIVING ME THE WINGS, TRAINING ME TO BECOME THE NEW HAWKGIRL--

--HE GAVE ME SOMETHING TO REACH FOR. TO WORK TOWARDS.

AND I'M GLAD HE LOVES YOU SO SELFLESSLY--

--BECAUSE A MAN LIKE ME COULD NEVER DO THAT!

A MAN ...LIKE ME...

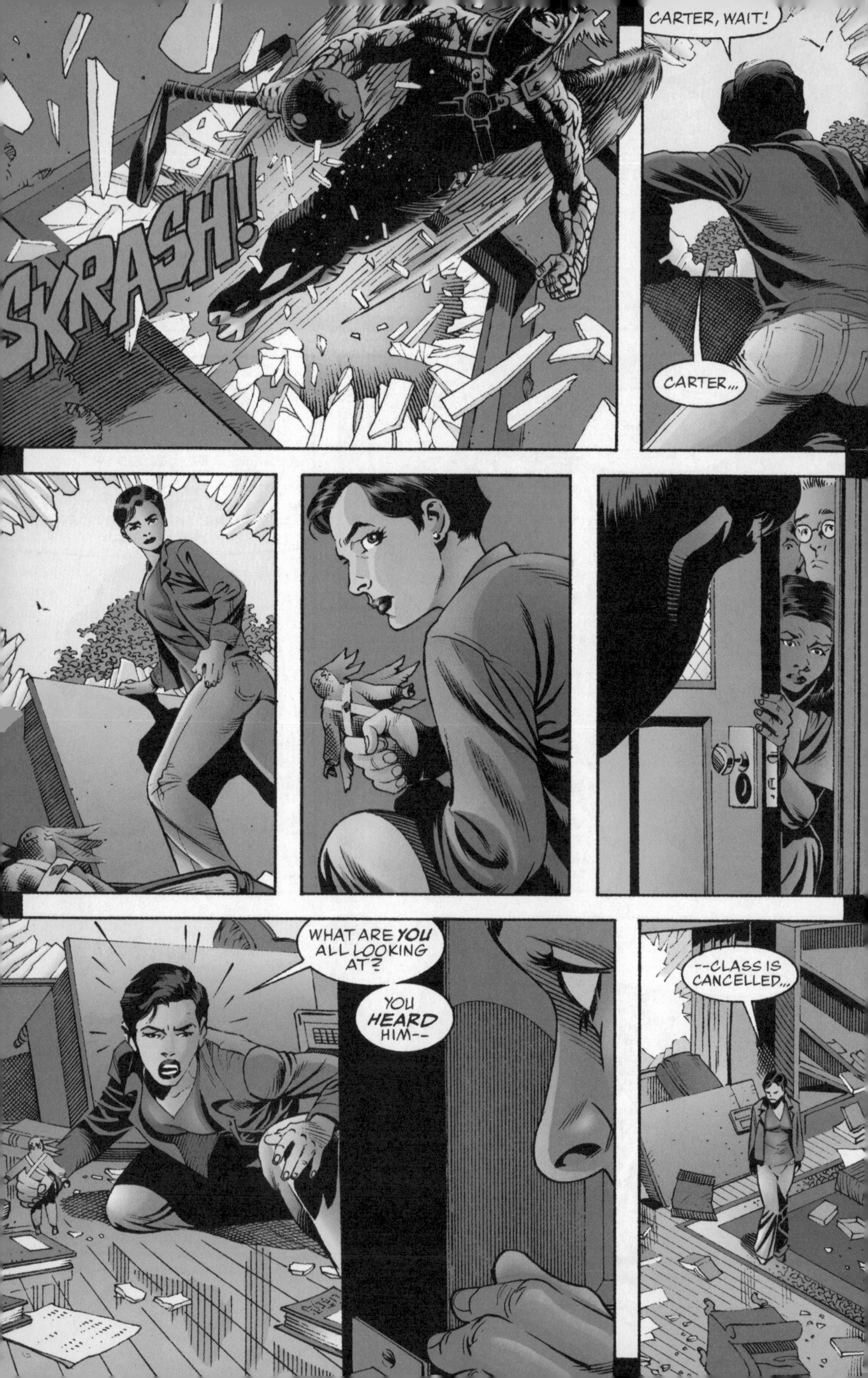
SKRASH!
CARTER, WAIT!
CARTER...
WHAT ARE YOU ALL LOOKING AT?
YOU HEARD HIM--
--CLASS IS CANCELLED...

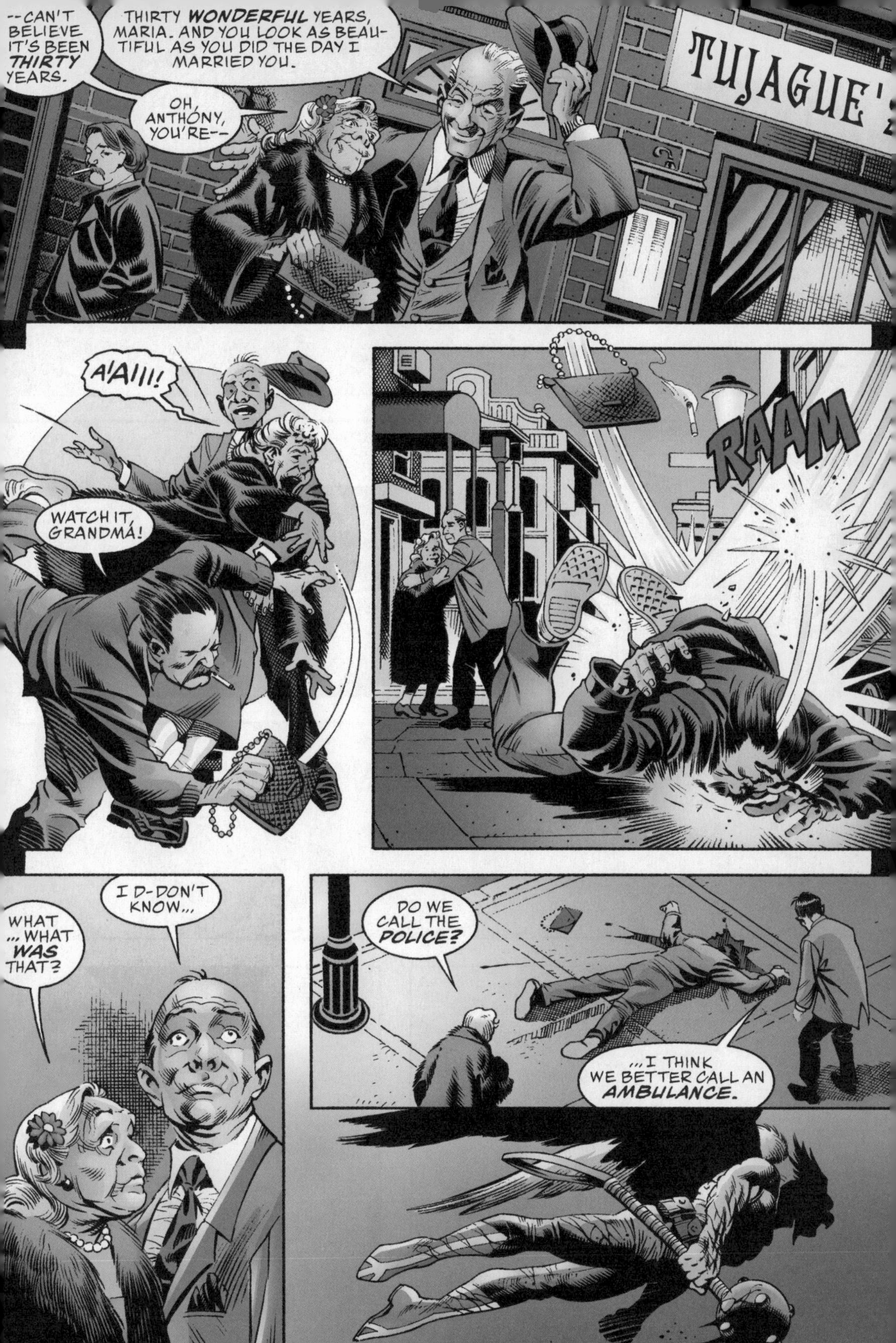
--CAN'T BELIEVE IT'S BEEN THIRTY YEARS.
THIRTY WONDERFUL YEARS, MARIA. AND YOU LOOK AS BEAUTIFUL AS YOU DID THE DAY I MARRIED YOU.
OH, ANTHONY, YOU'RE--
TUJAGUE'S
AAIII!
WATCH IT, GRANDMA!
RAAM
WHAT ...WHAT WAS THAT?
I D-DON'T KNOW...
DO WE CALL THE POLICE?
...I THINK WE BETTER CALL AN AMBULANCE.

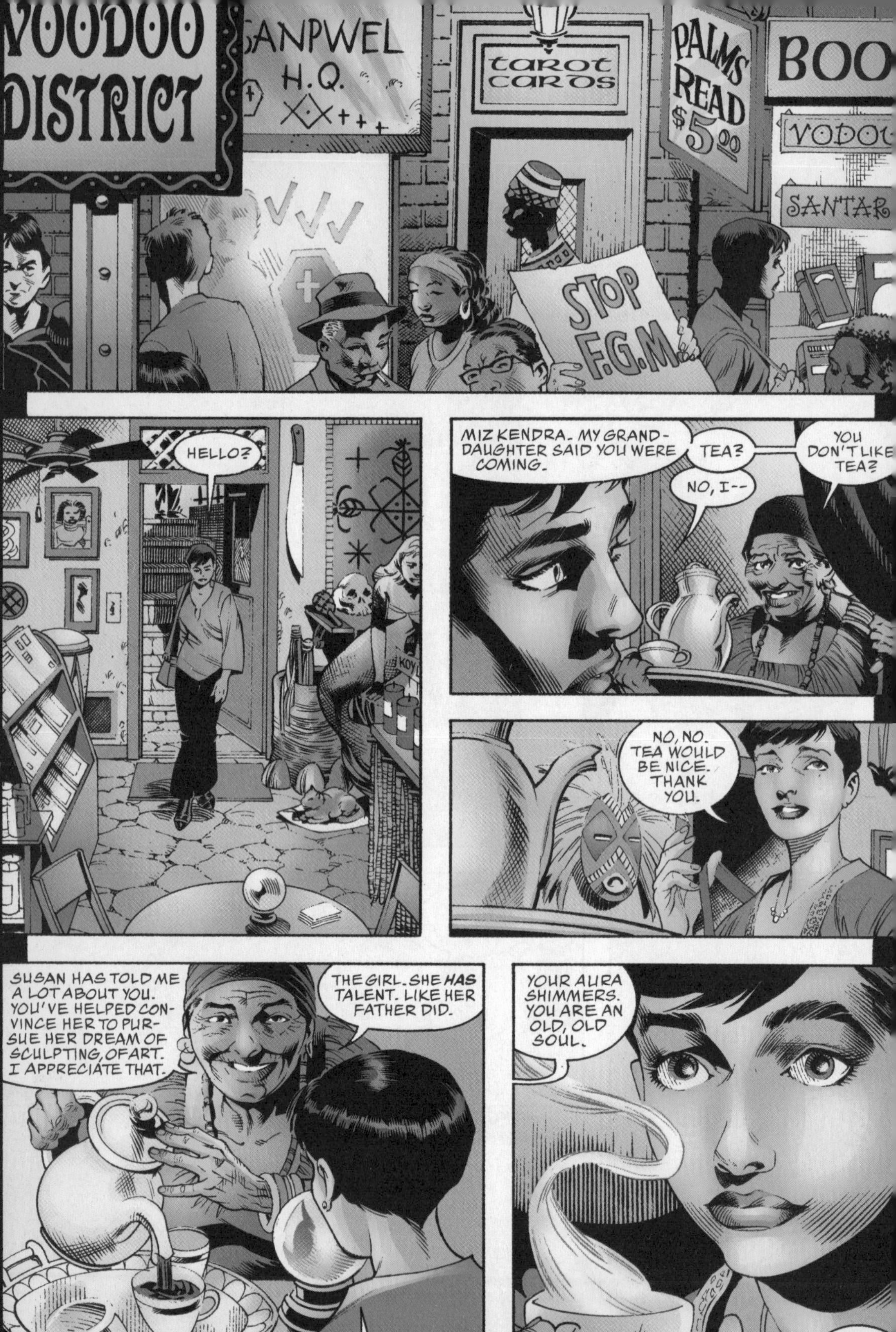
VOODOO DISTRICT
SANPWEL H.Q.
tarot cards
PALMS READ $5.00
BOO
VODOU
SANTAR
STOP F.G.M.
HELLO?
MIZ KENDRA. MY GRAND-DAUGHTER SAID YOU WERE COMING.
TEA?
NO, I--
YOU DON'T LIKE TEA?
NO, NO. TEA WOULD BE NICE. THANK YOU.
SUSAN HAS TOLD ME A LOT ABOUT YOU. YOU'VE HELPED CONVINCE HER TO PURSUE HER DREAM OF SCULPTING, OF ART. I APPRECIATE THAT.
THE GIRL. SHE HAS TALENT. LIKE HER FATHER DID.
THE MUSEUM'S LUCKY TO HAVE HER...
YOUR AURA SHIMMERS. YOU ARE AN OLD, OLD SOUL.
WITH A FRESH LOOK ON LIFE.

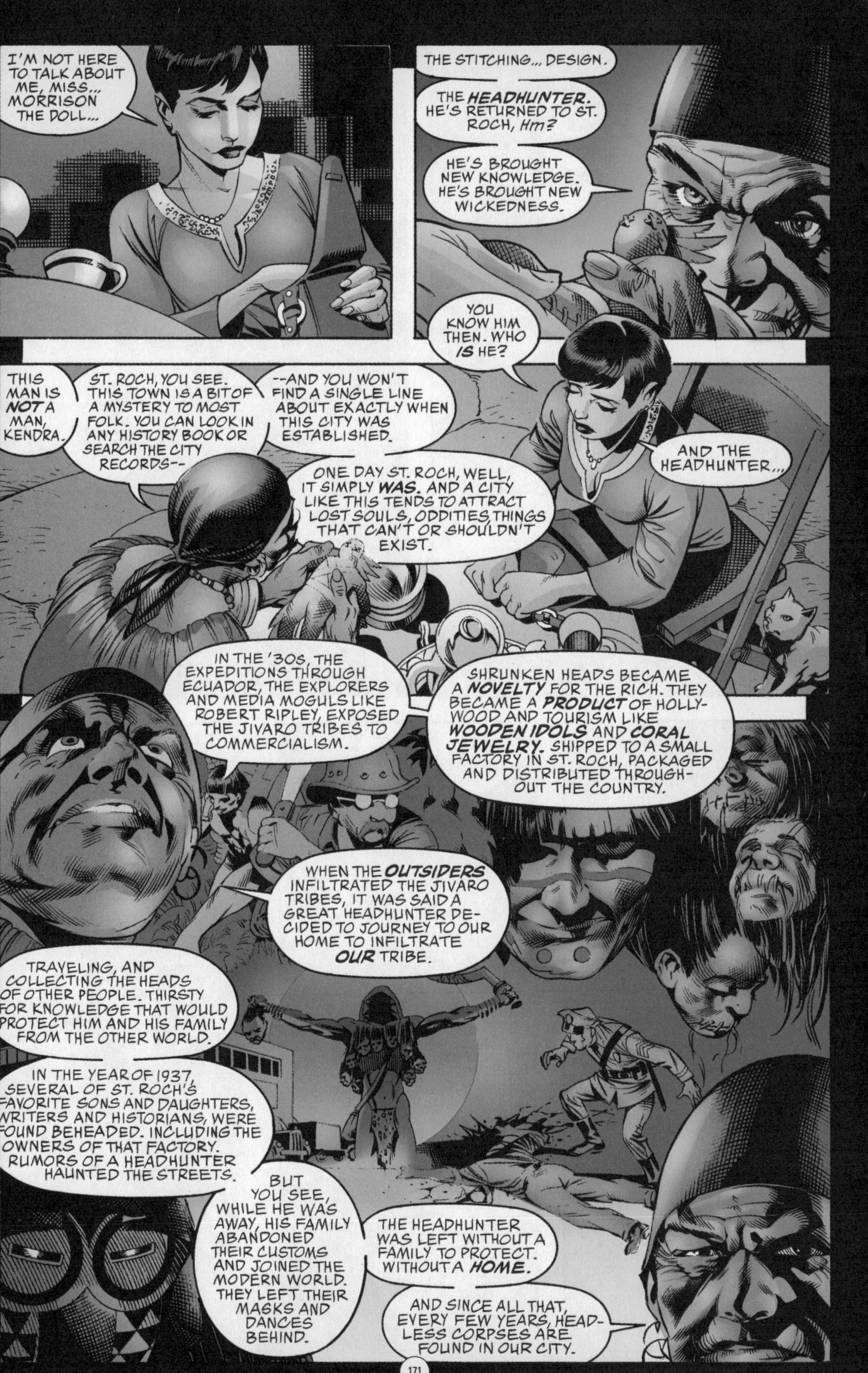
I'M NOT HERE TO TALK ABOUT ME, MISS... MORRISON THE DOLL...
THE STITCHING... DESIGN.
THE HEADHUNTER. HE'S RETURNED TO ST. ROCH, Hm?
HE'S BROUGHT NEW KNOWLEDGE. HE'S BROUGHT NEW WICKEDNESS.
YOU KNOW HIM THEN. WHO IS HE?
THIS MAN IS NOT A MAN, KENDRA.
ST. ROCH, YOU SEE. THIS TOWN IS A BIT OF A MYSTERY TO MOST FOLK. YOU CAN LOOK IN ANY HISTORY BOOK OR SEARCH THE CITY RECORDS--
--AND YOU WON'T FIND A SINGLE LINE ABOUT EXACTLY WHEN THIS CITY WAS ESTABLISHED.
ONE DAY ST. ROCH, WELL, IT SIMPLY WAS. AND A CITY LIKE THIS TENDS TO ATTRACT LOST SOULS, ODDITIES, THINGS THAT CAN'T OR SHOULDN'T EXIST.
AND THE HEADHUNTER...
IN THE '30S, THE EXPEDITIONS THROUGH ECUADOR, THE EXPLORERS AND MEDIA MOGULS LIKE ROBERT RIPLEY, EXPOSED THE JIVARO TRIBES TO COMMERCIALISM.
SHRUNKEN HEADS BECAME A NOVELTY FOR THE RICH. THEY BECAME A PRODUCT OF HOLLYWOOD AND TOURISM LIKE WOODEN IDOLS AND CORAL JEWELRY. SHIPPED TO A SMALL FACTORY IN ST. ROCH, PACKAGED AND DISTRIBUTED THROUGHOUT THE COUNTRY.
WHEN THE OUTSIDERS INFILTRATED THE JIVARO TRIBES, IT WAS SAID A GREAT HEADHUNTER DECIDED TO JOURNEY TO OUR HOME TO INFILTRATE OUR TRIBE.
TRAVELING, AND COLLECTING THE HEADS OF OTHER PEOPLE. THIRSTY FOR KNOWLEDGE THAT WOULD PROTECT HIM AND HIS FAMILY FROM THE OTHER WORLD.
IN THE YEAR OF 1937, SEVERAL OF ST. ROCH'S FAVORITE SONS AND DAUGHTERS, WRITERS AND HISTORIANS, WERE FOUND BEHEADED. INCLUDING THE OWNERS OF THAT FACTORY. RUMORS OF A HEADHUNTER HAUNTED THE STREETS.
BUT YOU SEE, WHILE HE WAS AWAY, HIS FAMILY ABANDONED THEIR CUSTOMS AND JOINED THE MODERN WORLD. THEY LEFT THEIR MASKS AND DANCES BEHIND.
THE HEADHUNTER WAS LEFT WITHOUT A FAMILY TO PROTECT. WITHOUT A HOME.
AND SINCE ALL THAT, EVERY FEW YEARS, HEADLESS CORPSES ARE FOUND IN OUR CITY.

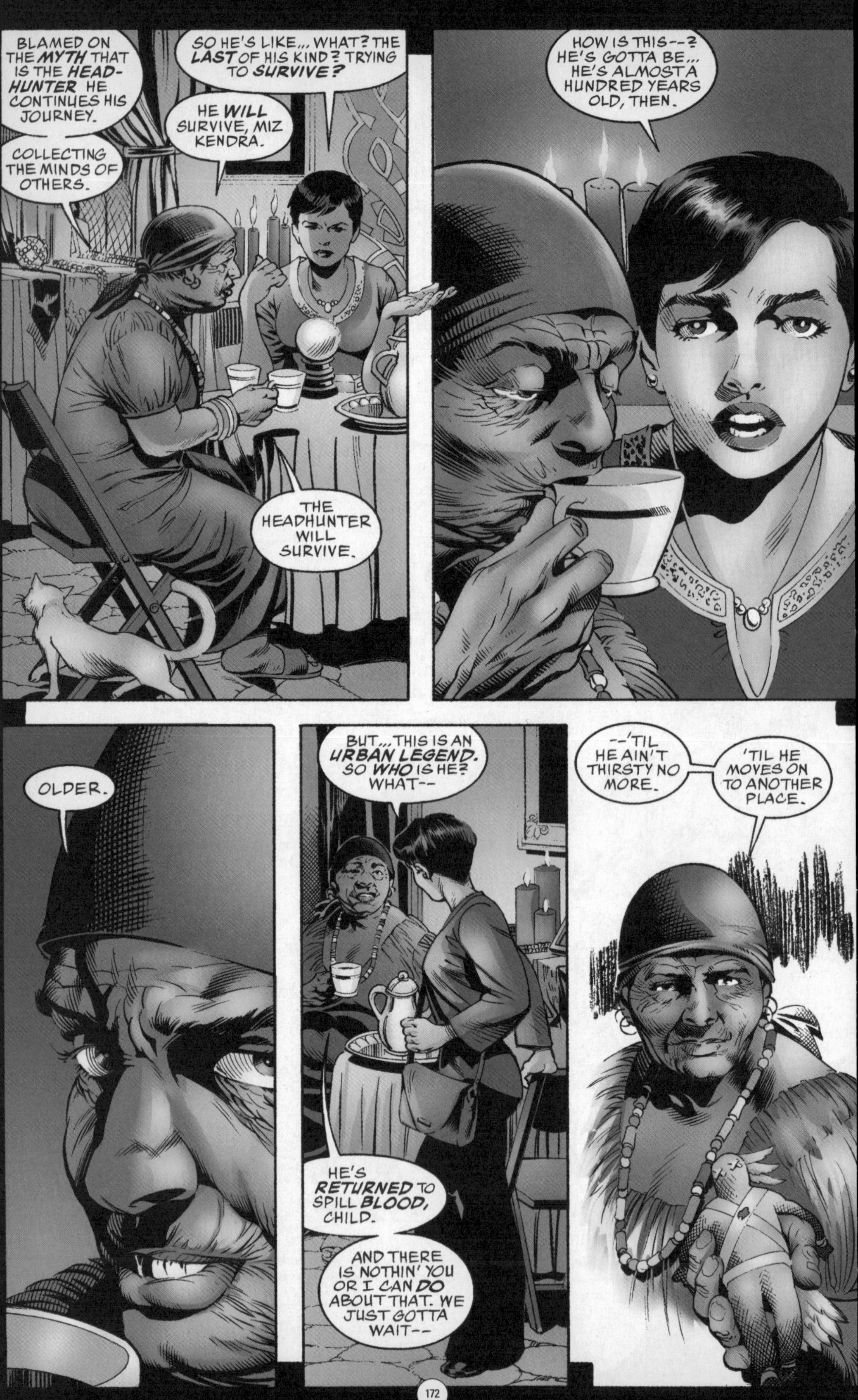
BLAMED ON THE MYTH THAT IS THE HEAD-HUNTER HE CONTINUES HIS JOURNEY.
COLLECTING THE MINDS OF OTHERS.
SO HE'S LIKE... WHAT? THE LAST OF HIS KIND? TRYING TO SURVIVE?
HE WILL SURVIVE, MIZ KENDRA.
THE HEADHUNTER WILL SURVIVE.
HOW IS THIS--? HE'S GOTTA BE... HE'S ALMOST A HUNDRED YEARS OLD, THEN.
OLDER.
BUT... THIS IS AN URBAN LEGEND. SO WHO IS HE? WHAT--
HE'S RETURNED TO SPILL BLOOD, CHILD.
AND THERE IS NOTHIN' YOU OR I CAN DO ABOUT THAT. WE JUST GOTTA WAIT--
--'TIL HE AIN'T THIRSTY NO MORE.
'TIL HE MOVES ON TO ANOTHER PLACE.

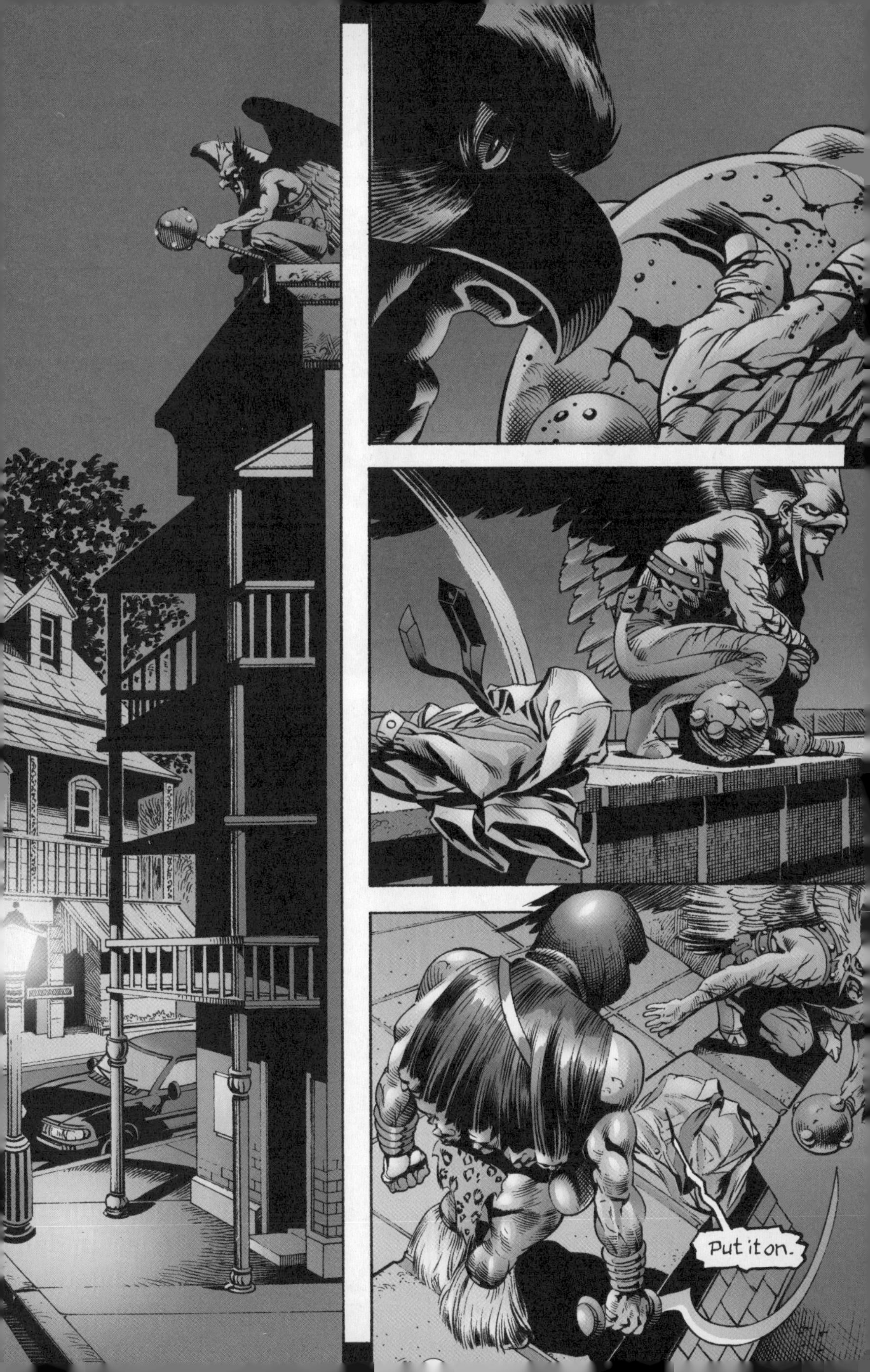
Put it on.

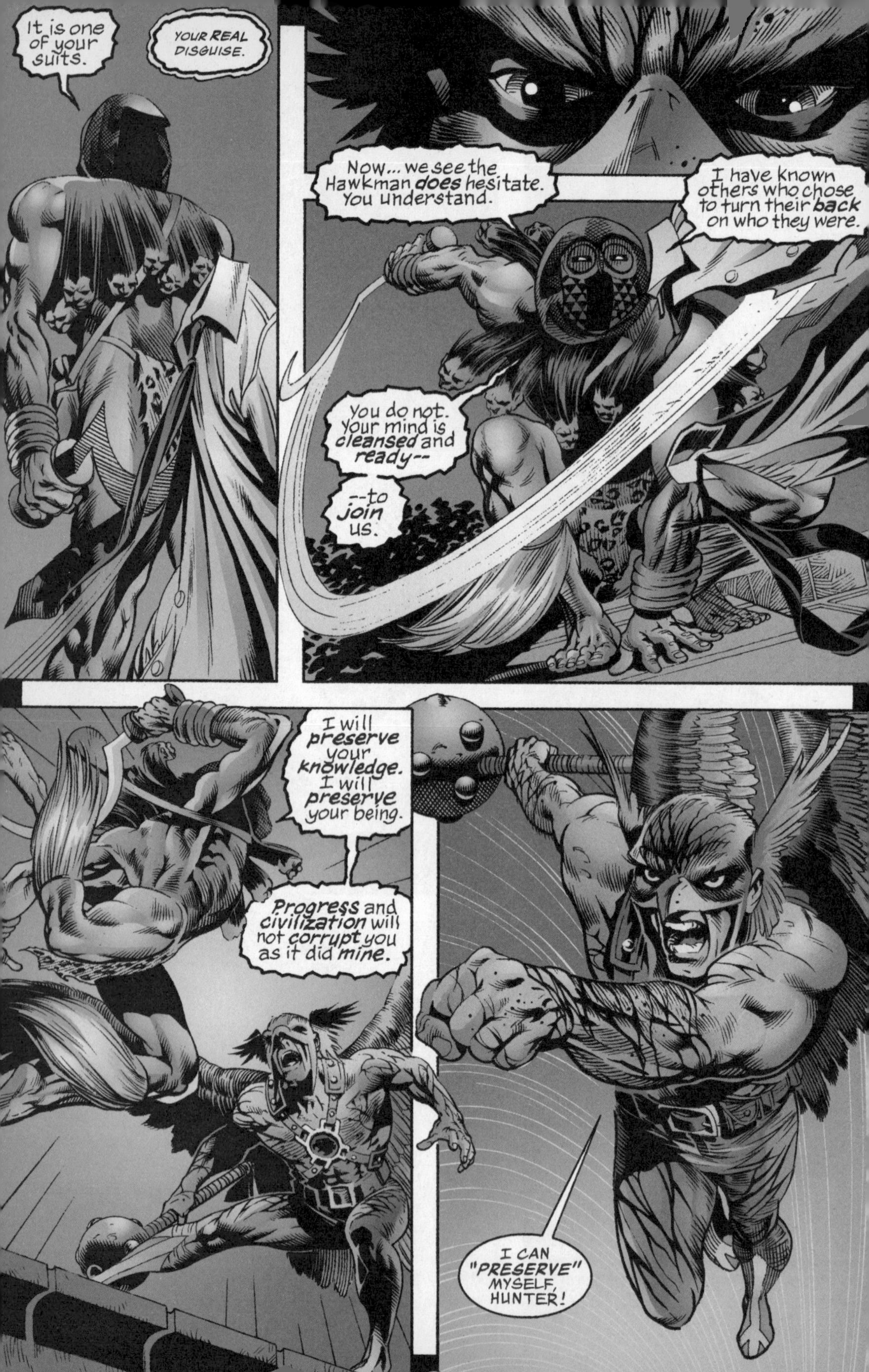
It is one of your suits.
YOUR REAL DISGUISE.
Now... we see the Hawkman does hesitate. You understand.
I have known others who chose to turn their back on who they were.
You do not. Your mind is cleansed and ready--
--to join us.
I will preserve your knowledge. I will preserve your being.
Progress and civilization will not corrupt you as it did mine.
I CAN "PRESERVE" MYSELF, HUNTER!

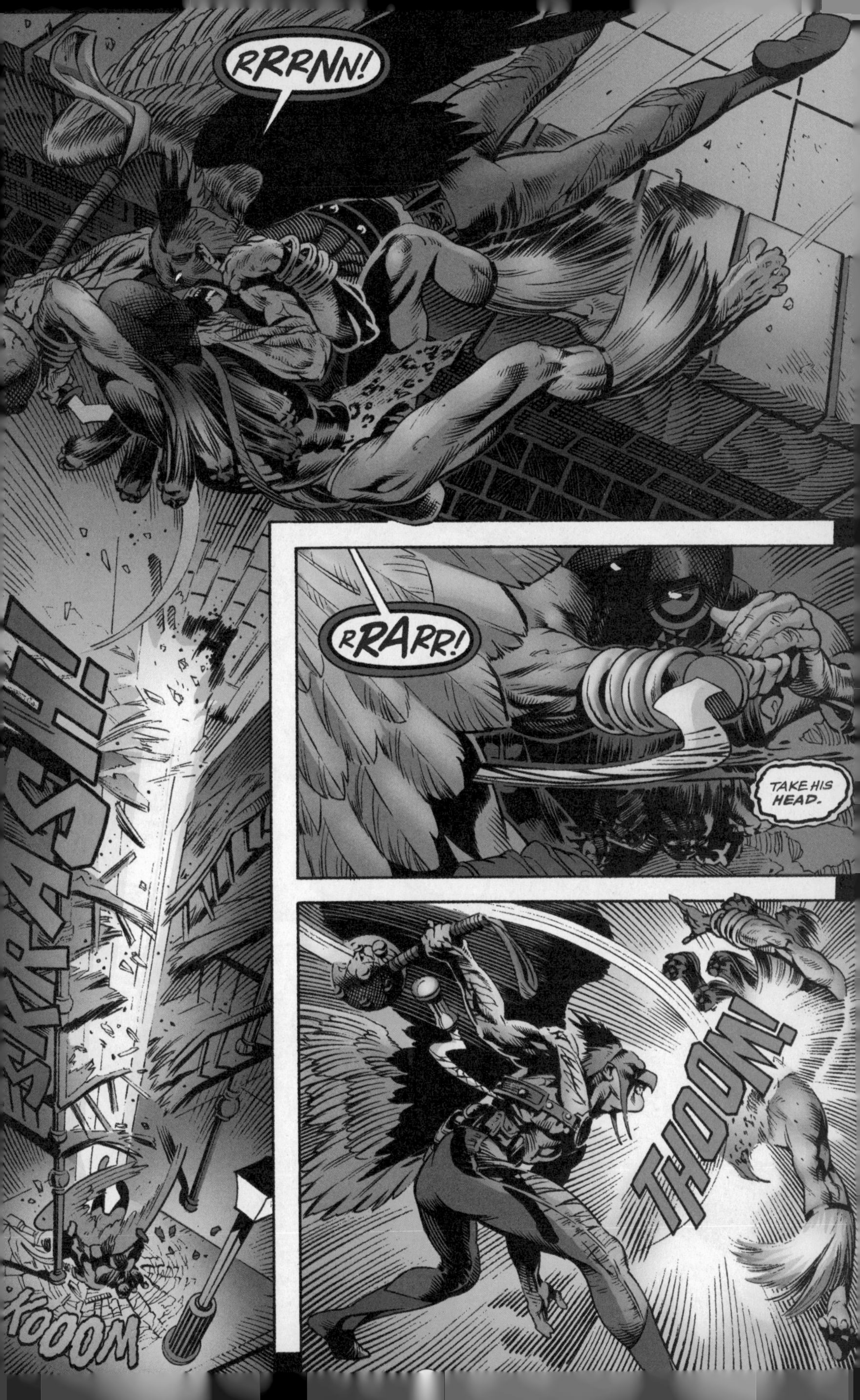
RRRNN!
SKRASH!
KOOOM
rRARR!
TAKE HIS HEAD.
THOOM!

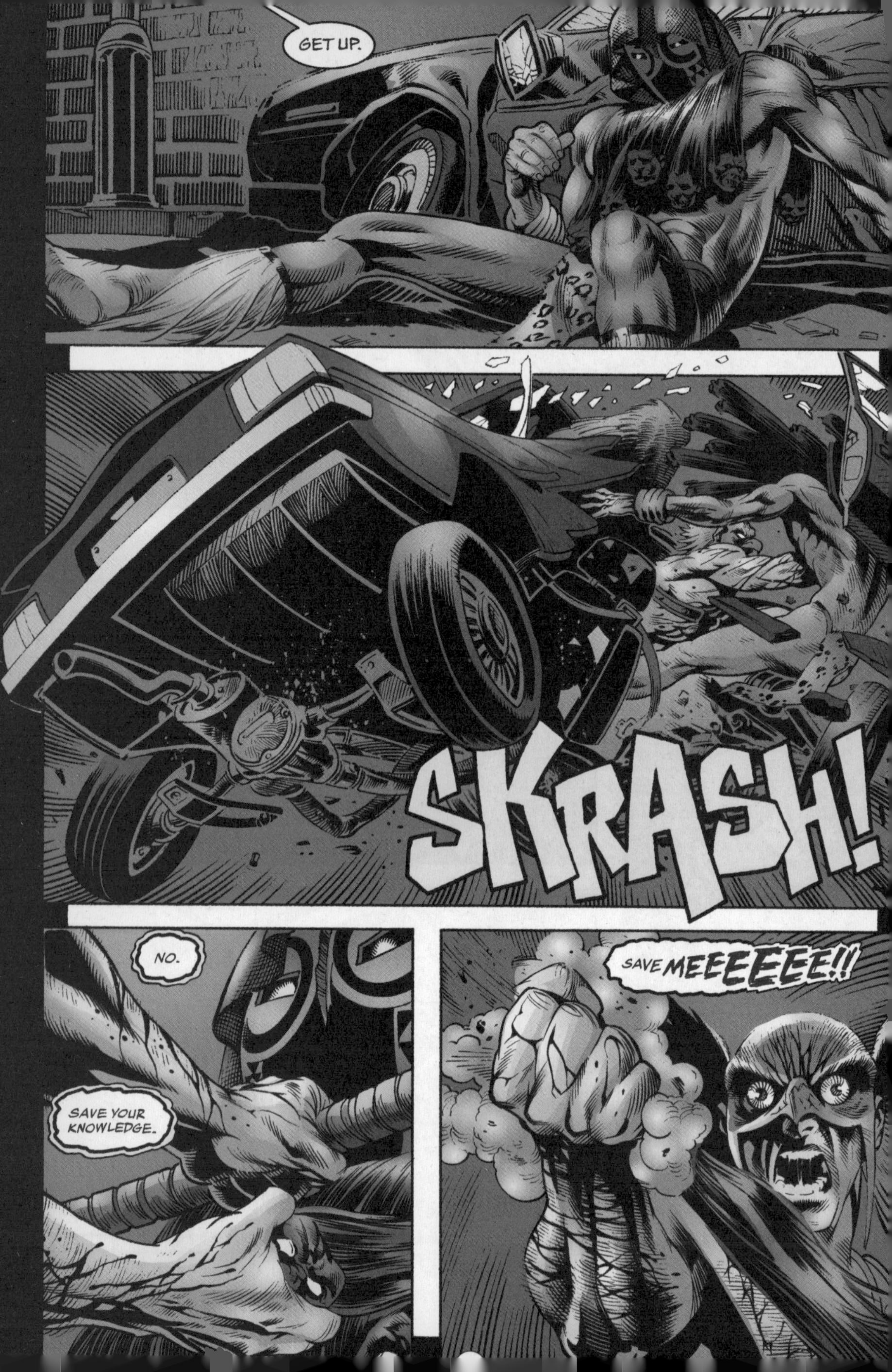
GET UP.
SKRASH!
NO.
SAVE YOUR KNOWLEDGE.
SAVE MEEEEEEE!!

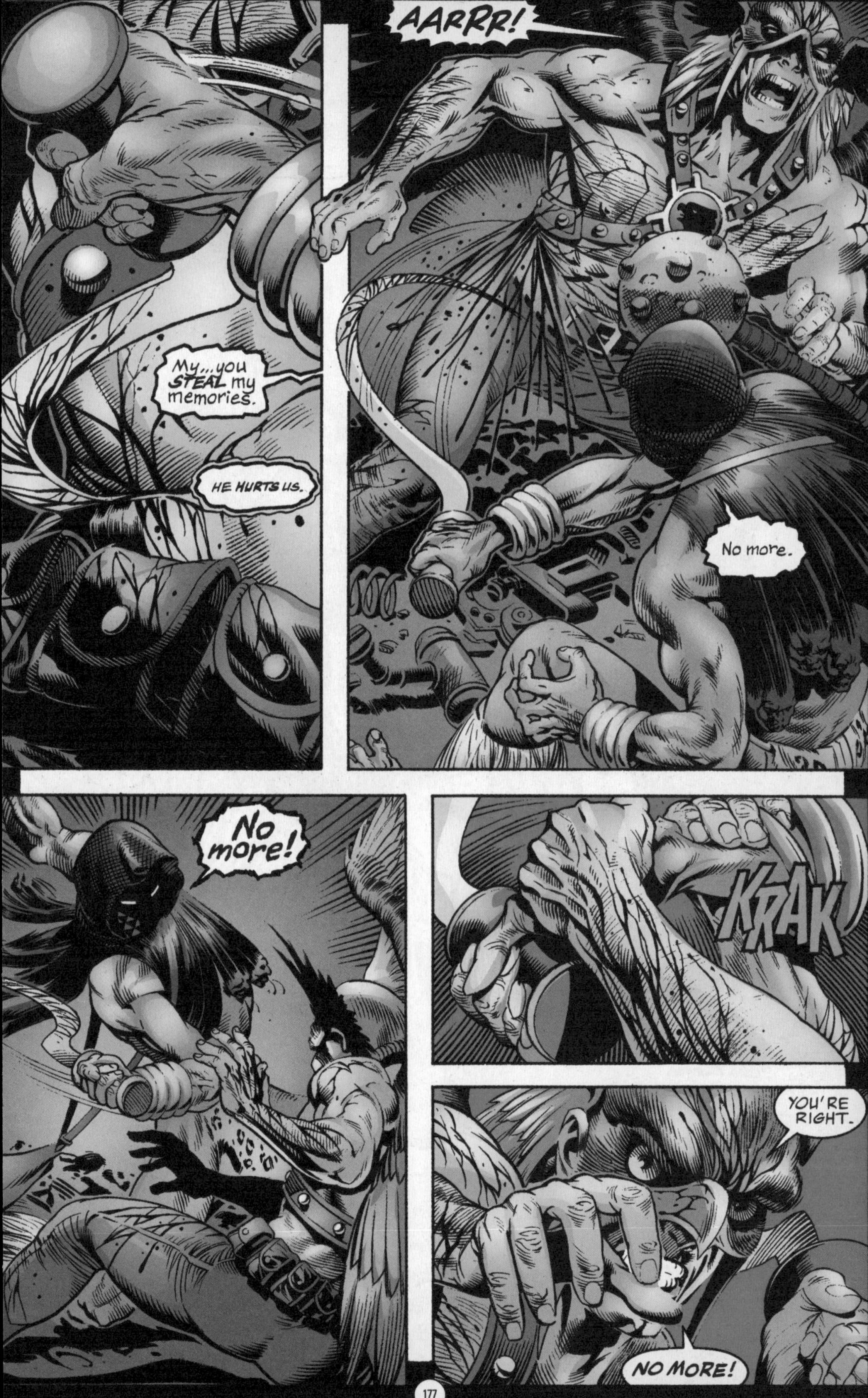

AARRR!
My...you STEAL my memories.
HE HURTS US.
No more.
No more!
KRAK
YOU'RE RIGHT.
NO MORE!

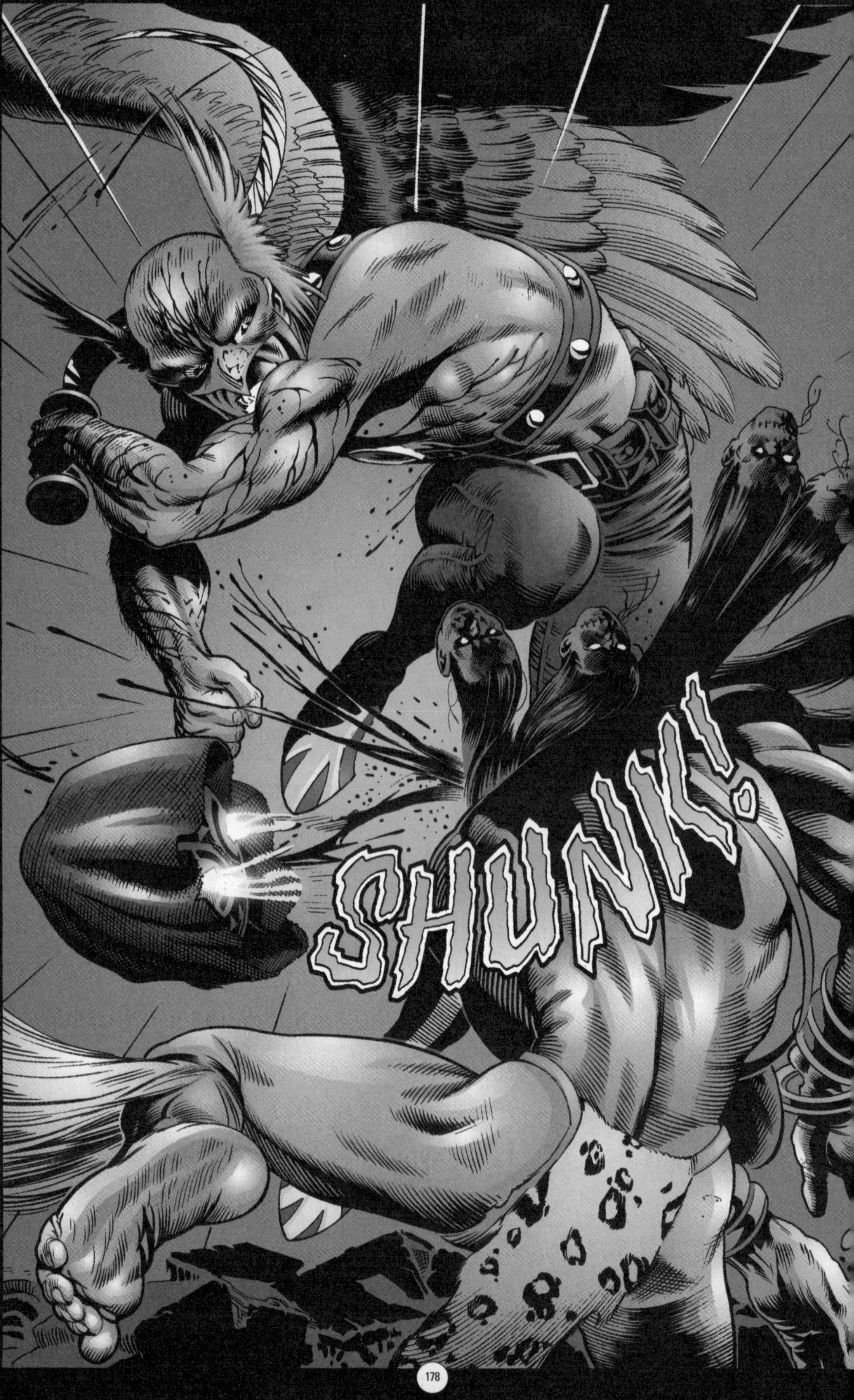
SHUNK!

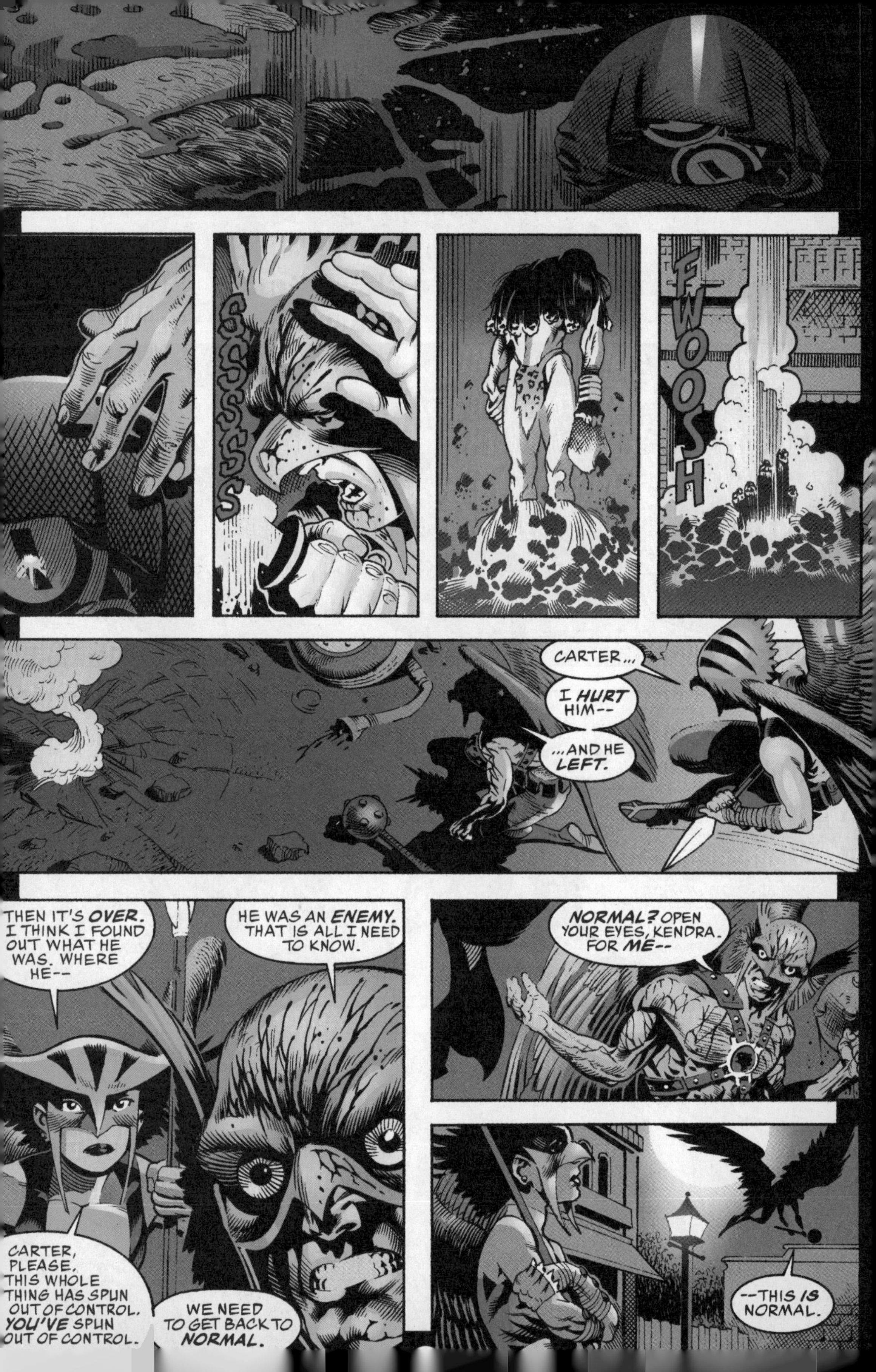
SSSSSSS
FWOOSH
CARTER...
I HURT HIM--
...AND HE LEFT.
THEN IT'S OVER. I THINK I FOUND OUT WHAT HE WAS. WHERE HE--
HE WAS AN ENEMY. THAT IS ALL I NEED TO KNOW.
CARTER, PLEASE. THIS WHOLE THING HAS SPUN OUT OF CONTROL. YOU'VE SPUN OUT OF CONTROL.
WE NEED TO GET BACK TO NORMAL.
NORMAL? OPEN YOUR EYES, KENDRA. FOR ME--
--THIS IS NORMAL.

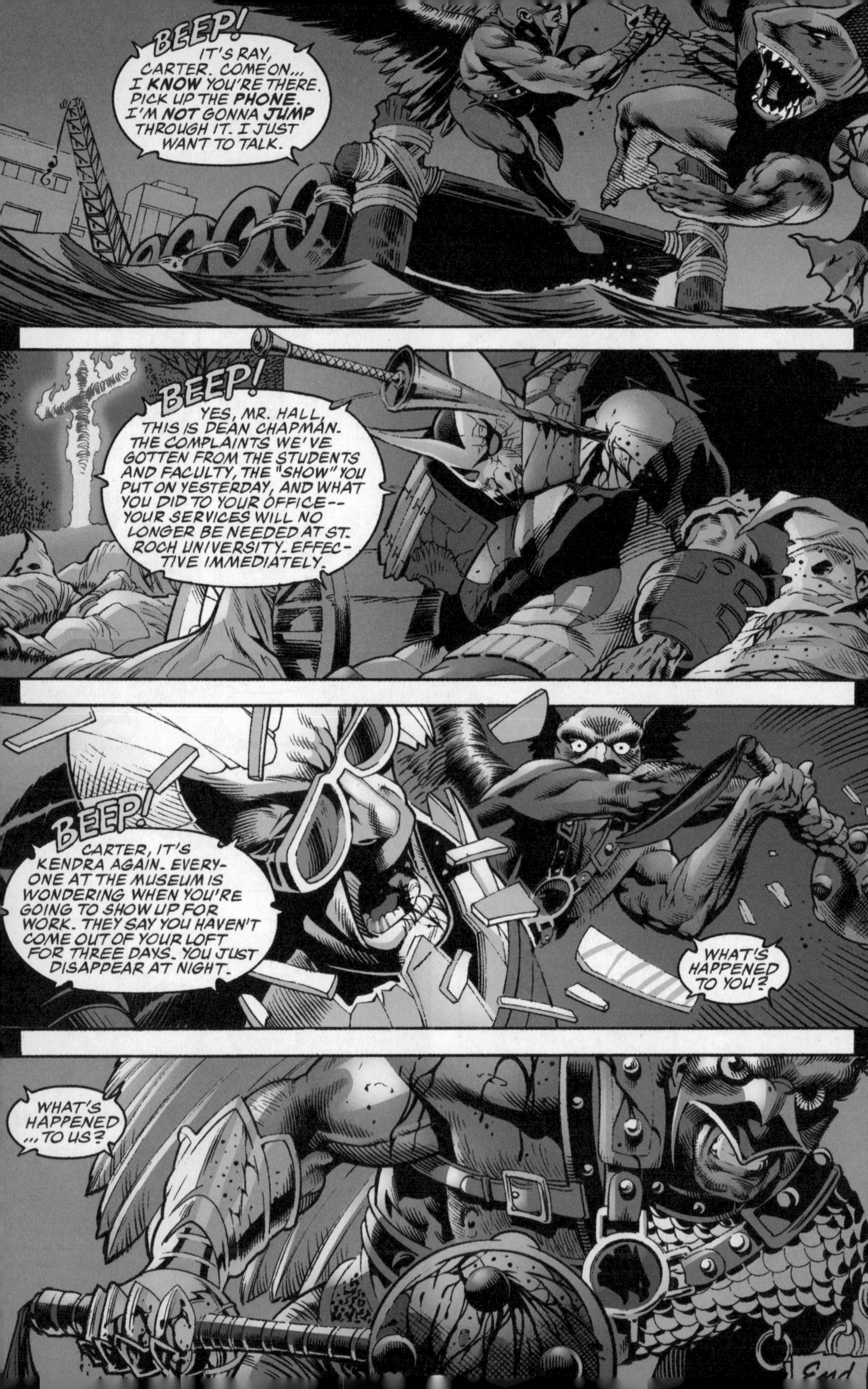
BEEP!
IT'S RAY, CARTER. COME ON... I KNOW YOU'RE THERE. PICK UP THE PHONE. I'M NOT GONNA JUMP THROUGH IT. I JUST WANT TO TALK.
BEEP!
YES, MR. HALL, THIS IS DEAN CHAPMAN. THE COMPLAINTS WE'VE GOTTEN FROM THE STUDENTS AND FACULTY, THE "SHOW" YOU PUT ON YESTERDAY, AND WHAT YOU DID TO YOUR OFFICE-- YOUR SERVICES WILL NO LONGER BE NEEDED AT ST. ROCH UNIVERSITY. EFFECTIVE IMMEDIATELY.
BEEP!
CARTER, IT'S KENDRA AGAIN. EVERYONE AT THE MUSEUM IS WONDERING WHEN YOU'RE GOING TO SHOW UP FOR WORK. THEY SAY YOU HAVEN'T COME OUT OF YOUR LOFT FOR THREE DAYS. YOU JUST DISAPPEAR AT NIGHT.
WHAT'S HAPPENED TO YOU?
WHAT'S HAPPENED ...TO US?
End

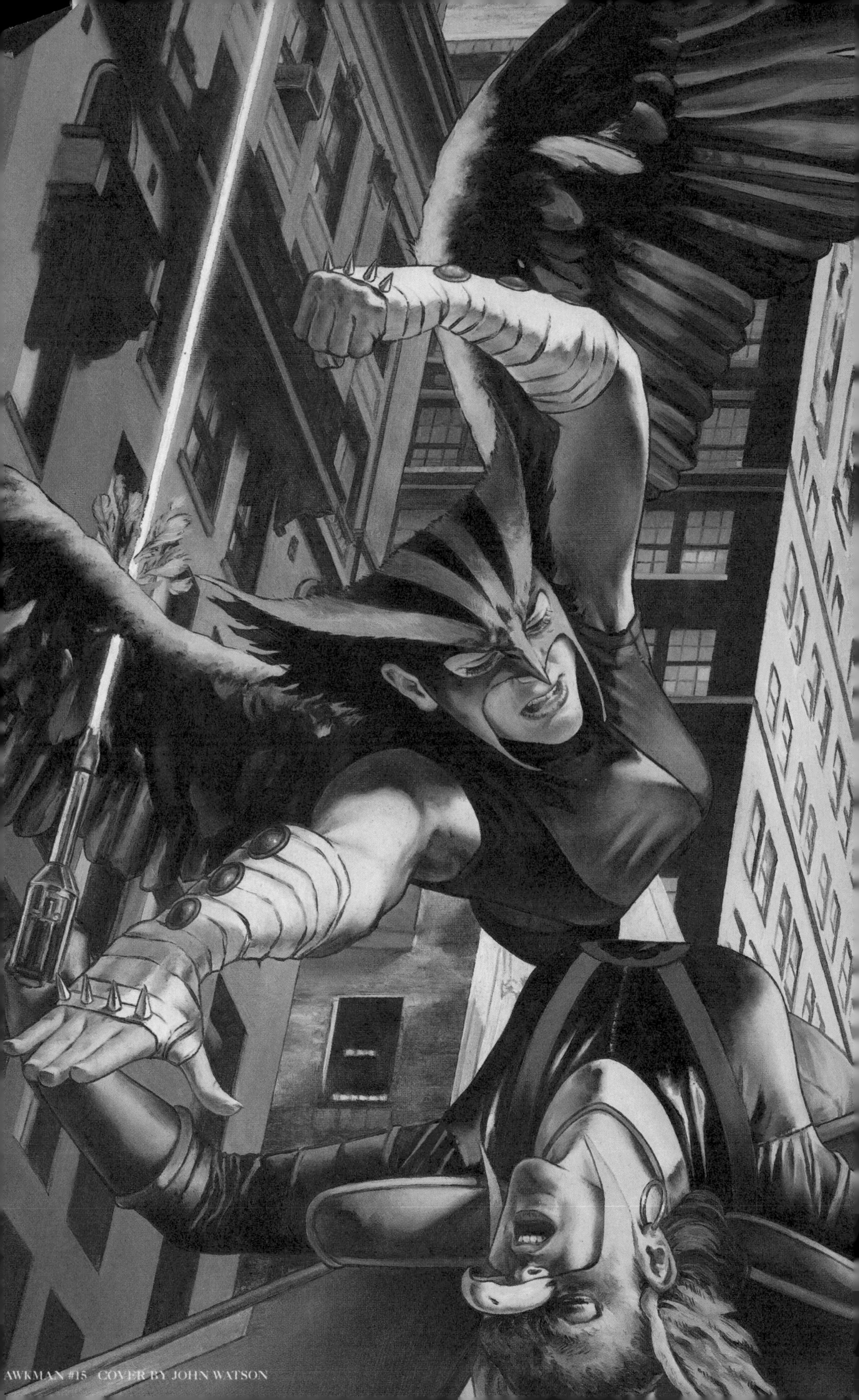

AWKMAN #15 COVER BY JOHN WATSON

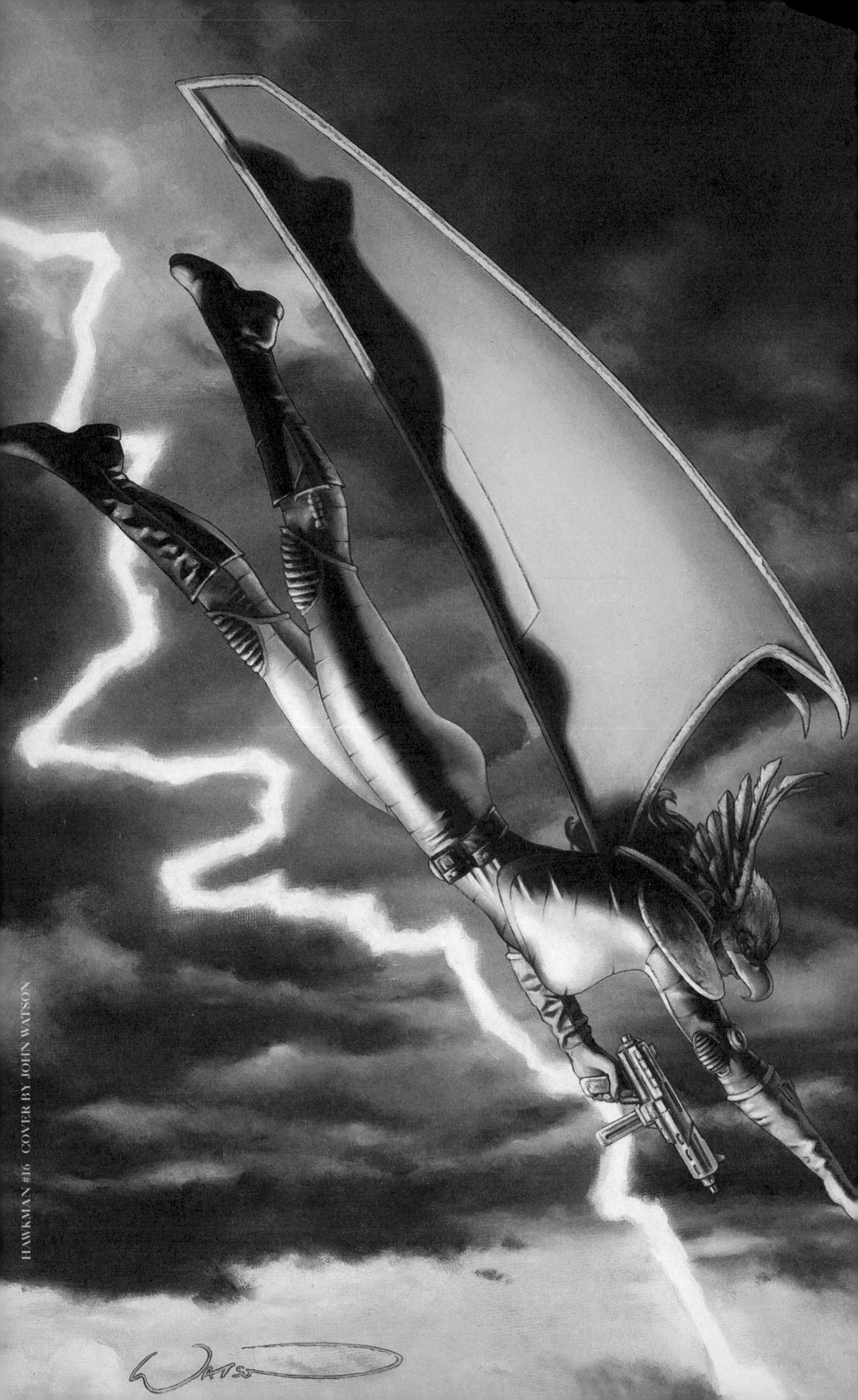

HAWKMAN #16 COVER BY JOHN WATSON

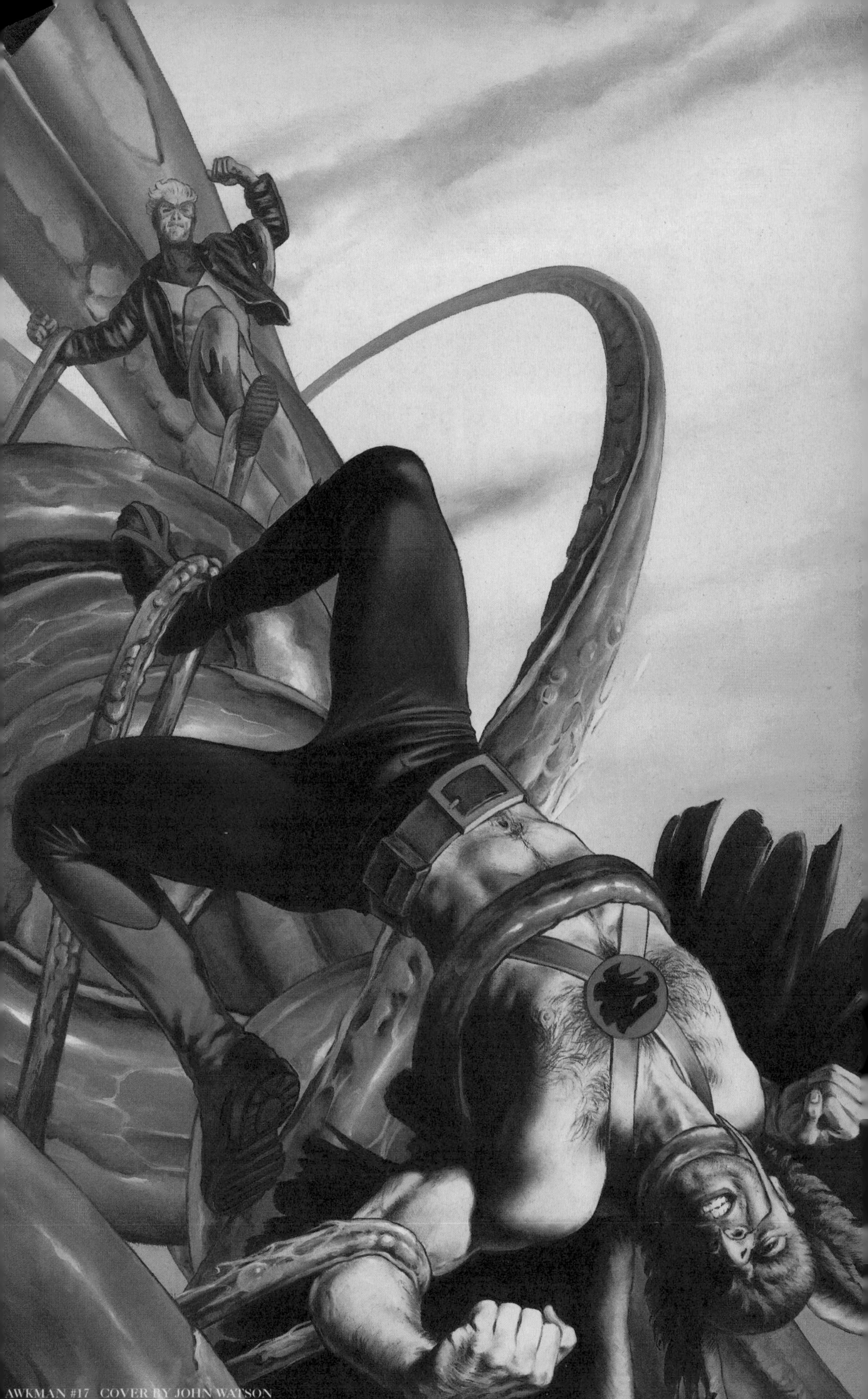

AWKMAN #17 COVER BY JOHN WATSON

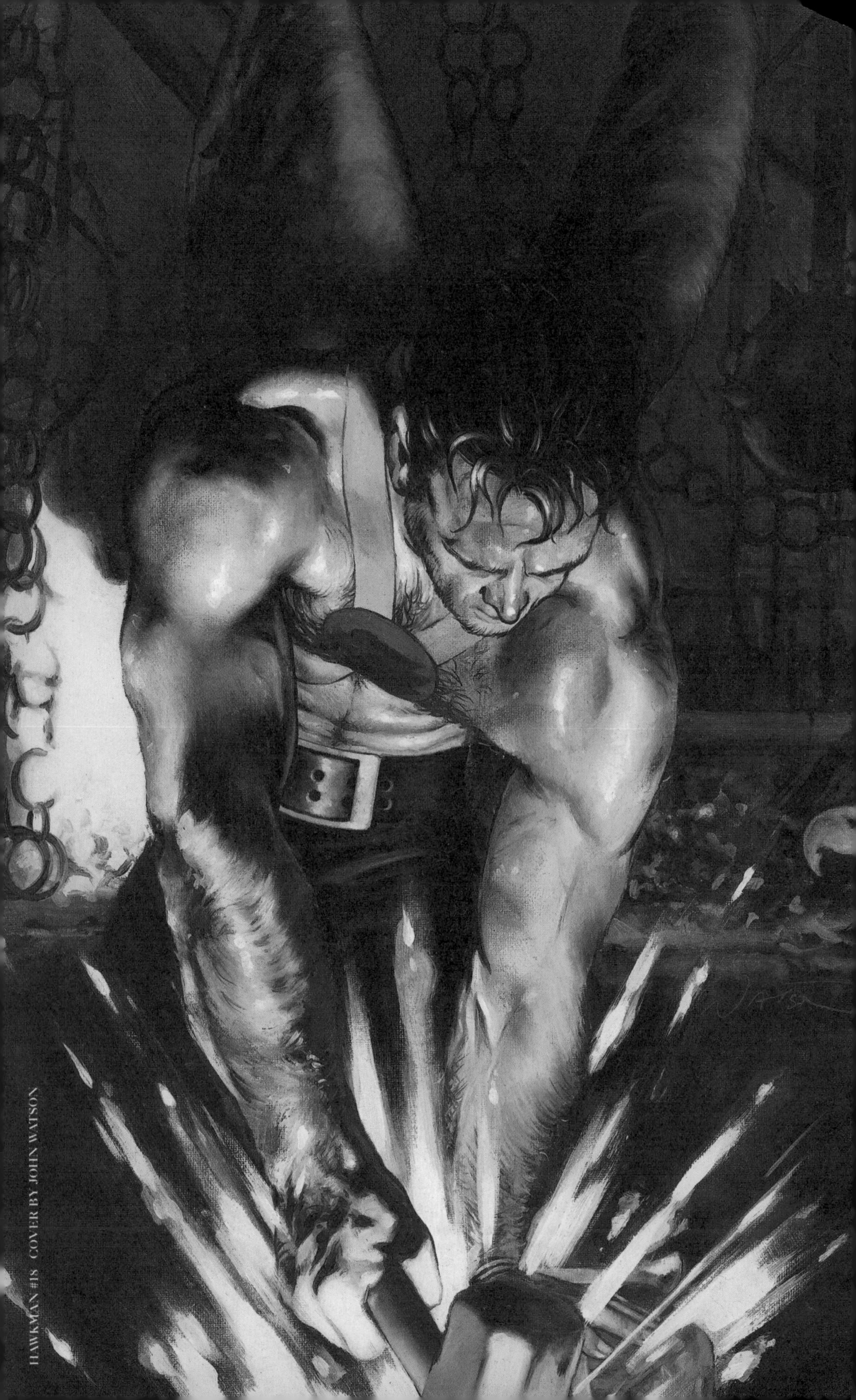

HAWKMAN #18 COVER BY JOHN WATSON

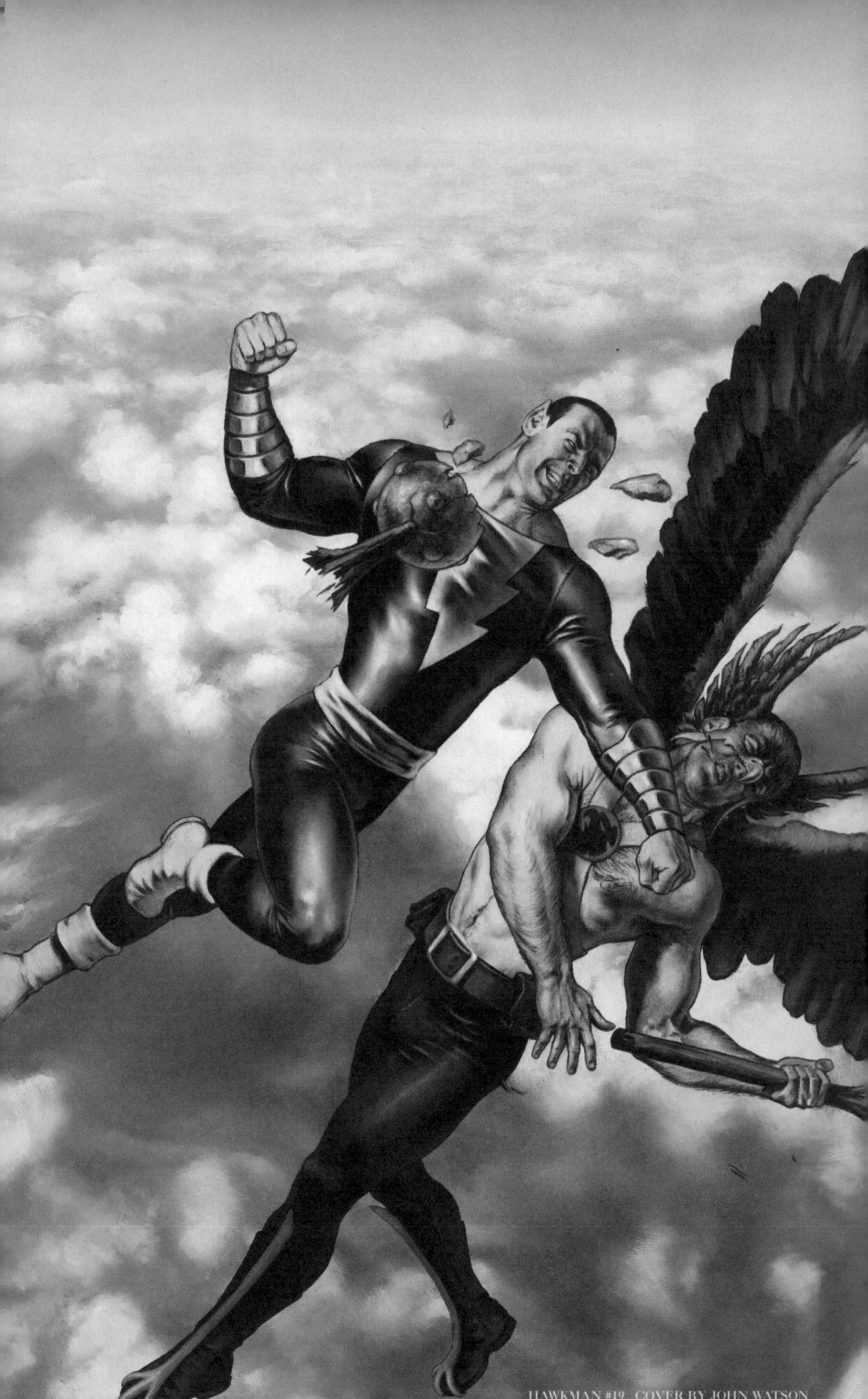

HAWKMAN #19 COVER BY JOHN WATSON

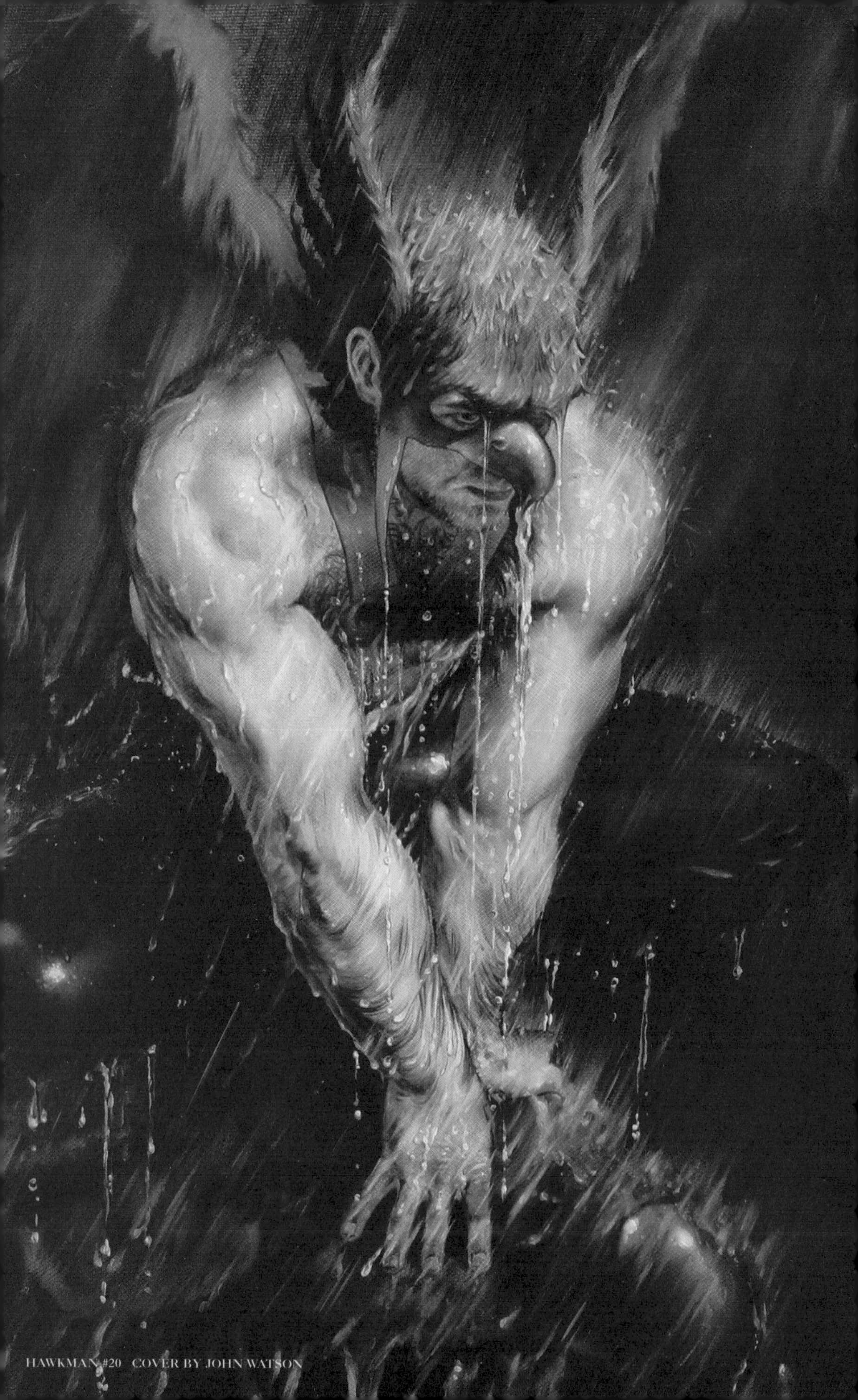
HAWKMAN #20 COVER BY JOHN WATSON

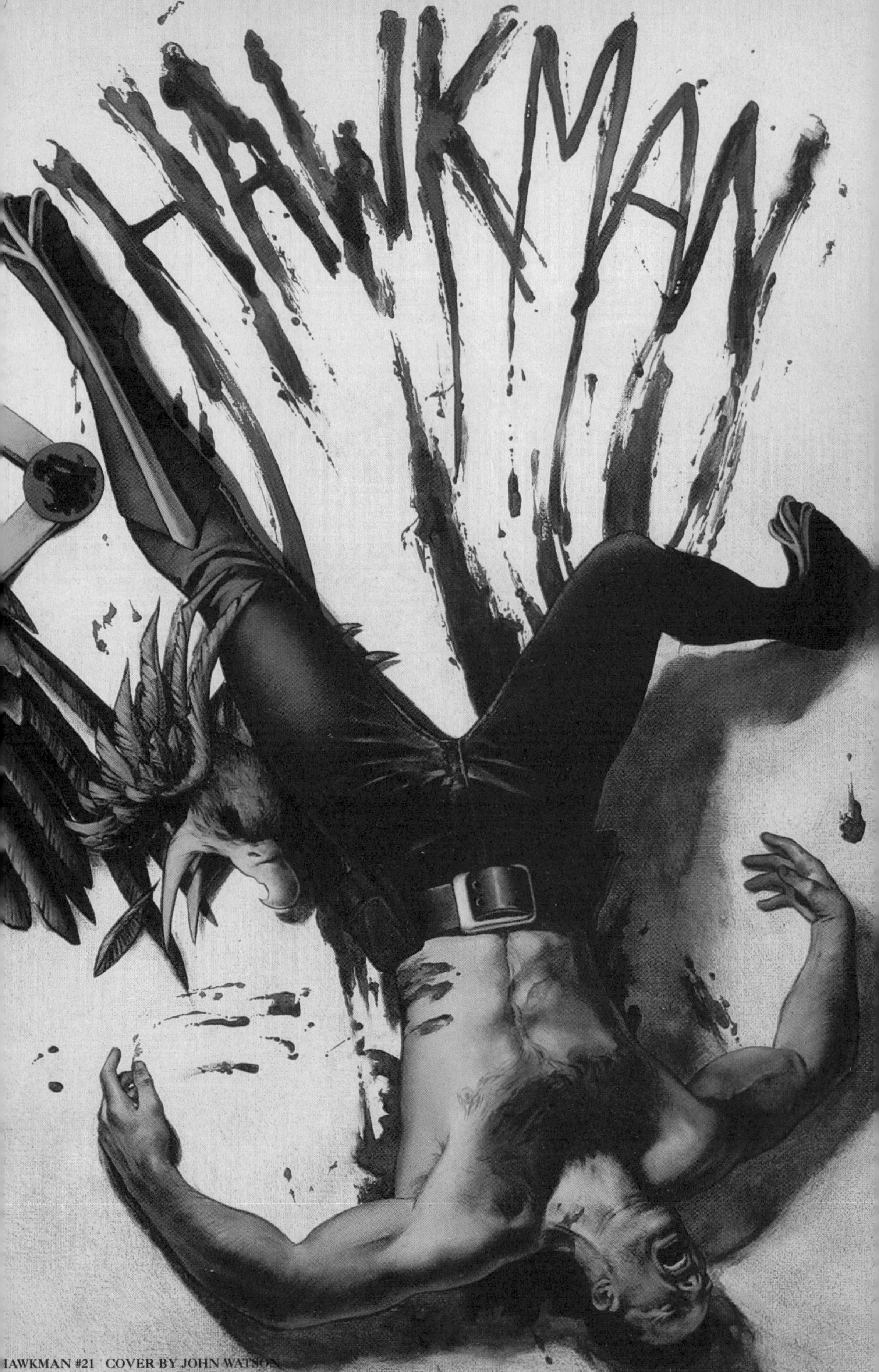
HAWKMAN

HAWKMAN #21 COVER BY JOHN WATSON

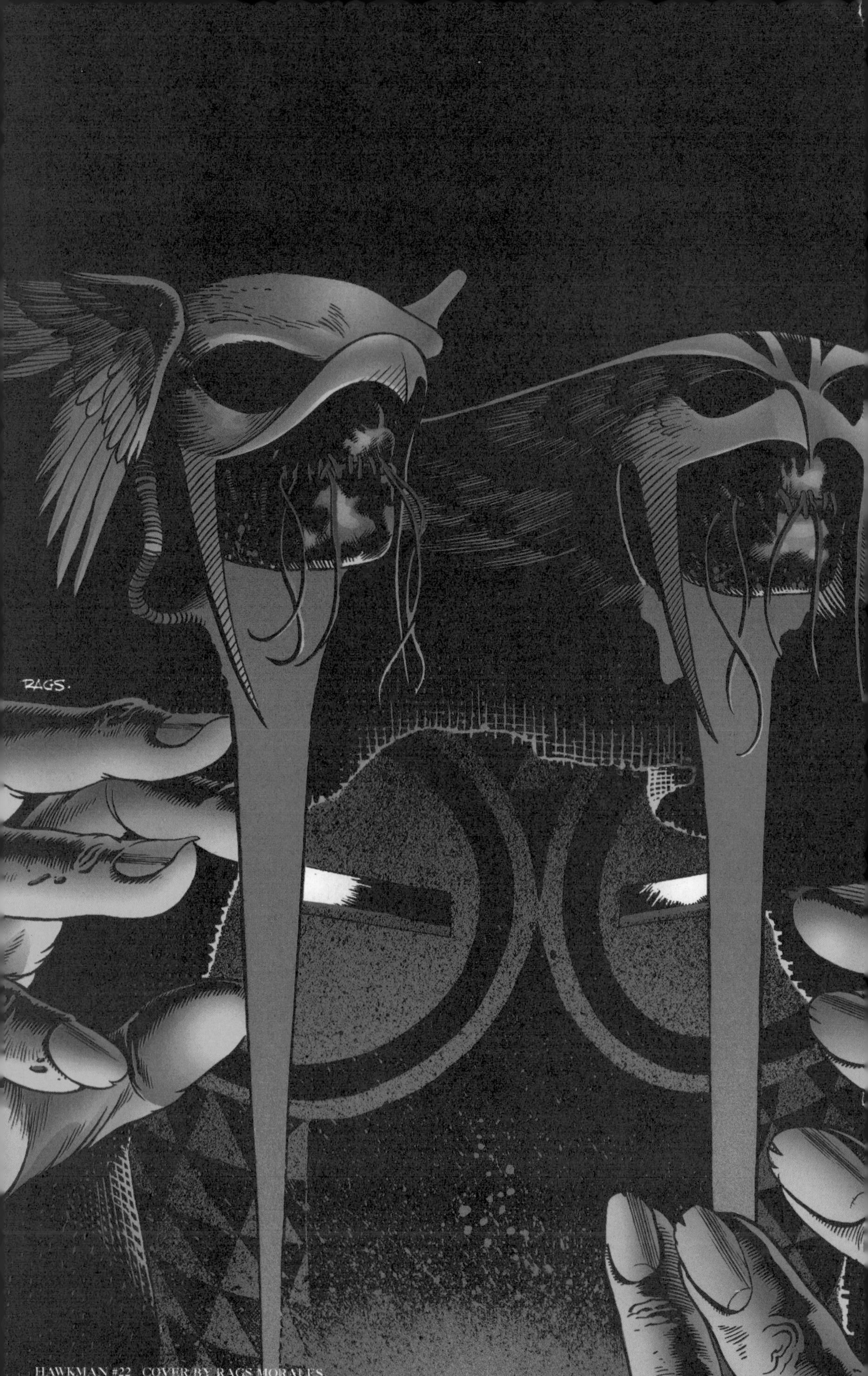
RAGS.

HAWKMAN #22   COVER BY RAGS MORALES

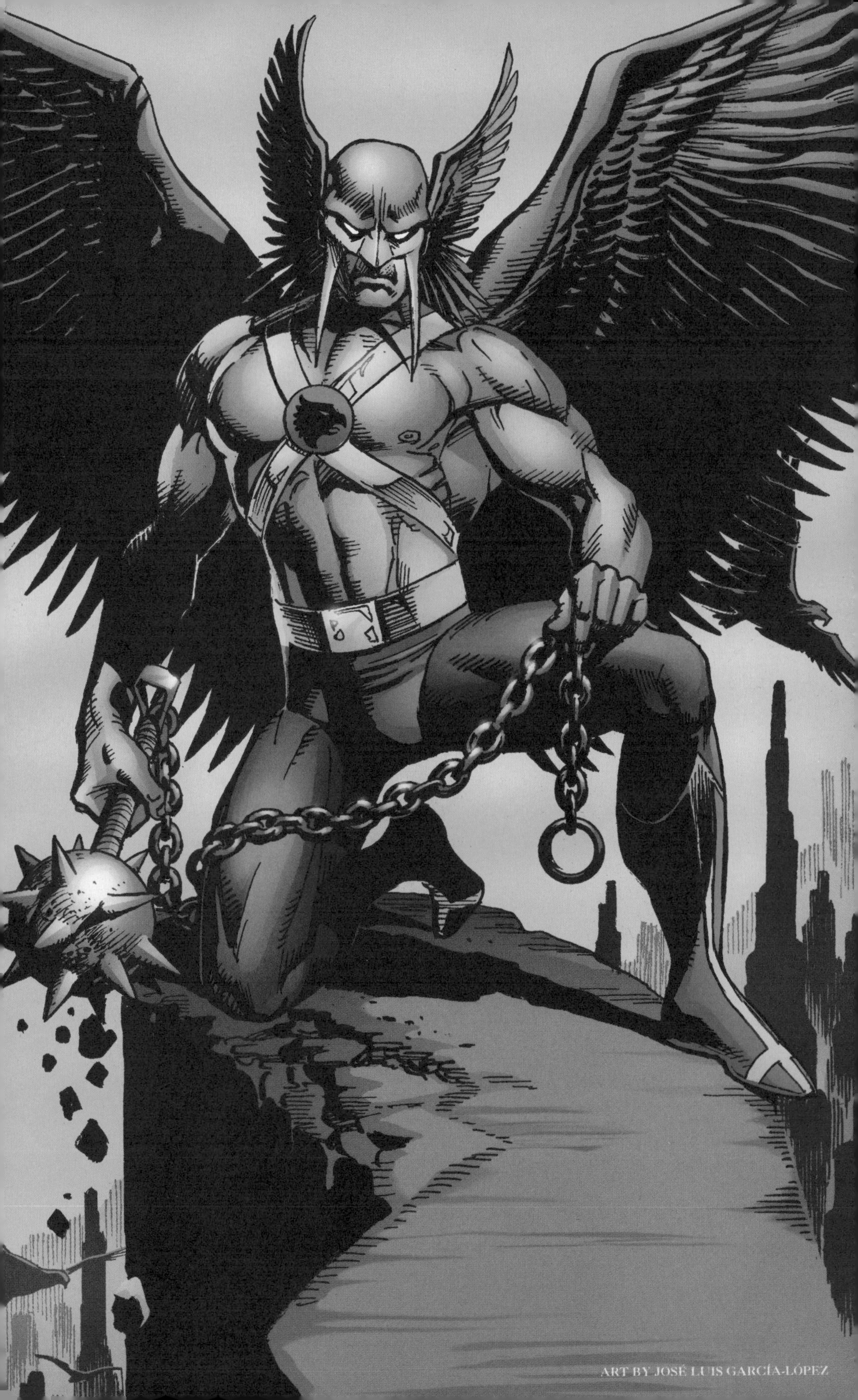

ART BY JOSÉ LUIS GARCÍA-LÓPEZ

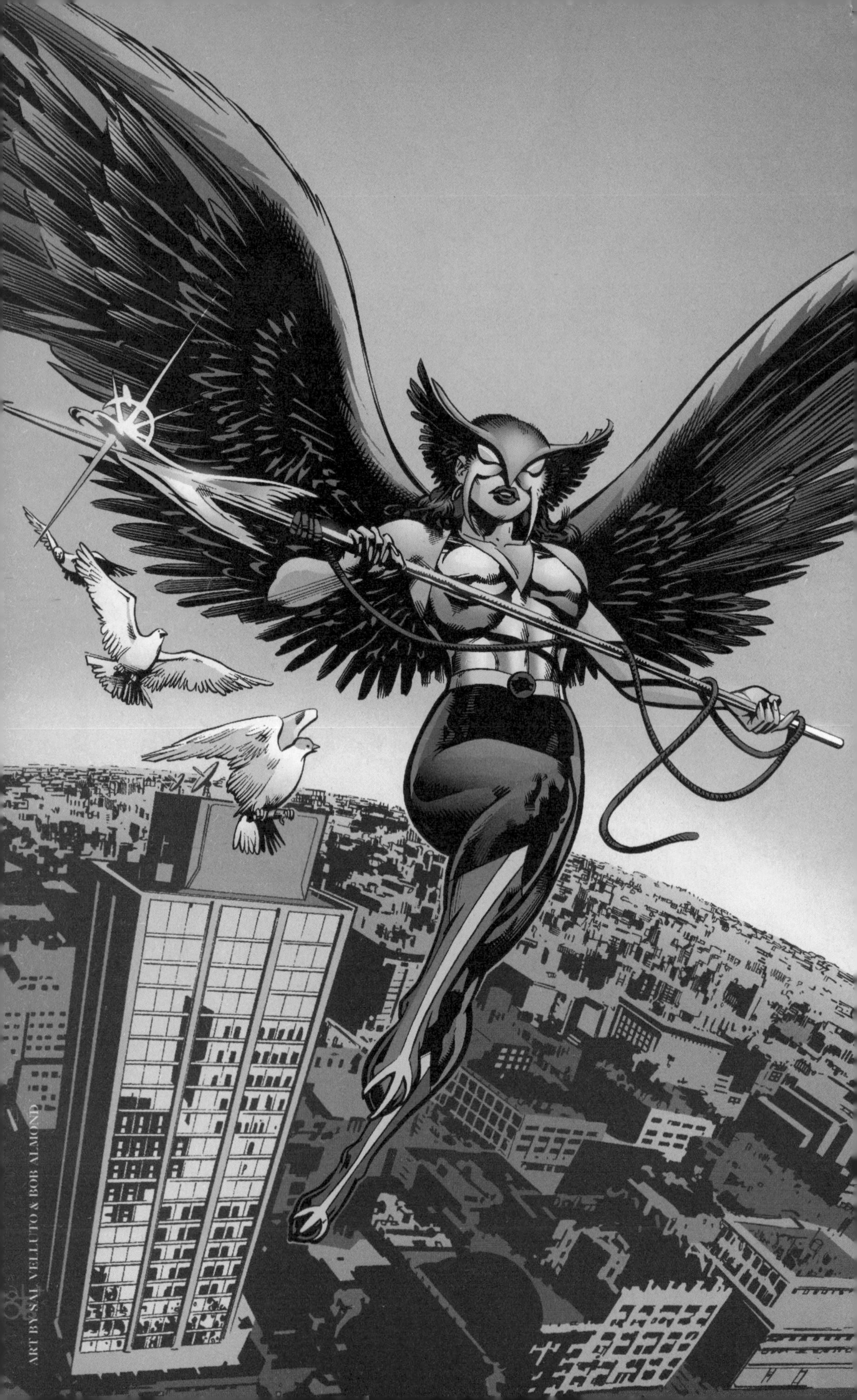

ART BY SAL VELLUTO & BOB ALMOND

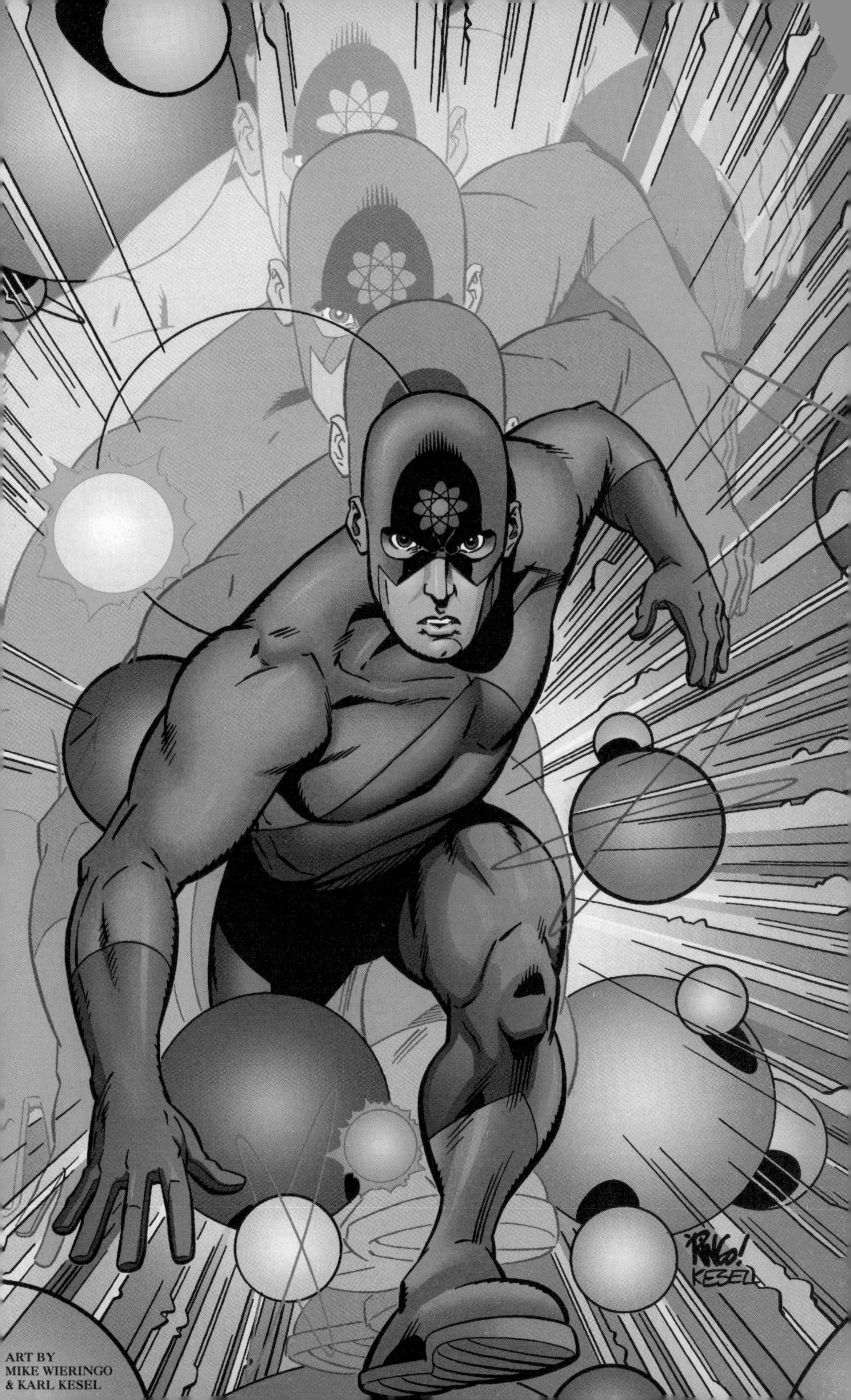
RINGO!
KESEL
ART BY
MIKE WIERINGO
& KARL KESEL